D1484158

Spell of Desire

Volume 2

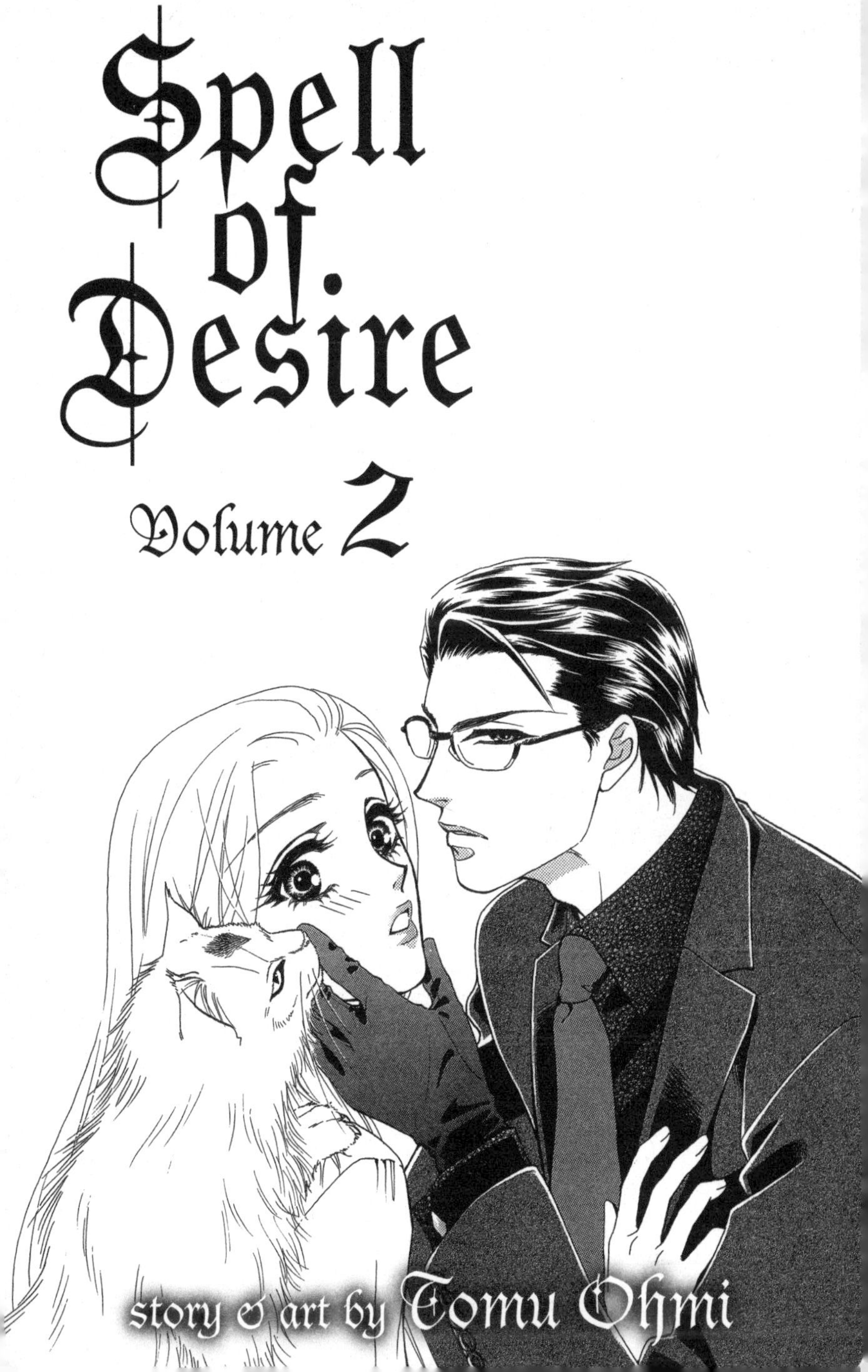

story & art by Tomu Ohmi

Spell of Desire

Volume 2

Contents

story

One day, Kaname, dressed all in black, appears in front of Kaoruko, who runs an herb shop. He tells her that her mother, whom she long thought was dead, is actually alive—and in fact, a Witch Queen. The power of the Witch Queen has been entrusted to Kaoruko's care, but this power also has a tendency to run rampant. Kaname helps Kaoruko control this power by kissing her, and she gradually finds herself drawn to him…

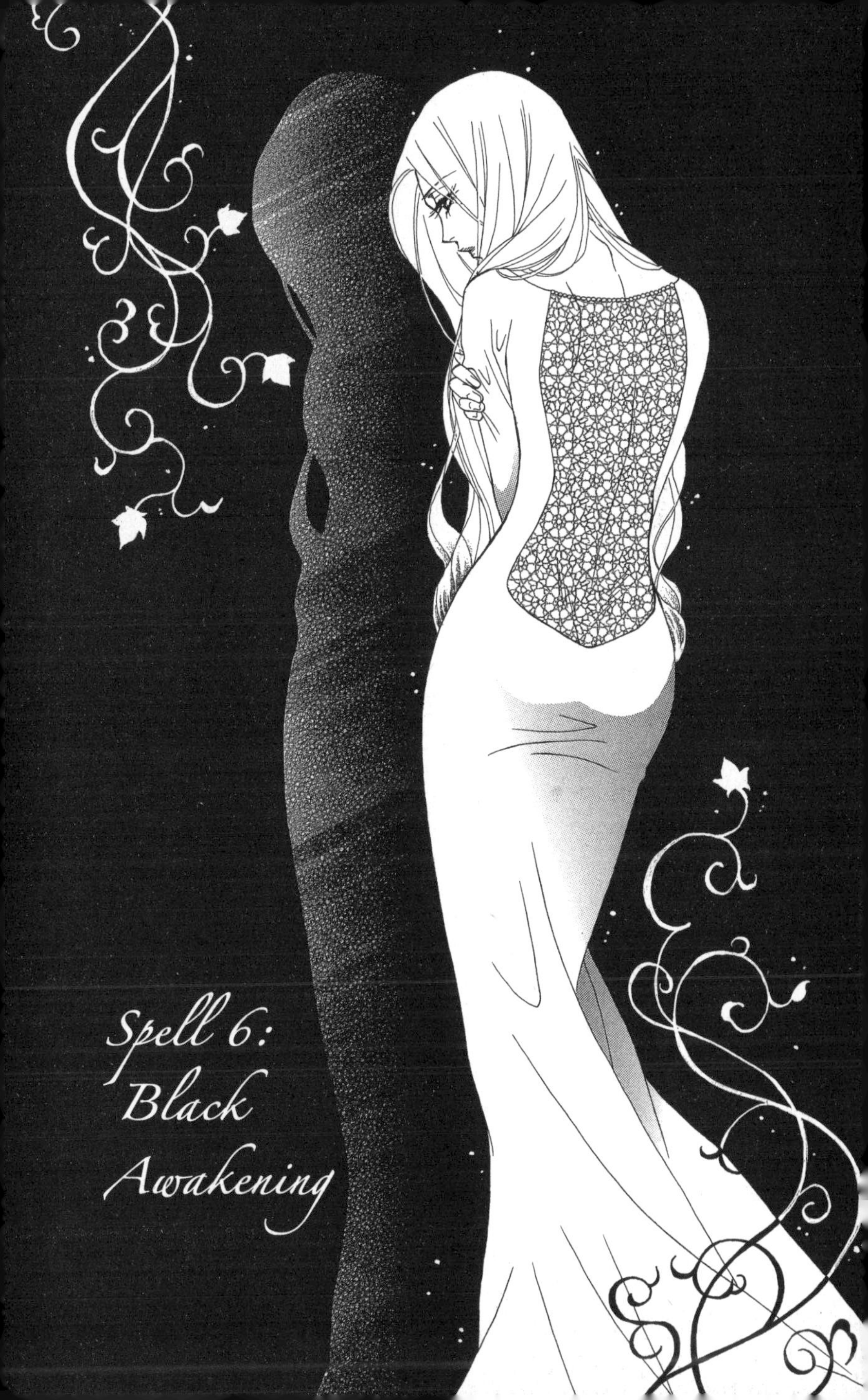
Spell 6:
Black
Awakening

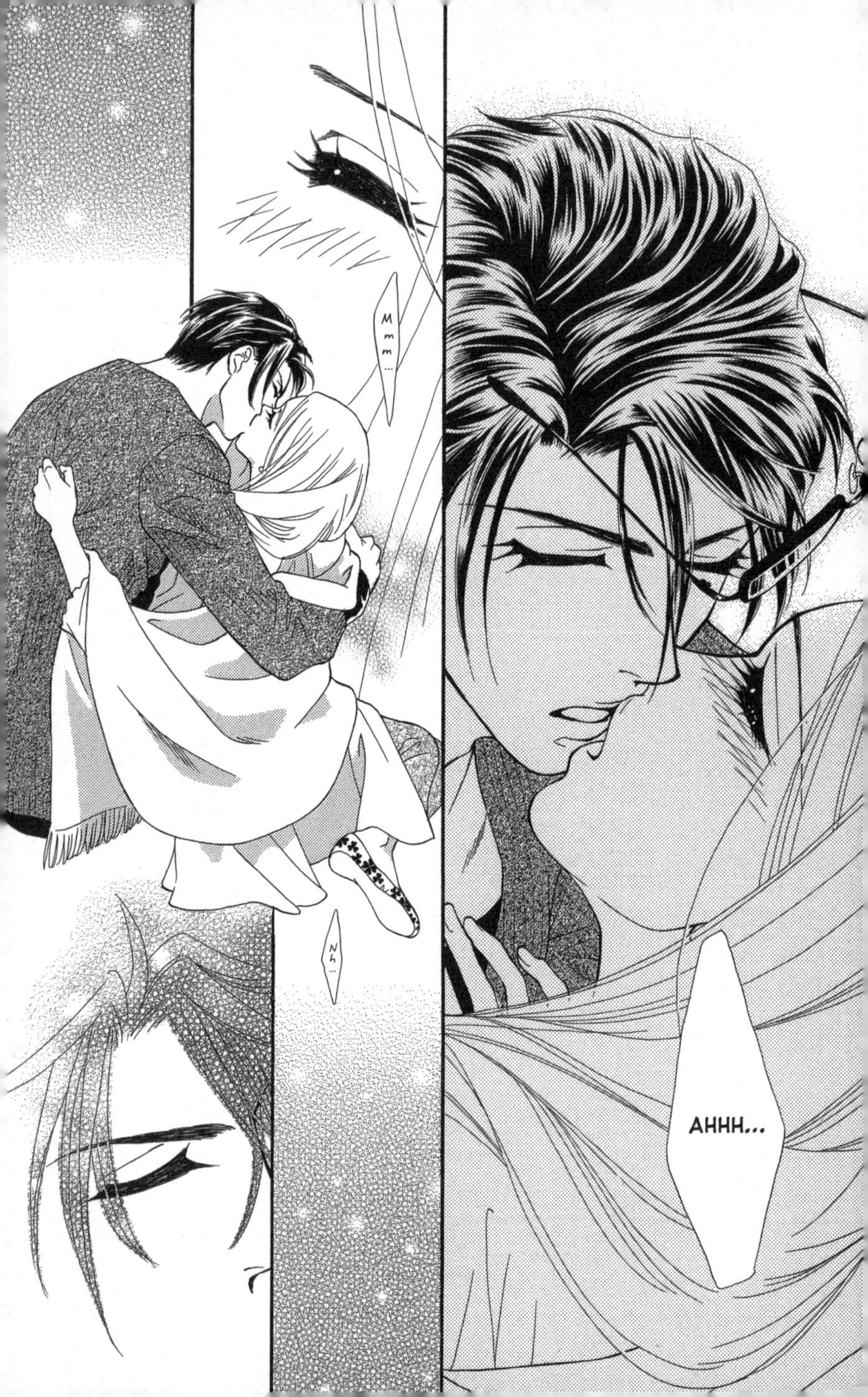
Mmm...
Nh...
AHHH...

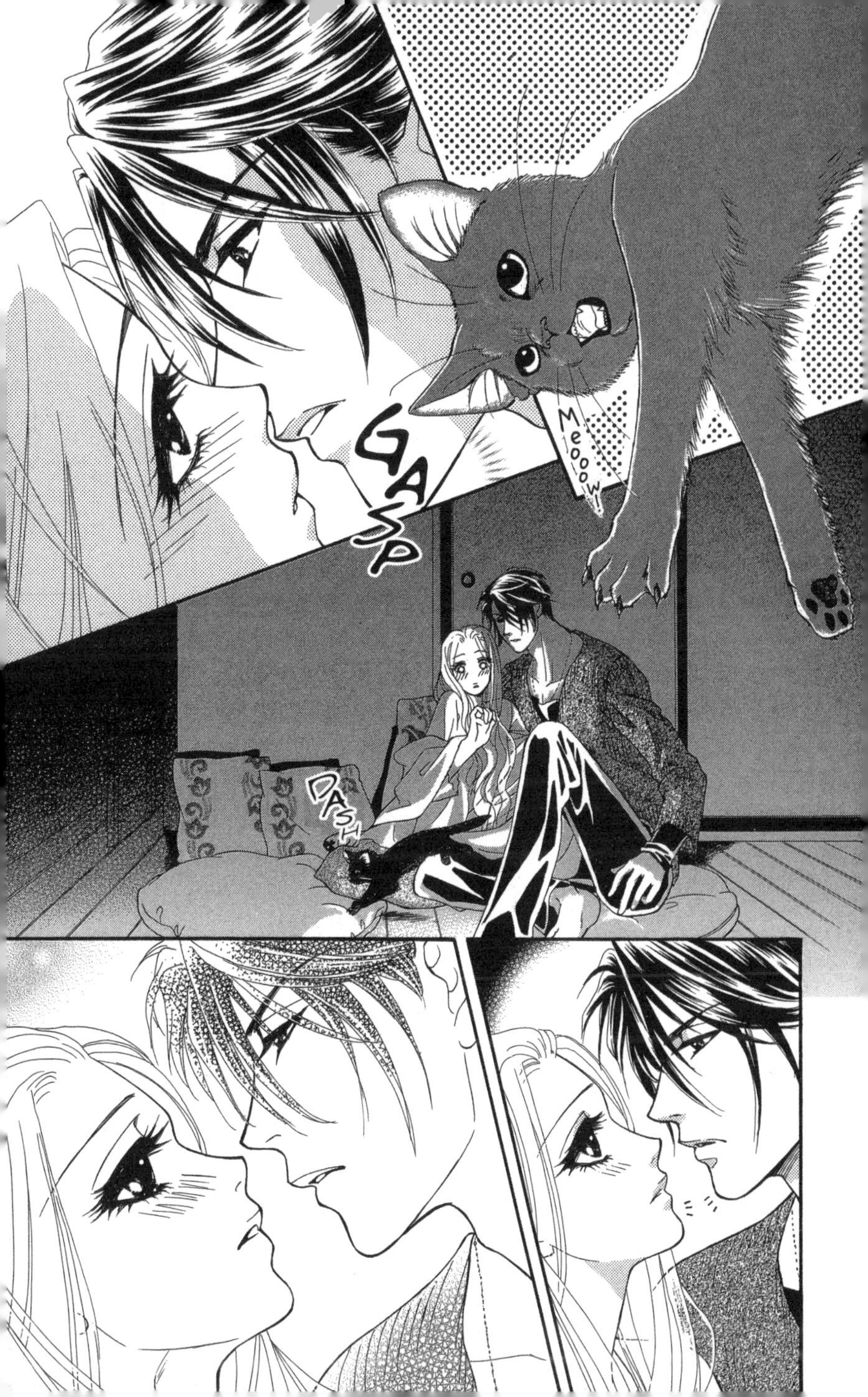
Meooow!
GASP
DASH

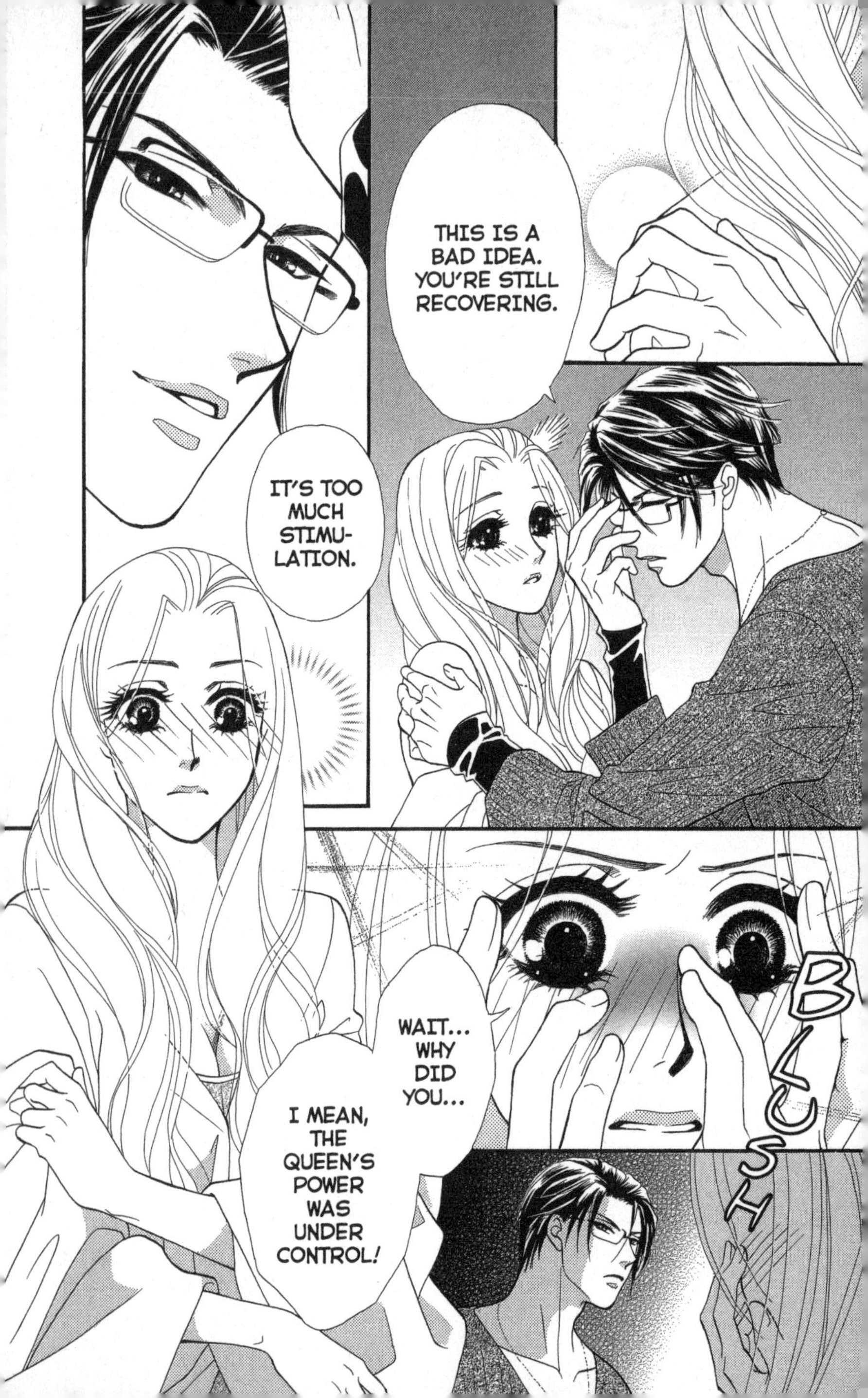
THIS IS A BAD IDEA. YOU'RE STILL RECOVERING.
IT'S TOO MUCH STIMU-LATION.
BLUSH
WAIT... WHY DID YOU...
I MEAN, THE QUEEN'S POWER WAS UNDER CONTROL!

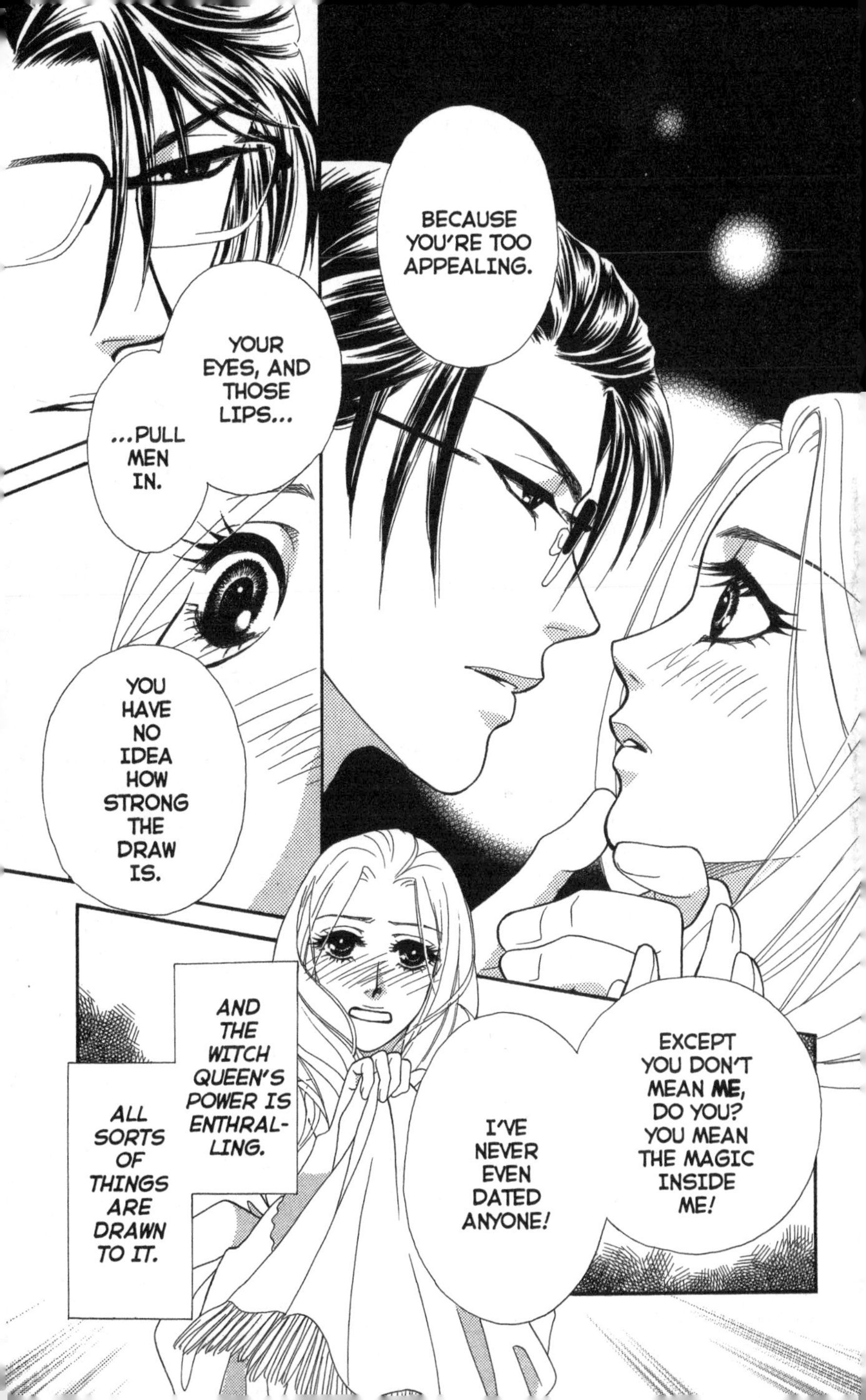
BECAUSE YOU'RE TOO APPEALING.
YOUR EYES, AND THOSE LIPS...
...PULL MEN IN.
YOU HAVE NO IDEA HOW STRONG THE DRAW IS.
EXCEPT YOU DON'T MEAN **ME**, DO YOU? YOU MEAN THE MAGIC INSIDE ME!
I'VE NEVER EVEN DATED ANYONE!
AND THE WITCH QUEEN'S POWER IS ENTHRAL-LING.
ALL SORTS OF THINGS ARE DRAWN TO IT.

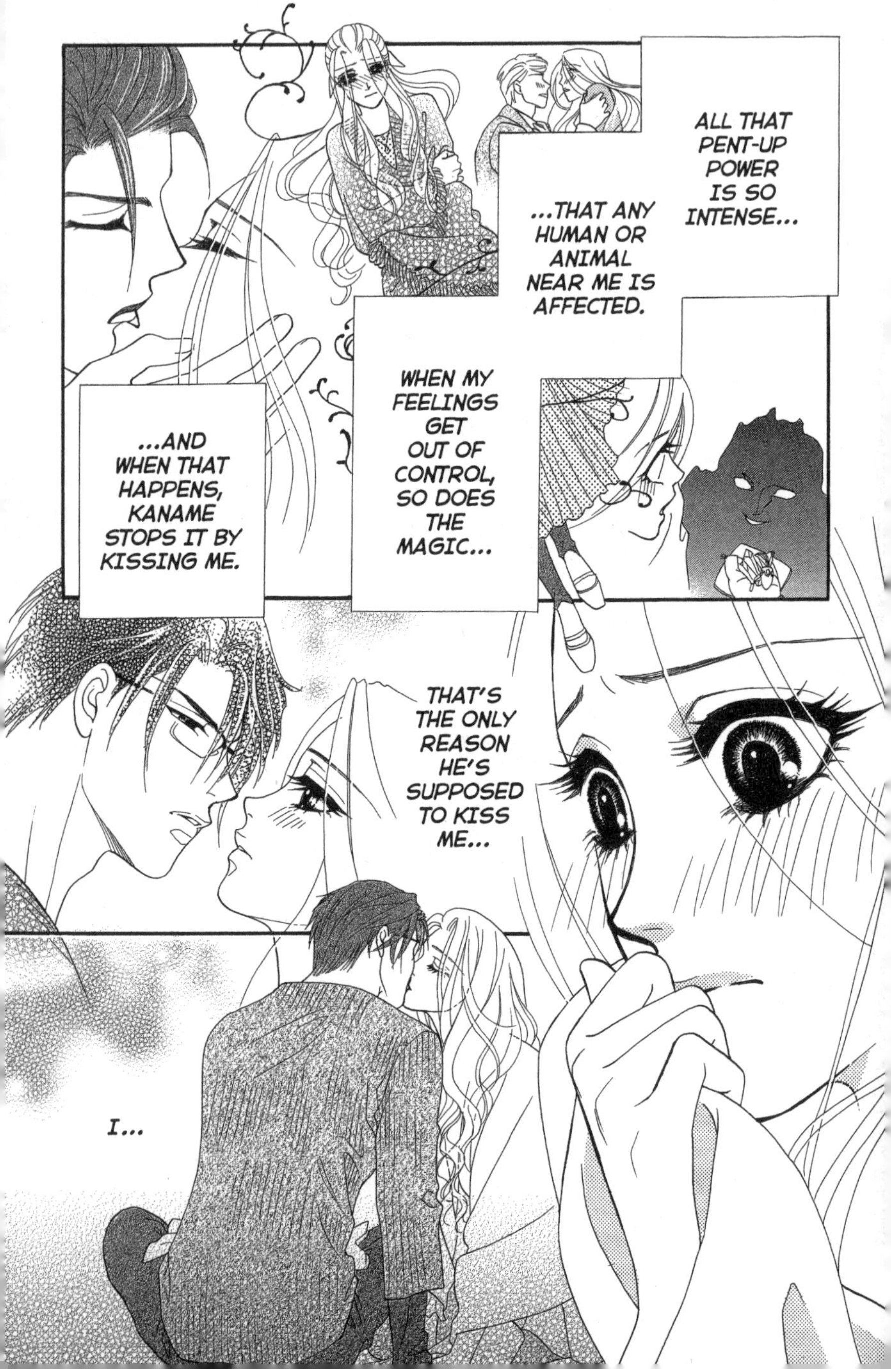
ALL THAT PENT-UP POWER IS SO INTENSE...
...THAT ANY HUMAN OR ANIMAL NEAR ME IS AFFECTED.
WHEN MY FEELINGS GET OUT OF CONTROL, SO DOES THE MAGIC...
...AND WHEN THAT HAPPENS, KANAME STOPS IT BY KISSING ME.
THAT'S THE ONLY REASON HE'S SUPPOSED TO KISS ME...
I...

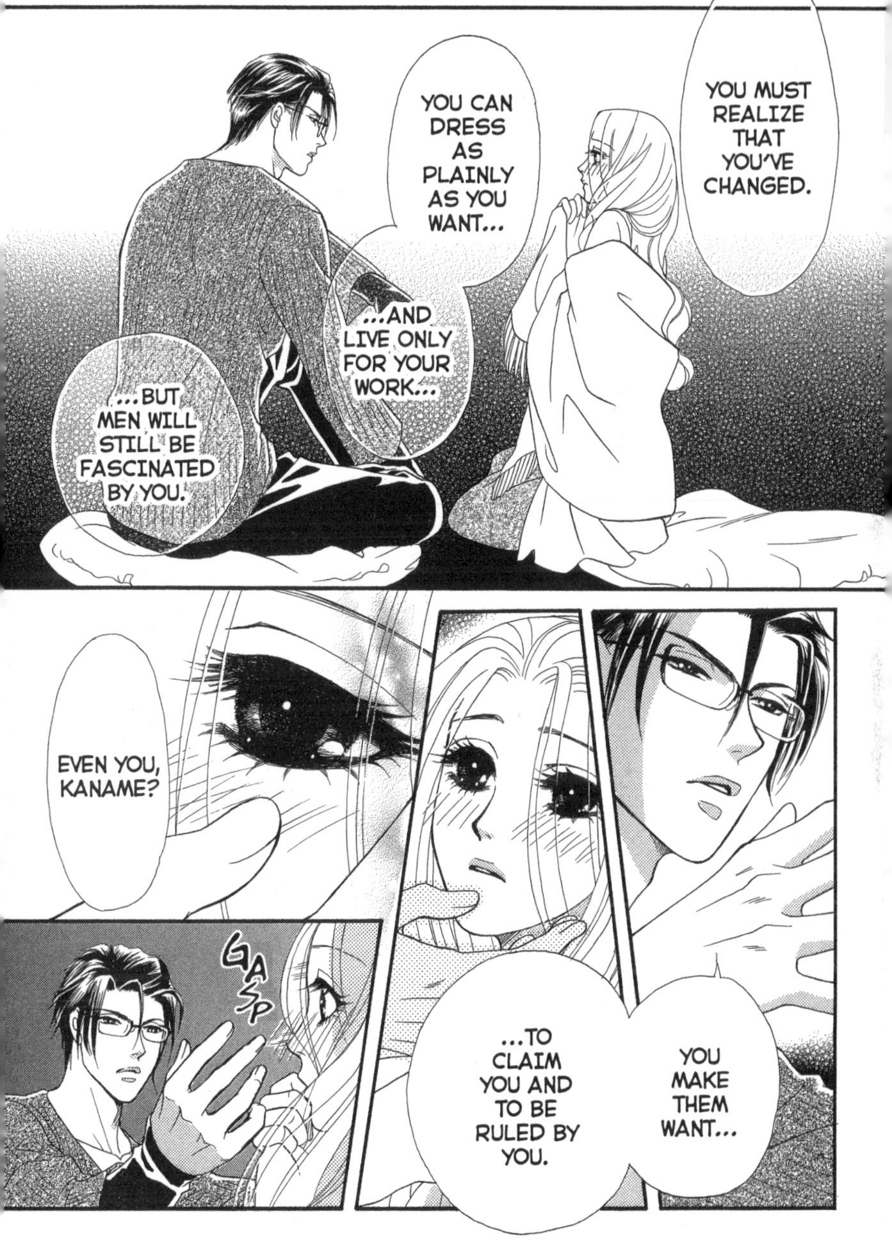
YOU MUST REALIZE THAT YOU'VE CHANGED.
YOU CAN DRESS AS PLAINLY AS YOU WANT...
...AND LIVE ONLY FOR YOUR WORK...
...BUT MEN WILL STILL BE FASCINATED BY YOU.
YOU MAKE THEM WANT...
...TO CLAIM YOU AND TO BE RULED BY YOU.
EVEN YOU, KANAME?
GASP

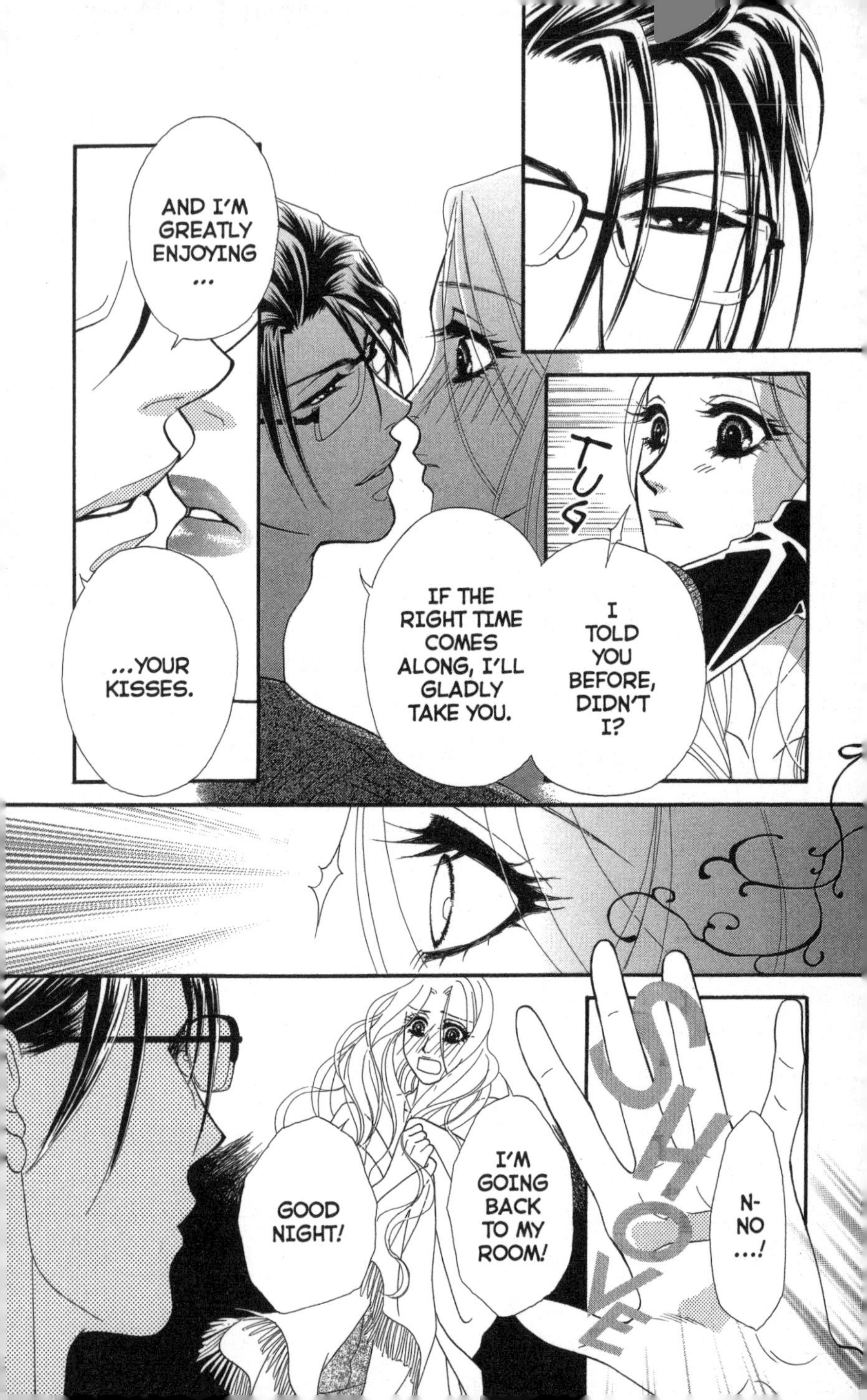
TUG
I TOLD YOU BEFORE, DIDN'T I?
IF THE RIGHT TIME COMES ALONG, I'LL GLADLY TAKE YOU.
AND I'M GREATLY ENJOYING ...
...YOUR KISSES.
SHOVE
N-NO ...!
I'M GOING BACK TO MY ROOM!
GOOD NIGHT!

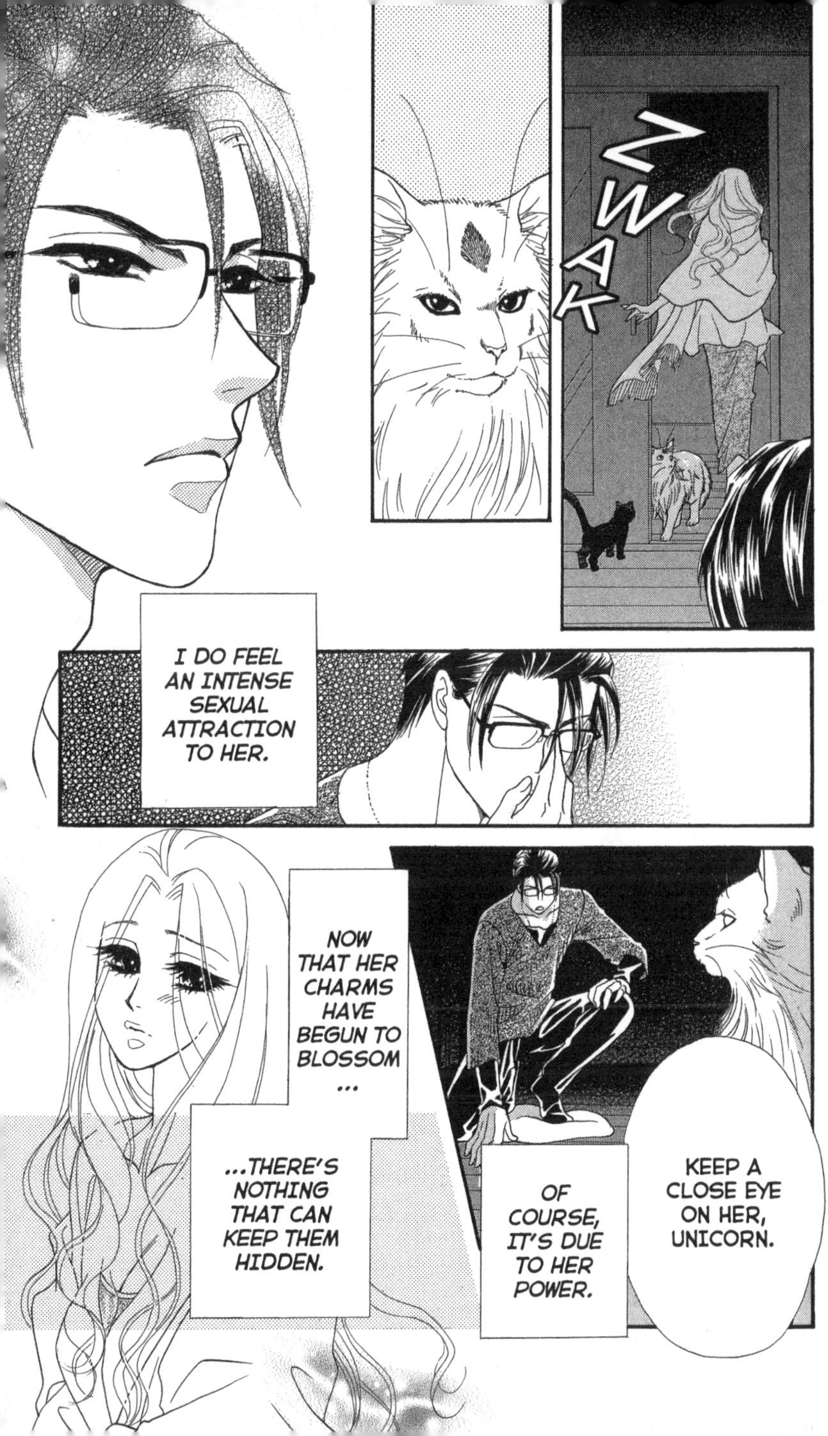
ZWAK
I DO FEEL AN INTENSE SEXUAL ATTRACTION TO HER.
KEEP A CLOSE EYE ON HER, UNICORN.
OF COURSE, IT'S DUE TO HER POWER.
NOW THAT HER CHARMS HAVE BEGUN TO BLOSSOM ...
...THERE'S NOTHING THAT CAN KEEP THEM HIDDEN.

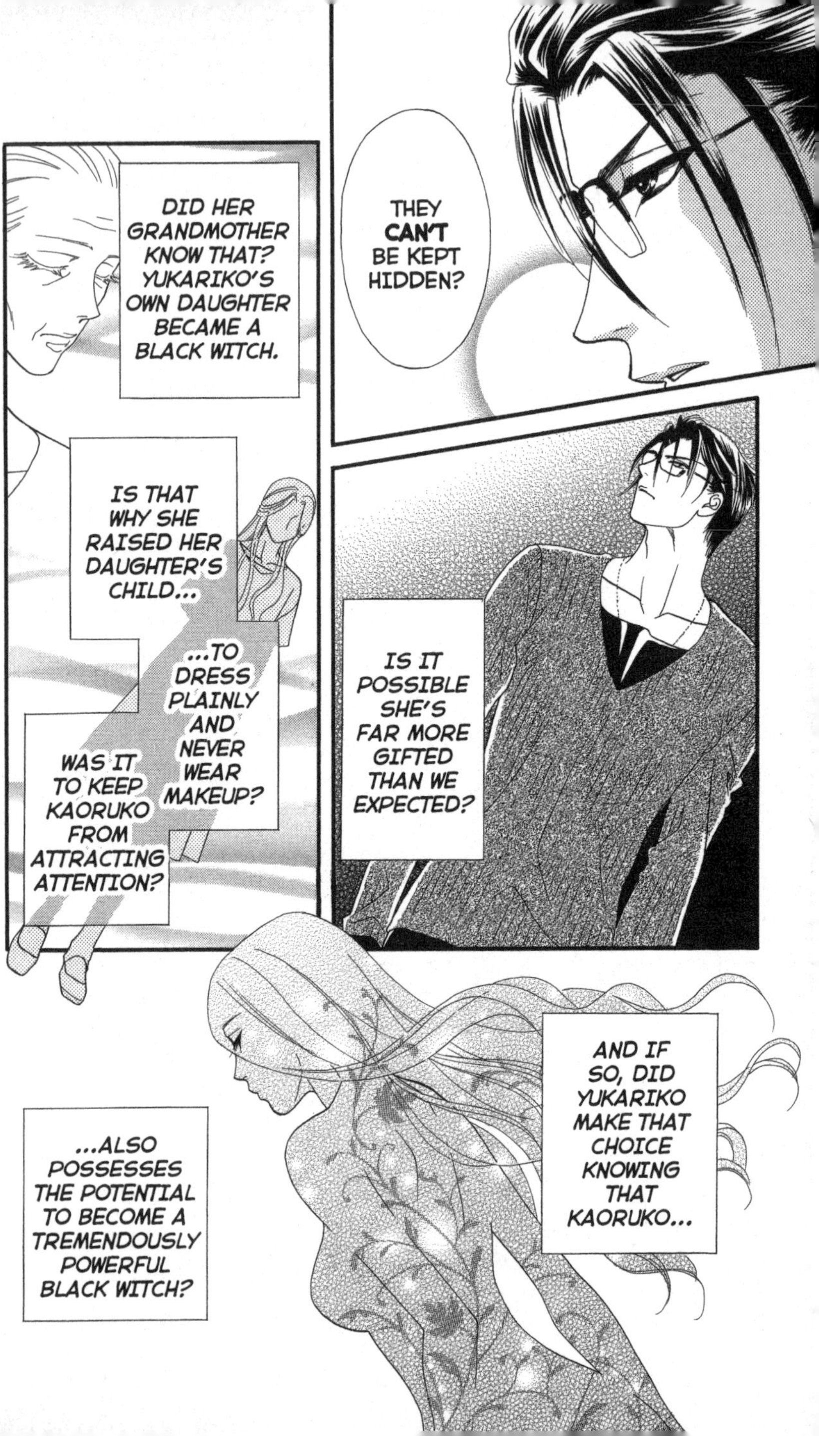
THEY **CAN'T** BE KEPT HIDDEN?
IS IT POSSIBLE SHE'S FAR MORE GIFTED THAN WE EXPECTED?
DID HER GRANDMOTHER KNOW THAT? YUKARIKO'S OWN DAUGHTER BECAME A BLACK WITCH.
IS THAT WHY SHE RAISED HER DAUGHTER'S CHILD...
...TO DRESS PLAINLY AND NEVER WEAR MAKEUP?
WAS IT TO KEEP KAORUKO FROM ATTRACTING ATTENTION?
AND IF SO, DID YUKARIKO MAKE THAT CHOICE KNOWING THAT KAORUKO...
...ALSO POSSESSES THE POTENTIAL TO BECOME A TREMENDOUSLY POWERFUL BLACK WITCH?

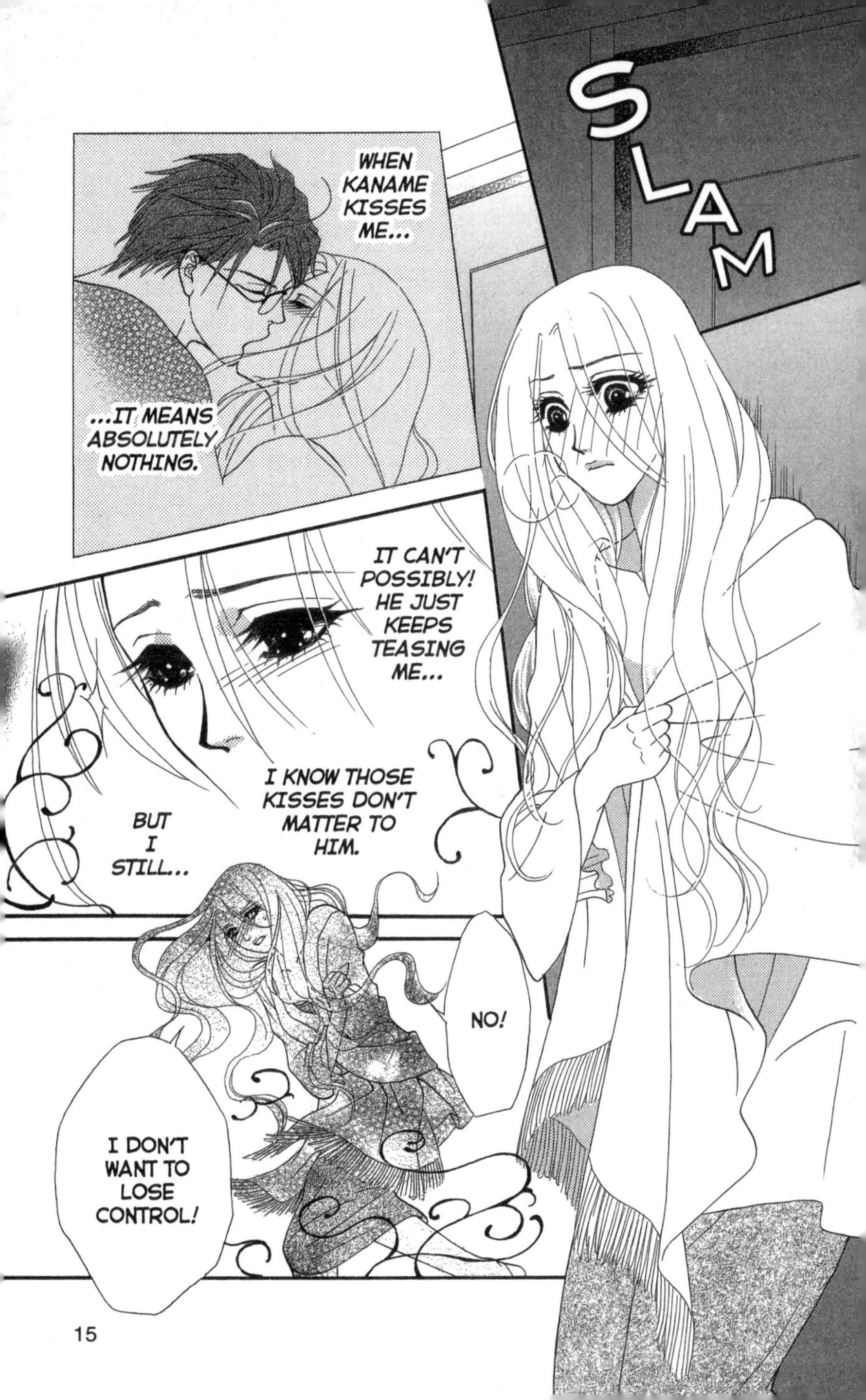
SLAM
WHEN KANAME KISSES ME...
...IT MEANS ABSOLUTELY NOTHING.
IT CAN'T POSSIBLY! HE JUST KEEPS TEASING ME...
I KNOW THOSE KISSES DON'T MATTER TO HIM.
BUT I STILL...
NO!
I DON'T WANT TO LOSE CONTROL!

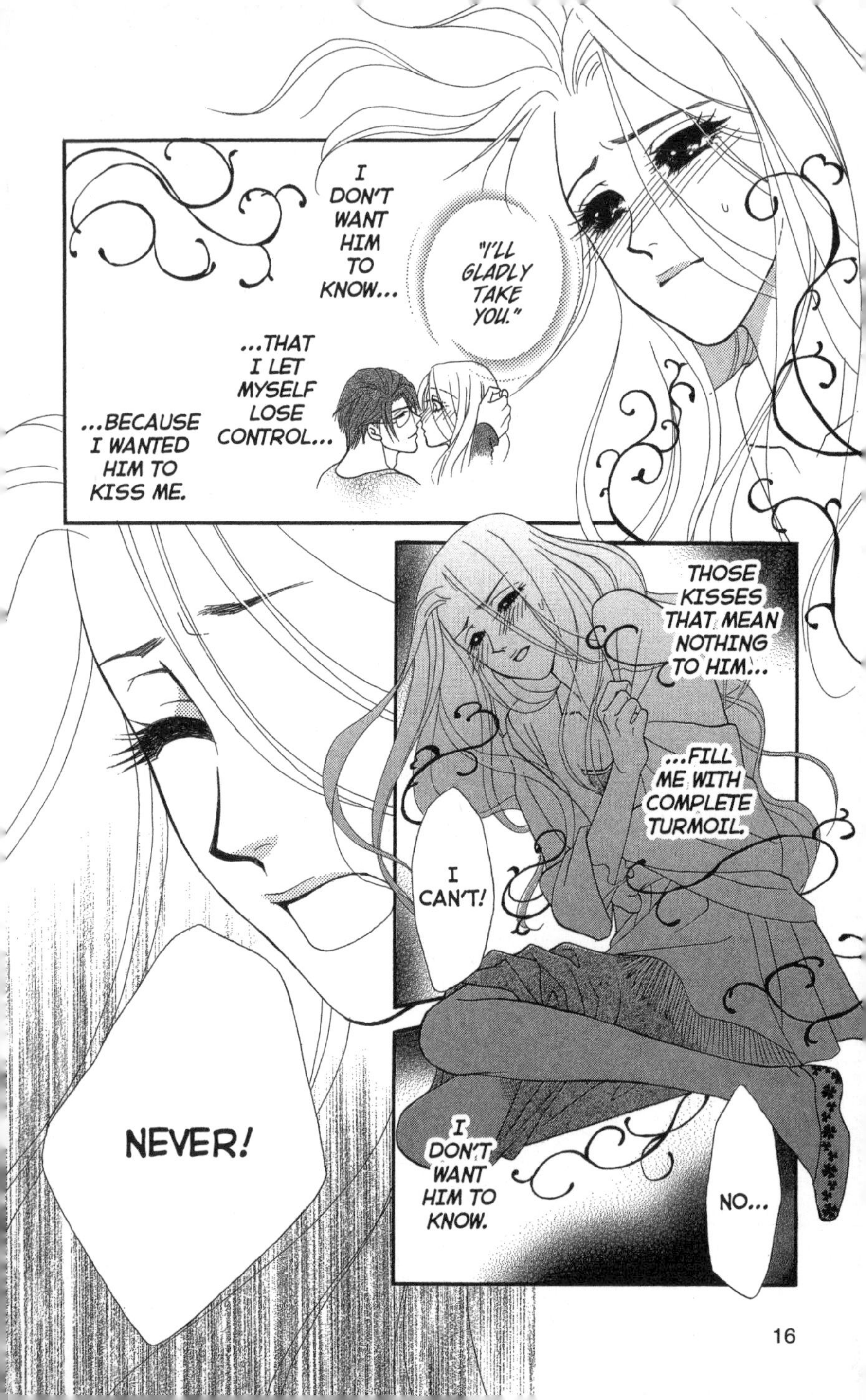
"I'LL GLADLY TAKE YOU."
I DON'T WANT HIM TO KNOW...
...THAT I LET MYSELF LOSE CONTROL...
...BECAUSE I WANTED HIM TO KISS ME.
THOSE KISSES THAT MEAN NOTHING TO HIM...
...FILL ME WITH COMPLETE TURMOIL.
I CAN'T!
NO...
I DON'T WANT HIM TO KNOW.
NEVER!

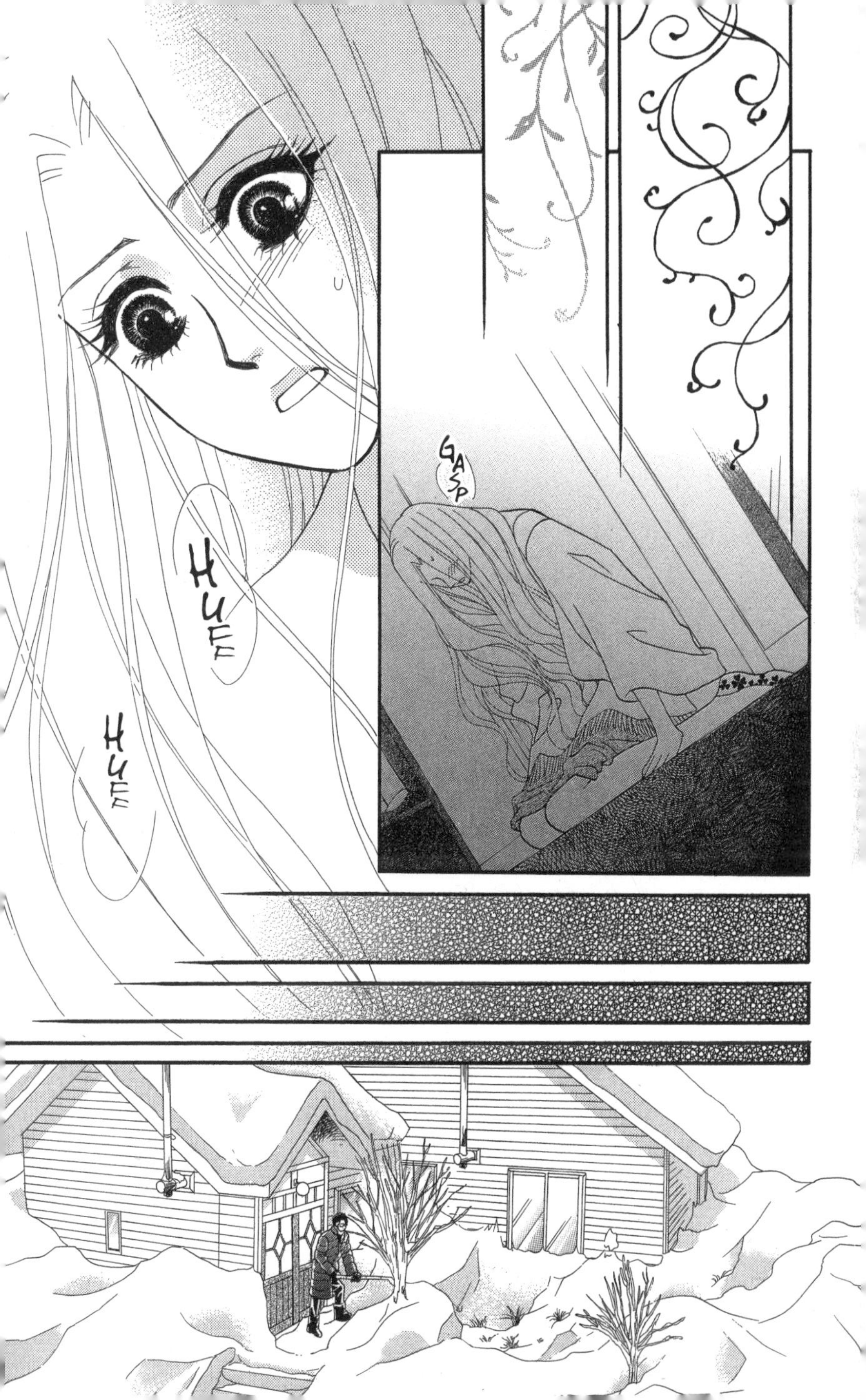
GASP
HUFF
HUFF

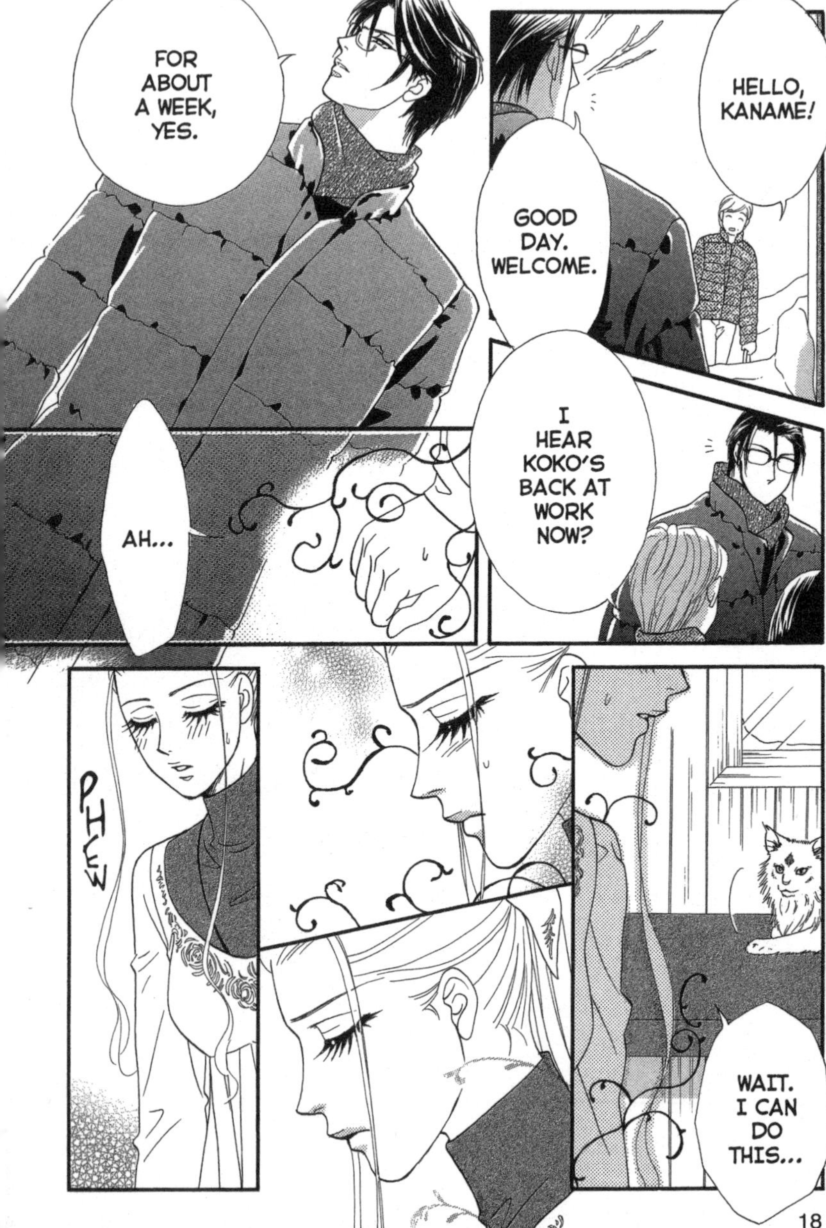
HELLO, KANAME!
GOOD DAY. WELCOME.
I HEAR KOKO'S BACK AT WORK NOW?
FOR ABOUT A WEEK, YES.
AH...
WAIT. I CAN DO THIS...
PHEW

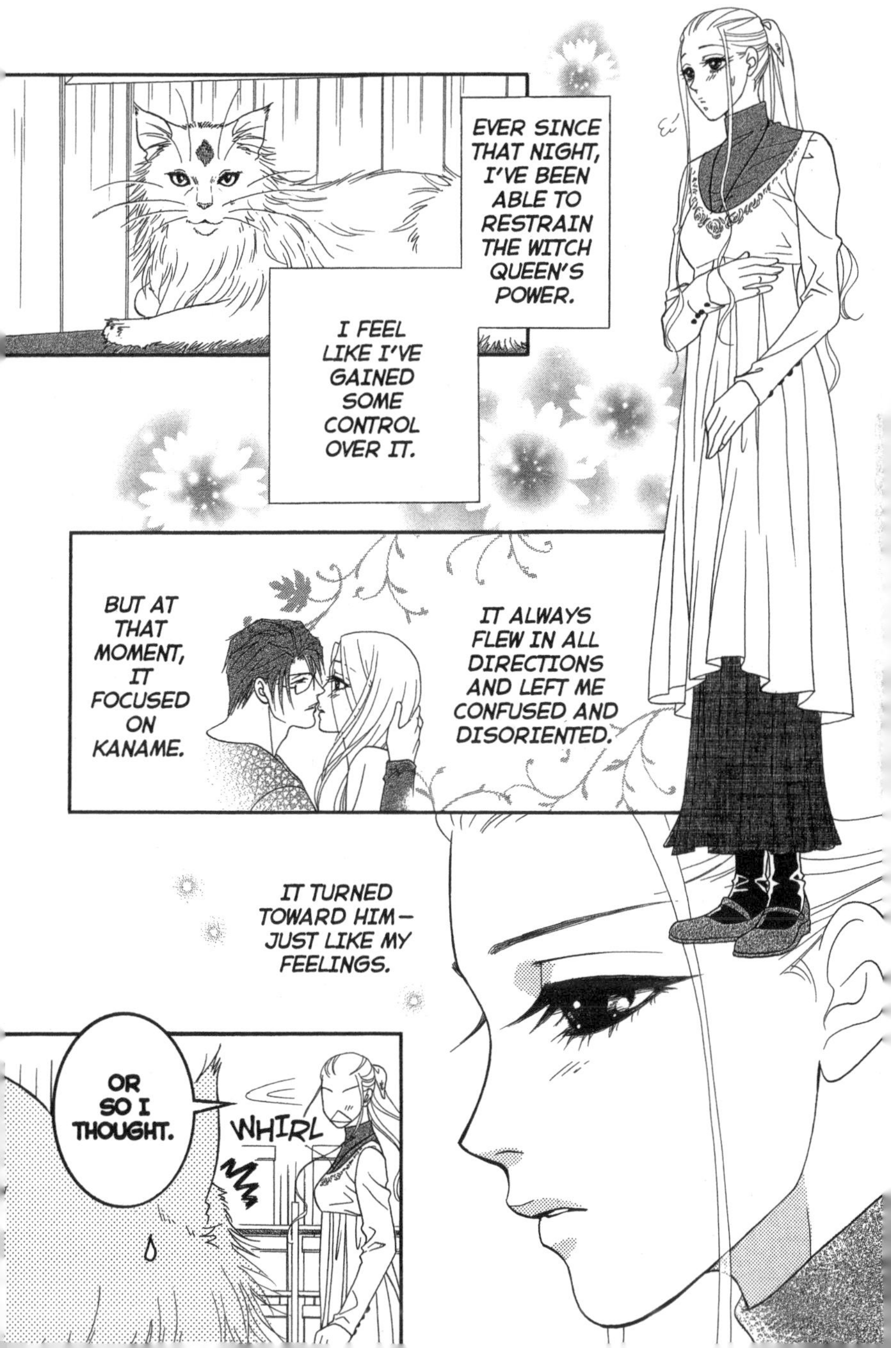
EVER SINCE THAT NIGHT, I'VE BEEN ABLE TO RESTRAIN THE WITCH QUEEN'S POWER.
I FEEL LIKE I'VE GAINED SOME CONTROL OVER IT.
IT ALWAYS FLEW IN ALL DIRECTIONS AND LEFT ME CONFUSED AND DISORIENTED.
BUT AT THAT MOMENT, IT FOCUSED ON KANAME.
IT TURNED TOWARD HIM—JUST LIKE MY FEELINGS.
OR SO I THOUGHT.
WHIRL

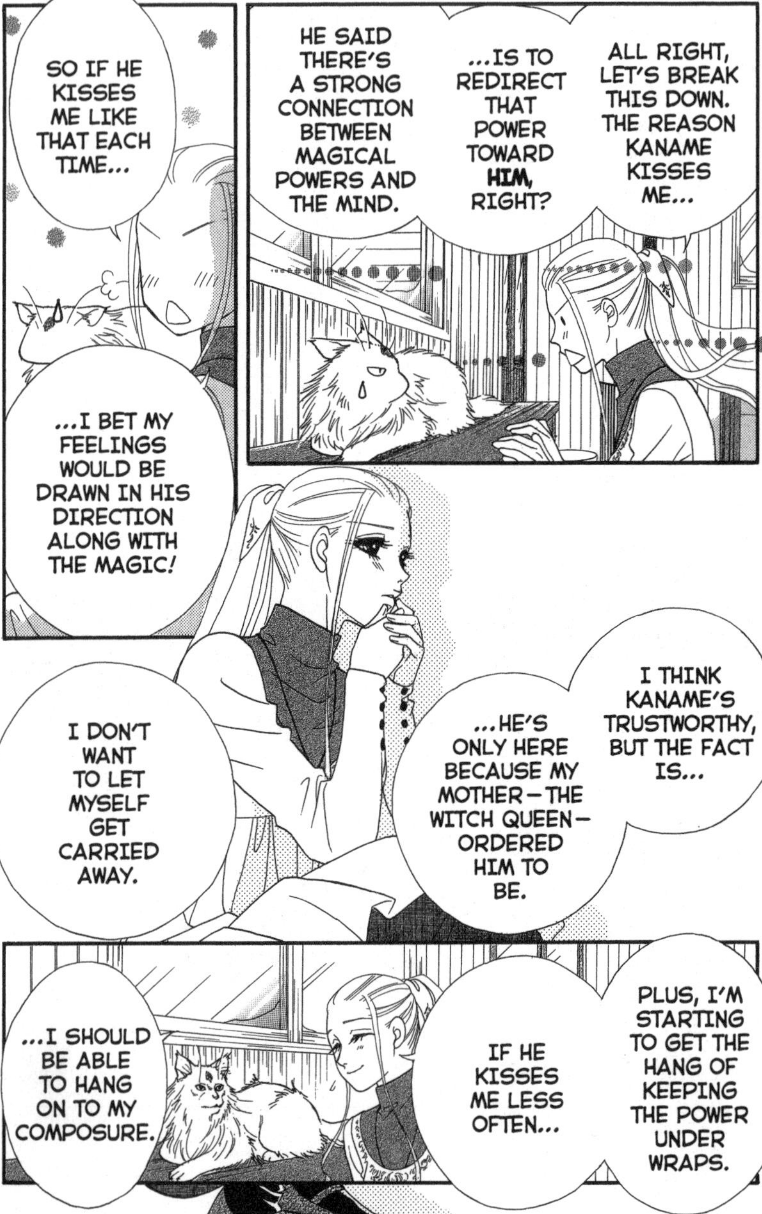
ALL RIGHT, LET'S BREAK THIS DOWN. THE REASON KANAME KISSES ME...
...IS TO REDIRECT THAT POWER TOWARD **HIM**, RIGHT?
HE SAID THERE'S A STRONG CONNECTION BETWEEN MAGICAL POWERS AND THE MIND.
SO IF HE KISSES ME LIKE THAT EACH TIME...
...I BET MY FEELINGS WOULD BE DRAWN IN HIS DIRECTION ALONG WITH THE MAGIC!
I THINK KANAME'S TRUSTWORTHY, BUT THE FACT IS...
...HE'S ONLY HERE BECAUSE MY MOTHER—THE WITCH QUEEN—ORDERED HIM TO BE.
I DON'T WANT TO LET MYSELF GET CARRIED AWAY.
PLUS, I'M STARTING TO GET THE HANG OF KEEPING THE POWER UNDER WRAPS.
IF HE KISSES ME LESS OFTEN...
...I SHOULD BE ABLE TO HANG ON TO MY COMPOSURE.

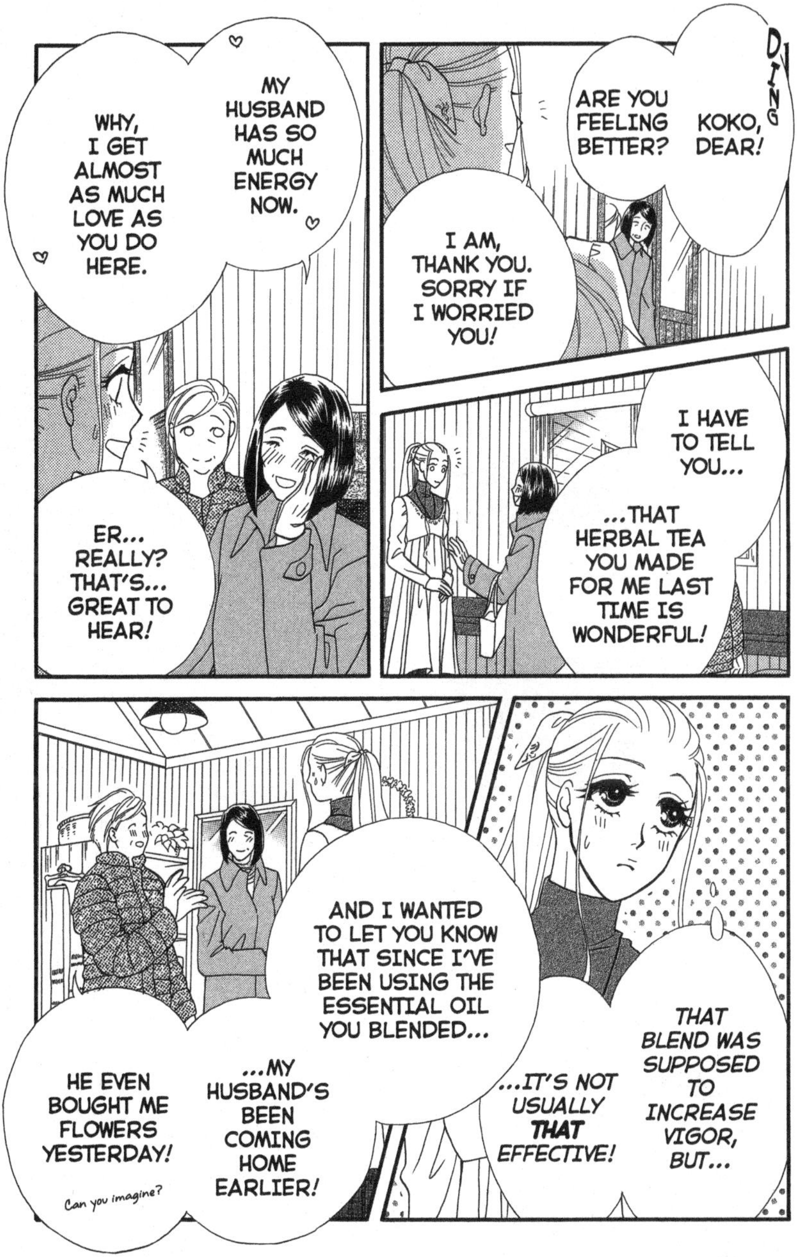
DING
KOKO, DEAR!
ARE YOU FEELING BETTER?
I AM, THANK YOU. SORRY IF I WORRIED YOU!
I HAVE TO TELL YOU...
...THAT HERBAL TEA YOU MADE FOR ME LAST TIME IS WONDERFUL!
MY HUSBAND HAS SO MUCH ENERGY NOW.
WHY, I GET ALMOST AS MUCH LOVE AS YOU DO HERE.
ER... REALLY? THAT'S... GREAT TO HEAR!
THAT BLEND WAS SUPPOSED TO INCREASE VIGOR, BUT...
...IT'S NOT USUALLY THAT EFFECTIVE!
AND I WANTED TO LET YOU KNOW THAT SINCE I'VE BEEN USING THE ESSENTIAL OIL YOU BLENDED...
...MY HUSBAND'S BEEN COMING HOME EARLIER!
HE EVEN BOUGHT ME FLOWERS YESTERDAY!
Can you imagine?

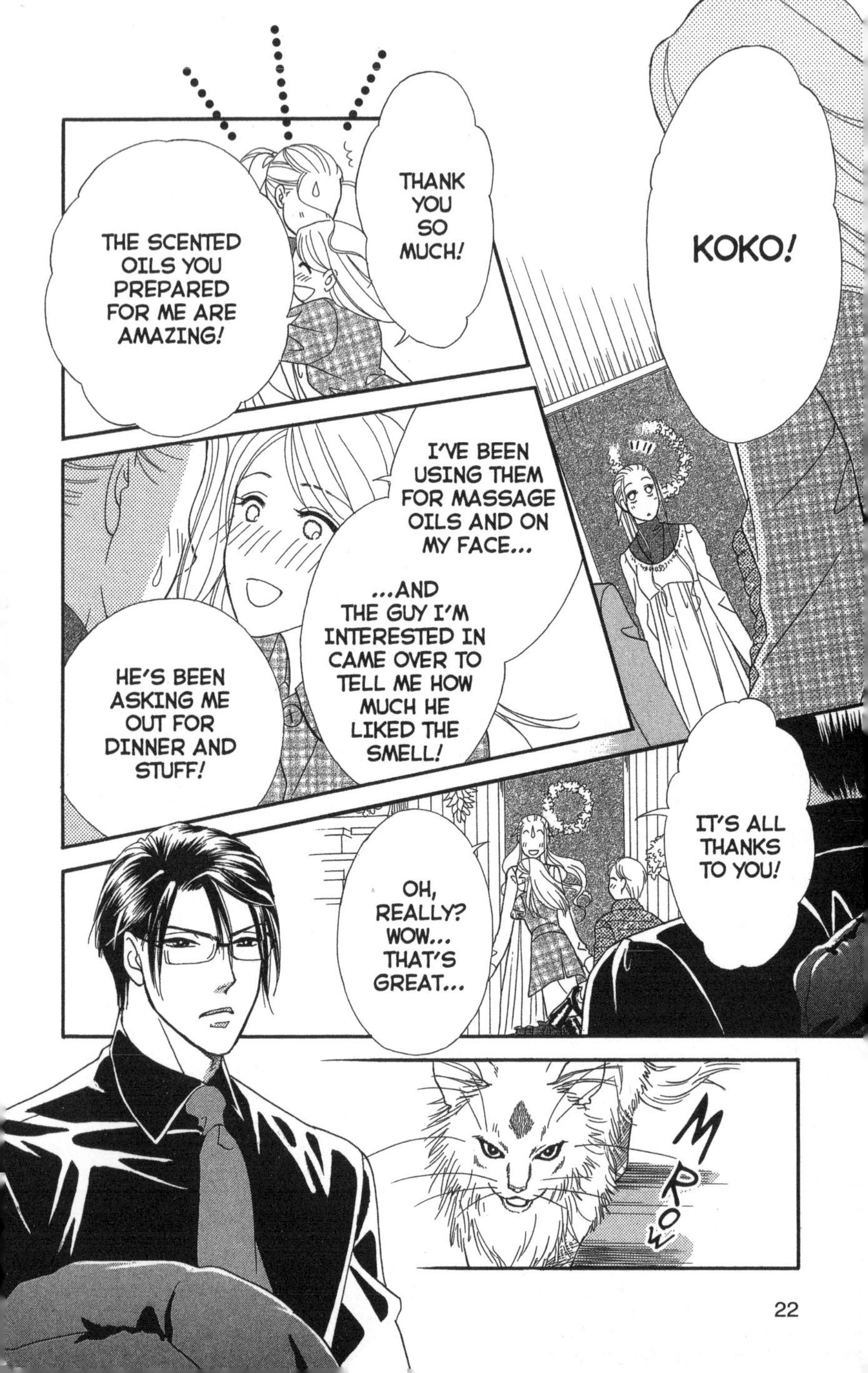
KOKO!
THANK YOU SO MUCH!
THE SCENTED OILS YOU PREPARED FOR ME ARE AMAZING!
I'VE BEEN USING THEM FOR MASSAGE OILS AND ON MY FACE...
...AND THE GUY I'M INTERESTED IN CAME OVER TO TELL ME HOW MUCH HE LIKED THE SMELL!
HE'S BEEN ASKING ME OUT FOR DINNER AND STUFF!
IT'S ALL THANKS TO YOU!
OH, REALLY? WOW... THAT'S GREAT...
MROW

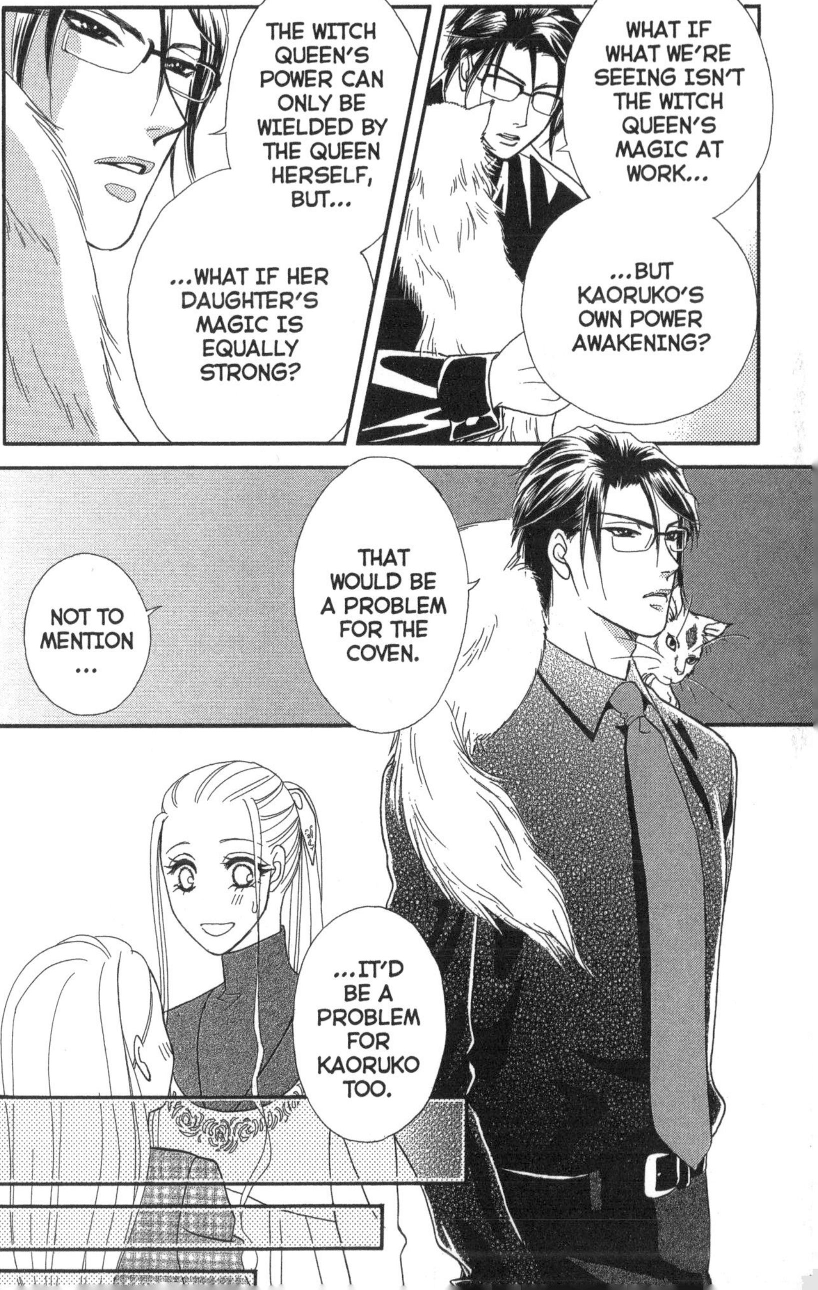
WHAT IF WHAT WE'RE SEEING ISN'T THE WITCH QUEEN'S MAGIC AT WORK...
...BUT KAORUKO'S OWN POWER AWAKENING?
THE WITCH QUEEN'S POWER CAN ONLY BE WIELDED BY THE QUEEN HERSELF, BUT...
...WHAT IF HER DAUGHTER'S MAGIC IS EQUALLY STRONG?
THAT WOULD BE A PROBLEM FOR THE COVEN.
NOT TO MENTION...
...IT'D BE A PROBLEM FOR KAORUKO TOO.

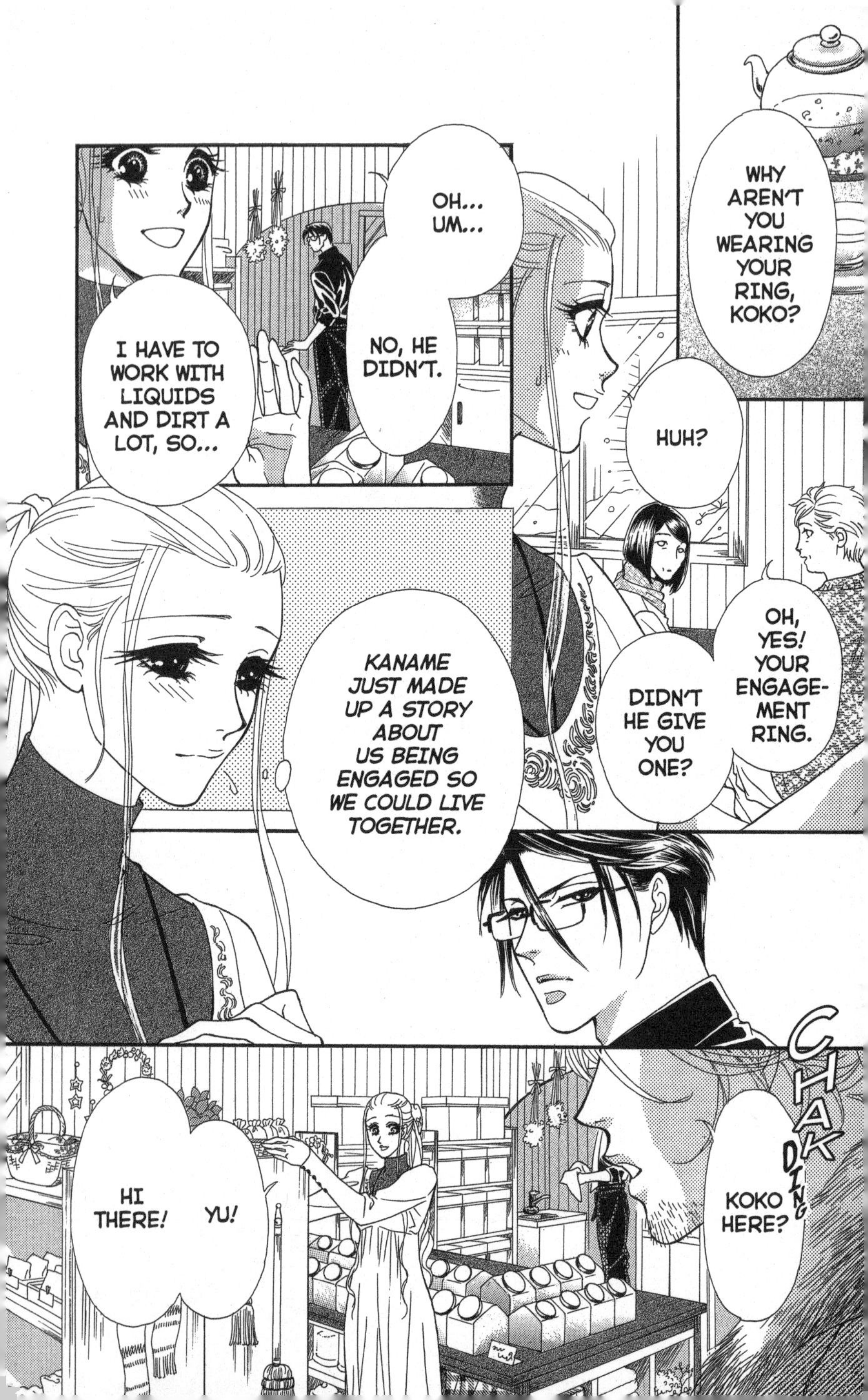
WHY AREN'T YOU WEARING YOUR RING, KOKO?
OH... UM...
NO, HE DIDN'T.
I HAVE TO WORK WITH LIQUIDS AND DIRT A LOT, SO...
HUH?
OH, YES! YOUR ENGAGE-MENT RING.
DIDN'T HE GIVE YOU ONE?
KANAME JUST MADE UP A STORY ABOUT US BEING ENGAGED SO WE COULD LIVE TOGETHER.
CHAK
DING
KOKO HERE?
HI THERE! YU!

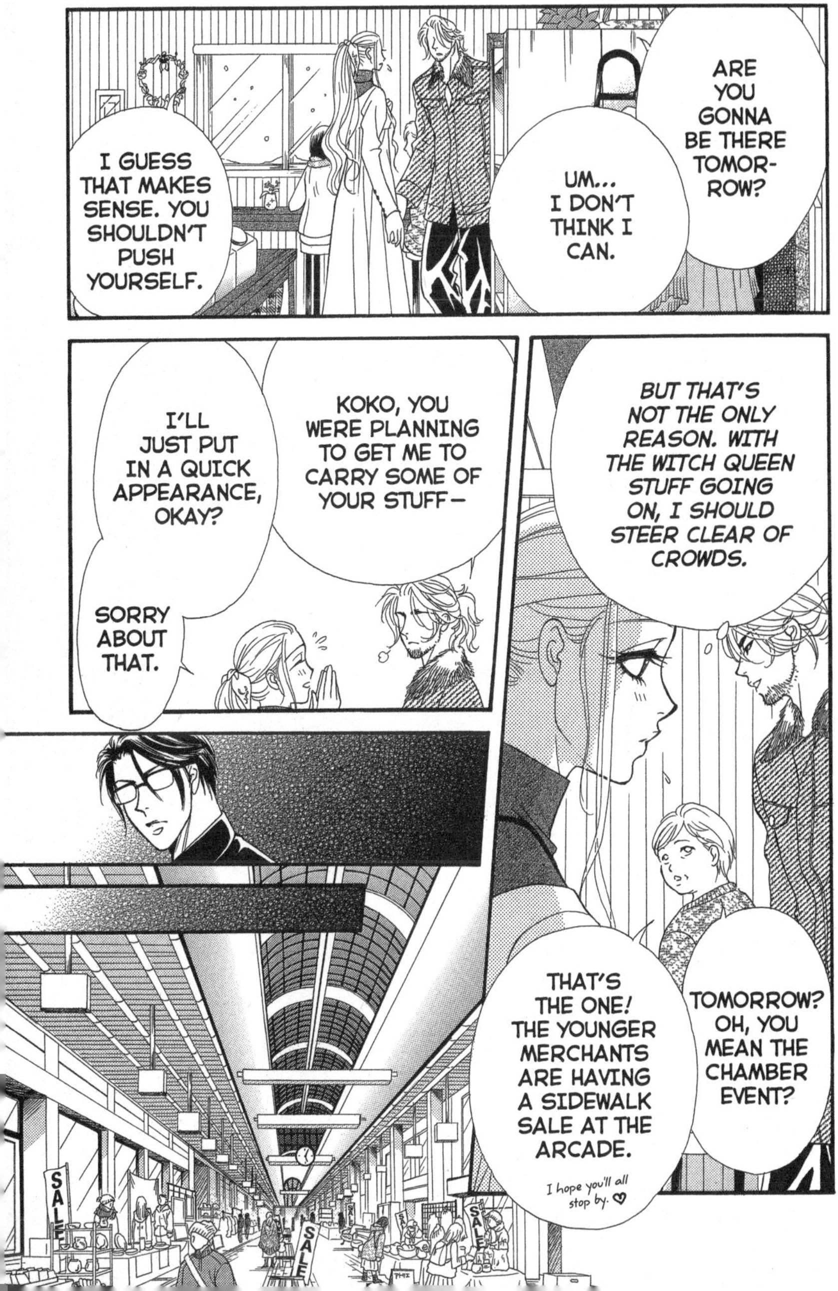
ARE YOU GONNA BE THERE TOMORROW?
UM... I DON'T THINK I CAN.
I GUESS THAT MAKES SENSE. YOU SHOULDN'T PUSH YOURSELF.
BUT THAT'S NOT THE ONLY REASON. WITH THE WITCH QUEEN STUFF GOING ON, I SHOULD STEER CLEAR OF CROWDS.
TOMORROW? OH, YOU MEAN THE CHAMBER EVENT?
THAT'S THE ONE! THE YOUNGER MERCHANTS ARE HAVING A SIDEWALK SALE AT THE ARCADE.
I hope you'll all stop by.
KOKO, YOU WERE PLANNING TO GET ME TO CARRY SOME OF YOUR STUFF—
I'LL JUST PUT IN A QUICK APPEARANCE, OKAY?
SORRY ABOUT THAT.
SALE
SALE
SALE

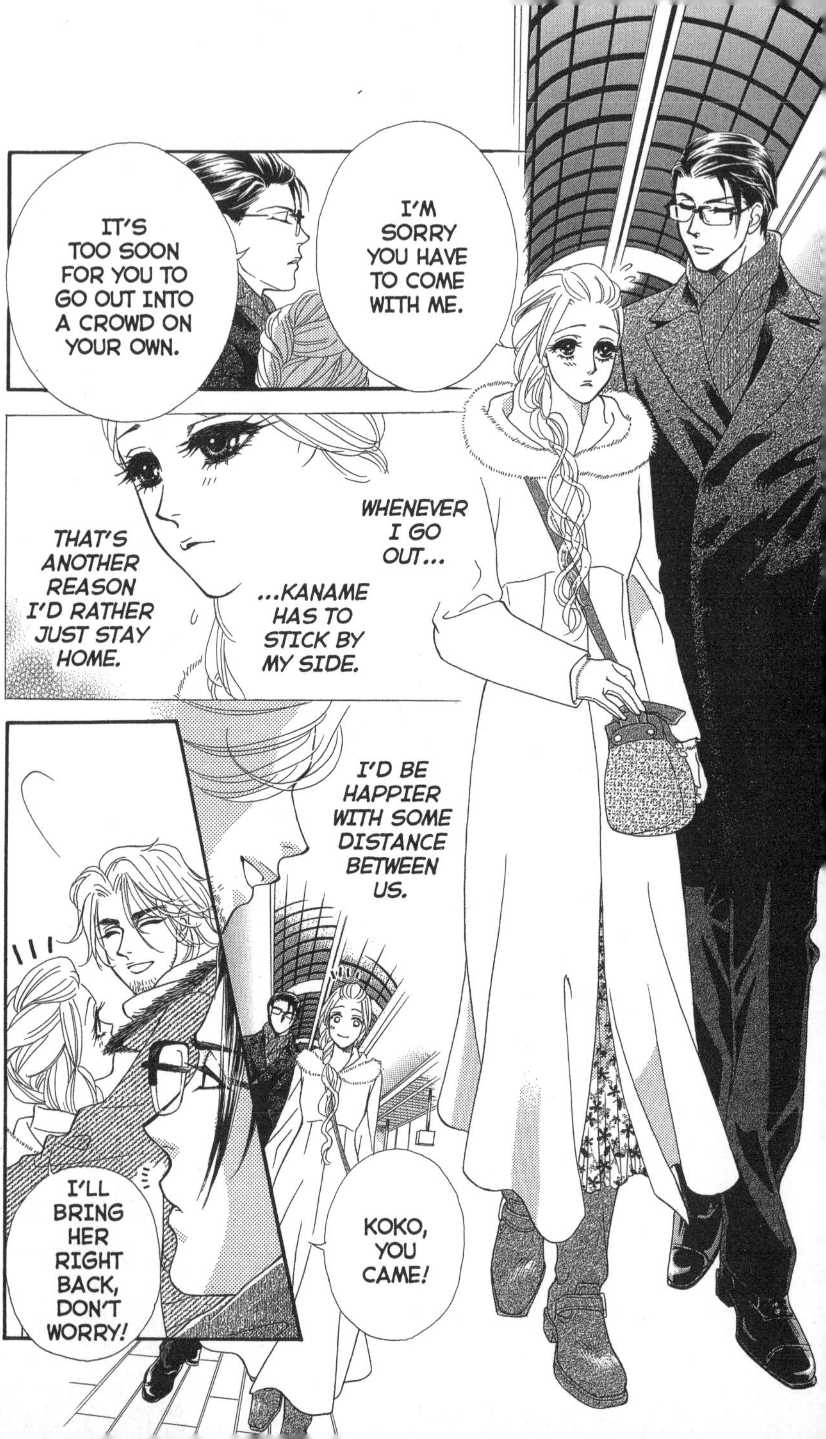
I'M SORRY YOU HAVE TO COME WITH ME.
IT'S TOO SOON FOR YOU TO GO OUT INTO A CROWD ON YOUR OWN.
WHENEVER I GO OUT...
...KANAME HAS TO STICK BY MY SIDE.
THAT'S ANOTHER REASON I'D RATHER JUST STAY HOME.
I'D BE HAPPIER WITH SOME DISTANCE BETWEEN US.
KOKO, YOU CAME!
I'LL BRING HER RIGHT BACK, DON'T WORRY!

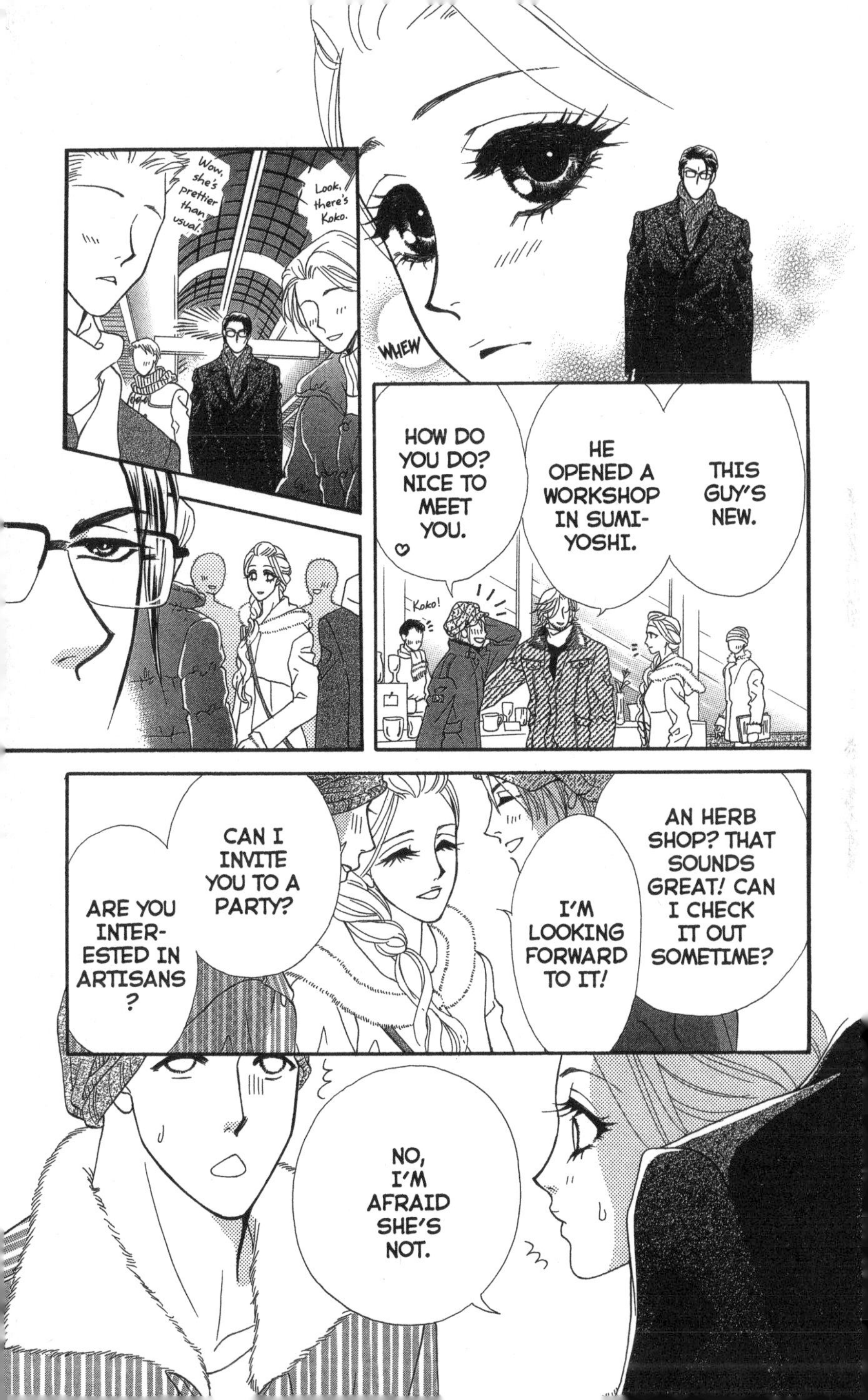
WHEW
Look, there's Koko.
Wow, she's prettier than usual!
THIS GUY'S NEW.
HE OPENED A WORKSHOP IN SUMI-YOSHI.
HOW DO YOU DO? NICE TO MEET YOU.
Koko!
AN HERB SHOP? THAT SOUNDS GREAT! CAN I CHECK IT OUT SOMETIME?
I'M LOOKING FORWARD TO IT!
CAN I INVITE YOU TO A PARTY?
ARE YOU INTER-ESTED IN ARTISANS?
NO, I'M AFRAID SHE'S NOT.

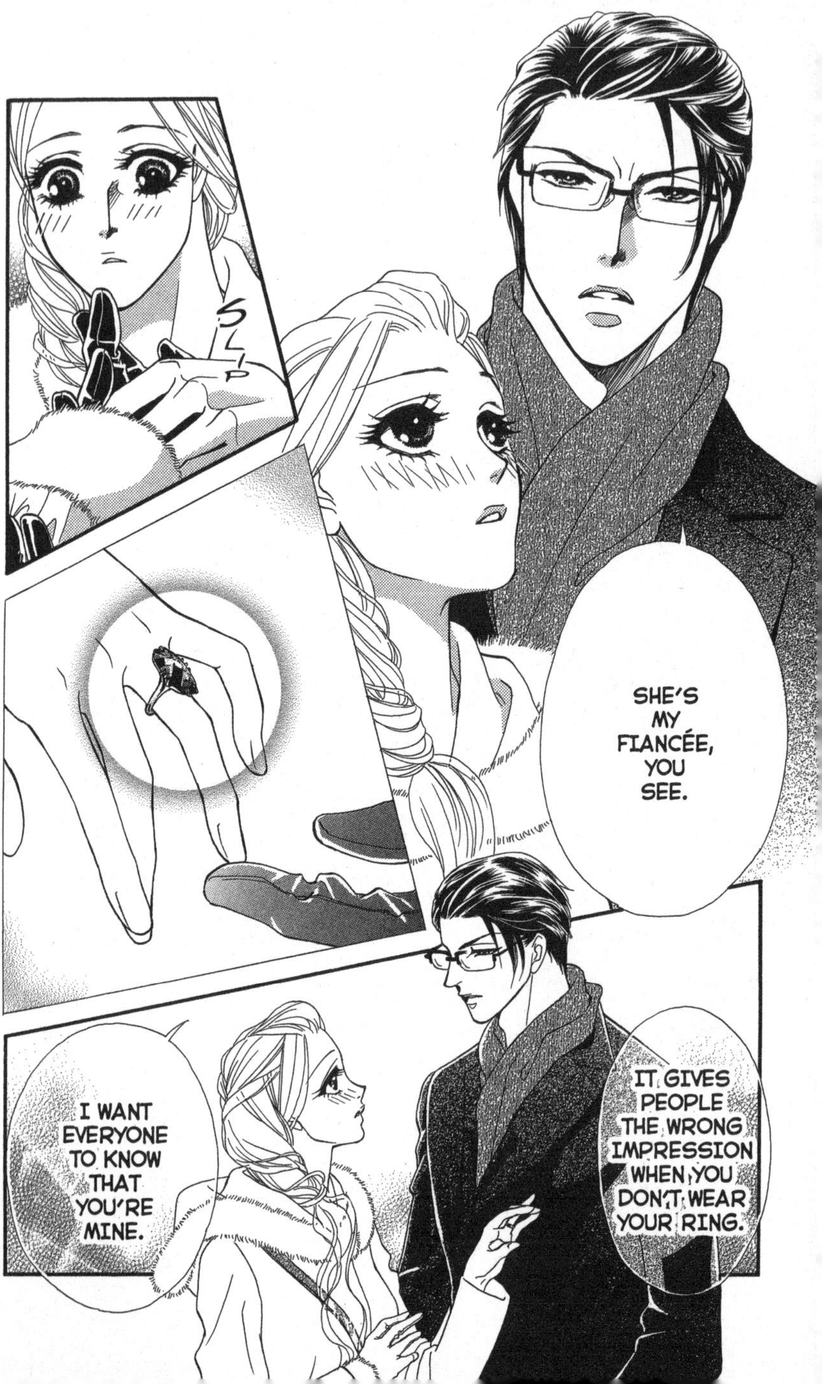
SHE'S MY FIANCÉE, YOU SEE.
SLIP
IT GIVES PEOPLE THE WRONG IMPRESSION WHEN YOU DON'T WEAR YOUR RING.
I WANT EVERYONE TO KNOW THAT YOU'RE MINE.

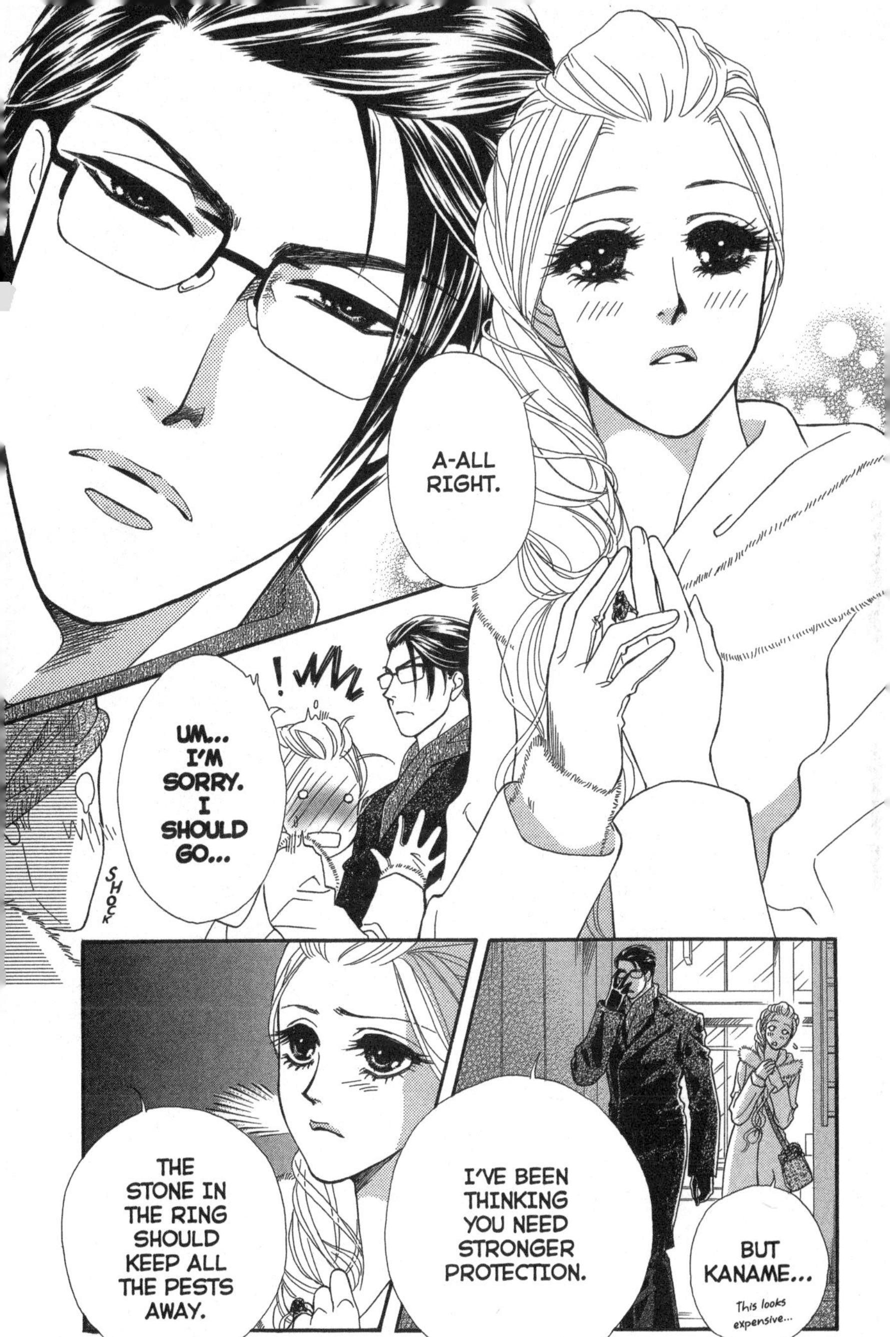
A-ALL RIGHT.
!
UM... I'M SORRY. I SHOULD GO...
SHOCK
BUT KANAME...
This looks expensive...
I'VE BEEN THINKING YOU NEED STRONGER PROTECTION.
THE STONE IN THE RING SHOULD KEEP ALL THE PESTS AWAY.

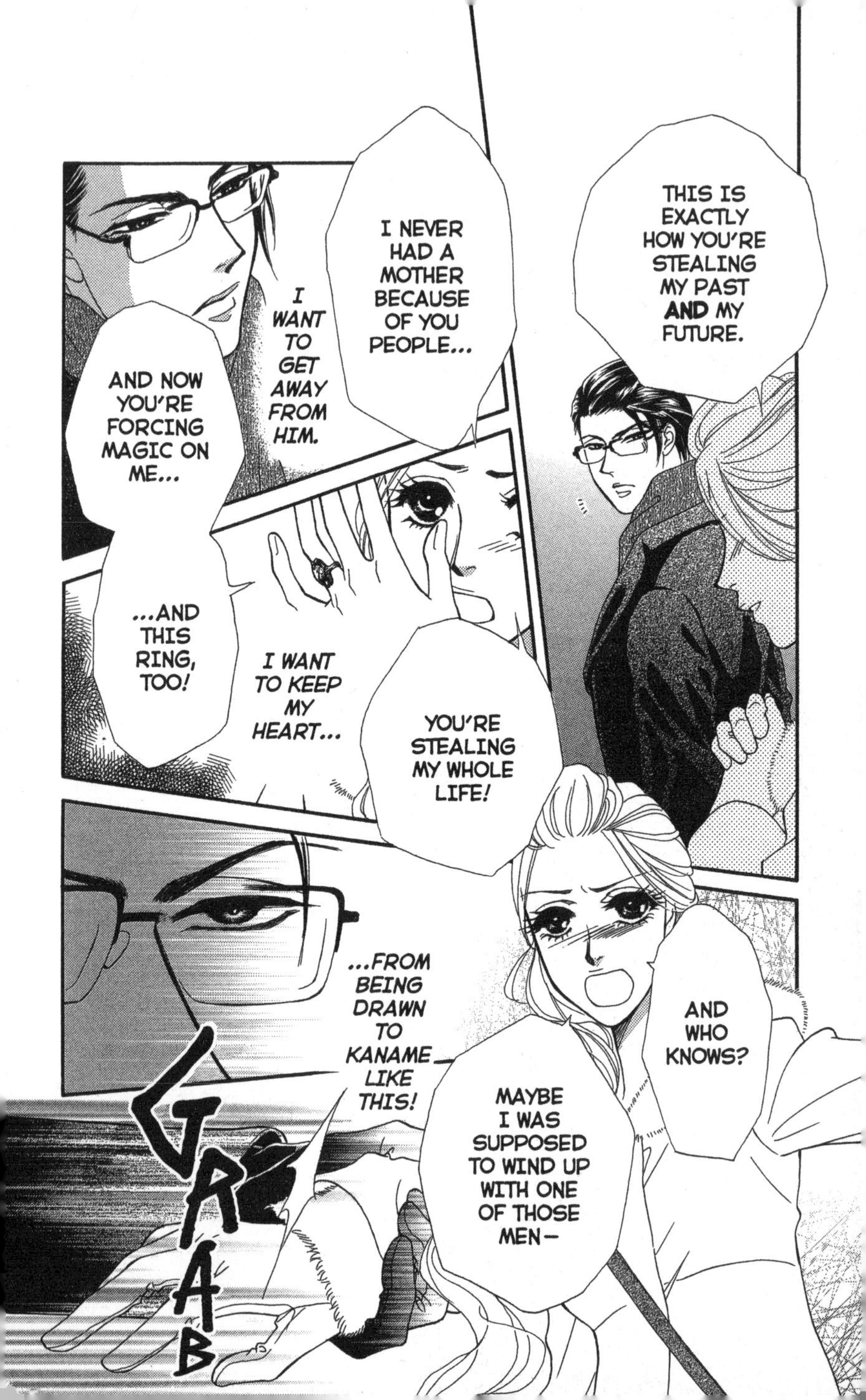
THIS IS EXACTLY HOW YOU'RE STEALING MY PAST **AND** MY FUTURE.
I NEVER HAD A MOTHER BECAUSE OF YOU PEOPLE...
I WANT TO GET AWAY FROM HIM.
AND NOW YOU'RE FORCING MAGIC ON ME...
...AND THIS RING, TOO!
I WANT TO KEEP MY HEART...
YOU'RE STEALING MY WHOLE LIFE!
AND WHO KNOWS?
MAYBE I WAS SUPPOSED TO WIND UP WITH ONE OF THOSE MEN–
...FROM BEING DRAWN TO KANAME LIKE THIS!
GRAB

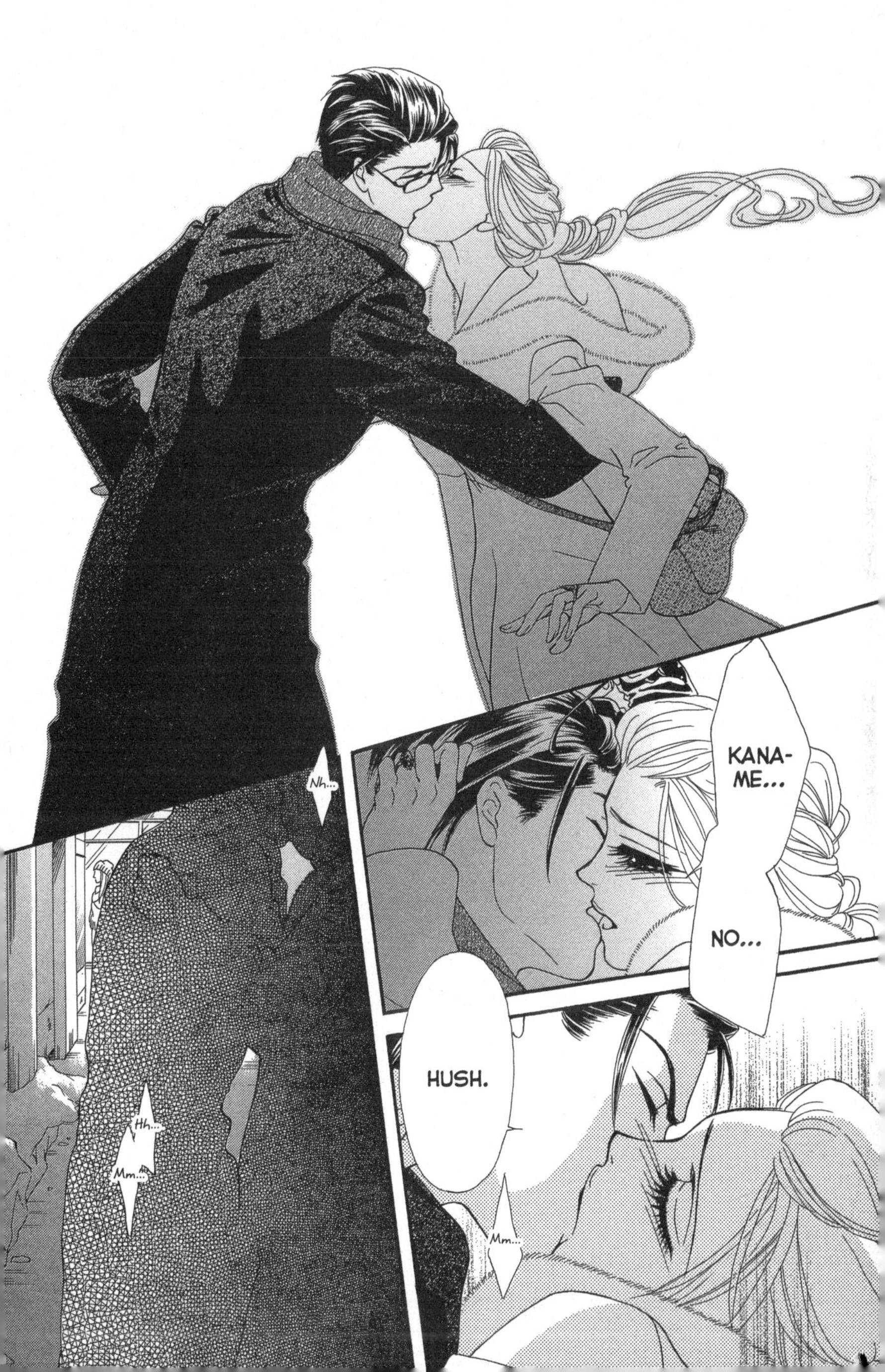

KANA-
ME...
NO...
HUSH.
Mm...
Nh...
Hh...
Mm...

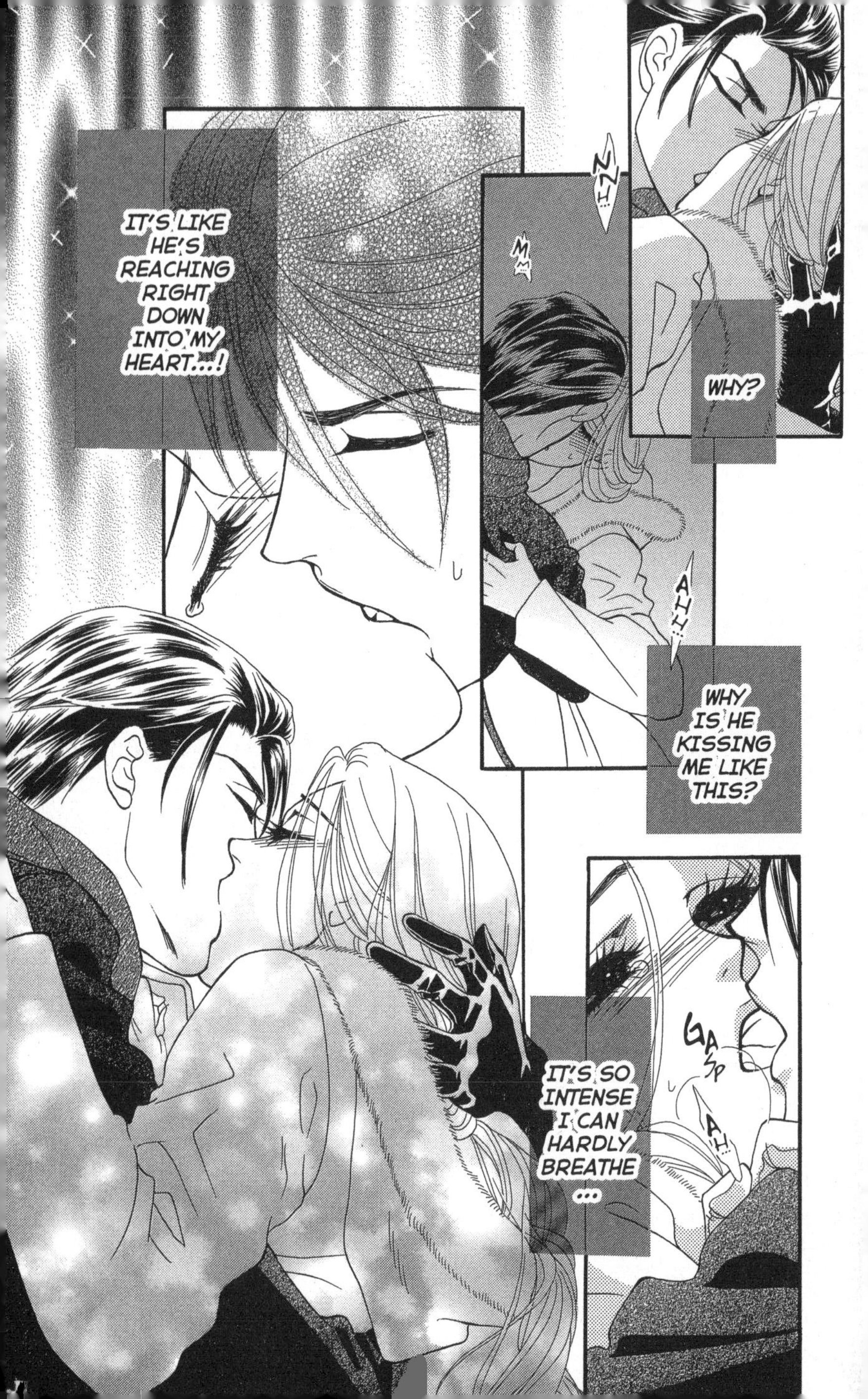
NNH...
WHY?
MM
AHH...
WHY IS HE KISSING ME LIKE THIS?
GASP
AH...
IT'S SO INTENSE I CAN HARDLY BREATHE...
IT'S LIKE HE'S REACHING RIGHT DOWN INTO MY HEART...!

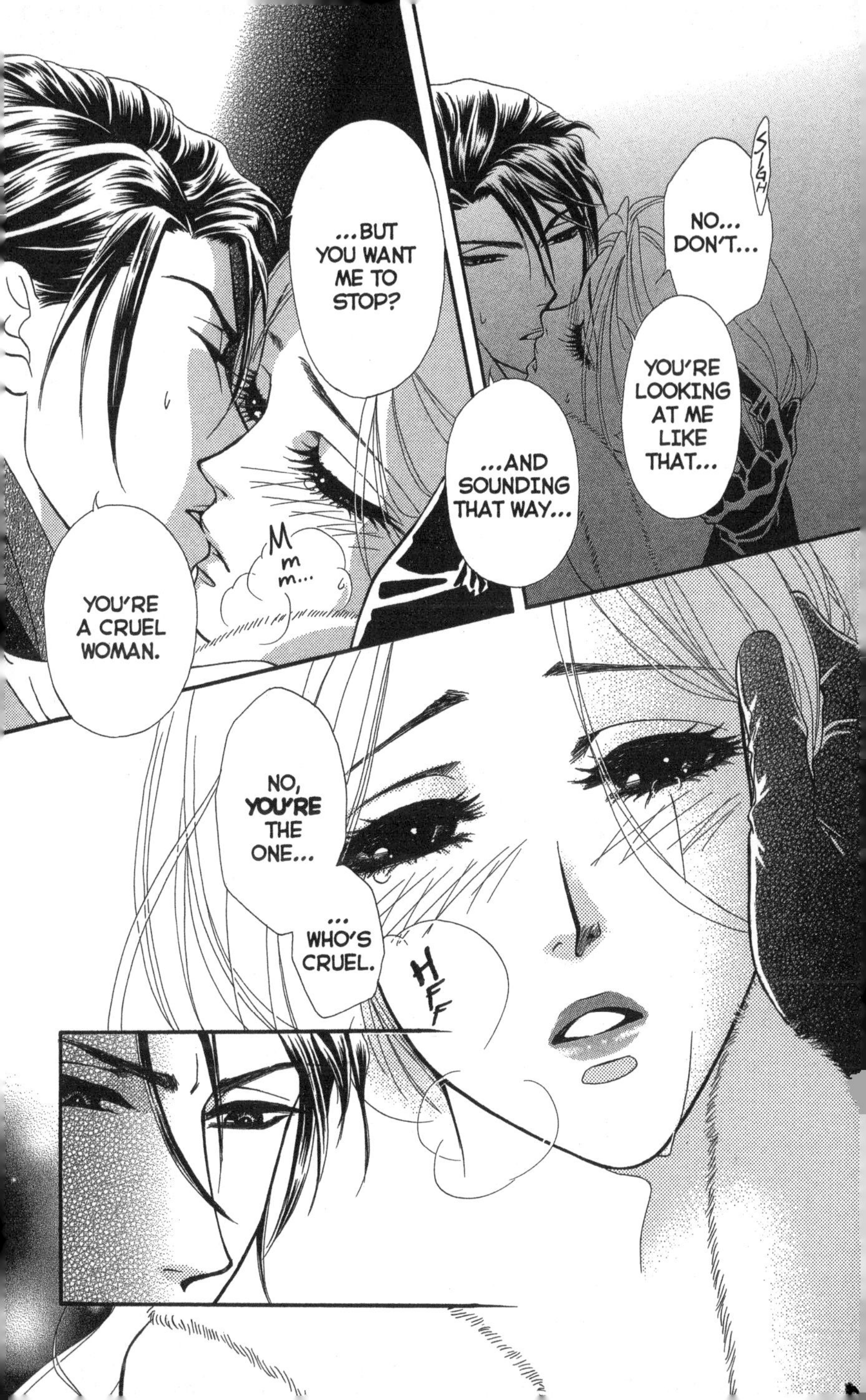
SIGH
NO... DON'T...
YOU'RE LOOKING AT ME LIKE THAT...
...AND SOUNDING THAT WAY...
...BUT YOU WANT ME TO STOP?
Mmm...
YOU'RE A CRUEL WOMAN.
NO, **YOU'RE** THE ONE...
...WHO'S CRUEL.
HFF

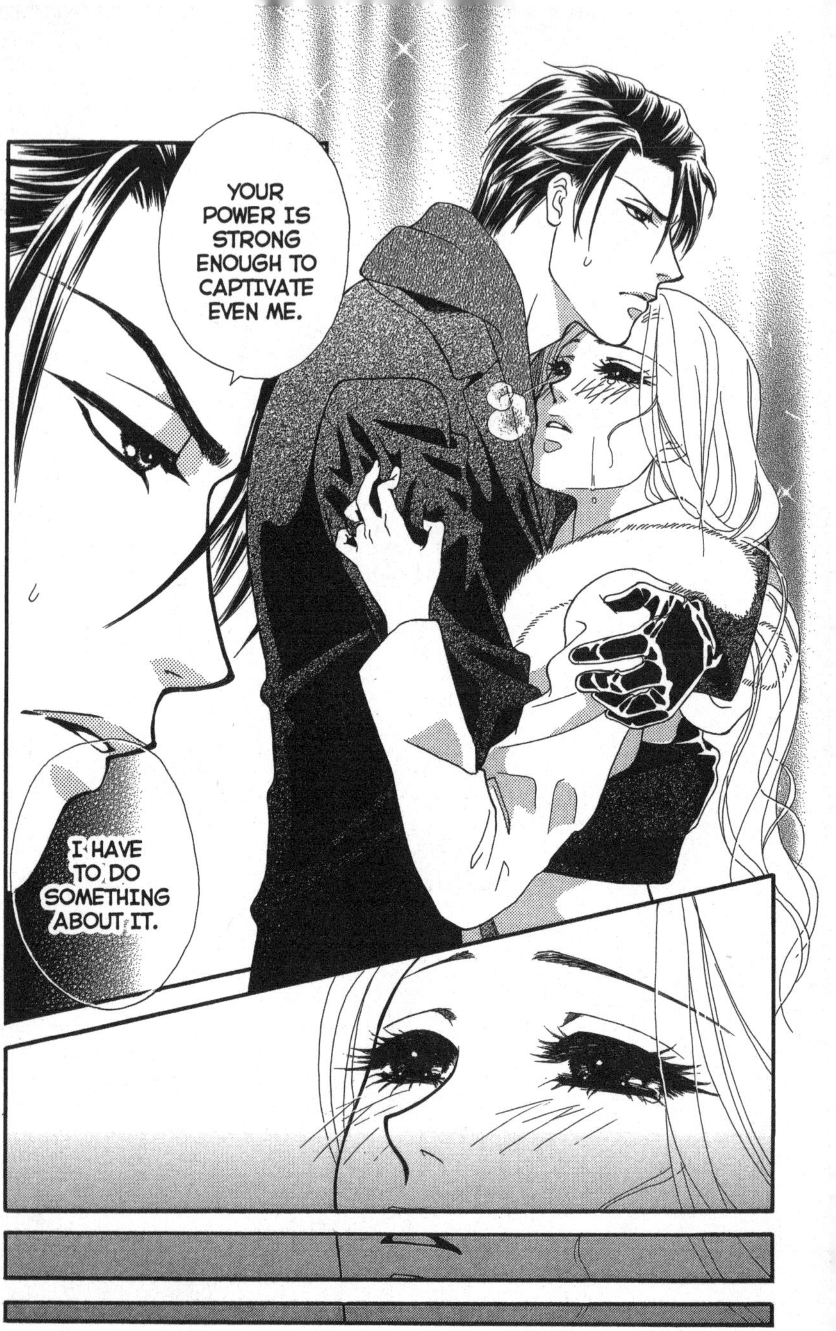
YOUR POWER IS STRONG ENOUGH TO CAPTIVATE EVEN ME.
I HAVE TO DO SOMETHING ABOUT IT.

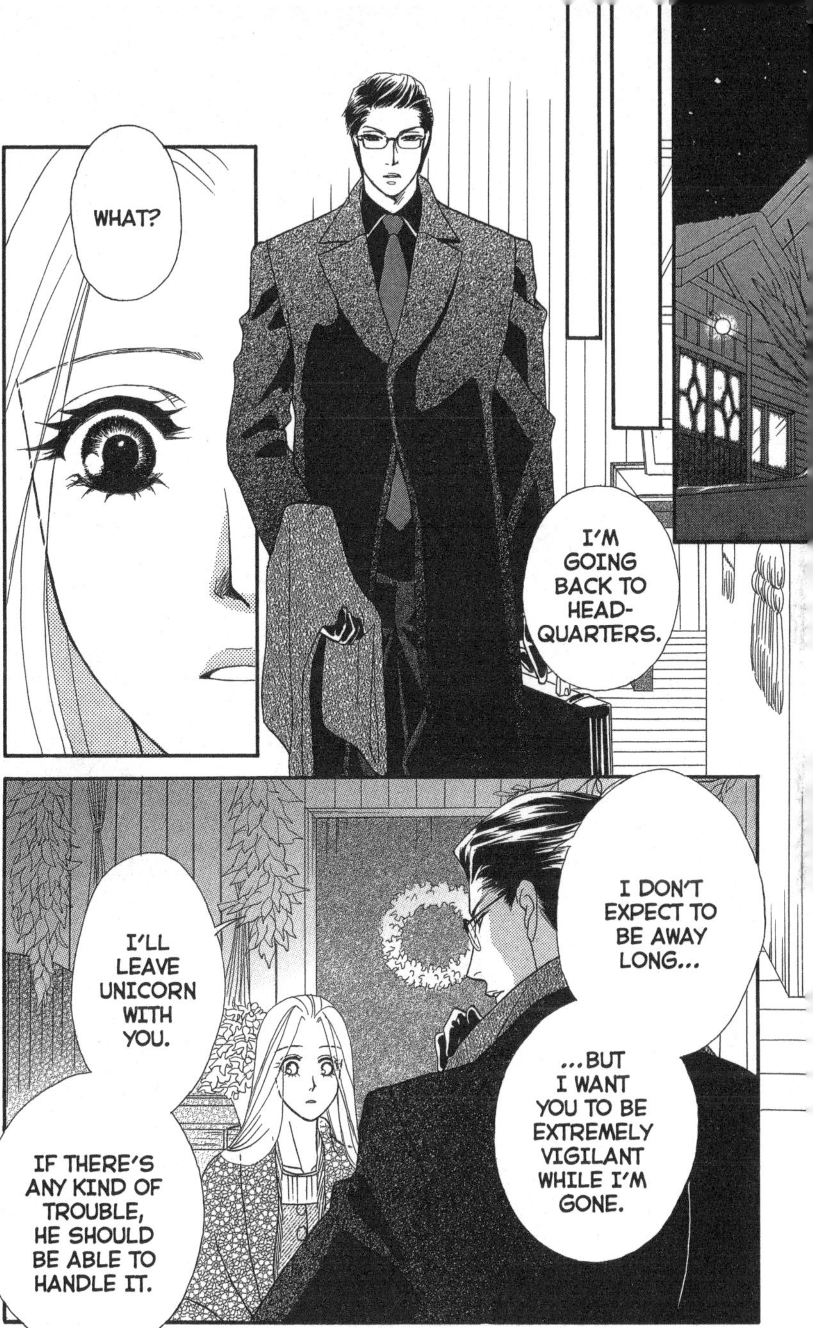
I'M GOING BACK TO HEAD-QUARTERS.
WHAT?
I DON'T EXPECT TO BE AWAY LONG...
...BUT I WANT YOU TO BE EXTREMELY VIGILANT WHILE I'M GONE.
I'LL LEAVE UNICORN WITH YOU.
IF THERE'S ANY KIND OF TROUBLE, HE SHOULD BE ABLE TO HANDLE IT.

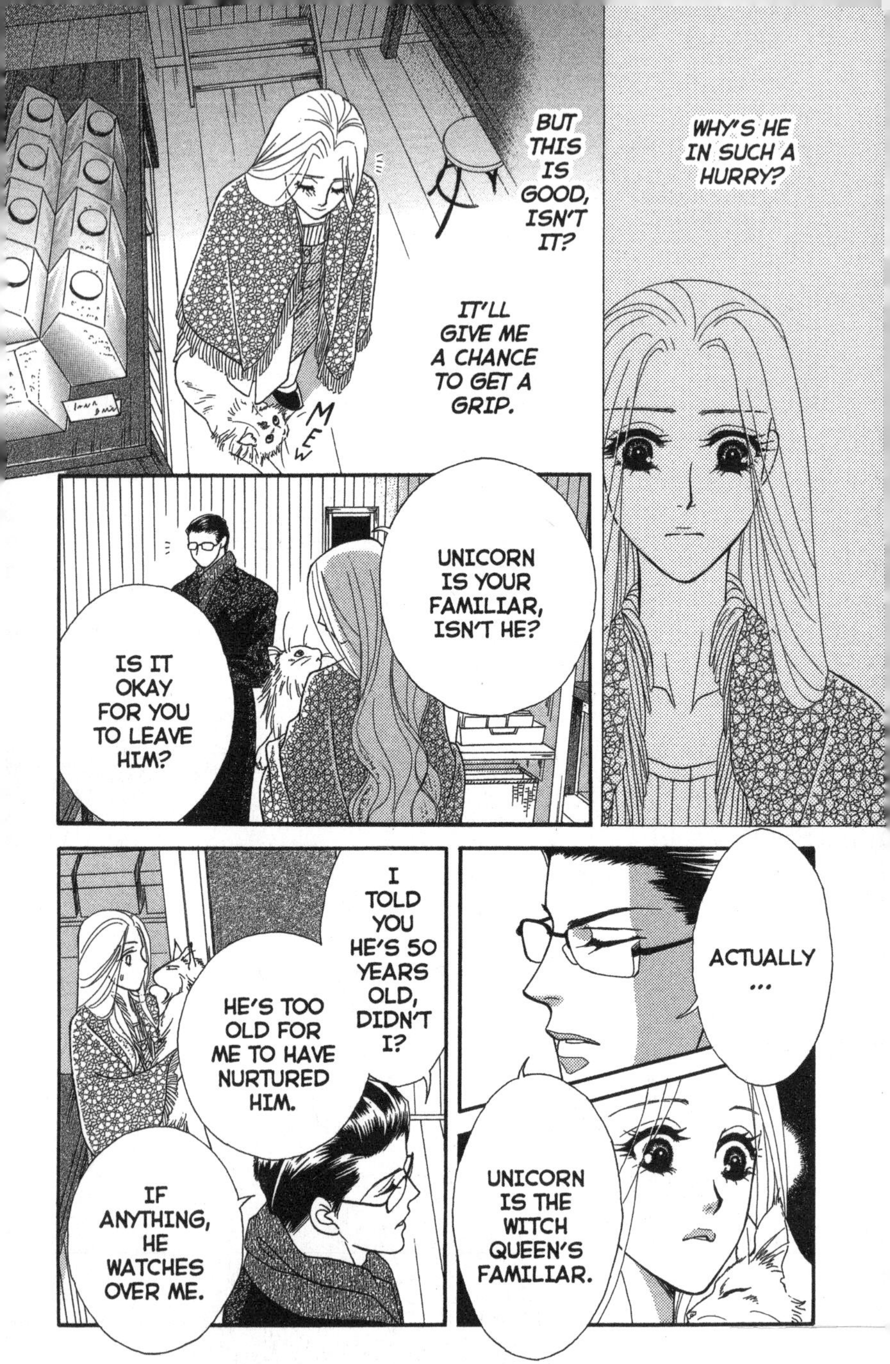
WHY'S HE IN SUCH A HURRY?
BUT THIS IS GOOD, ISN'T IT?
IT'LL GIVE ME A CHANCE TO GET A GRIP.
MEW
UNICORN IS YOUR FAMILIAR, ISN'T HE?
IS IT OKAY FOR YOU TO LEAVE HIM?
ACTUALLY...
UNICORN IS THE WITCH QUEEN'S FAMILIAR.
I TOLD YOU HE'S 50 YEARS OLD, DIDN'T I?
HE'S TOO OLD FOR ME TO HAVE NURTURED HIM.
IF ANYTHING, HE WATCHES OVER ME.

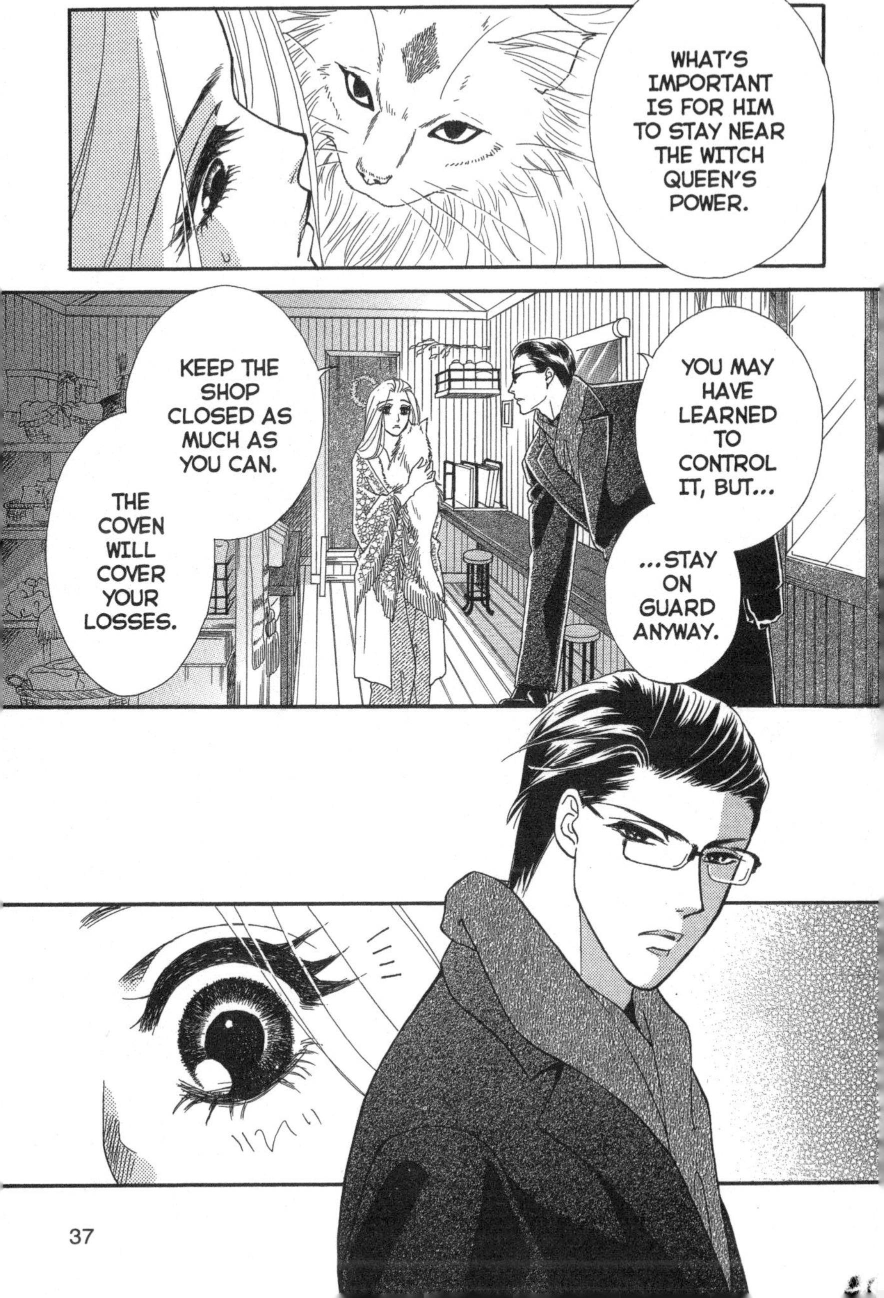
WHAT'S IMPORTANT IS FOR HIM TO STAY NEAR THE WITCH QUEEN'S POWER.
YOU MAY HAVE LEARNED TO CONTROL IT, BUT...
...STAY ON GUARD ANYWAY.
KEEP THE SHOP CLOSED AS MUCH AS YOU CAN.
THE COVEN WILL COVER YOUR LOSSES.

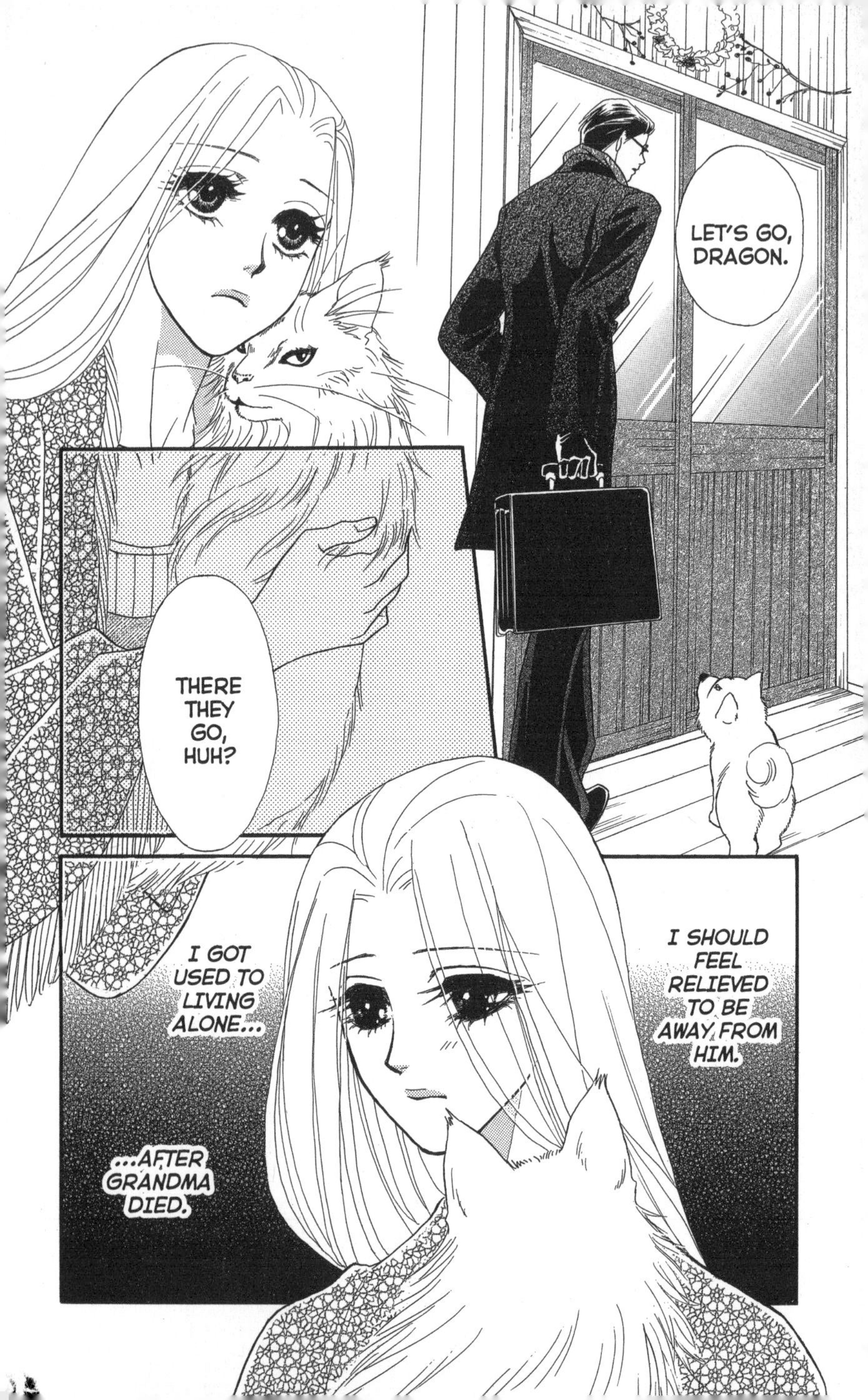
LET'S GO, DRAGON.
THERE THEY GO, HUH?
I SHOULD FEEL RELIEVED TO BE AWAY FROM HIM.
I GOT USED TO LIVING ALONE...
...AFTER GRANDMA DIED.

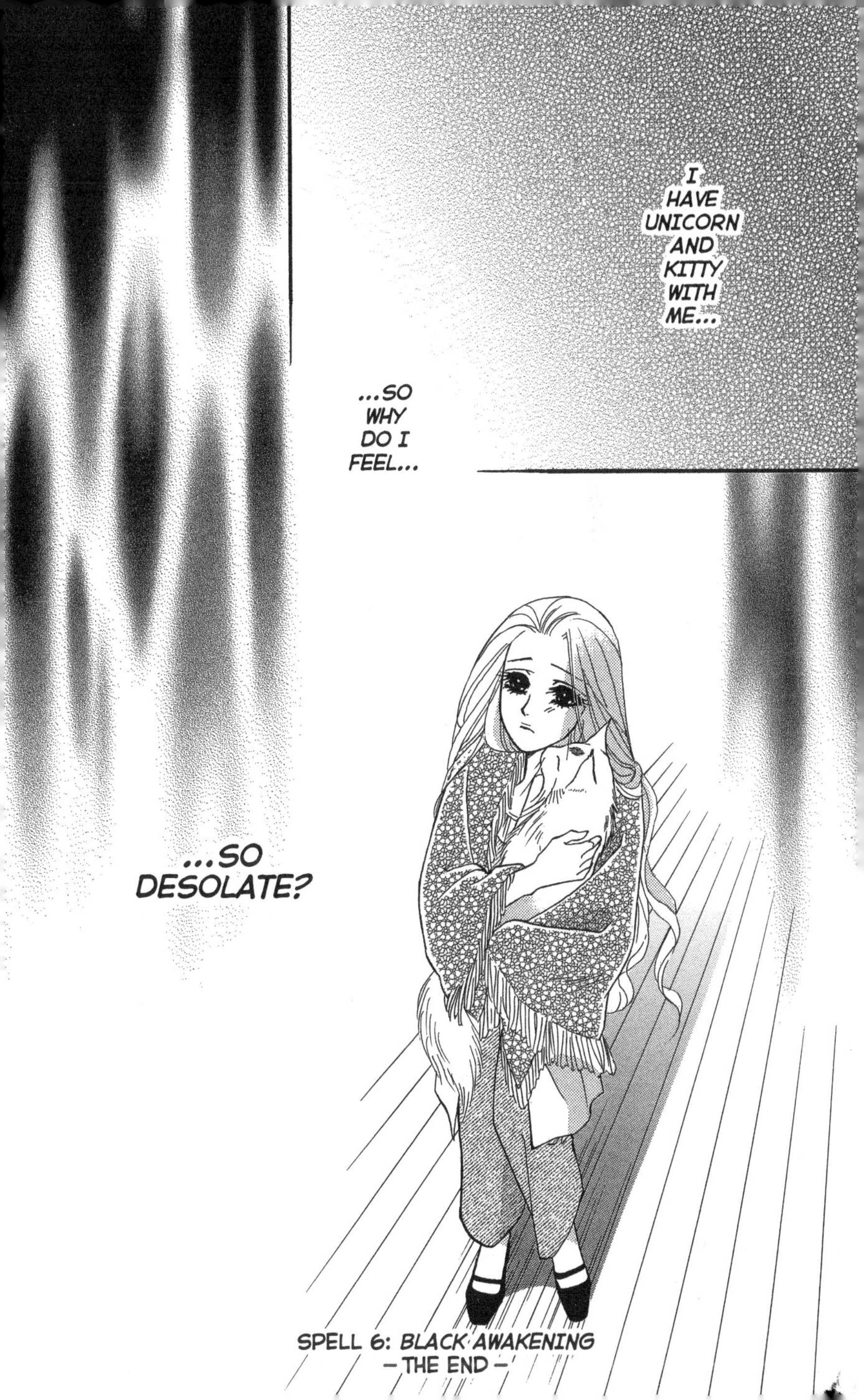
I HAVE UNICORN AND KITTY WITH ME...
...SO WHY DO I FEEL...
...SO DESOLATE?
SPELL 6: BLACK AWAKENING
–THE END–

– BLACK AWAKENING –

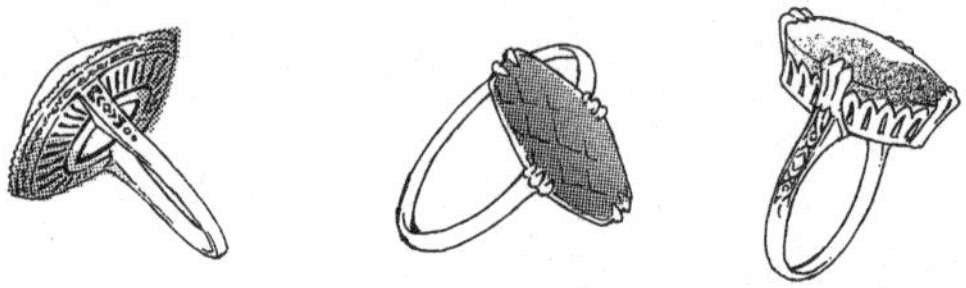

I love rings with retro designs! I like how the embellishments on the metal are designed so precisely. I'm drawn to objects where you can really sense all the work that went into them.

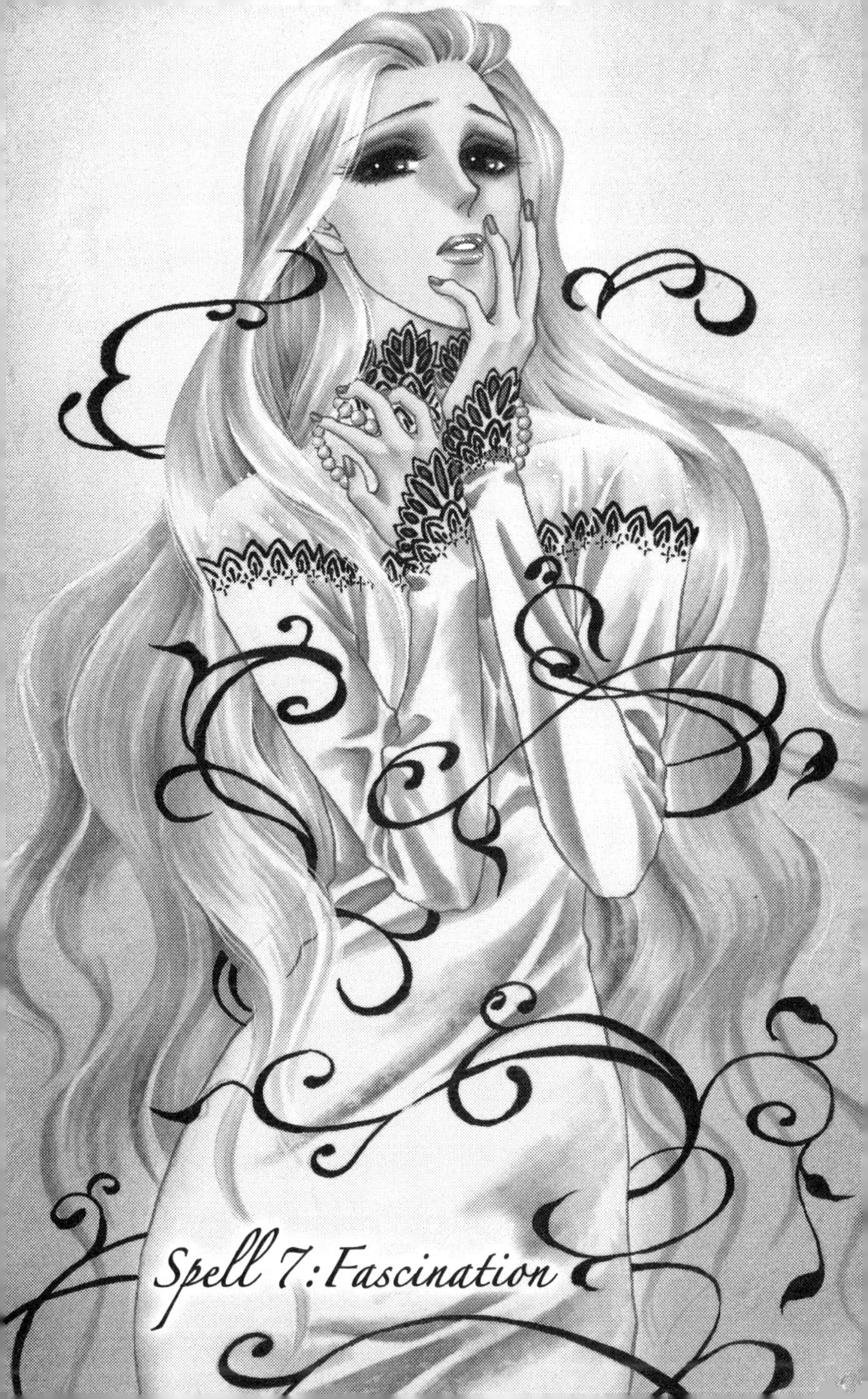
Spell 7: Fascination

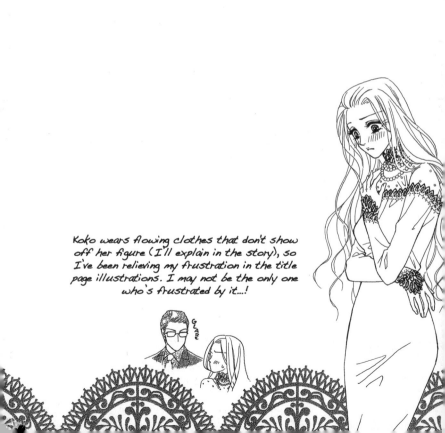

Koko wears flowing clothes that don't show off her figure (I'll explain in the story), so I've been relieving my frustration in the title page illustrations. I may not be the only one who's frustrated by it...!

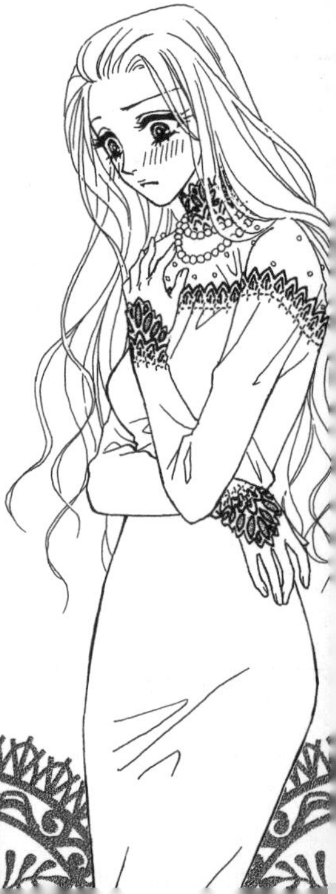

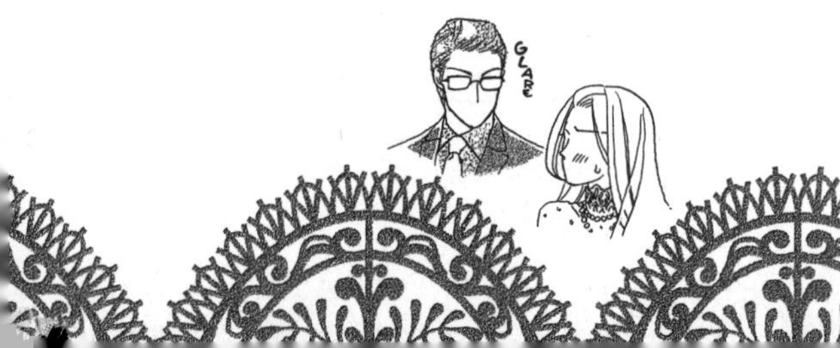
GLARE

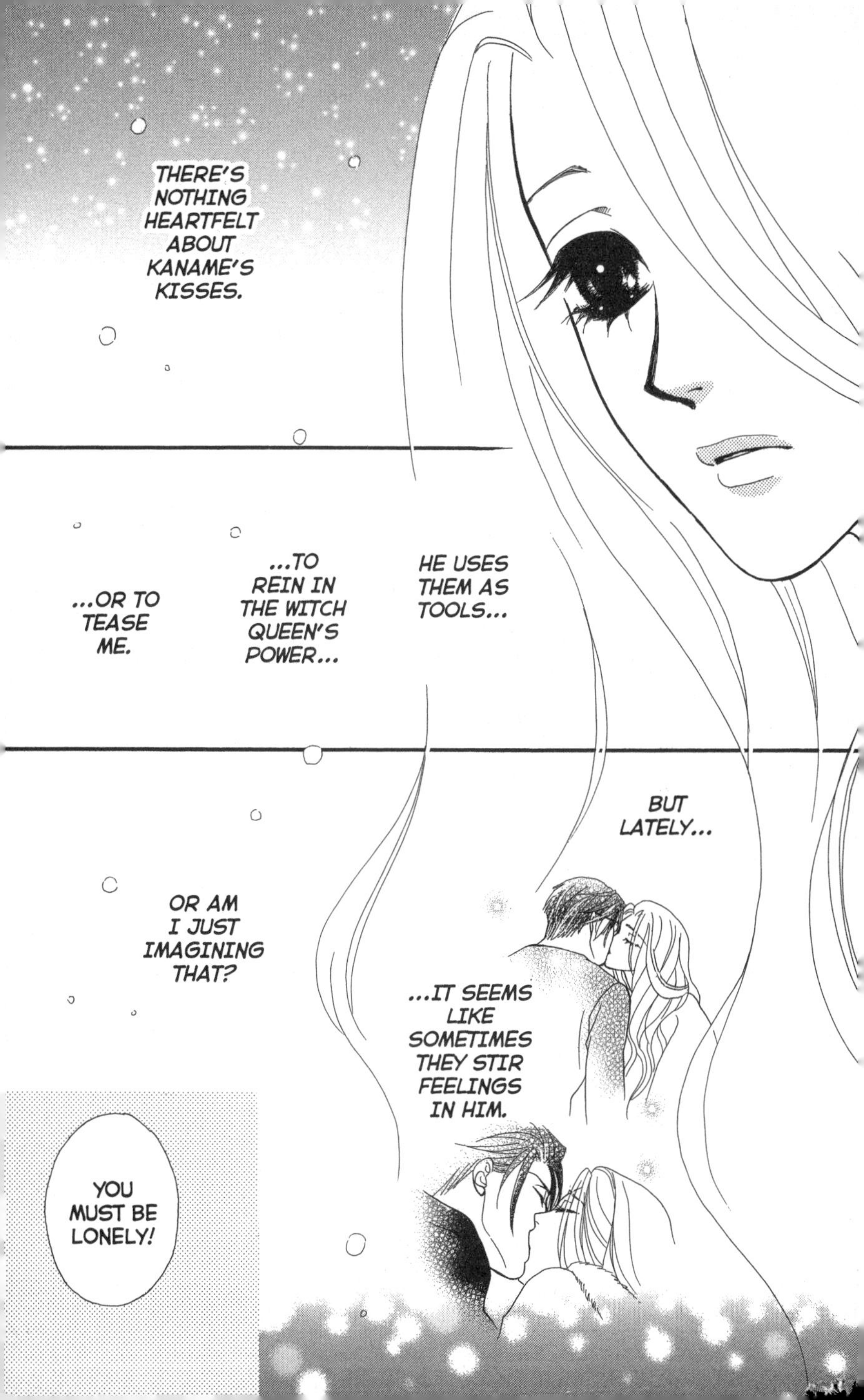
THERE'S NOTHING HEARTFELT ABOUT KANAME'S KISSES.
HE USES THEM AS TOOLS...
...TO REIN IN THE WITCH QUEEN'S POWER...
...OR TO TEASE ME.
BUT LATELY...
...IT SEEMS LIKE SOMETIMES THEY STIR FEELINGS IN HIM.
OR AM I JUST IMAGINING THAT?
YOU MUST BE LONELY!

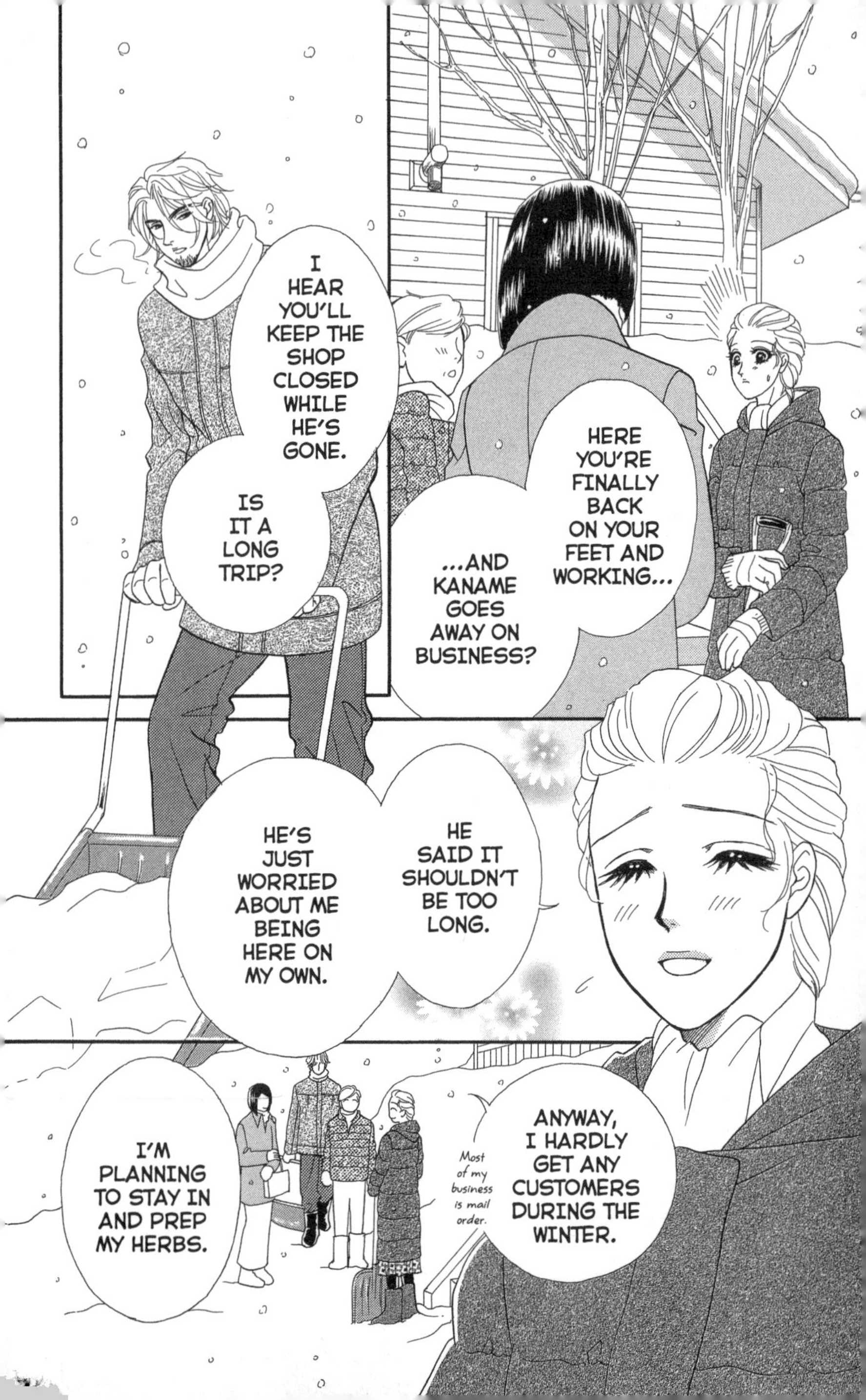
HERE YOU'RE FINALLY BACK ON YOUR FEET AND WORKING...
...AND KANAME GOES AWAY ON BUSINESS?
I HEAR YOU'LL KEEP THE SHOP CLOSED WHILE HE'S GONE.
IS IT A LONG TRIP?
HE SAID IT SHOULDN'T BE TOO LONG.
HE'S JUST WORRIED ABOUT ME BEING HERE ON MY OWN.
ANYWAY, I HARDLY GET ANY CUSTOMERS DURING THE WINTER.
Most of my business is mail order.
I'M PLANNING TO STAY IN AND PREP MY HERBS.

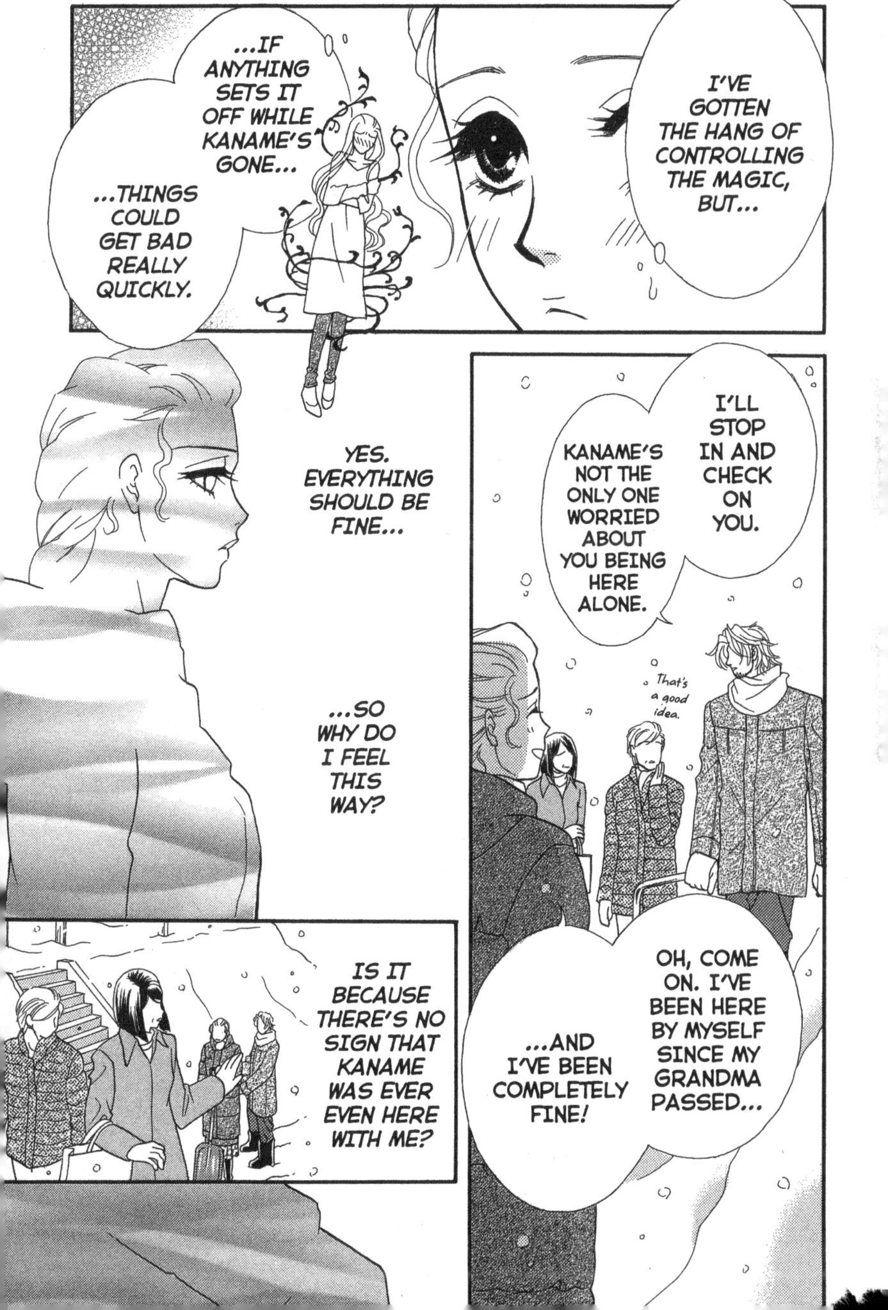
I'VE GOTTEN THE HANG OF CONTROLLING THE MAGIC, BUT...
...IF ANYTHING SETS IT OFF WHILE KANAME'S GONE...
...THINGS COULD GET BAD REALLY QUICKLY.
I'LL STOP IN AND CHECK ON YOU.
KANAME'S NOT THE ONLY ONE WORRIED ABOUT YOU BEING HERE ALONE.
That's a good idea.
OH, COME ON. I'VE BEEN HERE BY MYSELF SINCE MY GRANDMA PASSED...
...AND I'VE BEEN COMPLETELY FINE!
YES. EVERYTHING SHOULD BE FINE...
...SO WHY DO I FEEL THIS WAY?
IS IT BECAUSE THERE'S NO SIGN THAT KANAME WAS EVER EVEN HERE WITH ME?

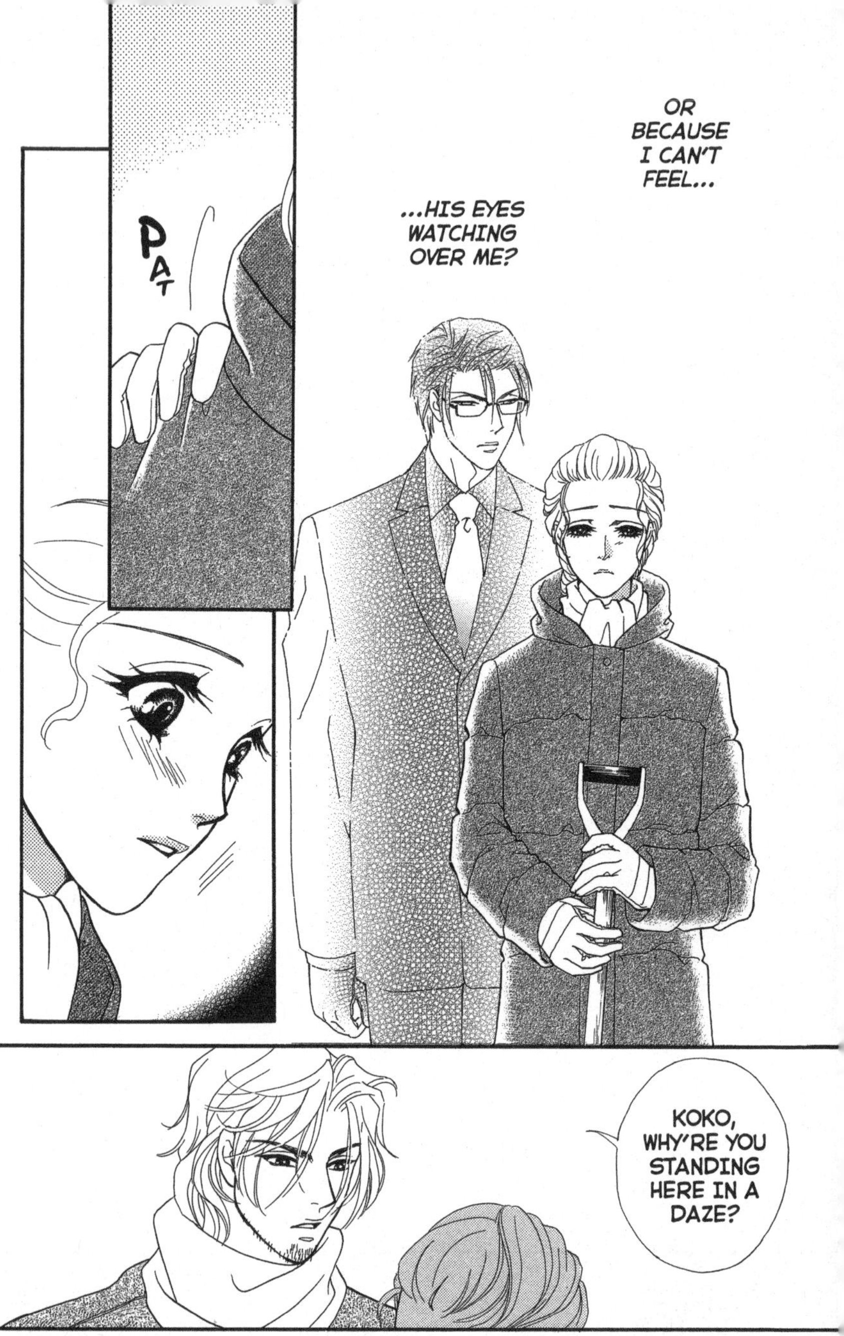
OR BECAUSE I CAN'T FEEL...
...HIS EYES WATCHING OVER ME?
PAT
KOKO, WHY'RE YOU STANDING HERE IN A DAZE?

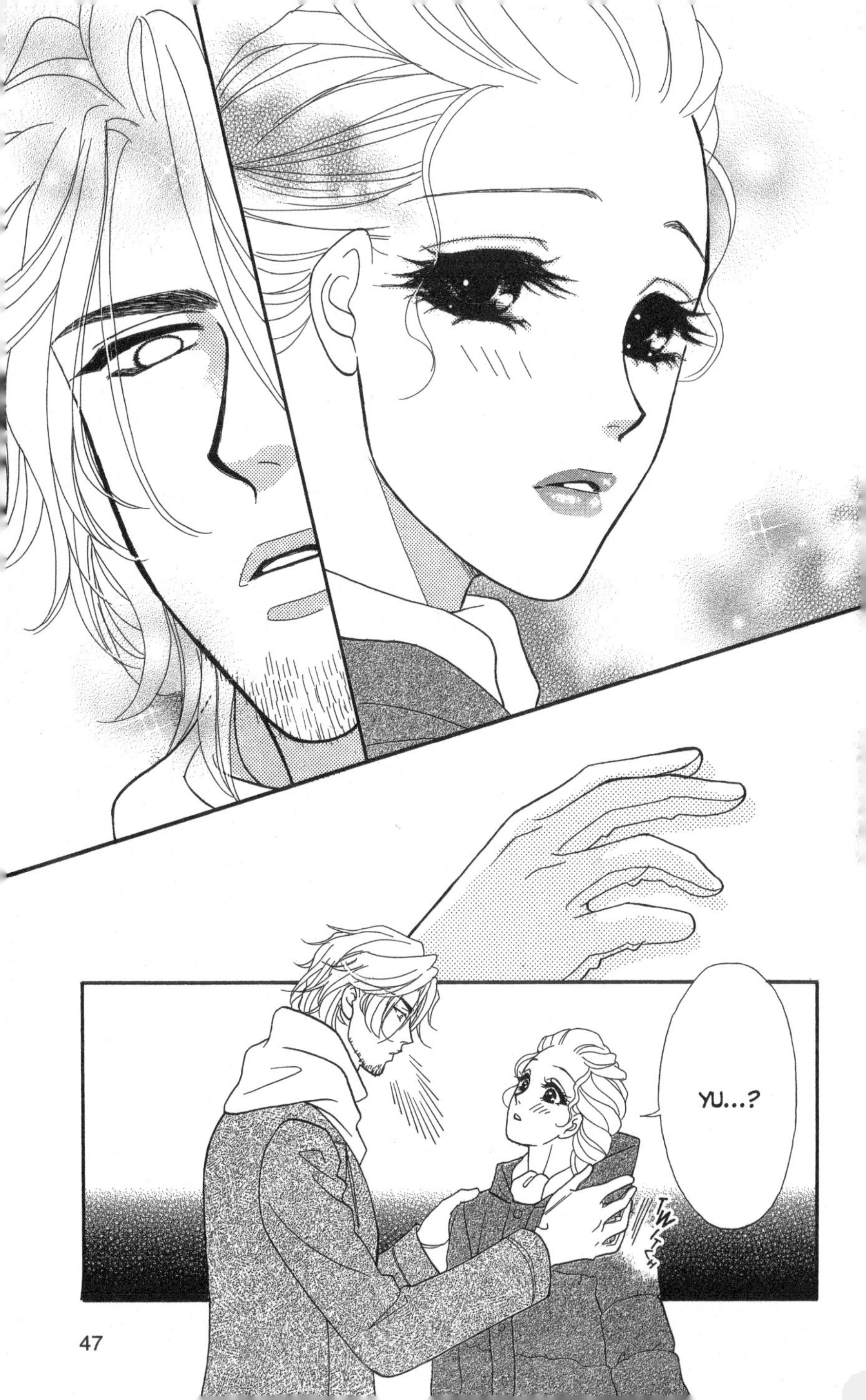
YU...?
TWITCH

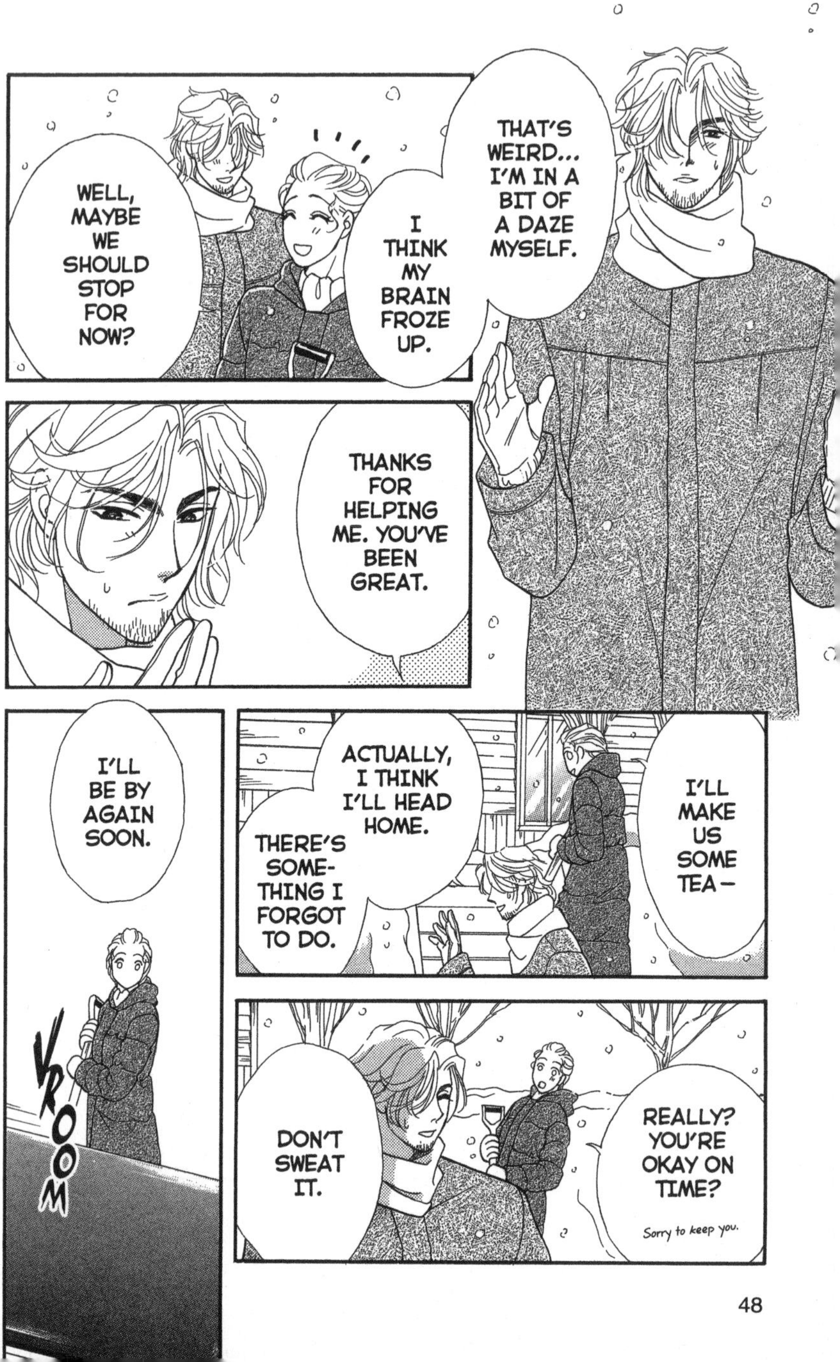
THAT'S WEIRD... I'M IN A BIT OF A DAZE MYSELF.
I THINK MY BRAIN FROZE UP.
WELL, MAYBE WE SHOULD STOP FOR NOW?
THANKS FOR HELPING ME. YOU'VE BEEN GREAT.
I'LL MAKE US SOME TEA—
ACTUALLY, I THINK I'LL HEAD HOME.
THERE'S SOME-THING I FORGOT TO DO.
REALLY? YOU'RE OKAY ON TIME?
Sorry to keep you.
DON'T SWEAT IT.
I'LL BE BY AGAIN SOON.
VROOM

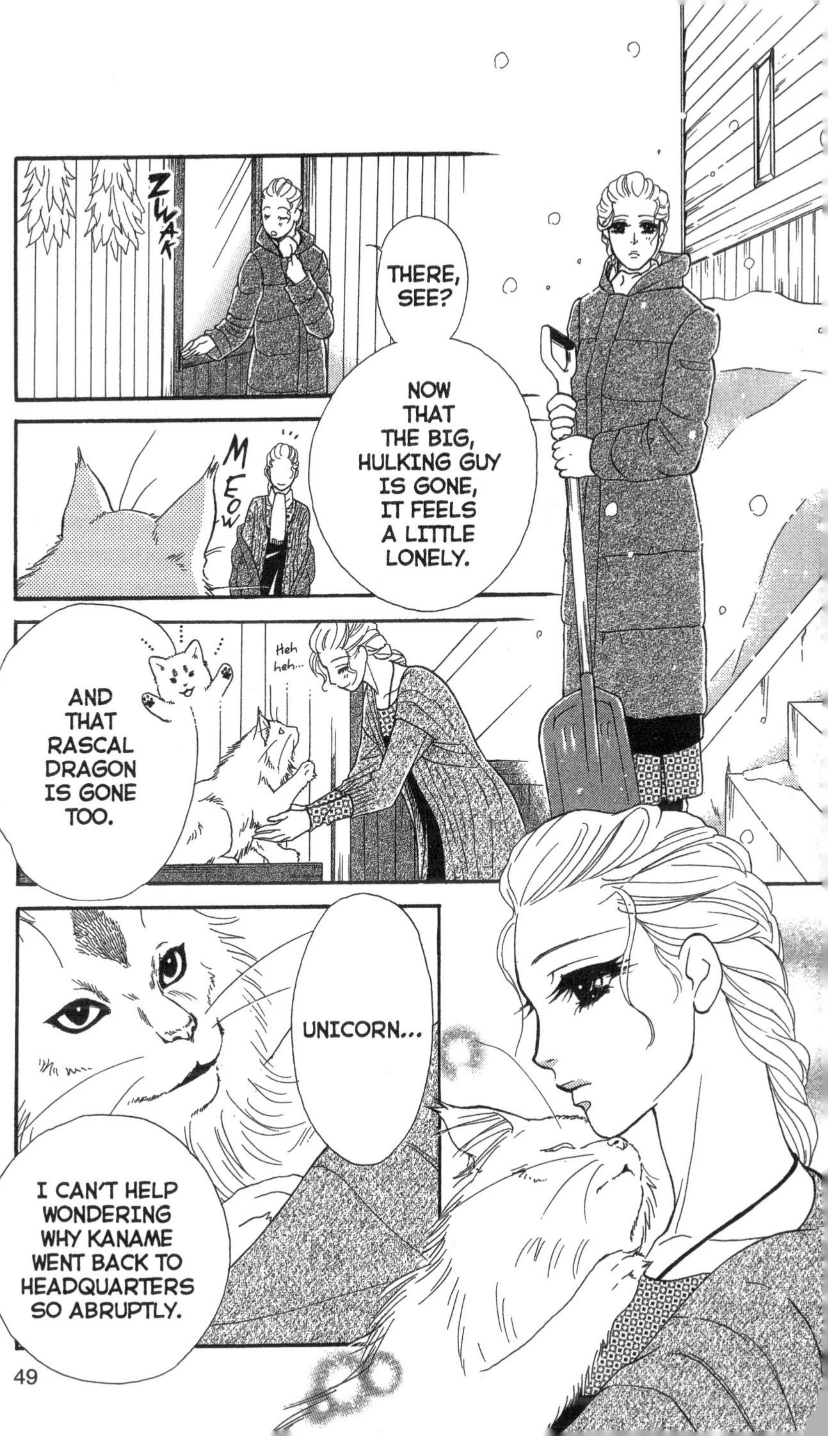
THERE, SEE?
NOW THAT THE BIG, HULKING GUY IS GONE, IT FEELS A LITTLE LONELY.
ZWAK
MEOW
Heh heh...
AND THAT RASCAL DRAGON IS GONE TOO.
UNICORN...
I CAN'T HELP WONDERING WHY KANAME WENT BACK TO HEADQUARTERS SO ABRUPTLY.

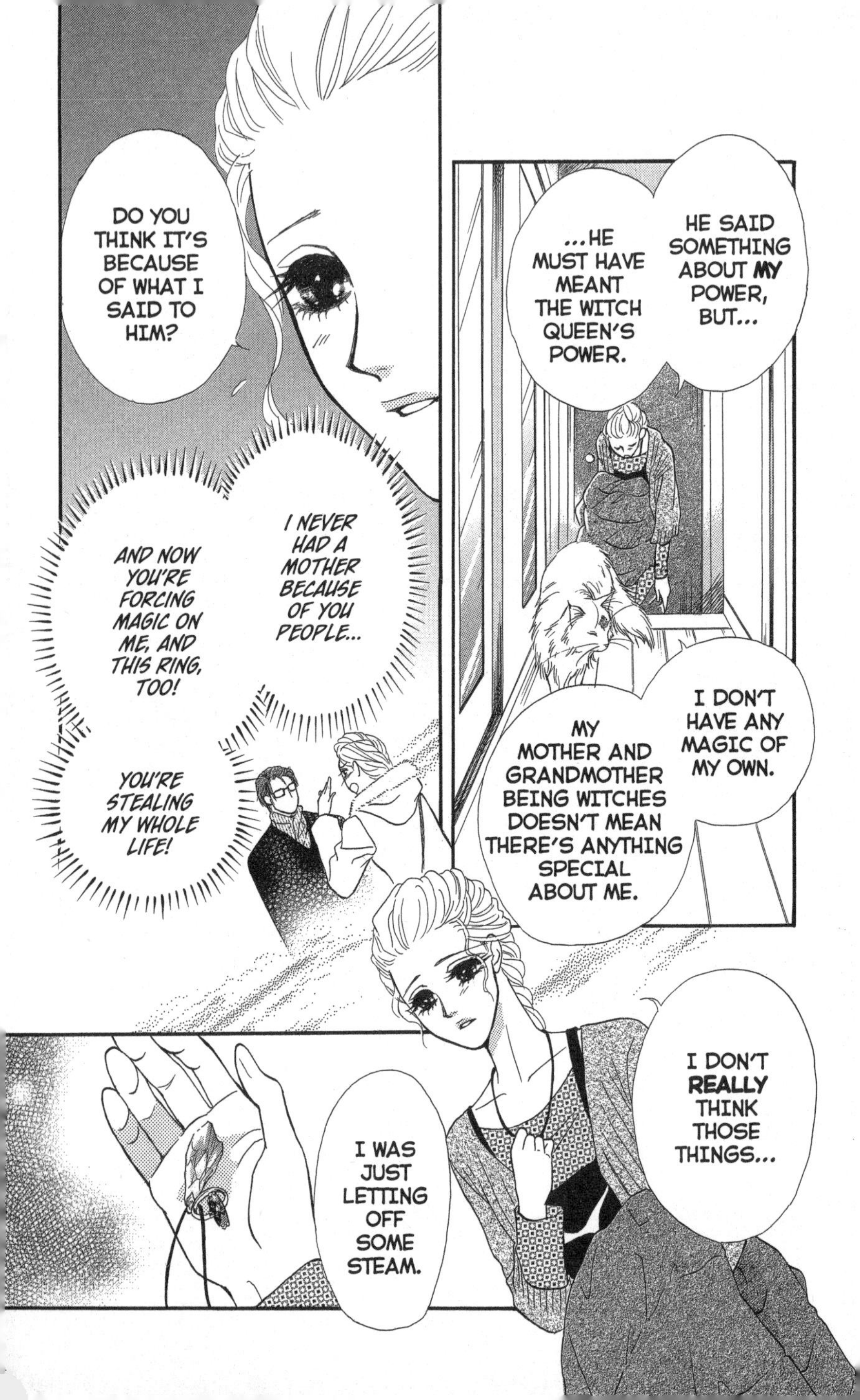

HE SAID SOMETHING ABOUT **MY** POWER, BUT...
...HE MUST HAVE MEANT THE WITCH QUEEN'S POWER.
I DON'T HAVE ANY MAGIC OF MY OWN.
MY MOTHER AND GRANDMOTHER BEING WITCHES DOESN'T MEAN THERE'S ANYTHING SPECIAL ABOUT ME.
DO YOU THINK IT'S BECAUSE OF WHAT I SAID TO HIM?
I NEVER HAD A MOTHER BECAUSE OF YOU PEOPLE...
AND NOW YOU'RE FORCING MAGIC ON ME, AND THIS RING, TOO!
YOU'RE STEALING MY WHOLE LIFE!
I DON'T **REALLY** THINK THOSE THINGS...
I WAS JUST LETTING OFF SOME STEAM.

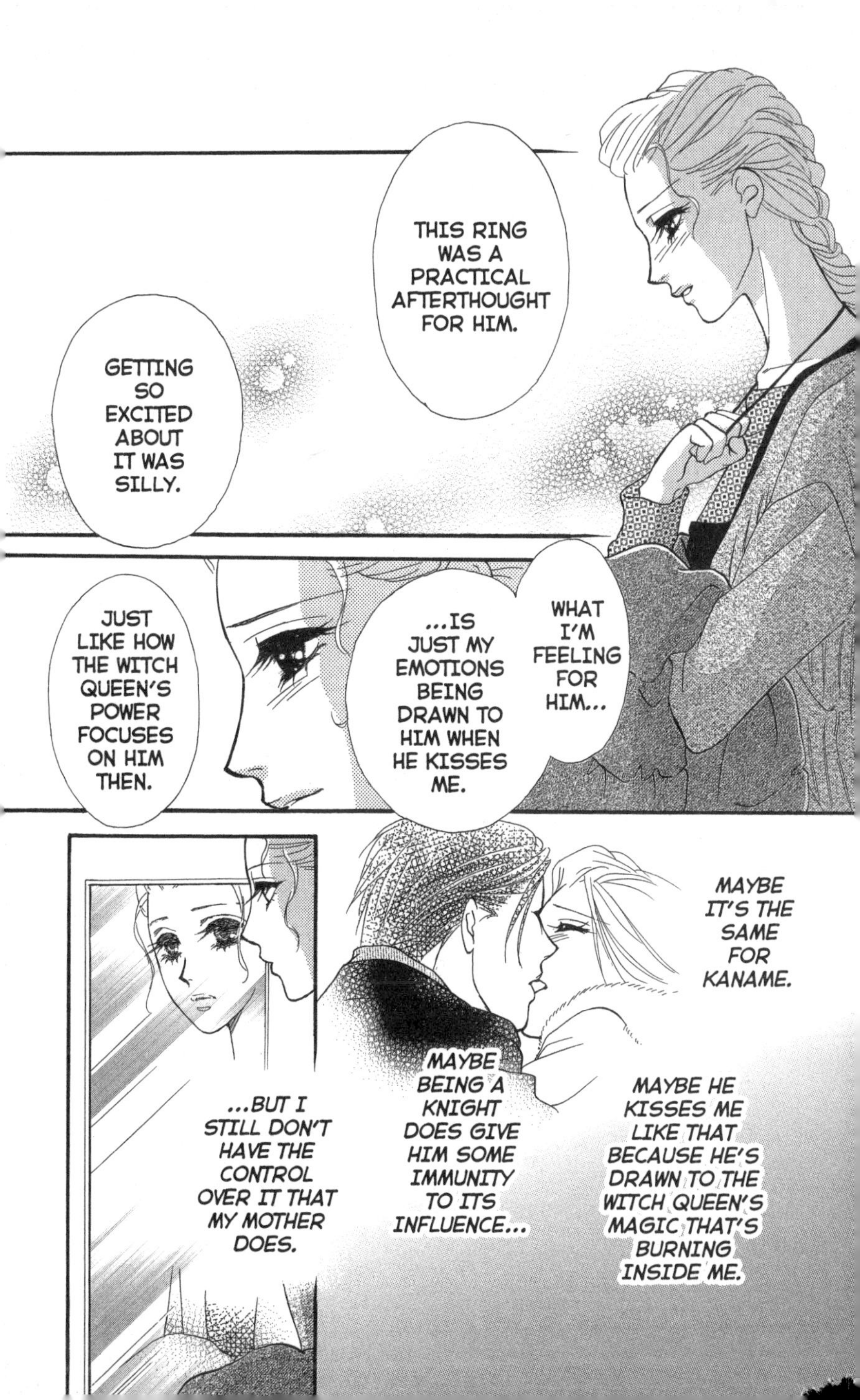
THIS RING WAS A PRACTICAL AFTERTHOUGHT FOR HIM.
GETTING SO EXCITED ABOUT IT WAS SILLY.
WHAT I'M FEELING FOR HIM...
...IS JUST MY EMOTIONS BEING DRAWN TO HIM WHEN HE KISSES ME.
JUST LIKE HOW THE WITCH QUEEN'S POWER FOCUSES ON HIM THEN.
MAYBE IT'S THE SAME FOR KANAME.
MAYBE HE KISSES ME LIKE THAT BECAUSE HE'S DRAWN TO THE WITCH QUEEN'S MAGIC THAT'S BURNING INSIDE ME.
MAYBE BEING A KNIGHT DOES GIVE HIM SOME IMMUNITY TO ITS INFLUENCE...
...BUT I STILL DON'T HAVE THE CONTROL OVER IT THAT MY MOTHER DOES.

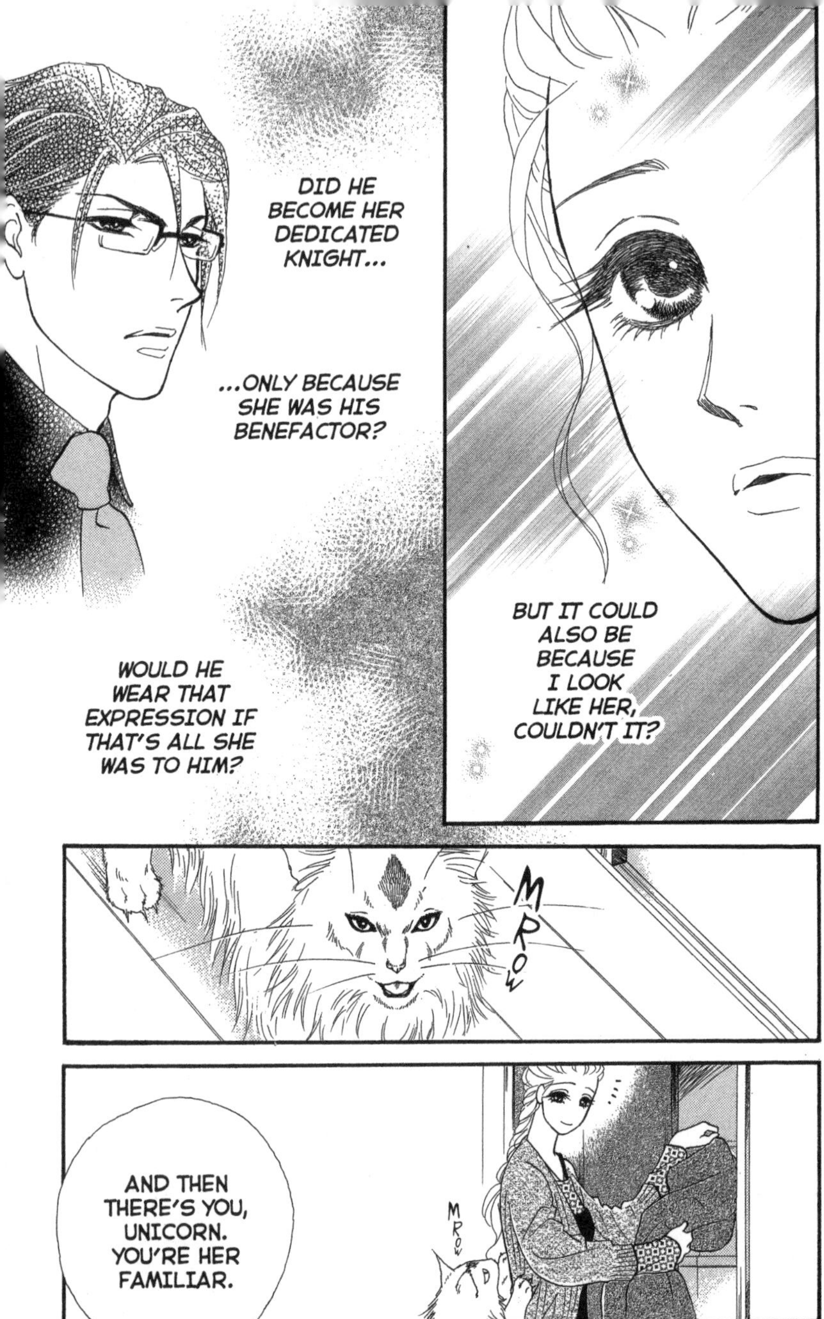
BUT IT COULD ALSO BE BECAUSE I LOOK LIKE HER, COULDN'T IT?
DID HE BECOME HER DEDICATED KNIGHT...
...ONLY BECAUSE SHE WAS HIS BENEFACTOR?
WOULD HE WEAR THAT EXPRESSION IF THAT'S ALL SHE WAS TO HIM?
MROW
...
MROW
AND THEN THERE'S YOU, UNICORN. YOU'RE HER FAMILIAR.

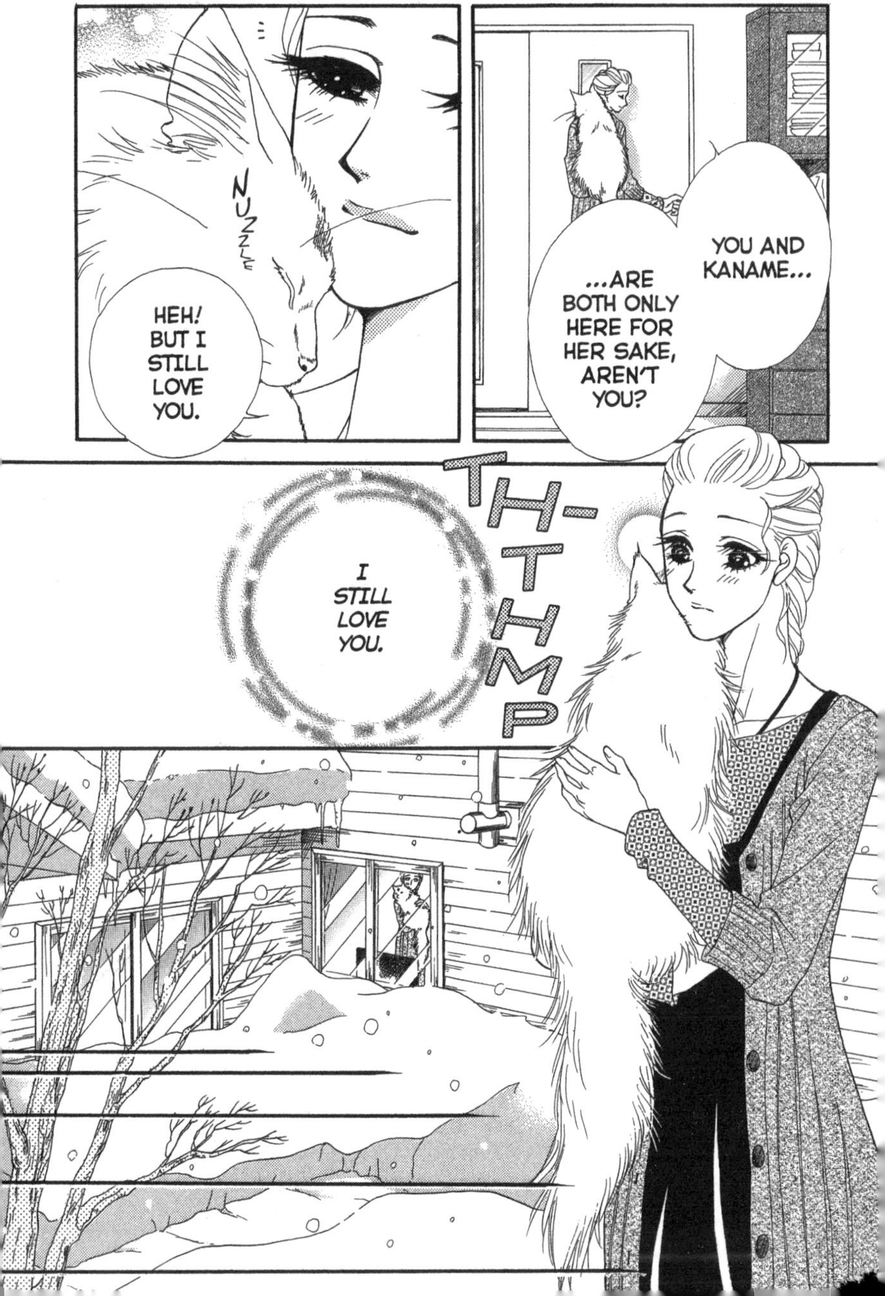
YOU AND KANAME...
...ARE BOTH ONLY HERE FOR HER SAKE, AREN'T YOU?
NUZZLE
HEH! BUT I STILL LOVE YOU.
TH-THMP
I STILL LOVE YOU.

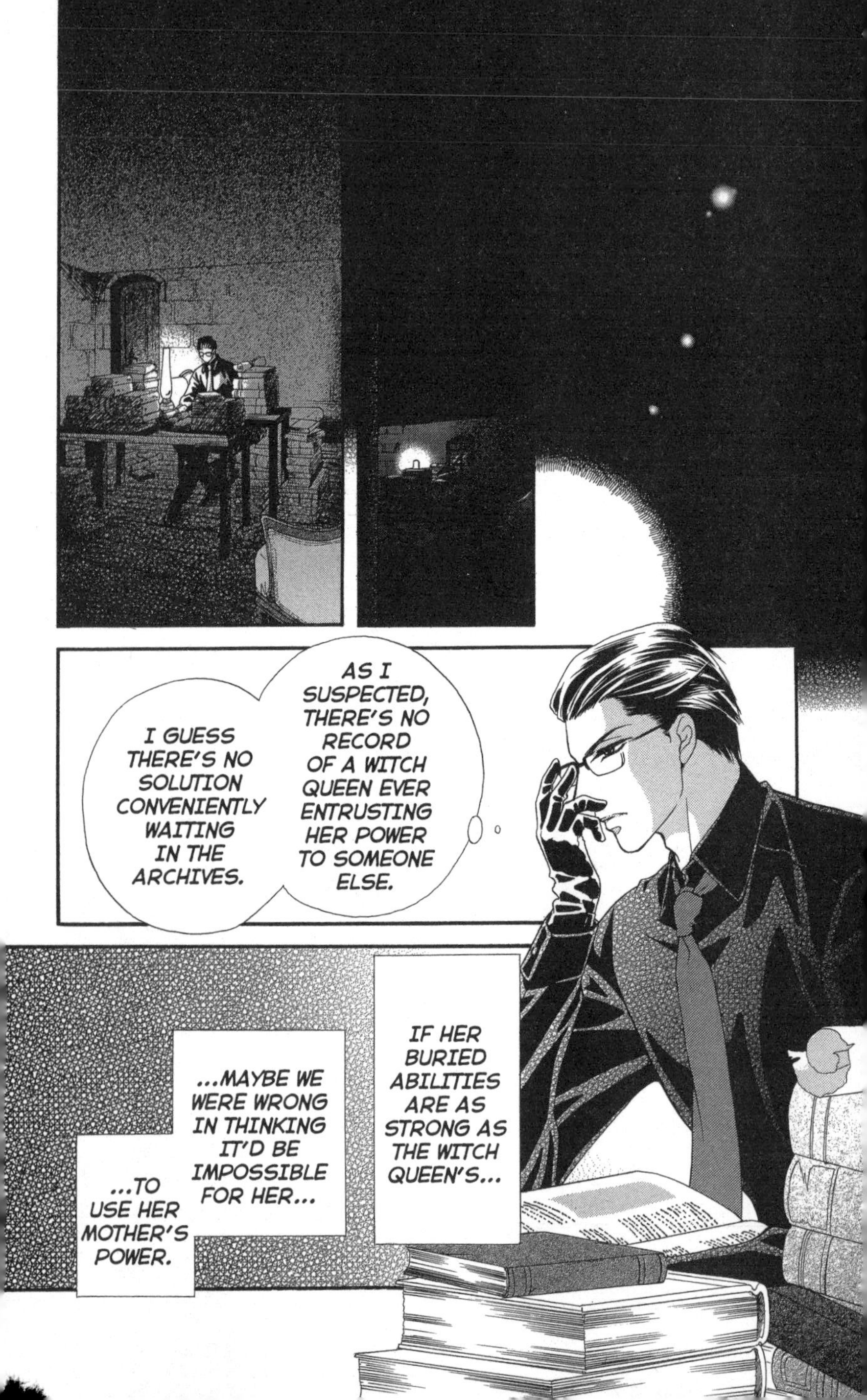
AS I SUSPECTED, THERE'S NO RECORD OF A WITCH QUEEN EVER ENTRUSTING HER POWER TO SOMEONE ELSE.
I GUESS THERE'S NO SOLUTION CONVENIENTLY WAITING IN THE ARCHIVES.
IF HER BURIED ABILITIES ARE AS STRONG AS THE WITCH QUEEN'S...
...MAYBE WE WERE WRONG IN THINKING IT'D BE IMPOSSIBLE FOR HER...
...TO USE HER MOTHER'S POWER.

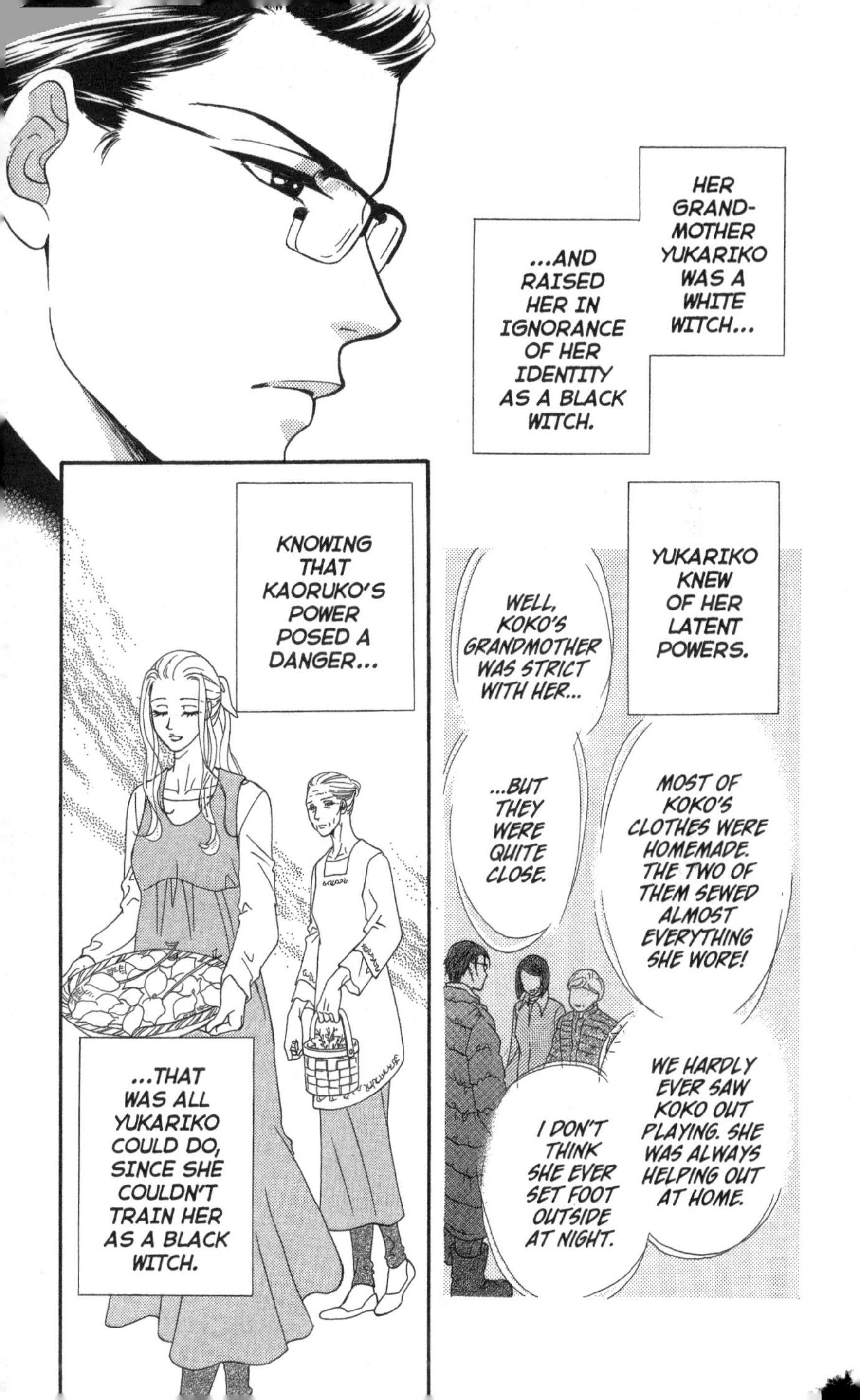
HER GRANDMOTHER YUKARIKO WAS A WHITE WITCH...
...AND RAISED HER IN IGNORANCE OF HER IDENTITY AS A BLACK WITCH.
YUKARIKO KNEW OF HER LATENT POWERS.
WELL, KOKO'S GRANDMOTHER WAS STRICT WITH HER...
MOST OF KOKO'S CLOTHES WERE HOMEMADE. THE TWO OF THEM SEWED ALMOST EVERYTHING SHE WORE!
...BUT THEY WERE QUITE CLOSE.
WE HARDLY EVER SAW KOKO OUT PLAYING. SHE WAS ALWAYS HELPING OUT AT HOME.
I DON'T THINK SHE EVER SET FOOT OUTSIDE AT NIGHT.
KNOWING THAT KAORUKO'S POWER POSED A DANGER...
...THAT WAS ALL YUKARIKO COULD DO, SINCE SHE COULDN'T TRAIN HER AS A BLACK WITCH.

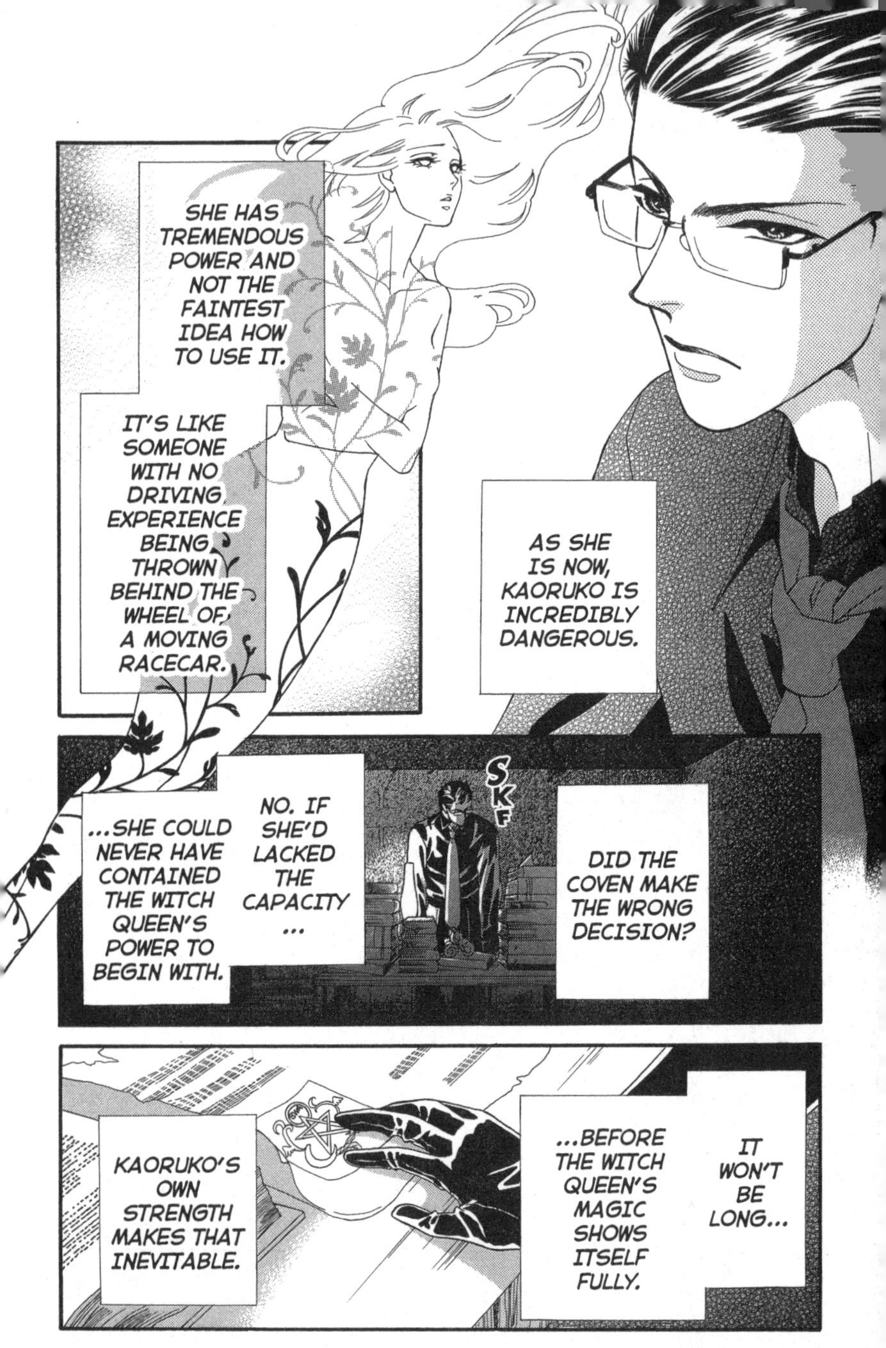
AS SHE IS NOW, KAORUKO IS INCREDIBLY DANGEROUS.
SHE HAS TREMENDOUS POWER AND NOT THE FAINTEST IDEA HOW TO USE IT.
IT'S LIKE SOMEONE WITH NO DRIVING EXPERIENCE BEING THROWN BEHIND THE WHEEL OF A MOVING RACECAR.
DID THE COVEN MAKE THE WRONG DECISION?
SKF
NO. IF SHE'D LACKED THE CAPACITY ...
...SHE COULD NEVER HAVE CONTAINED THE WITCH QUEEN'S POWER TO BEGIN WITH.
IT WON'T BE LONG...
...BEFORE THE WITCH QUEEN'S MAGIC SHOWS ITSELF FULLY.
KAORUKO'S OWN STRENGTH MAKES THAT INEVITABLE.

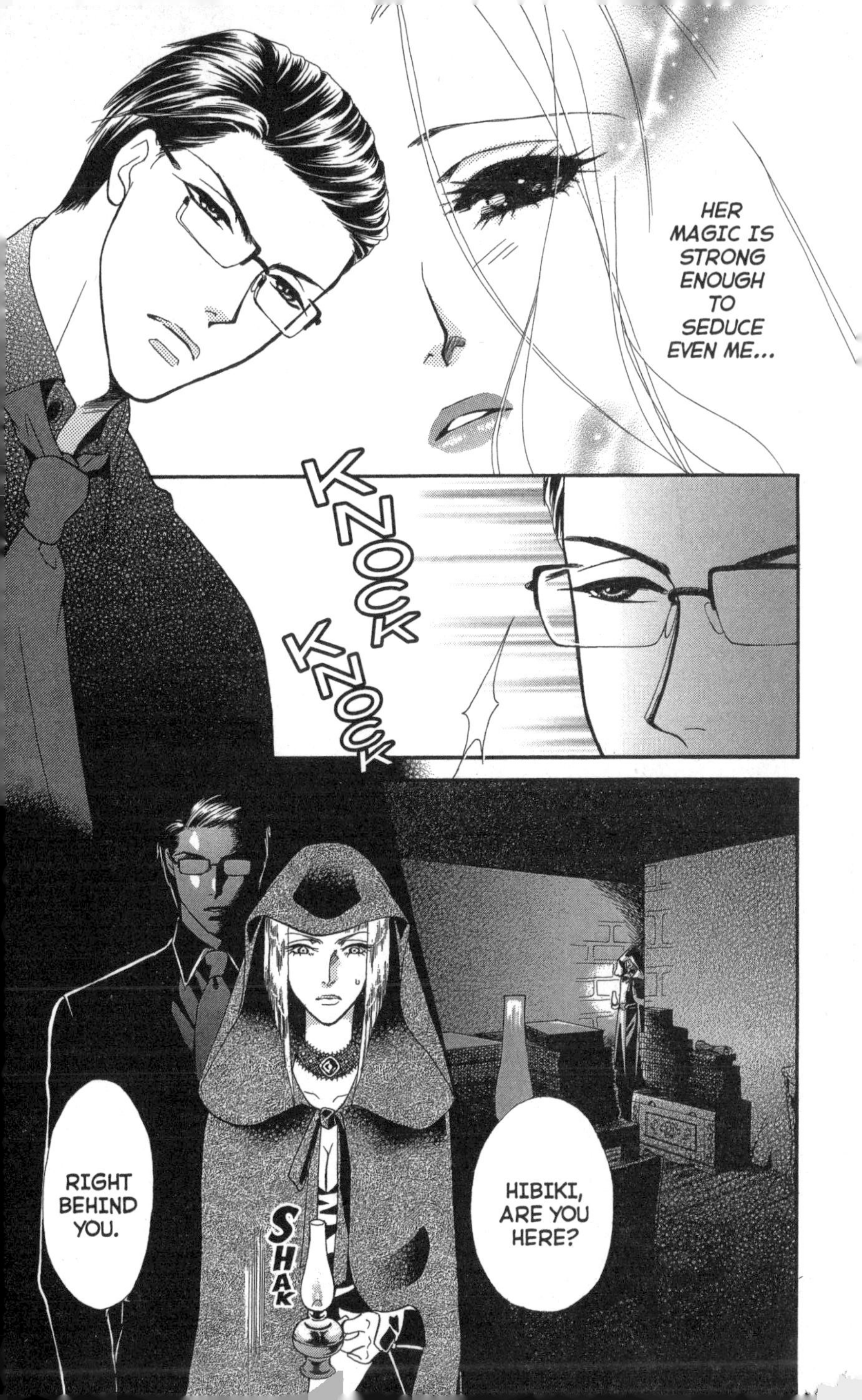
HER MAGIC IS STRONG ENOUGH TO SEDUCE EVEN ME...
KNOCK KNOCK
HIBIKI, ARE YOU HERE?
SHAK
RIGHT BEHIND YOU.

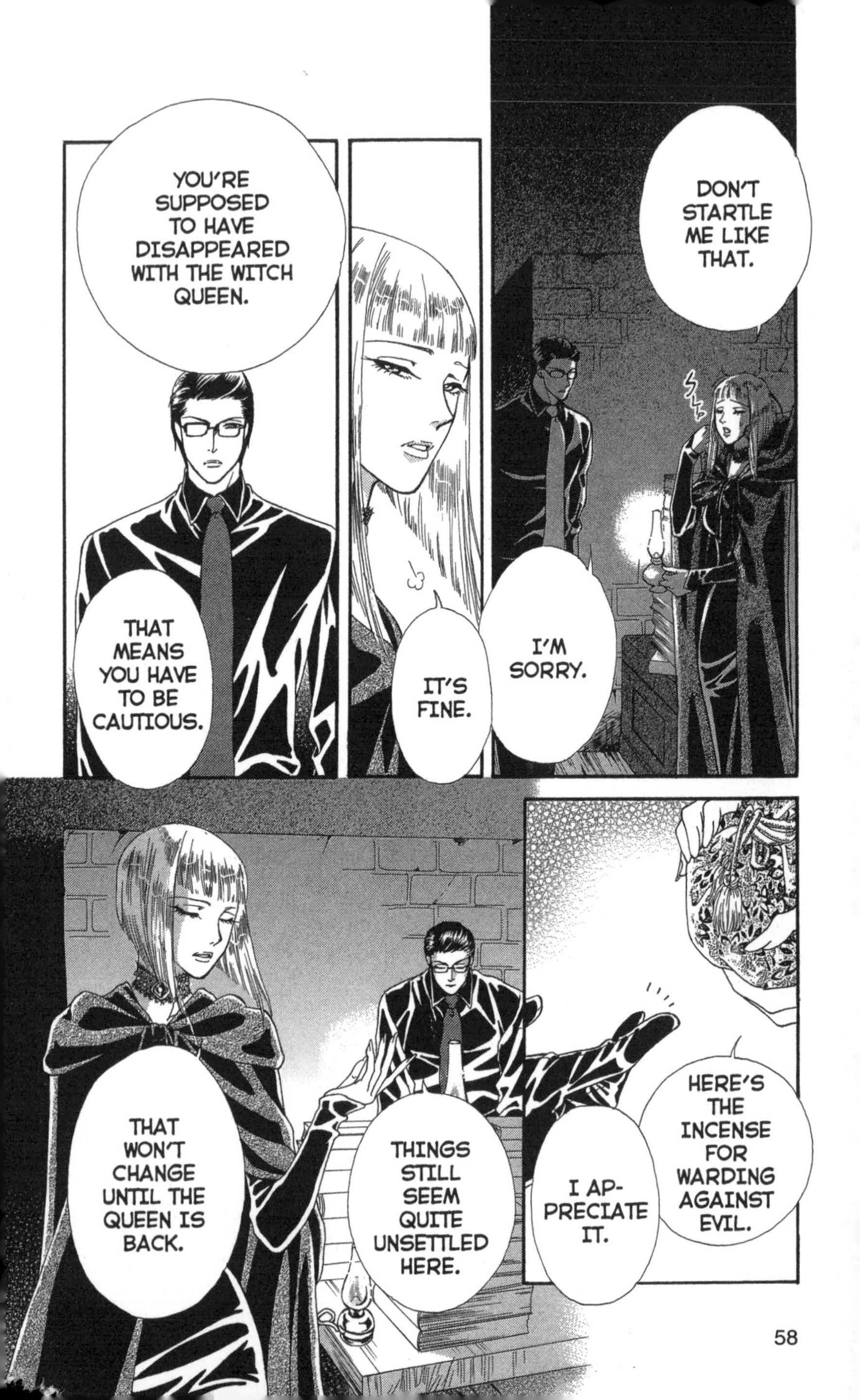

DON'T STARTLE ME LIKE THAT.
I'M SORRY.
IT'S FINE.
YOU'RE SUPPOSED TO HAVE DISAPPEARED WITH THE WITCH QUEEN.
THAT MEANS YOU HAVE TO BE CAUTIOUS.
HERE'S THE INCENSE FOR WARDING AGAINST EVIL.
I AP-PRECIATE IT.
THINGS STILL SEEM QUITE UNSETTLED HERE.
THAT WON'T CHANGE UNTIL THE QUEEN IS BACK.

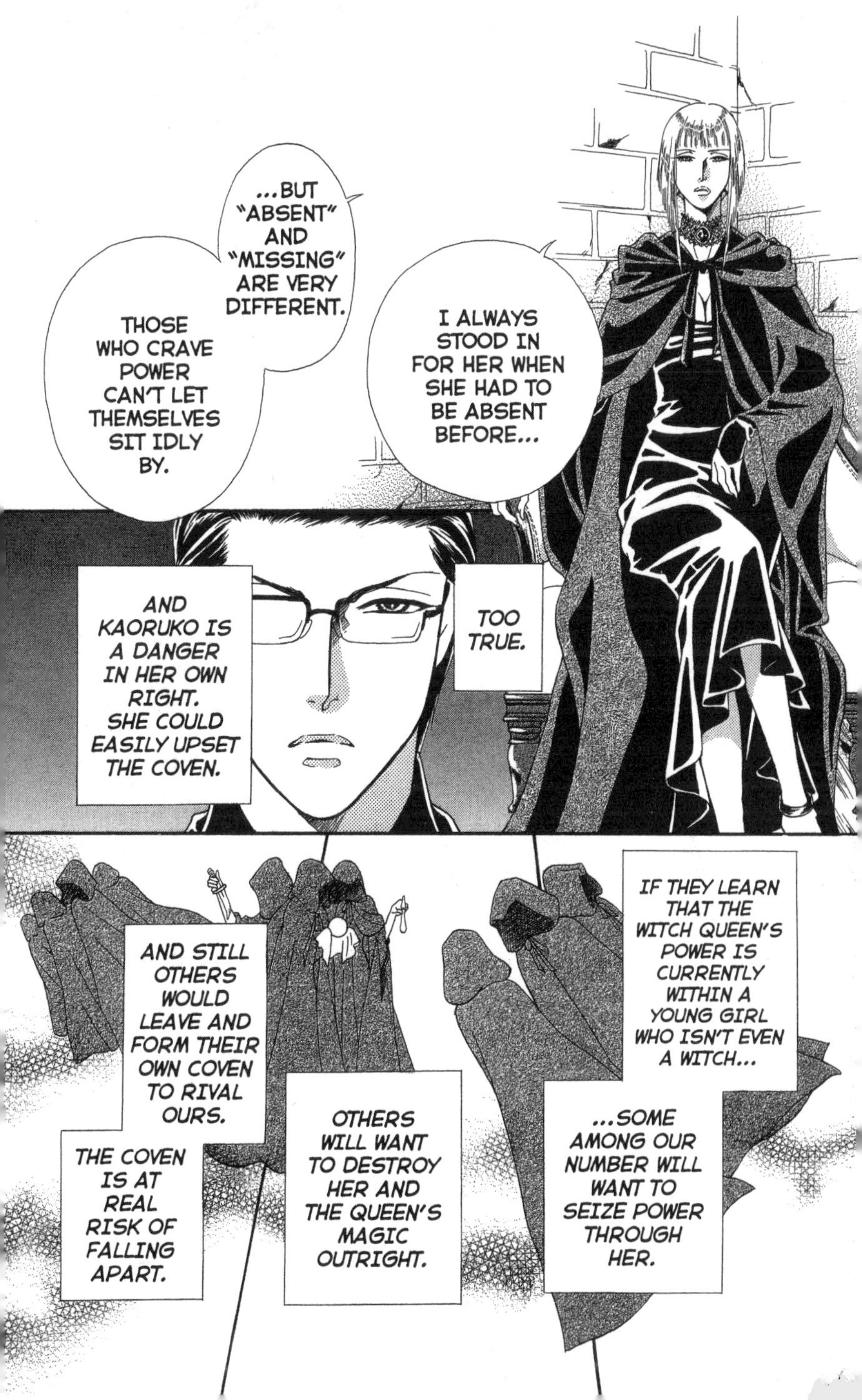
I ALWAYS STOOD IN FOR HER WHEN SHE HAD TO BE ABSENT BEFORE...
...BUT "ABSENT" AND "MISSING" ARE VERY DIFFERENT.
THOSE WHO CRAVE POWER CAN'T LET THEMSELVES SIT IDLY BY.
TOO TRUE.
AND KAORUKO IS A DANGER IN HER OWN RIGHT. SHE COULD EASILY UPSET THE COVEN.
IF THEY LEARN THAT THE WITCH QUEEN'S POWER IS CURRENTLY WITHIN A YOUNG GIRL WHO ISN'T EVEN A WITCH...
...SOME AMONG OUR NUMBER WILL WANT TO SEIZE POWER THROUGH HER.
OTHERS WILL WANT TO DESTROY HER AND THE QUEEN'S MAGIC OUTRIGHT.
AND STILL OTHERS WOULD LEAVE AND FORM THEIR OWN COVEN TO RIVAL OURS.
THE COVEN IS AT REAL RISK OF FALLING APART.

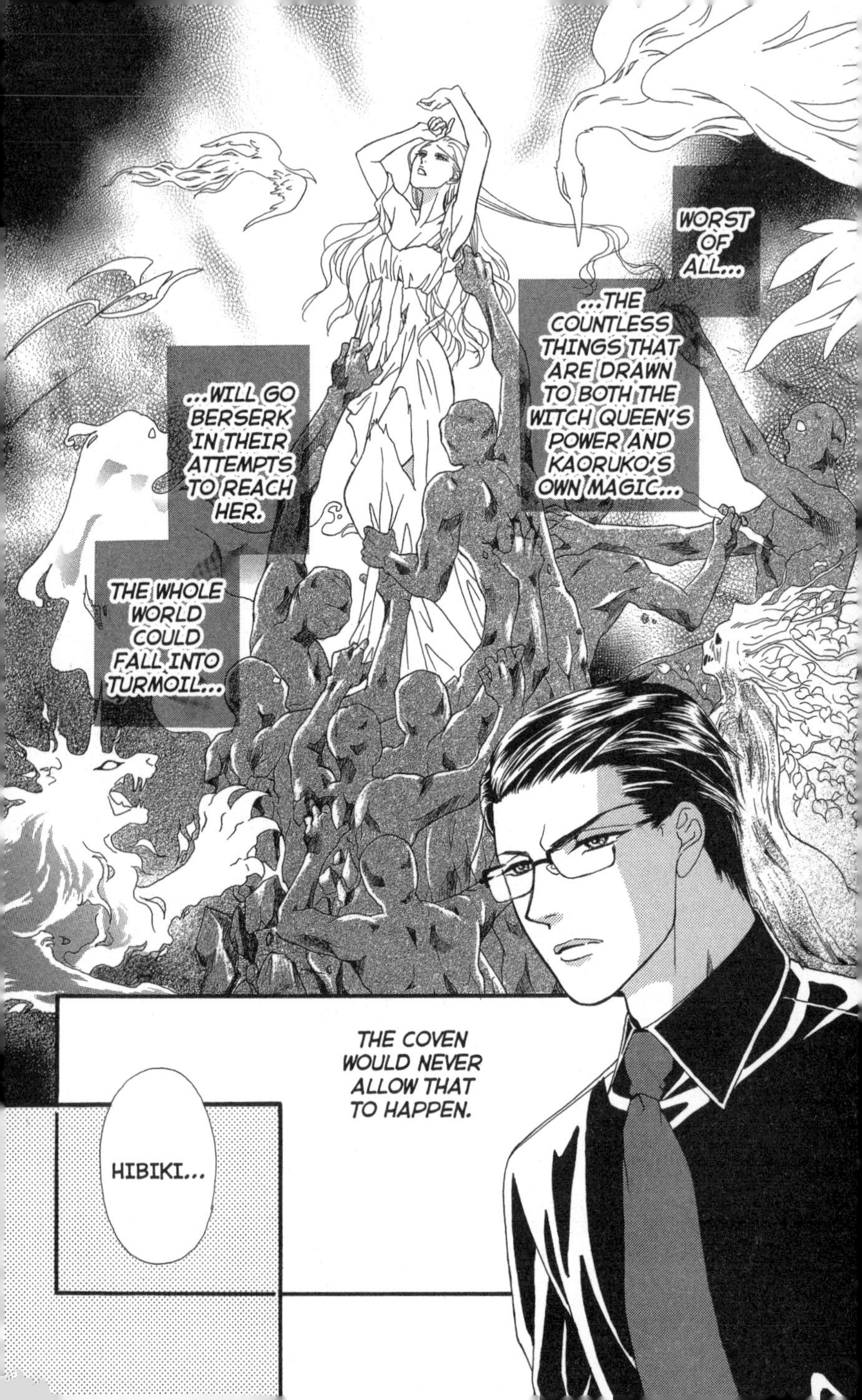
WORST OF ALL...
...THE COUNTLESS THINGS THAT ARE DRAWN TO BOTH THE WITCH QUEEN'S POWER AND KAORUKO'S OWN MAGIC...
...WILL GO BERSERK IN THEIR ATTEMPTS TO REACH HER.
THE WHOLE WORLD COULD FALL INTO TURMOIL...
THE COVEN WOULD NEVER ALLOW THAT TO HAPPEN.
HIBIKI...

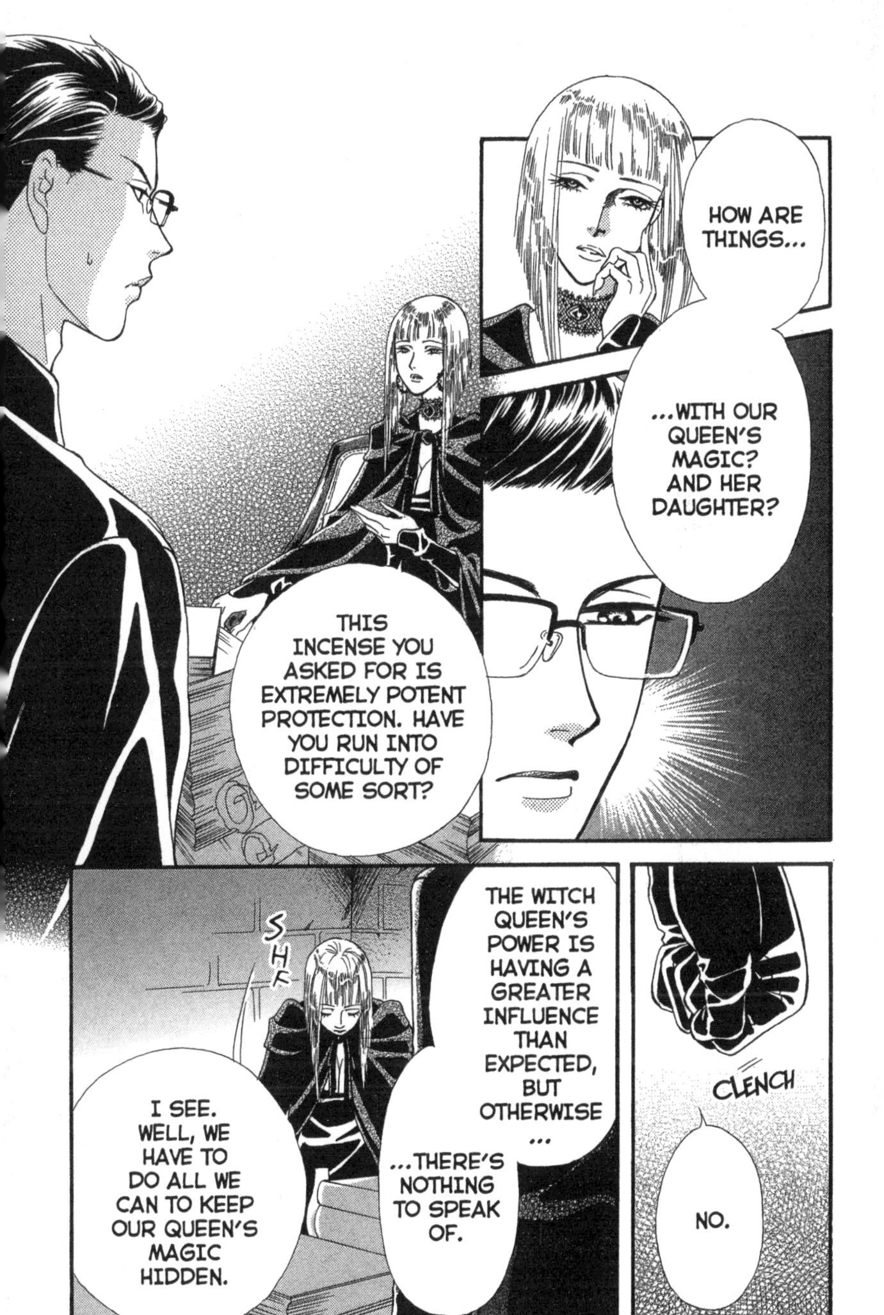
HOW ARE THINGS...
...WITH OUR QUEEN'S MAGIC? AND HER DAUGHTER?
THIS INCENSE YOU ASKED FOR IS EXTREMELY POTENT PROTECTION. HAVE YOU RUN INTO DIFFICULTY OF SOME SORT?
CLENCH
NO.
THE WITCH QUEEN'S POWER IS HAVING A GREATER INFLUENCE THAN EXPECTED, BUT OTHERWISE ...
...THERE'S NOTHING TO SPEAK OF.
SHF
I SEE. WELL, WE HAVE TO DO ALL WE CAN TO KEEP OUR QUEEN'S MAGIC HIDDEN.

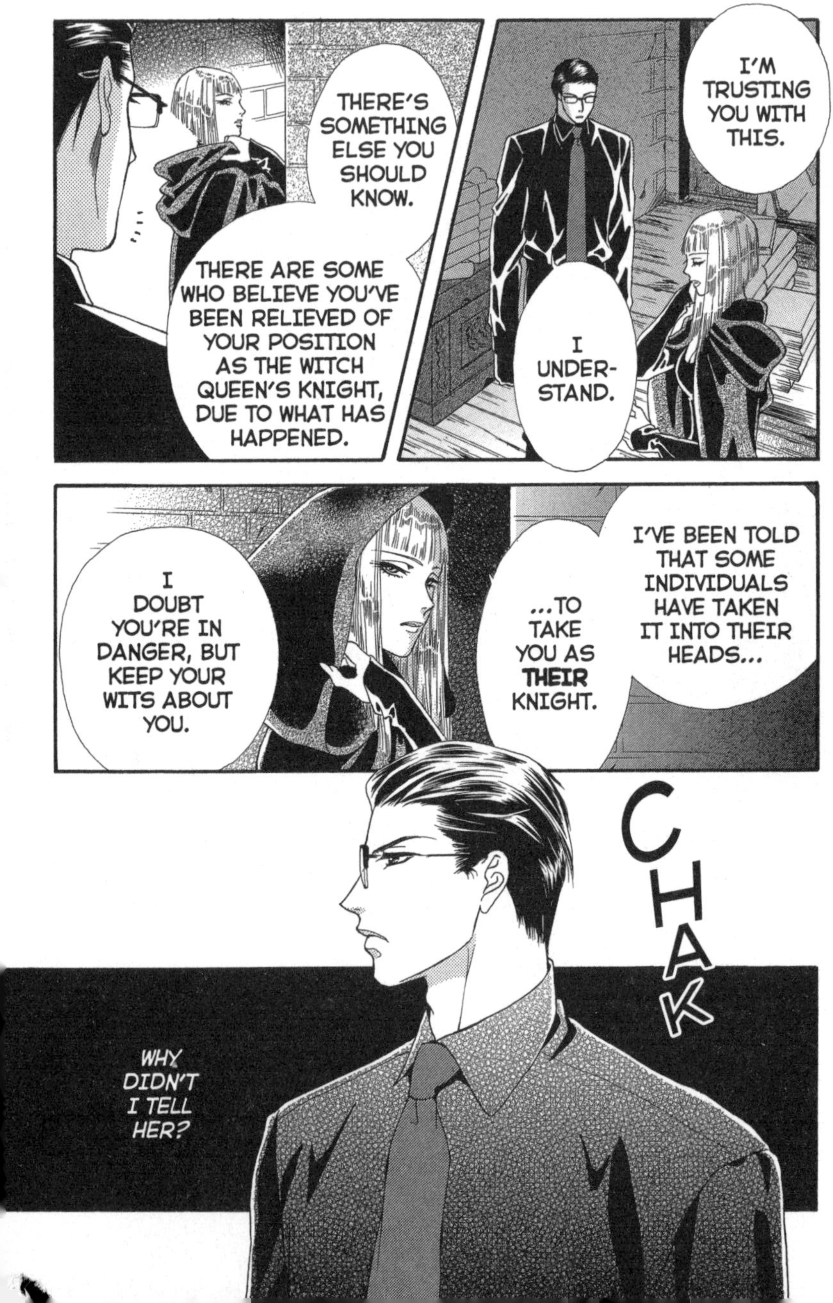
I'M TRUSTING YOU WITH THIS.
I UNDER-STAND.
THERE'S SOMETHING ELSE YOU SHOULD KNOW.
THERE ARE SOME WHO BELIEVE YOU'VE BEEN RELIEVED OF YOUR POSITION AS THE WITCH QUEEN'S KNIGHT, DUE TO WHAT HAS HAPPENED.
I'VE BEEN TOLD THAT SOME INDIVIDUALS HAVE TAKEN IT INTO THEIR HEADS...
...TO TAKE YOU AS **THEIR** KNIGHT.
I DOUBT YOU'RE IN DANGER, BUT KEEP YOUR WITS ABOUT YOU.
CHAK
WHY DIDN'T I TELL HER?

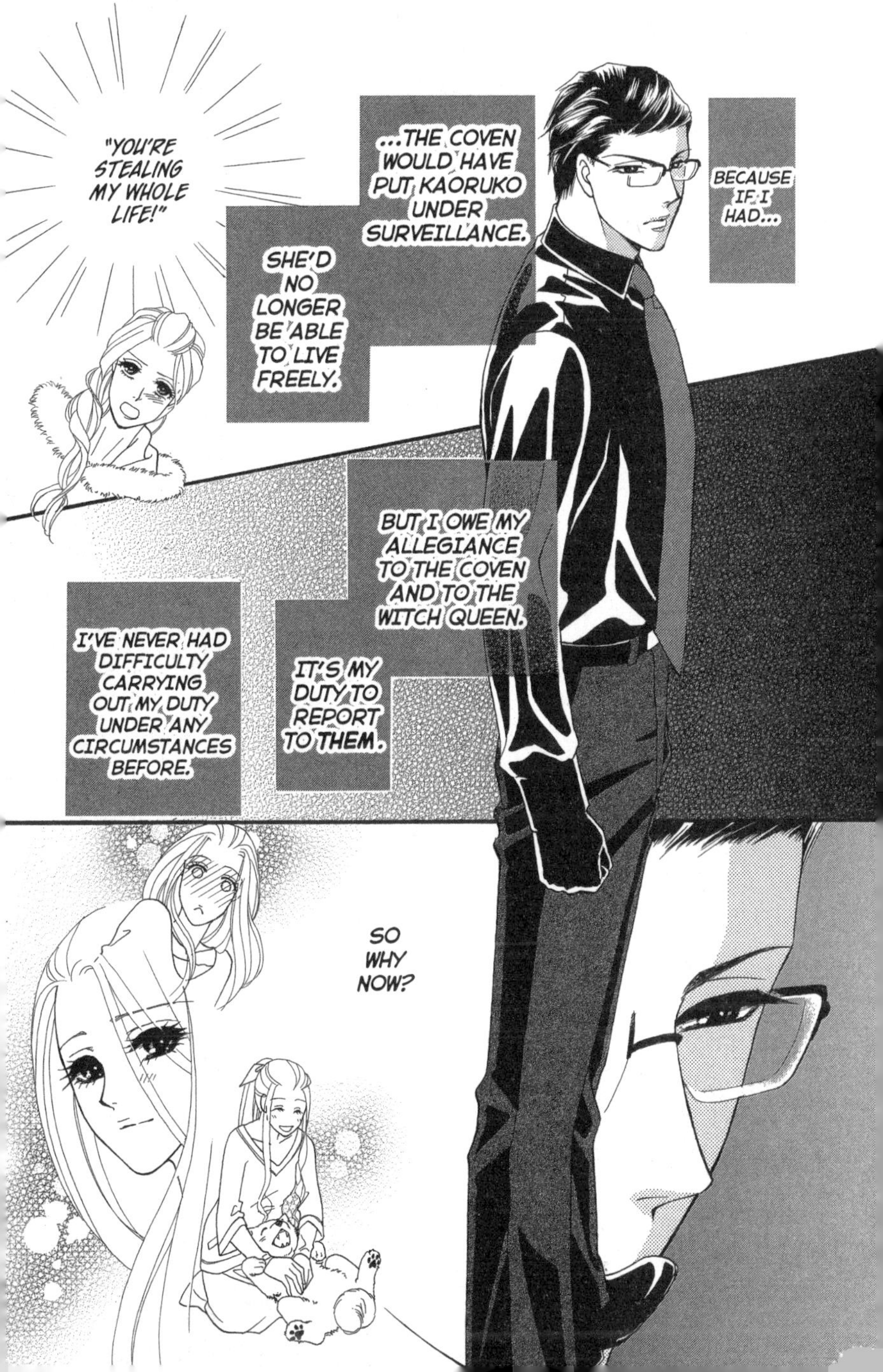
BECAUSE IF I HAD...
...THE COVEN WOULD HAVE PUT KAORUKO UNDER SURVEILLANCE.
SHE'D NO LONGER BE ABLE TO LIVE FREELY.
"YOU'RE STEALING MY WHOLE LIFE!"
BUT I OWE MY ALLEGIANCE TO THE COVEN AND TO THE WITCH QUEEN.
IT'S MY DUTY TO REPORT TO THEM.
I'VE NEVER HAD DIFFICULTY CARRYING OUT MY DUTY UNDER ANY CIRCUMSTANCES BEFORE.
SO WHY NOW?

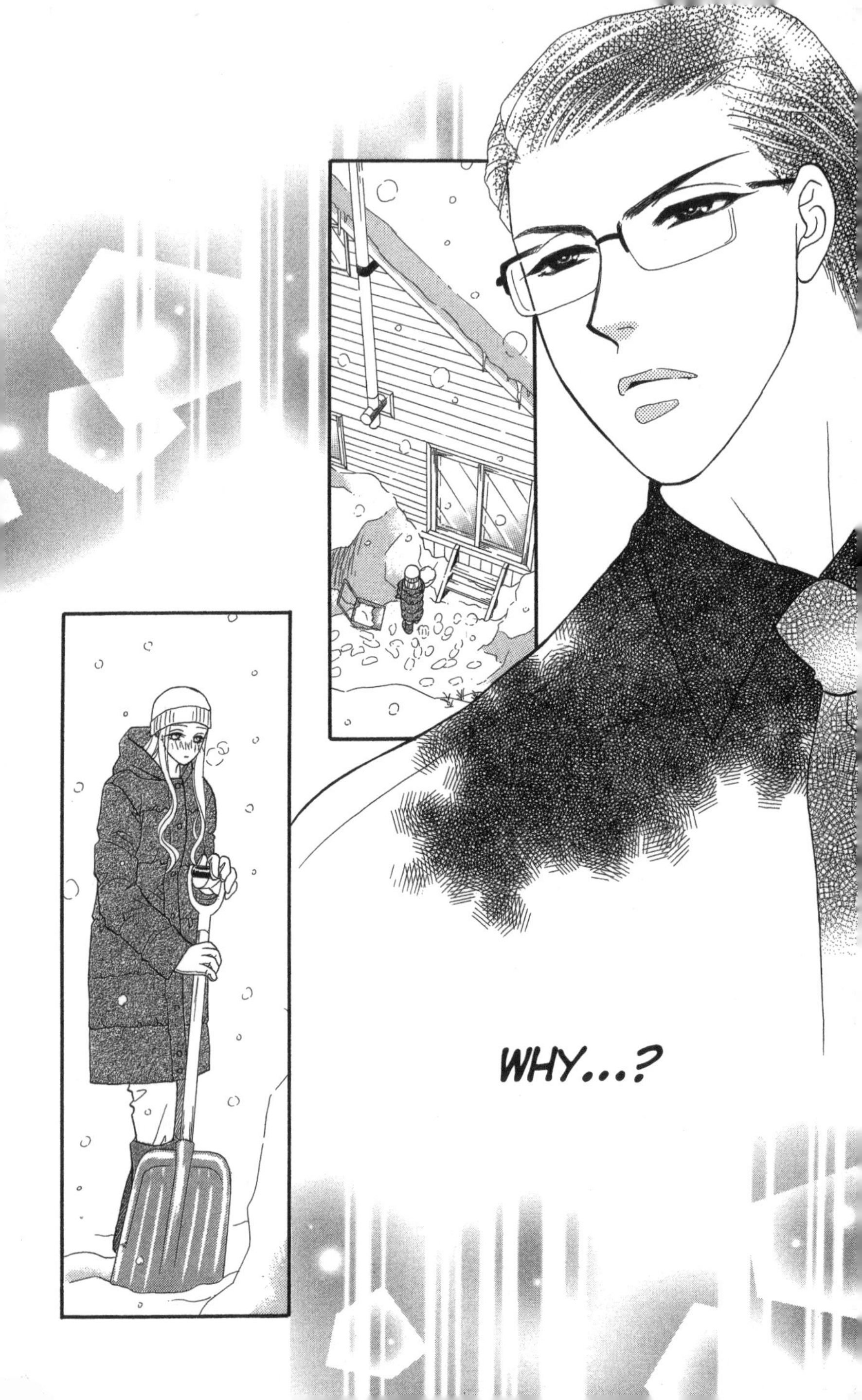
WHY...?

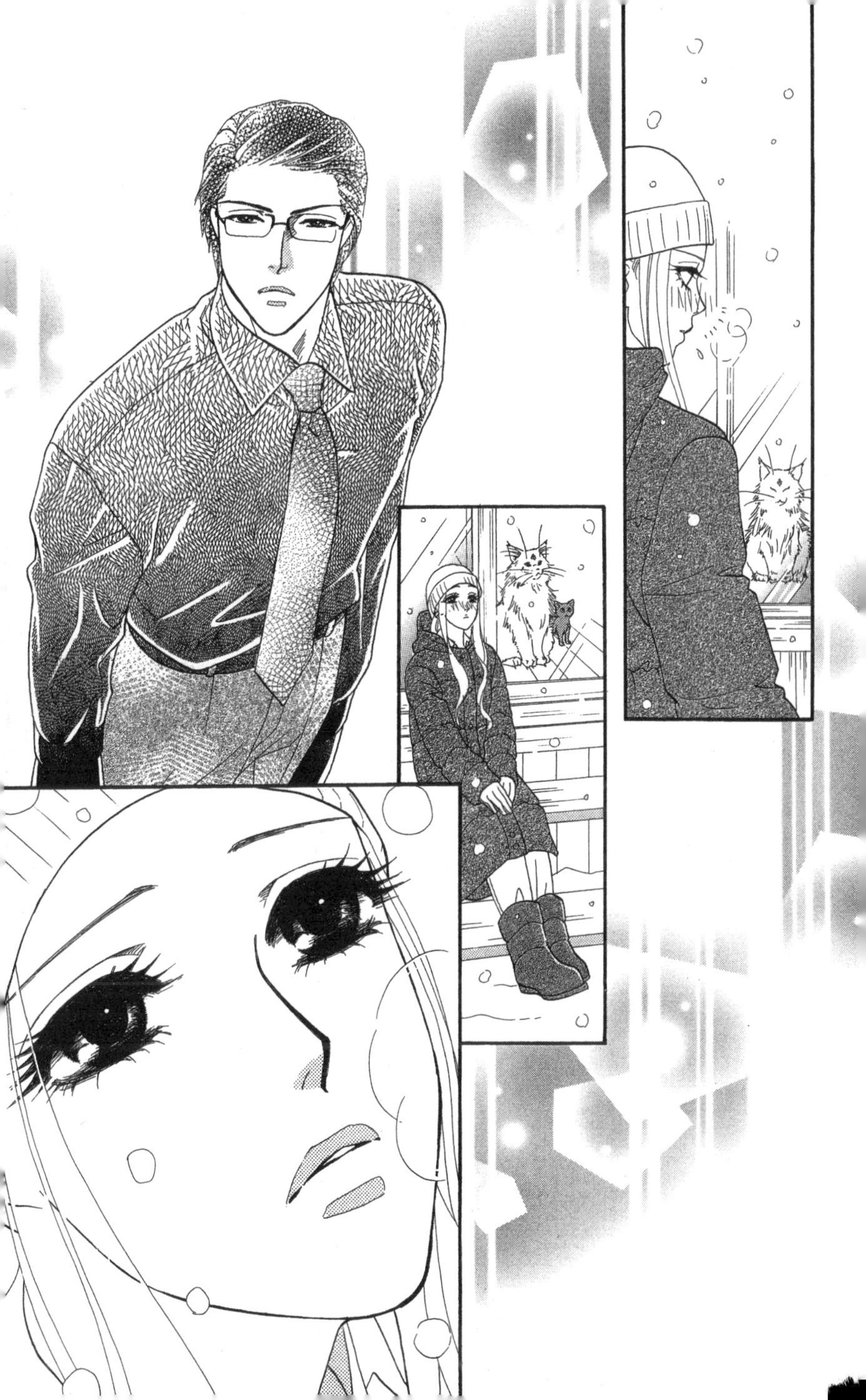

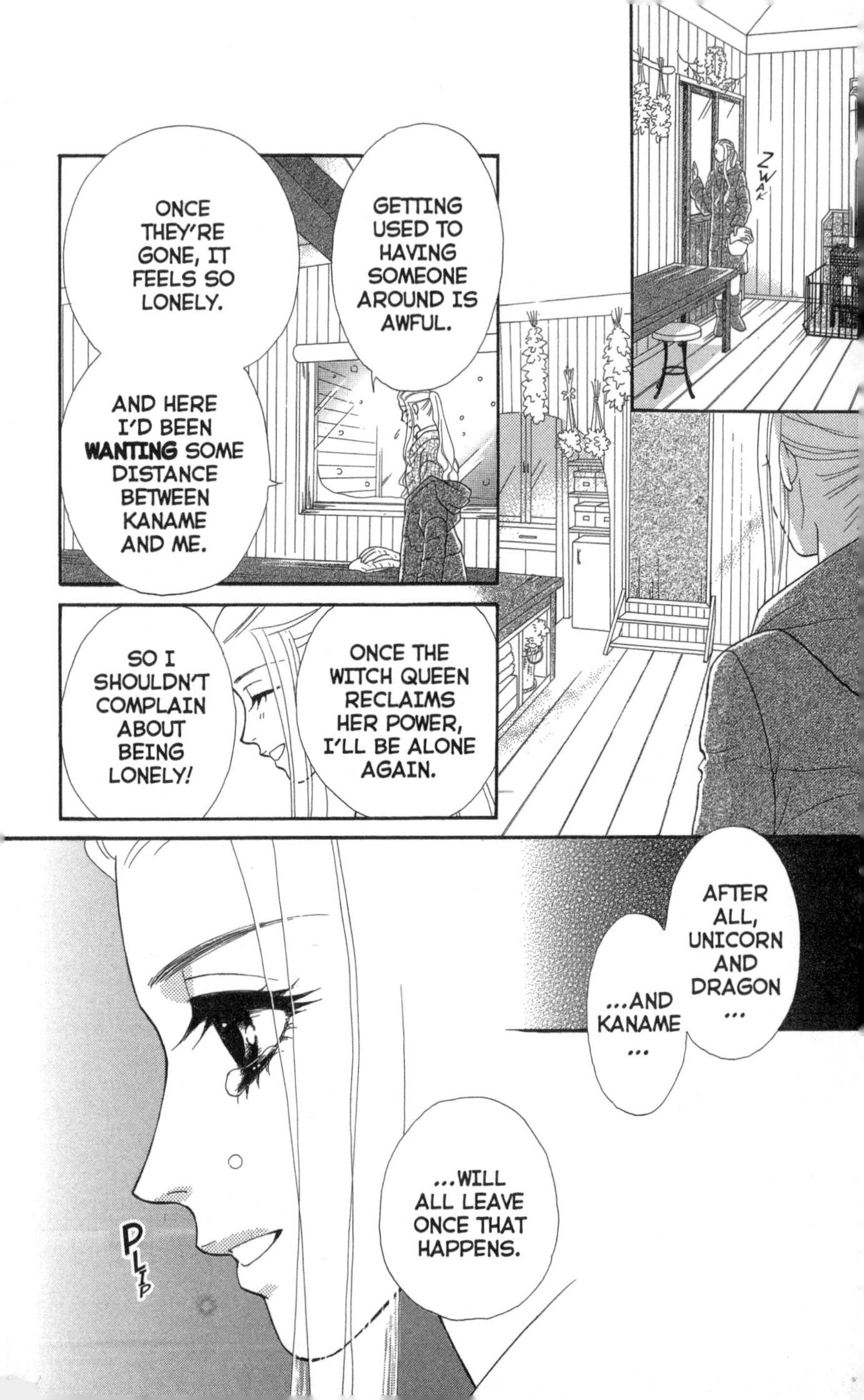
ZWAK
GETTING USED TO HAVING SOMEONE AROUND IS AWFUL.
ONCE THEY'RE GONE, IT FEELS SO LONELY.
AND HERE I'D BEEN **WANTING** SOME DISTANCE BETWEEN KANAME AND ME.
ONCE THE WITCH QUEEN RECLAIMS HER POWER, I'LL BE ALONE AGAIN.
SO I SHOULDN'T COMPLAIN ABOUT BEING LONELY!
AFTER ALL, UNICORN AND DRAGON...
...AND KANAME...
...WILL ALL LEAVE ONCE THAT HAPPENS.
PLIP

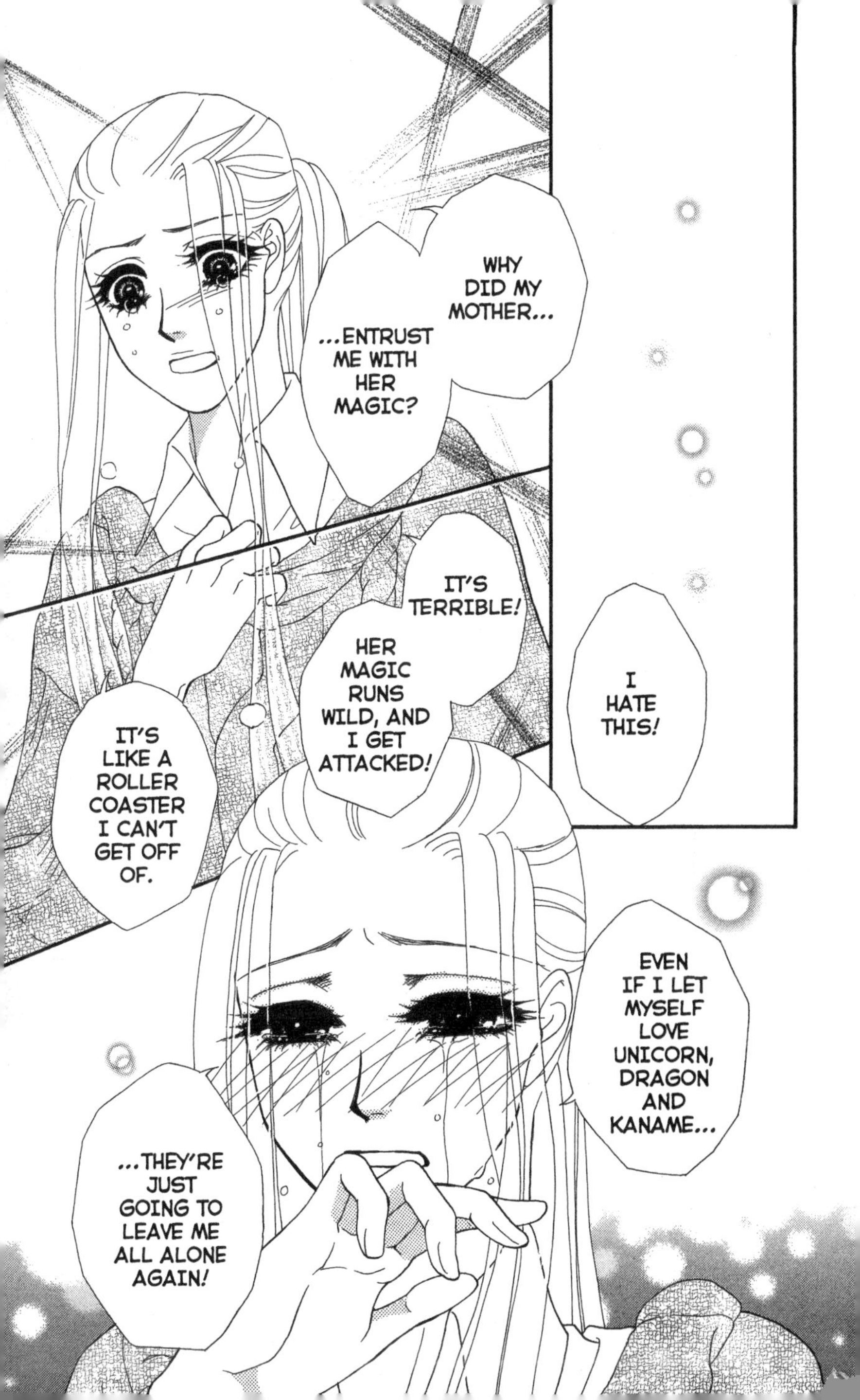
I HATE THIS!
WHY DID MY MOTHER...
...ENTRUST ME WITH HER MAGIC?
IT'S TERRIBLE!
HER MAGIC RUNS WILD, AND I GET ATTACKED!
IT'S LIKE A ROLLER COASTER I CAN'T GET OFF OF.
EVEN IF I LET MYSELF LOVE UNICORN, DRAGON AND KANAME...
...THEY'RE JUST GOING TO LEAVE ME ALL ALONE AGAIN!

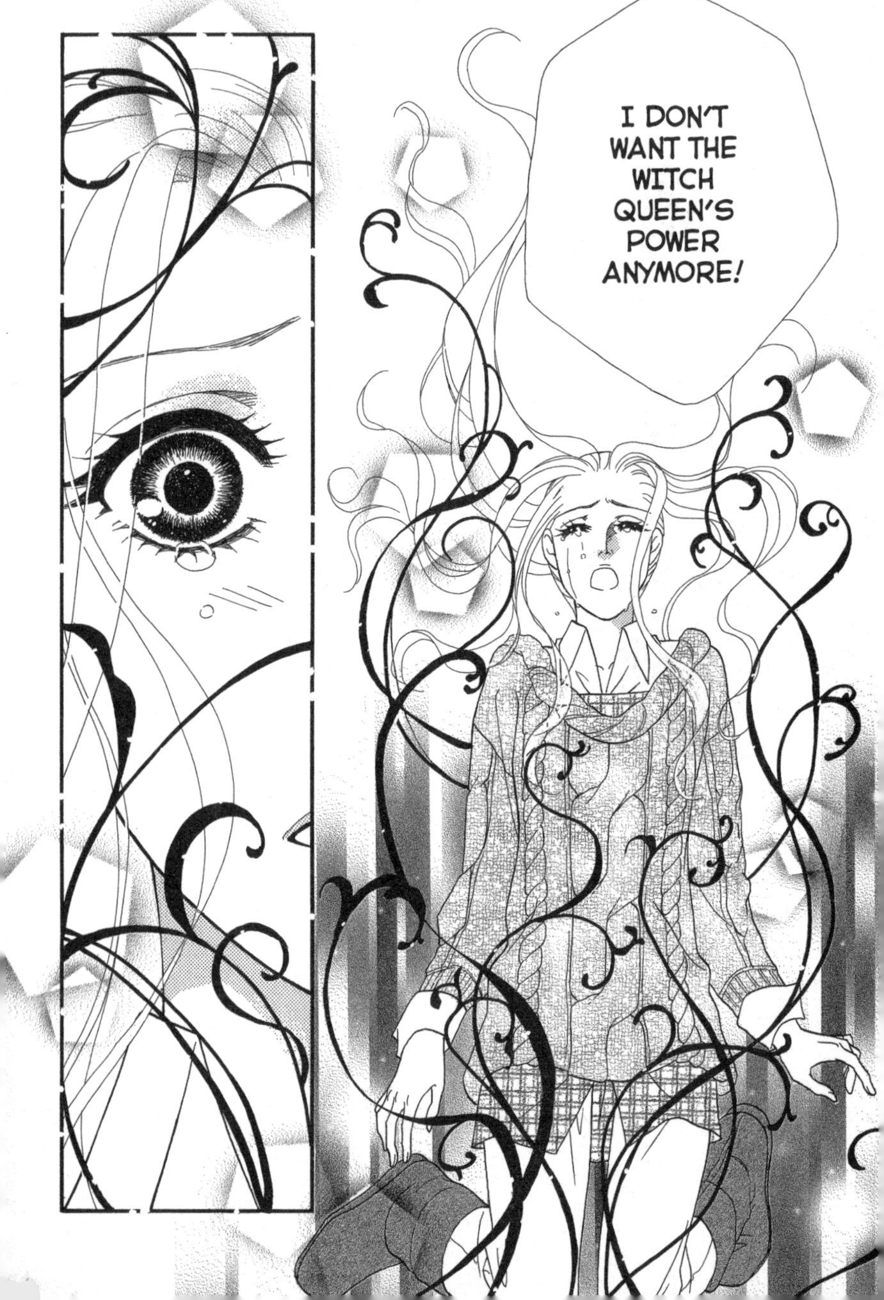
I DON'T WANT THE WITCH QUEEN'S POWER ANYMORE!

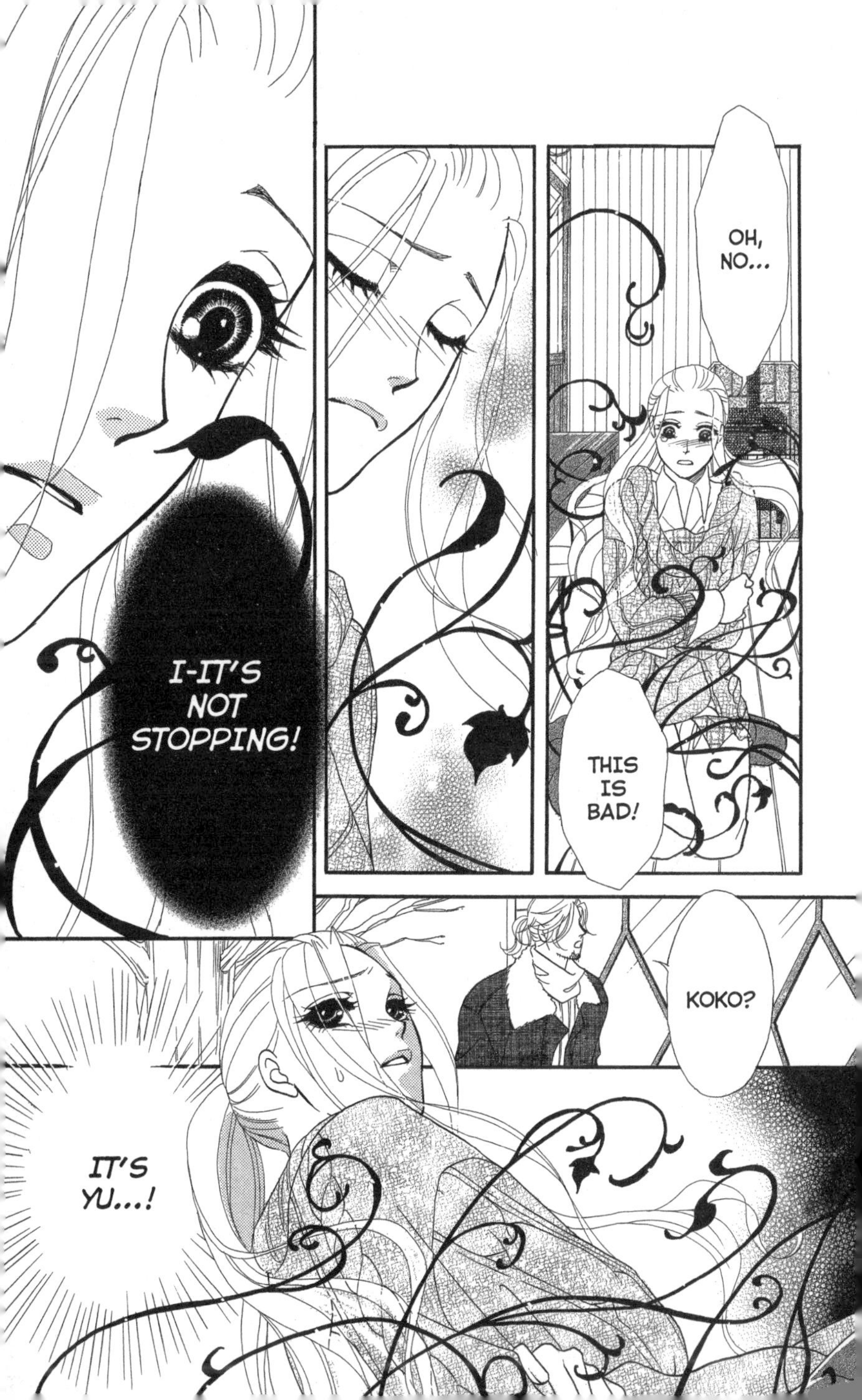
OH, NO...
THIS IS BAD!
I-IT'S NOT STOPPING!
KOKO?
IT'S YU...!

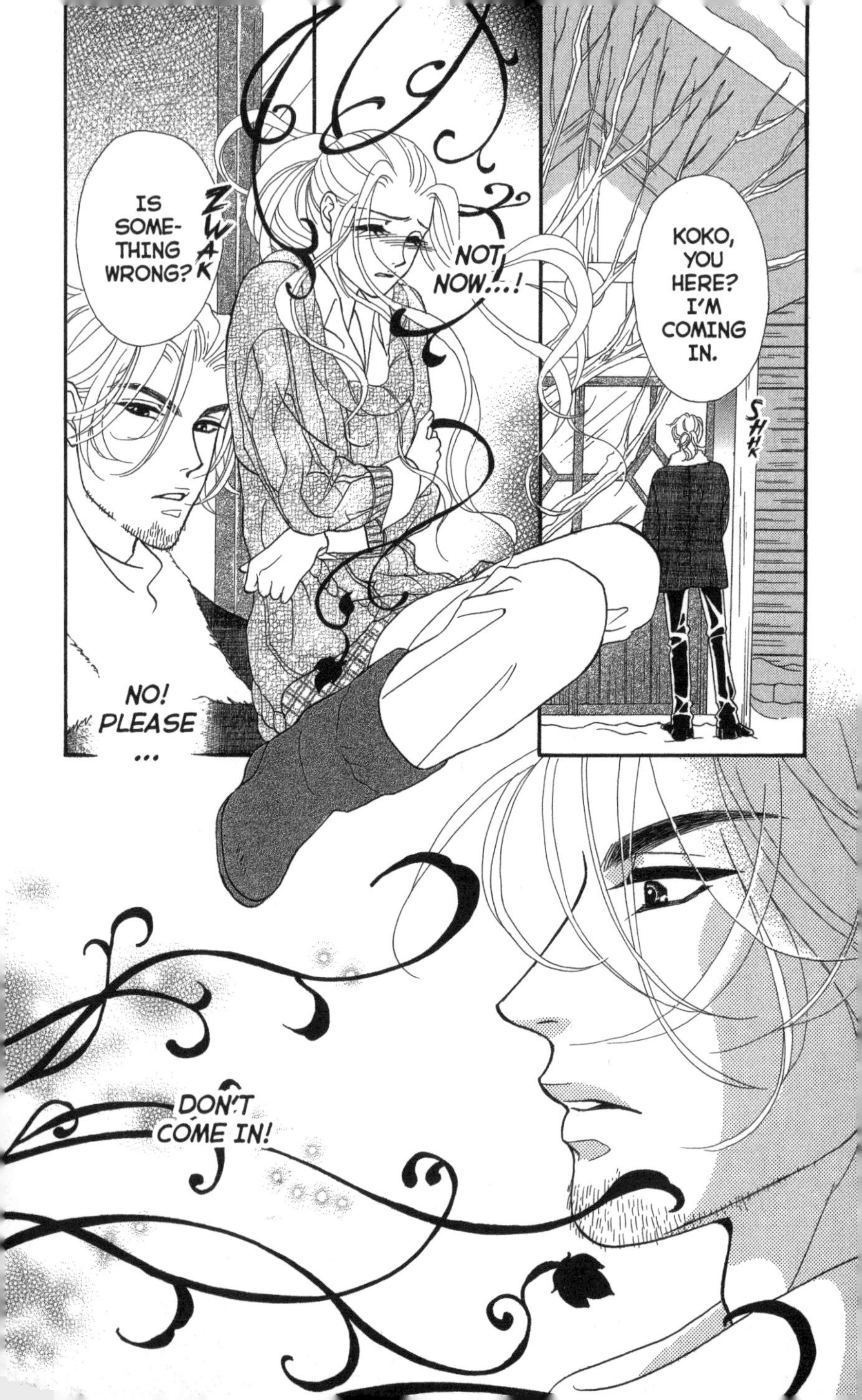
KOKO, YOU HERE? I'M COMING IN.
SHHK
NOT NOW...!
ZWAK
IS SOMETHING WRONG?
NO! PLEASE ...
DON'T COME IN!

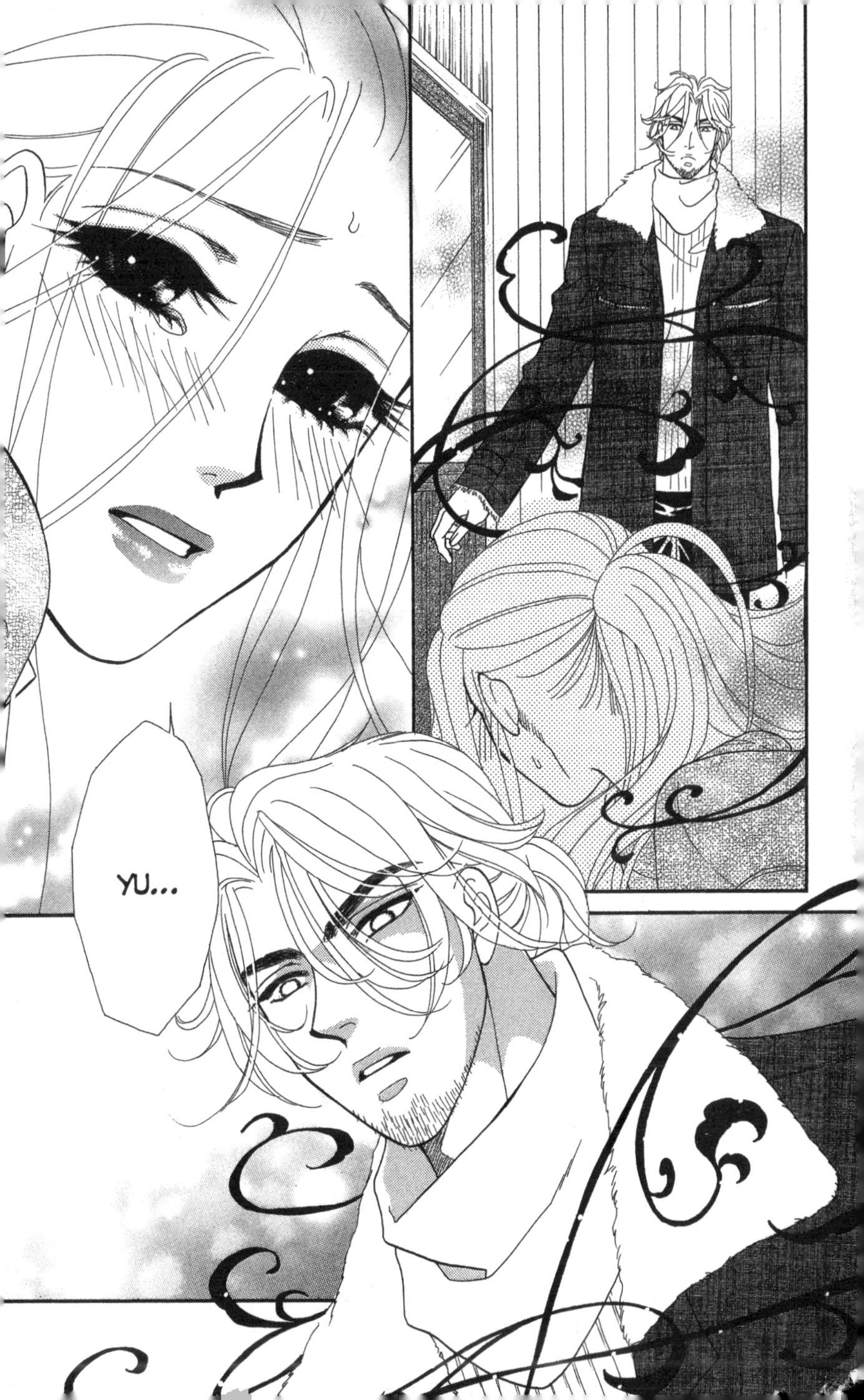
YU...

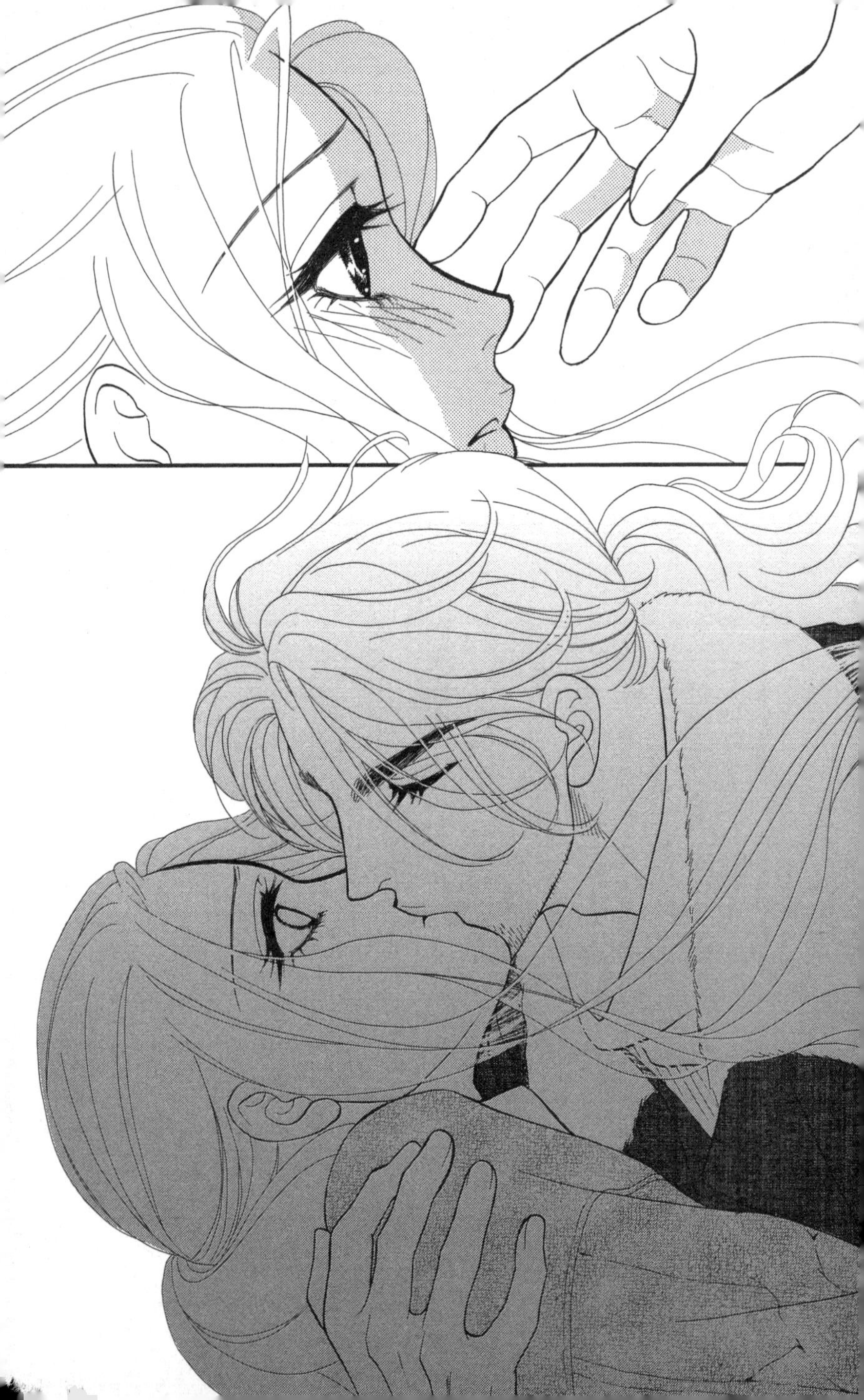

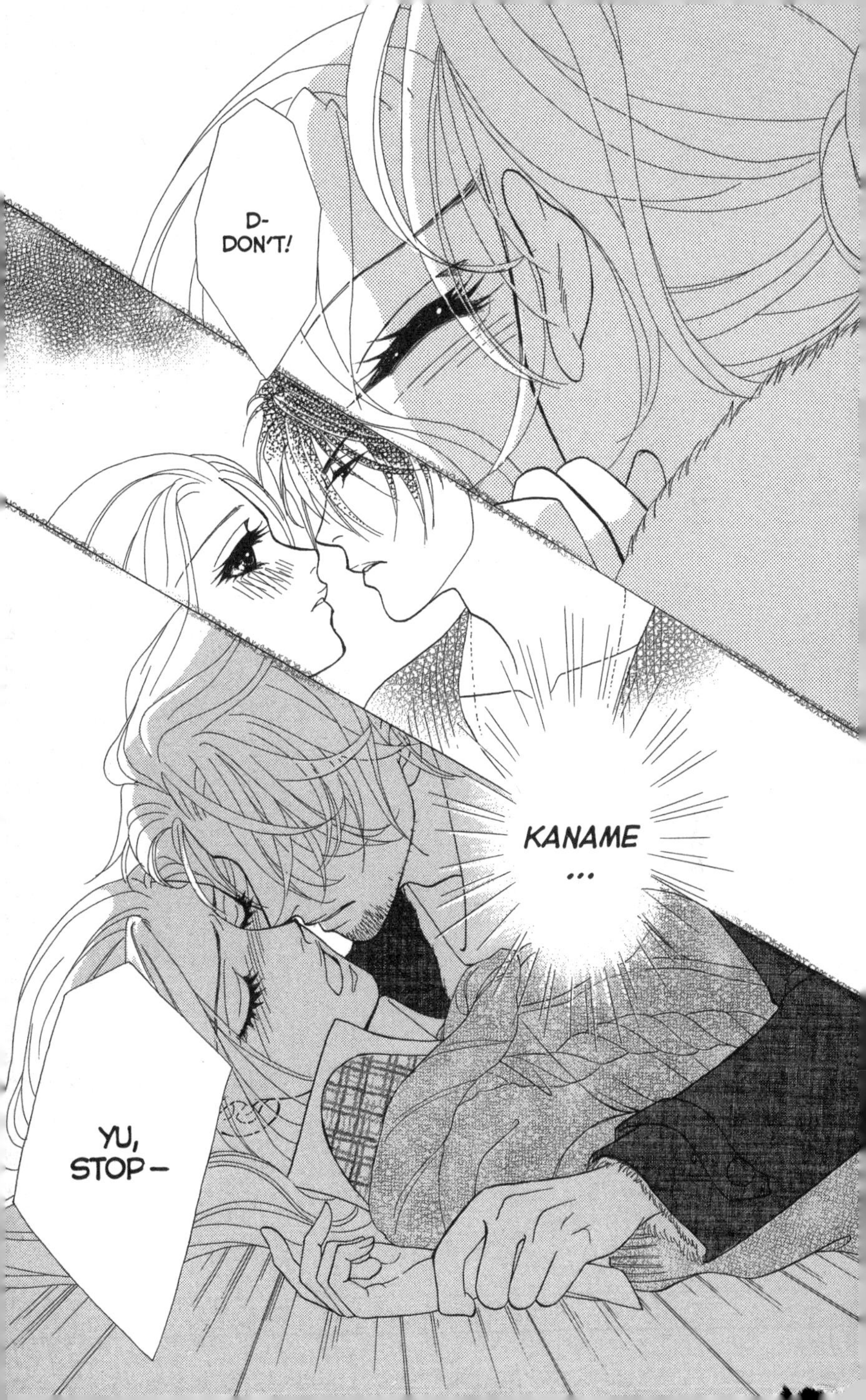
D-
DON'T!
KANAME
...
YU,
STOP–

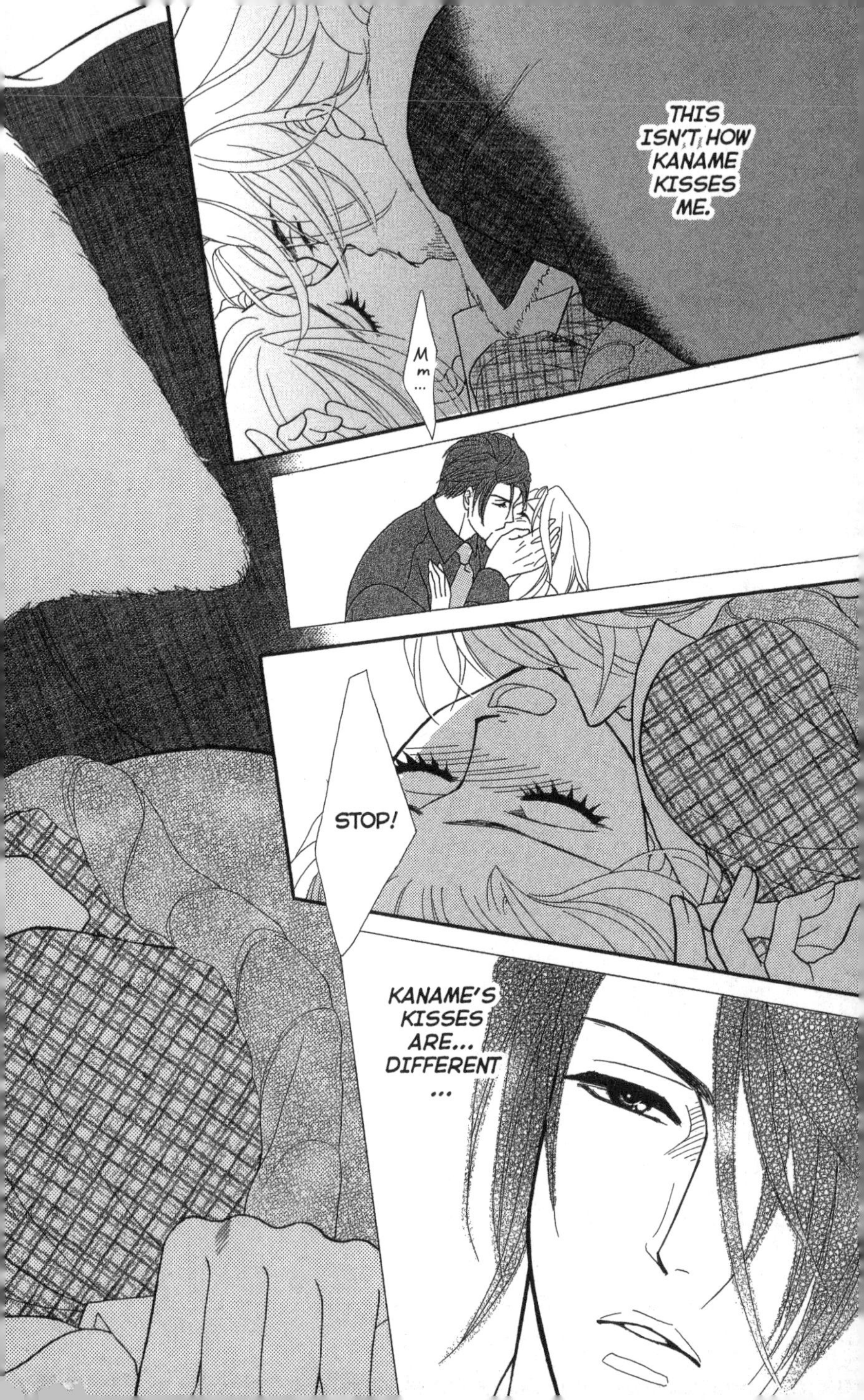
THIS ISN'T HOW KANAME KISSES ME.
Mm...
STOP!
KANAME'S KISSES ARE... DIFFERENT...

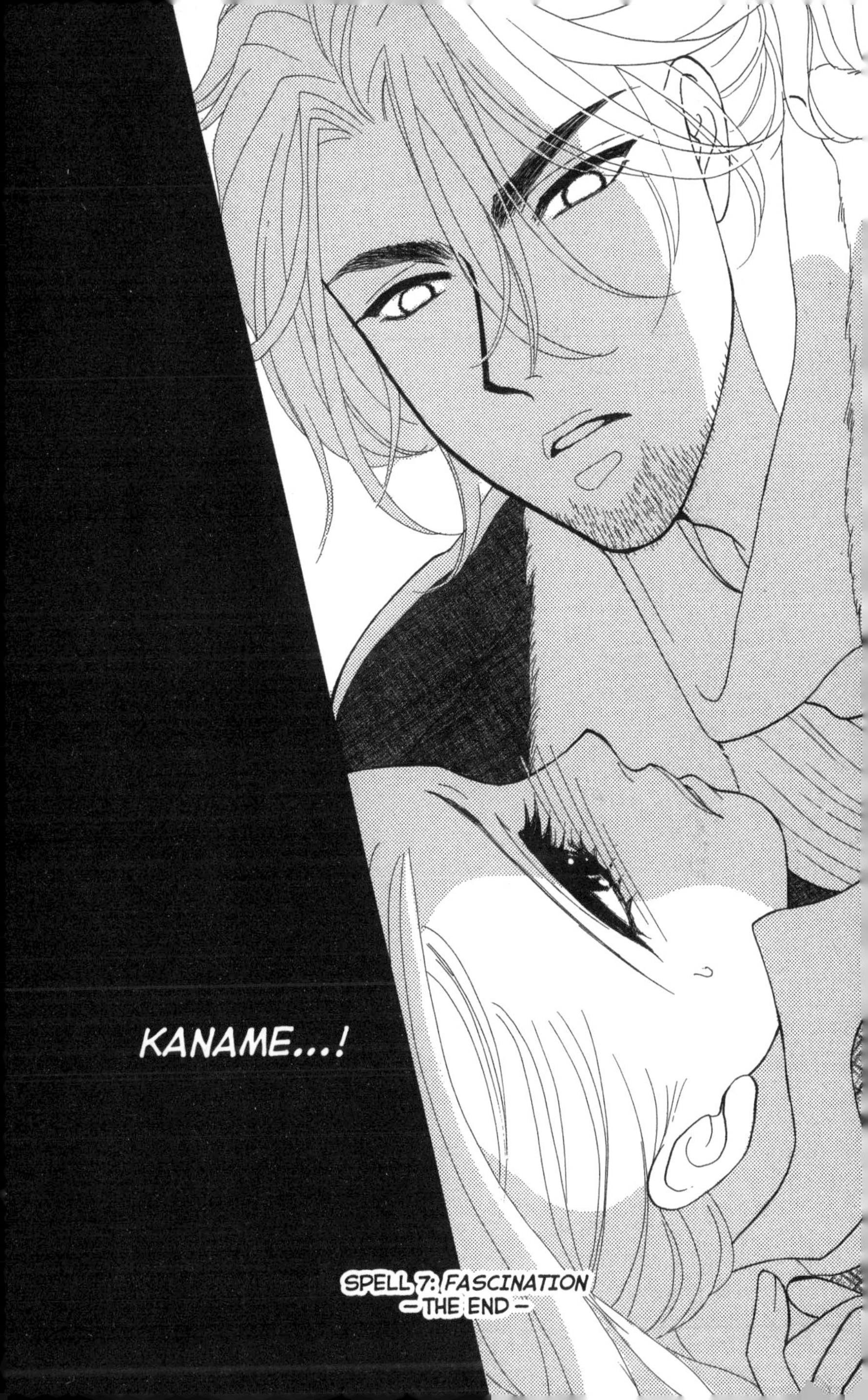
KANAME...!
SPELL 7: FASCINATION
–THE END–

Strong people wind up doing a lot of heavy labor.

— FASCINATION—

When you live in snow country, shoveling is a daily chore. I enjoy drawing activities like that! But I know that in reality, shoveling snow is hard work. (Wry smile)

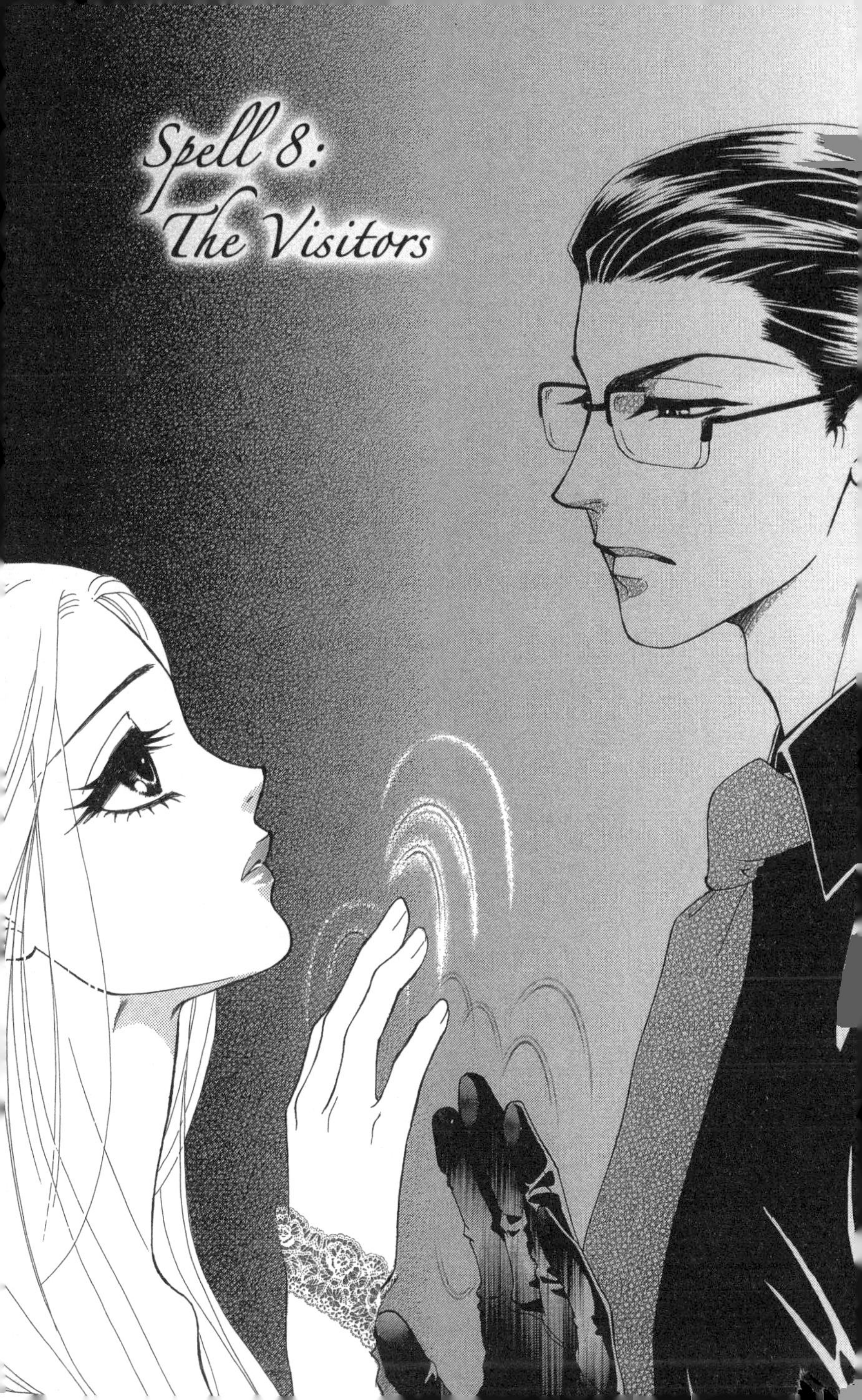
Spell 8:
The Visitors

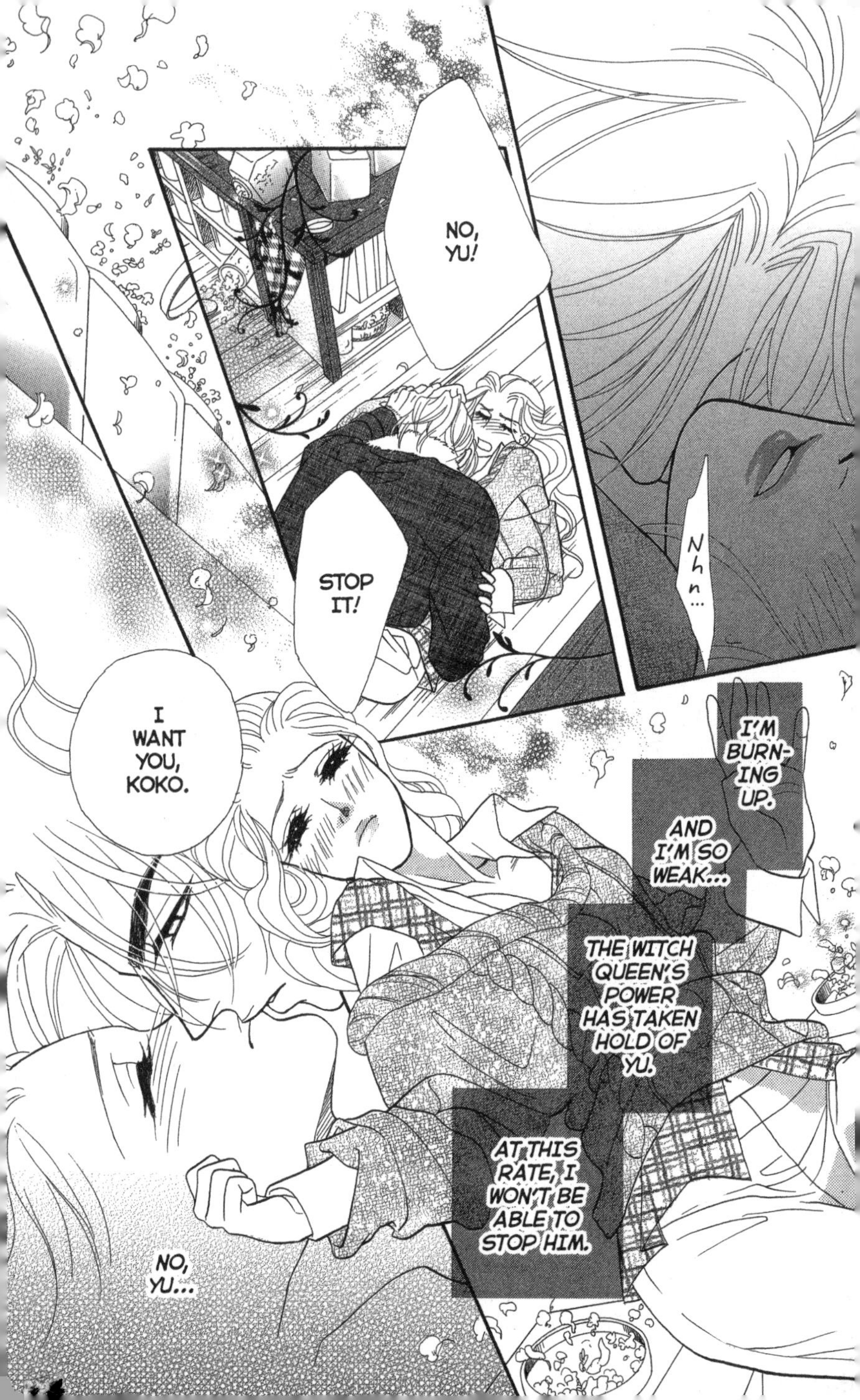
Nhn...
NO, YU!
STOP IT!
I'M BURNING UP.
AND I'M SO WEAK...
THE WITCH QUEEN'S POWER HAS TAKEN HOLD OF YU.
AT THIS RATE, I WON'T BE ABLE TO STOP HIM.
I WANT YOU, KOKO.
NO, YU...

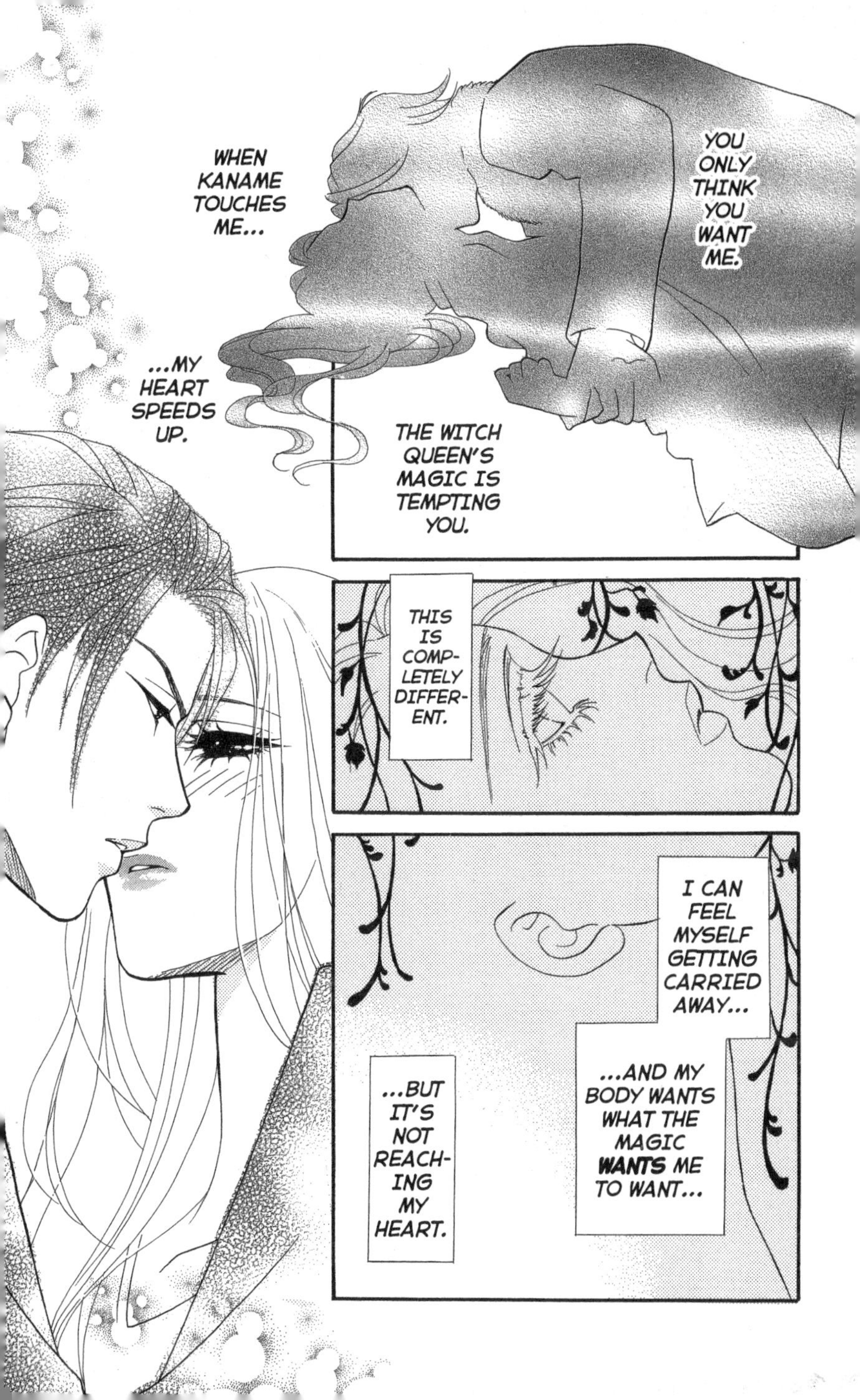

YOU ONLY THINK YOU WANT ME.
THE WITCH QUEEN'S MAGIC IS TEMPTING YOU.
WHEN KANAME TOUCHES ME...
...MY HEART SPEEDS UP.
THIS IS COMP-LETELY DIFFER-ENT.
I CAN FEEL MYSELF GETTING CARRIED AWAY...
...AND MY BODY WANTS WHAT THE MAGIC **WANTS** ME TO WANT...
...BUT IT'S NOT REACH-ING MY HEART.

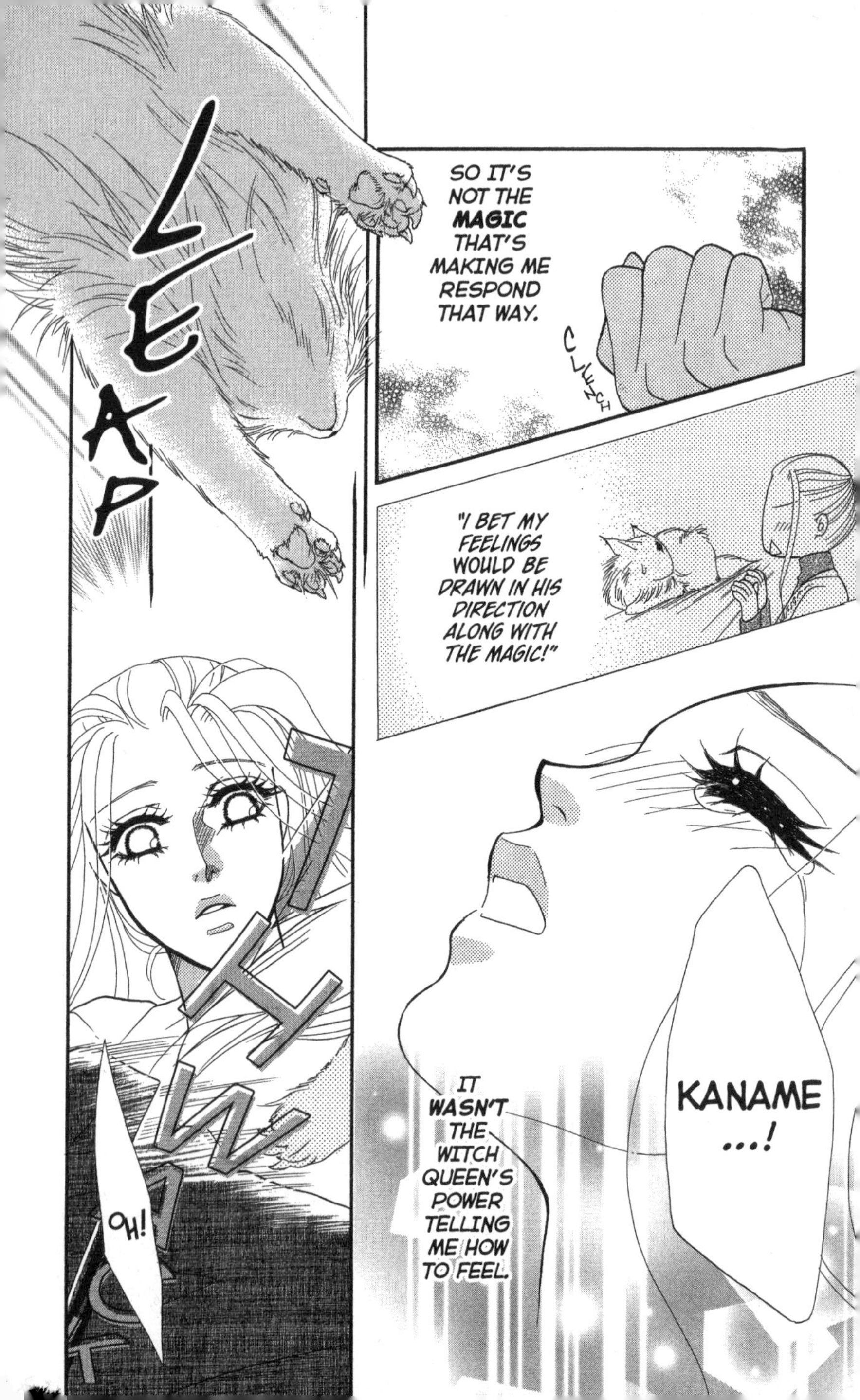
SO IT'S NOT THE **MAGIC** THAT'S MAKING ME RESPOND THAT WAY.
CLENCH
"I BET MY FEELINGS WOULD BE DRAWN IN HIS DIRECTION ALONG WITH THE MAGIC!"
IT **WASN'T** THE WITCH QUEEN'S POWER TELLING ME HOW TO FEEL.
KANAME ...!
LEAP
OH!

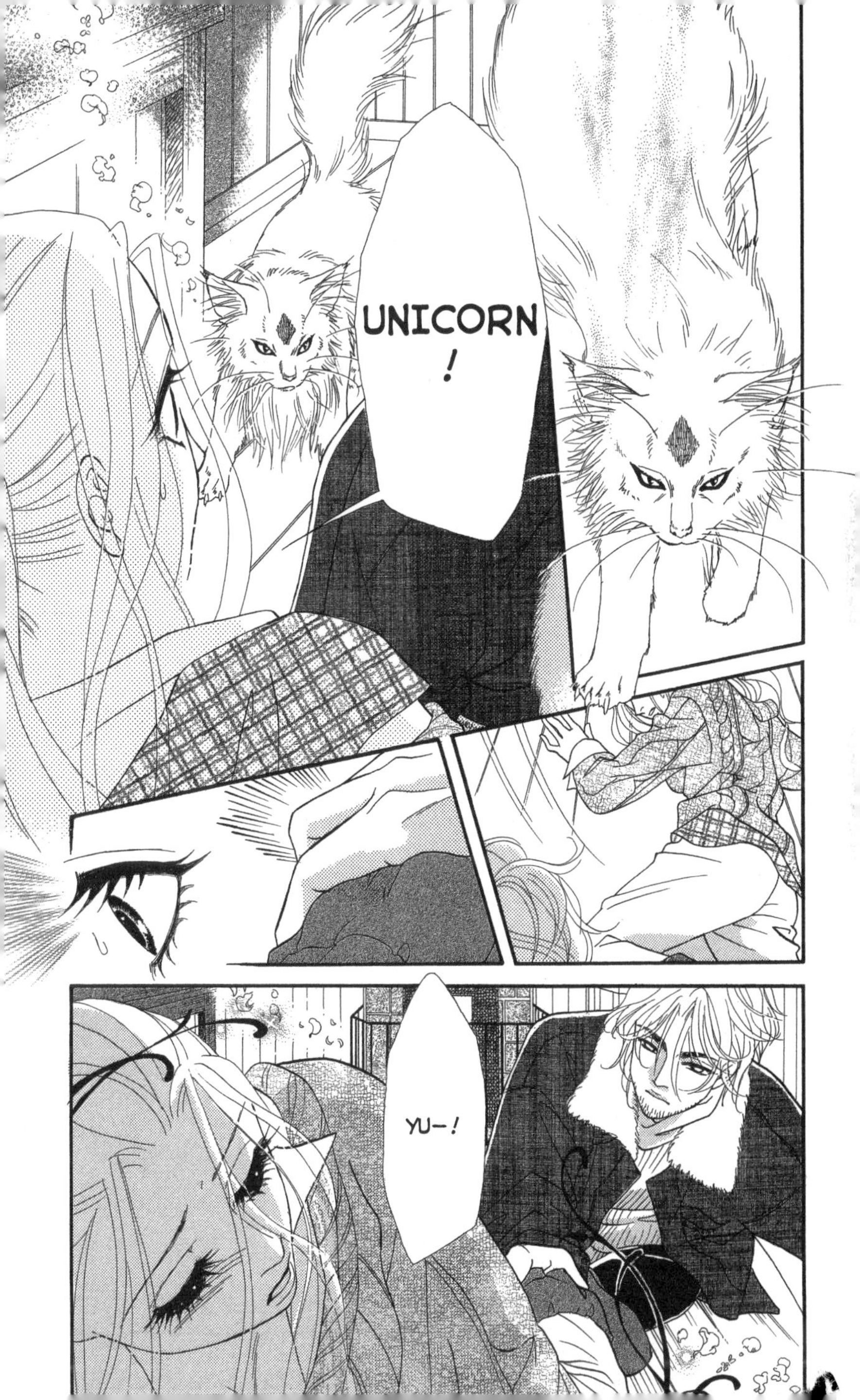
UNICORN!
YU-!

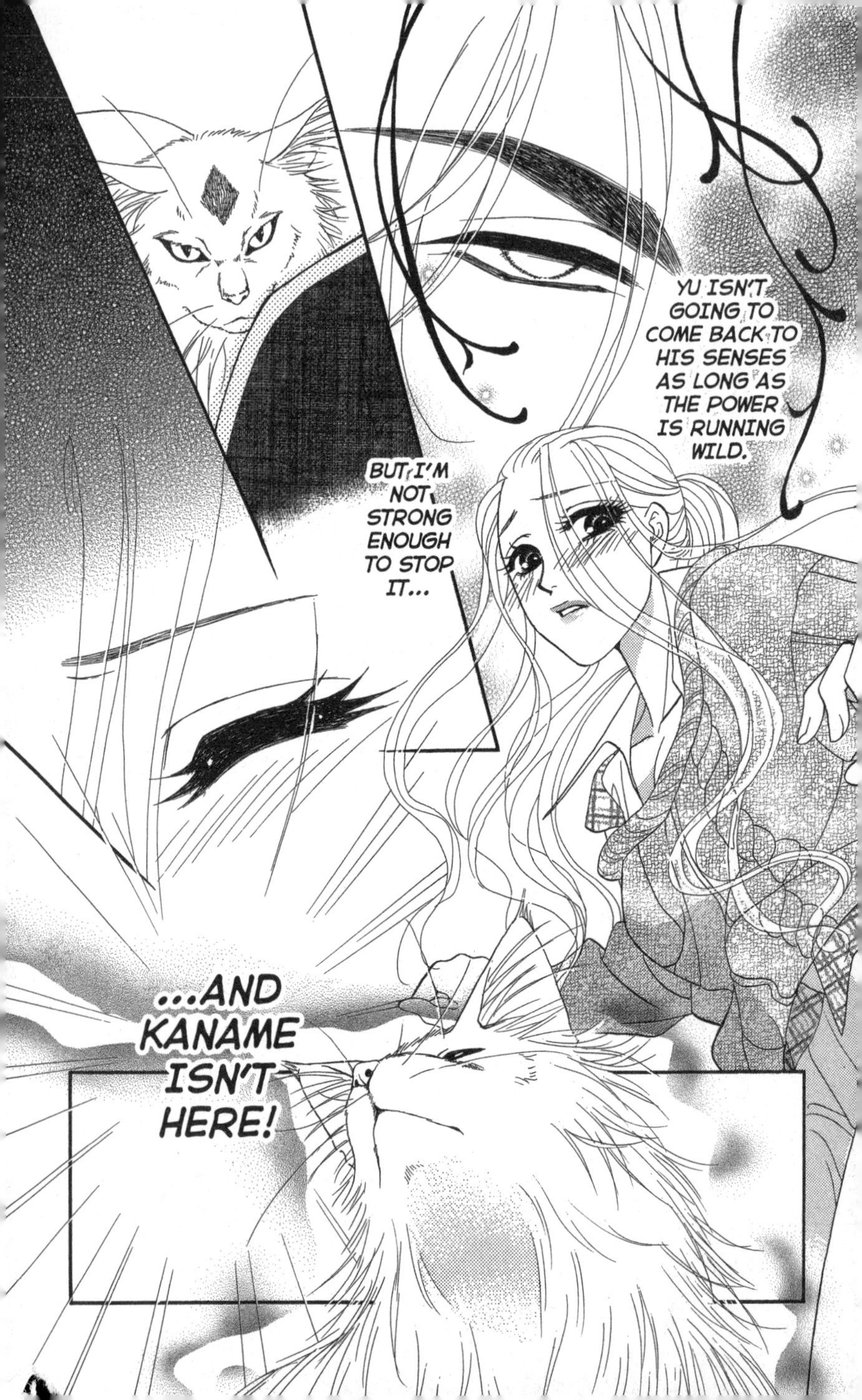
YU ISN'T GOING TO COME BACK TO HIS SENSES AS LONG AS THE POWER IS RUNNING WILD.
BUT I'M NOT STRONG ENOUGH TO STOP IT...
...AND KANAME ISN'T HERE!

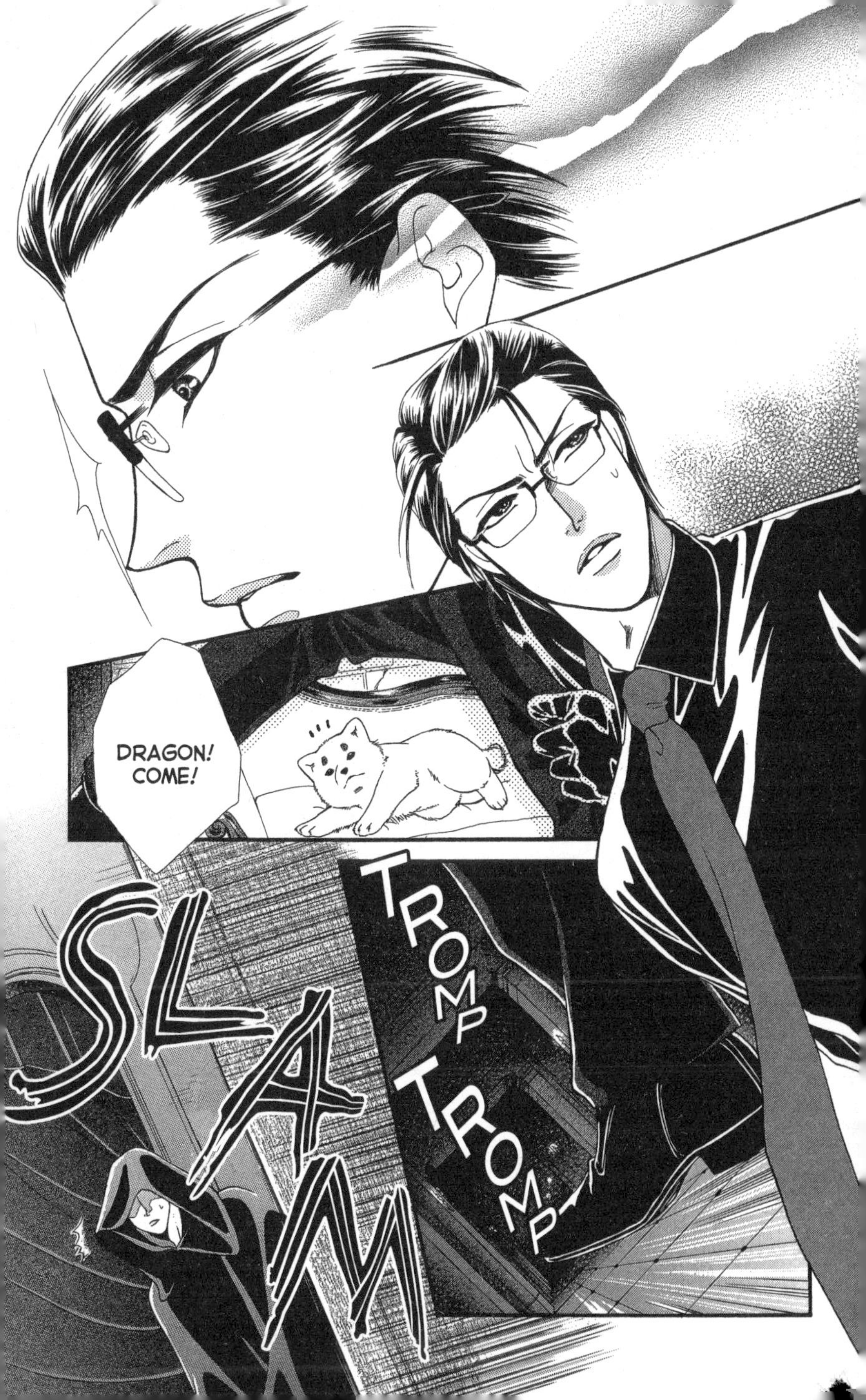
DRAGON! COME!
TROMP TROMP
SLAM

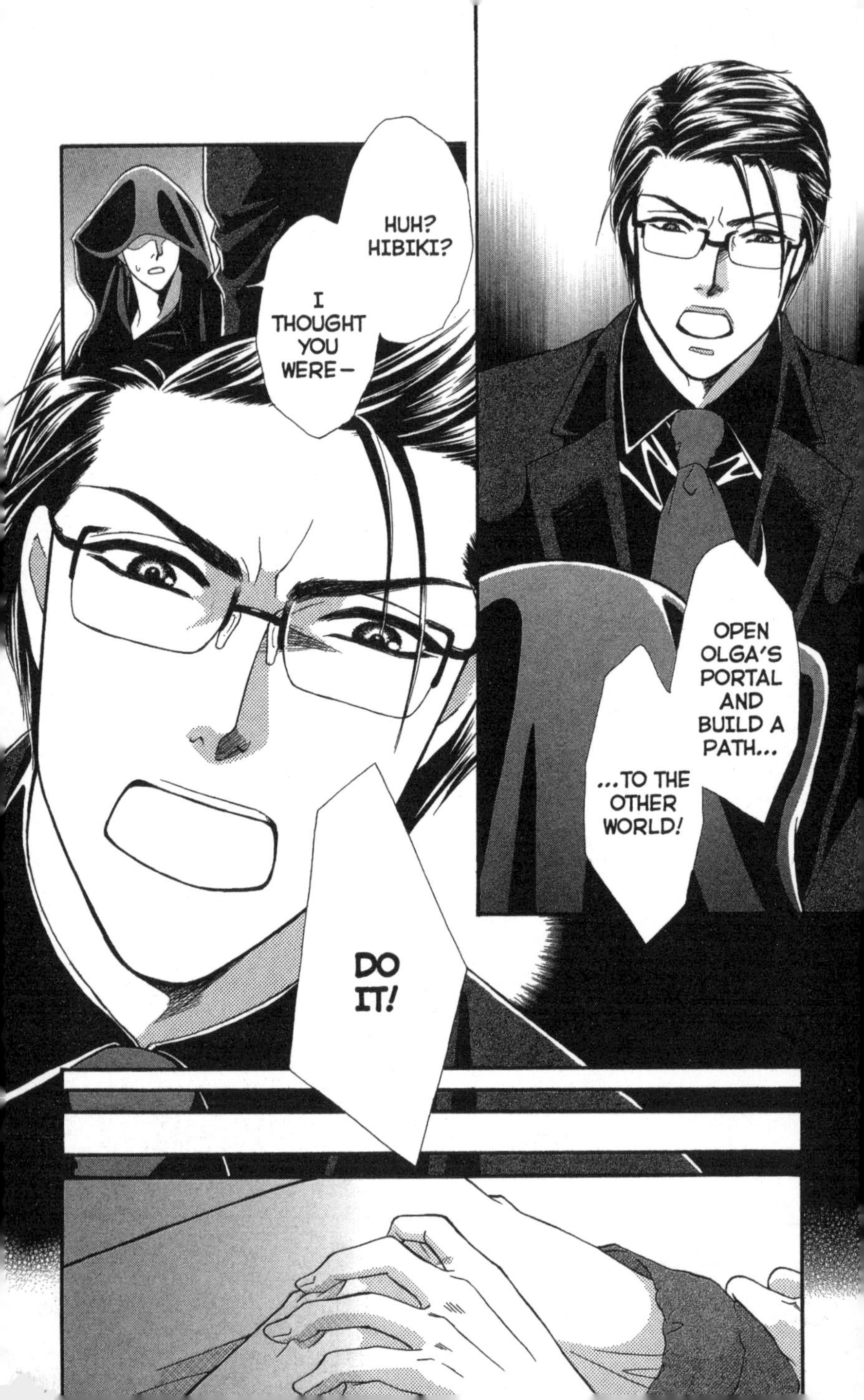
OPEN OLGA'S PORTAL AND BUILD A PATH...
...TO THE OTHER WORLD!
HUH? HIBIKI?
I THOUGHT YOU WERE—
DO IT!

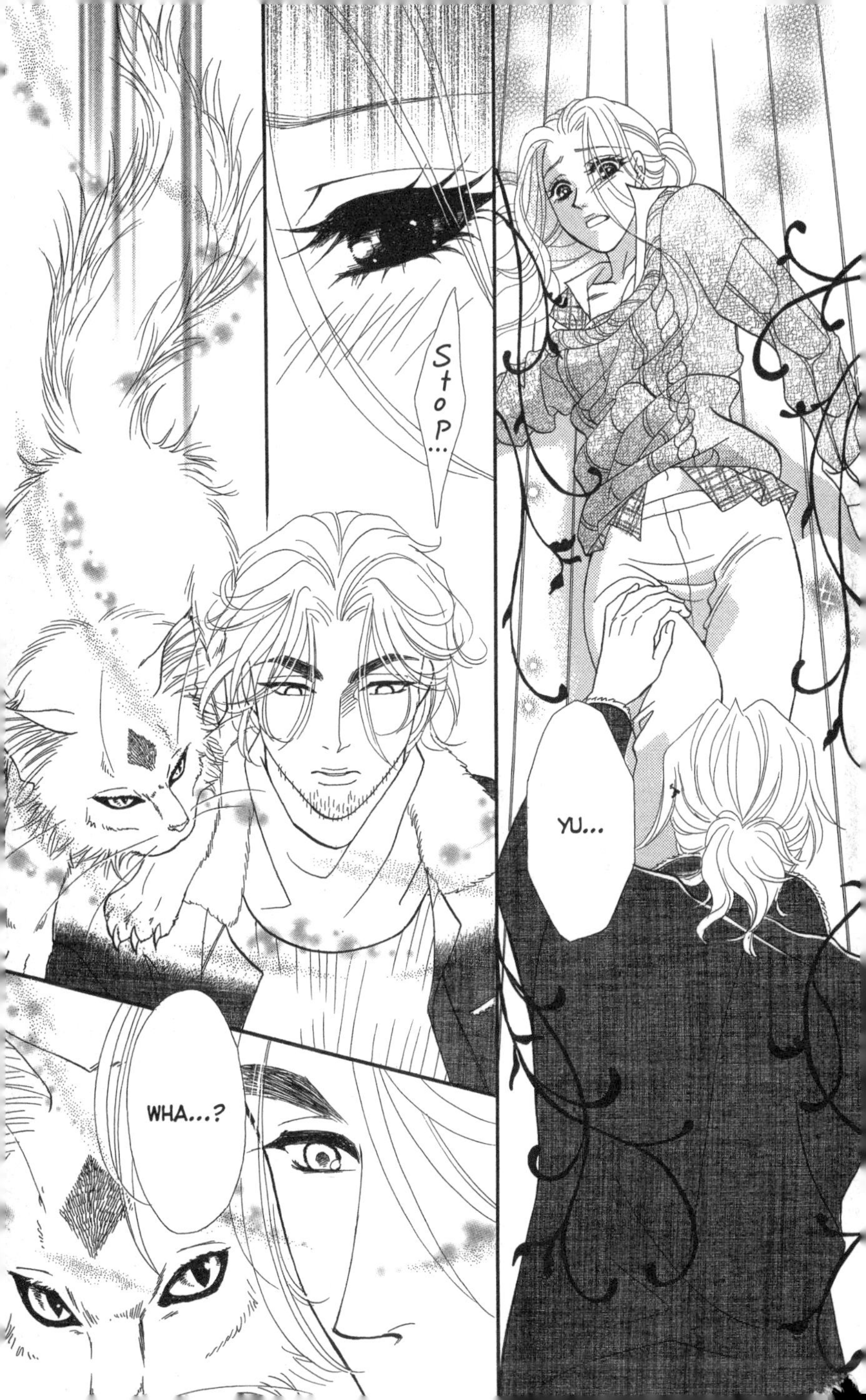
YU...
STOP...
WHA...?

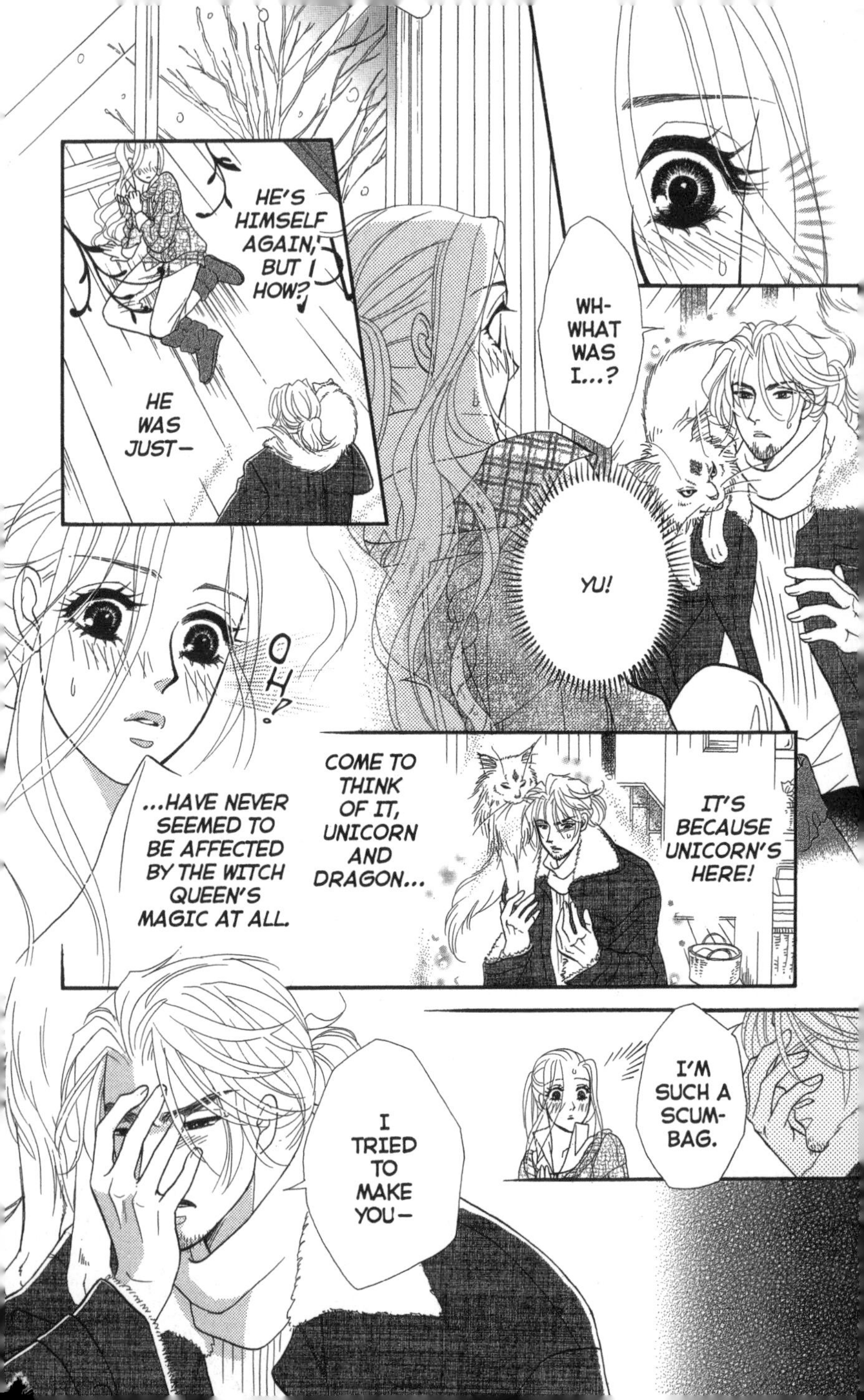
WH-WHAT WAS I...?
YU!
HE'S HIMSELF AGAIN, BUT HOW?
HE WAS JUST—
OH!?
IT'S BECAUSE UNICORN'S HERE!
COME TO THINK OF IT, UNICORN AND DRAGON...
...HAVE NEVER SEEMED TO BE AFFECTED BY THE WITCH QUEEN'S MAGIC AT ALL.
I'M SUCH A SCUM-BAG.
I TRIED TO MAKE YOU—

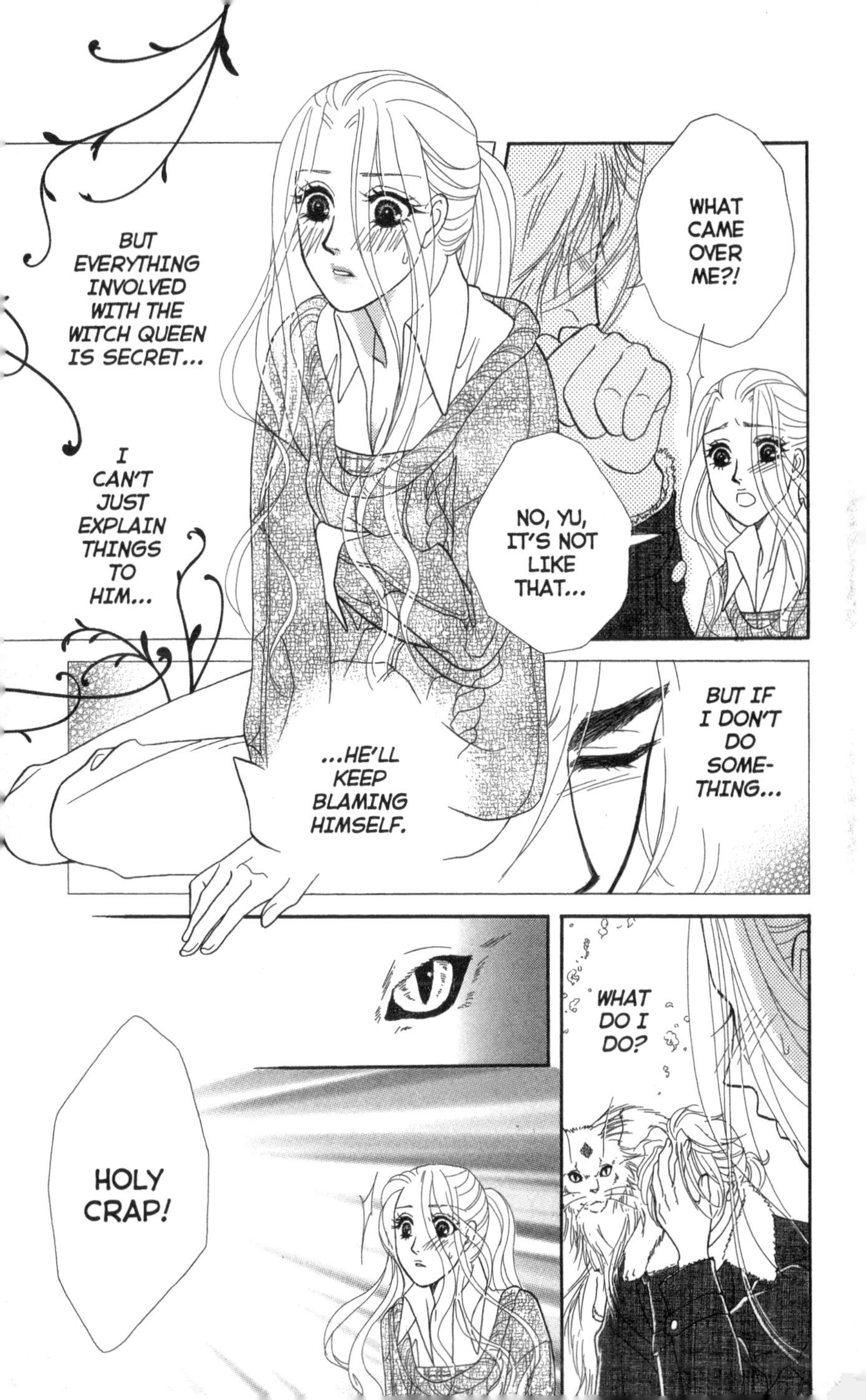
WHAT CAME OVER ME?!
NO, YU, IT'S NOT LIKE THAT...
BUT EVERYTHING INVOLVED WITH THE WITCH QUEEN IS SECRET...
I CAN'T JUST EXPLAIN THINGS TO HIM...
BUT IF I DON'T DO SOMETHING...
...HE'LL KEEP BLAMING HIMSELF.
WHAT DO I DO?
HOLY CRAP!

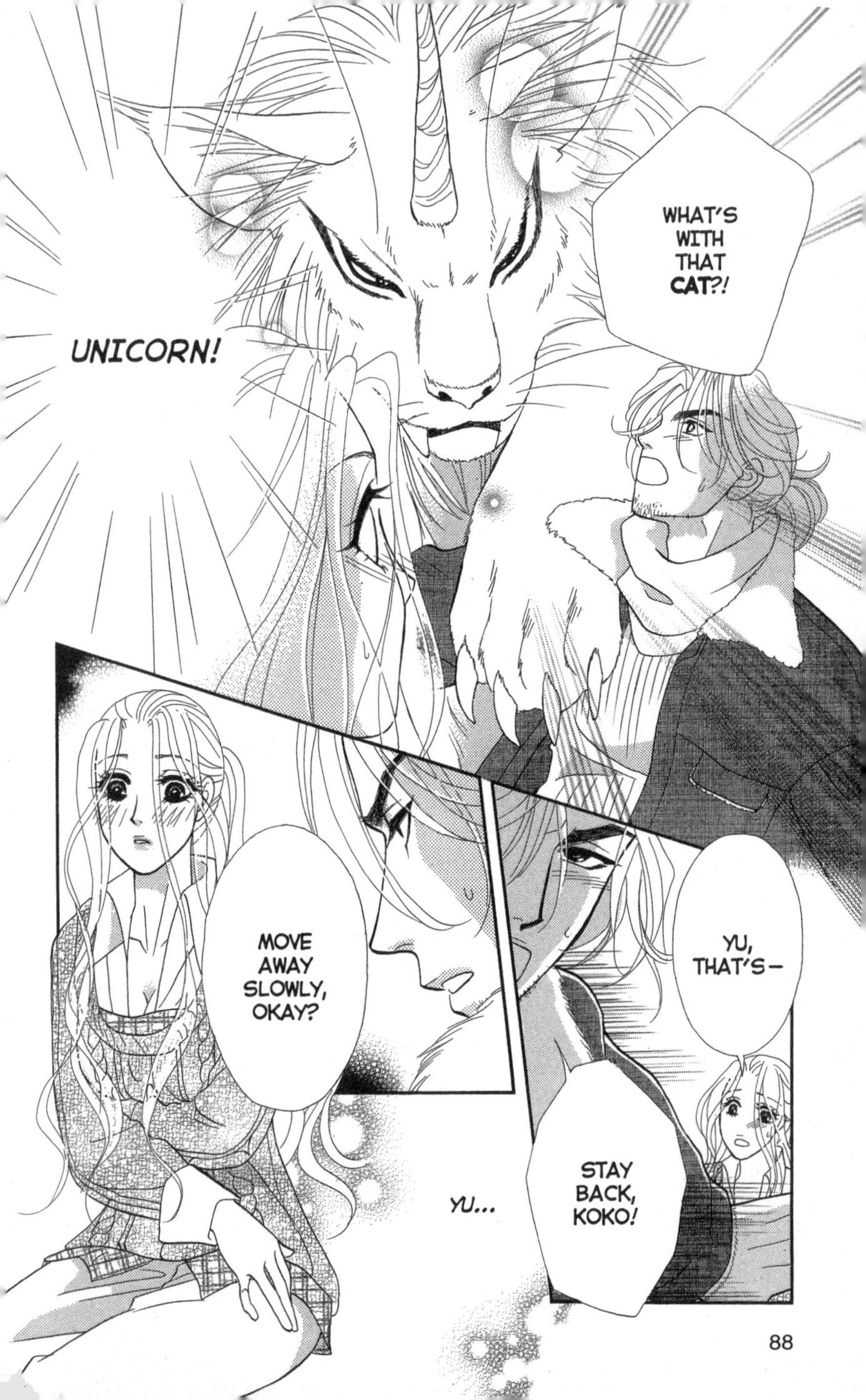
WHAT'S WITH THAT **CAT**?!
UNICORN!
YU, THAT'S—
STAY BACK, KOKO!
YU...
MOVE AWAY SLOWLY, OKAY?

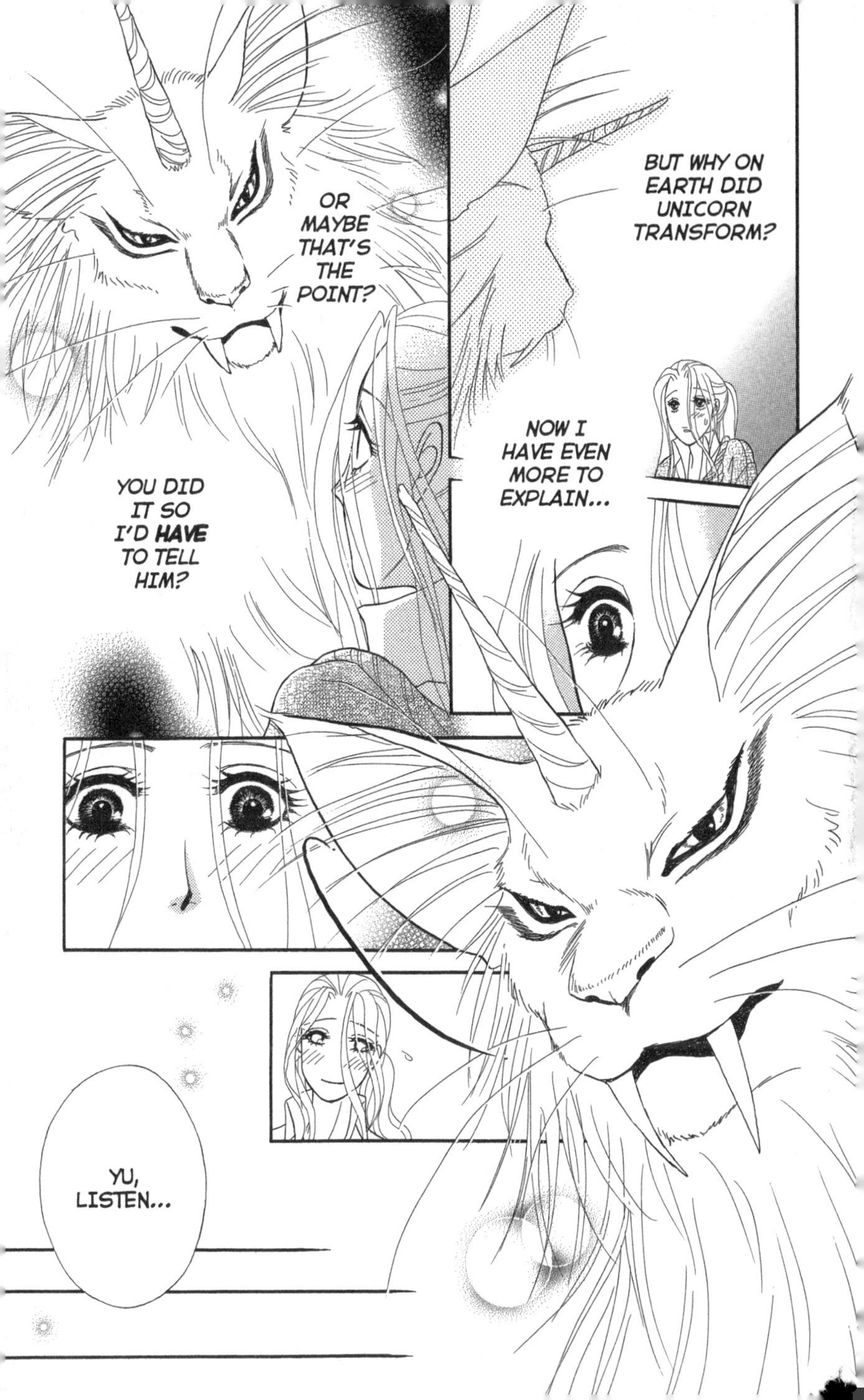
BUT WHY ON EARTH DID UNICORN TRANSFORM?
NOW I HAVE EVEN MORE TO EXPLAIN...
OR MAYBE THAT'S THE POINT?
YOU DID IT SO I'D **HAVE** TO TELL HIM?
YU, LISTEN...

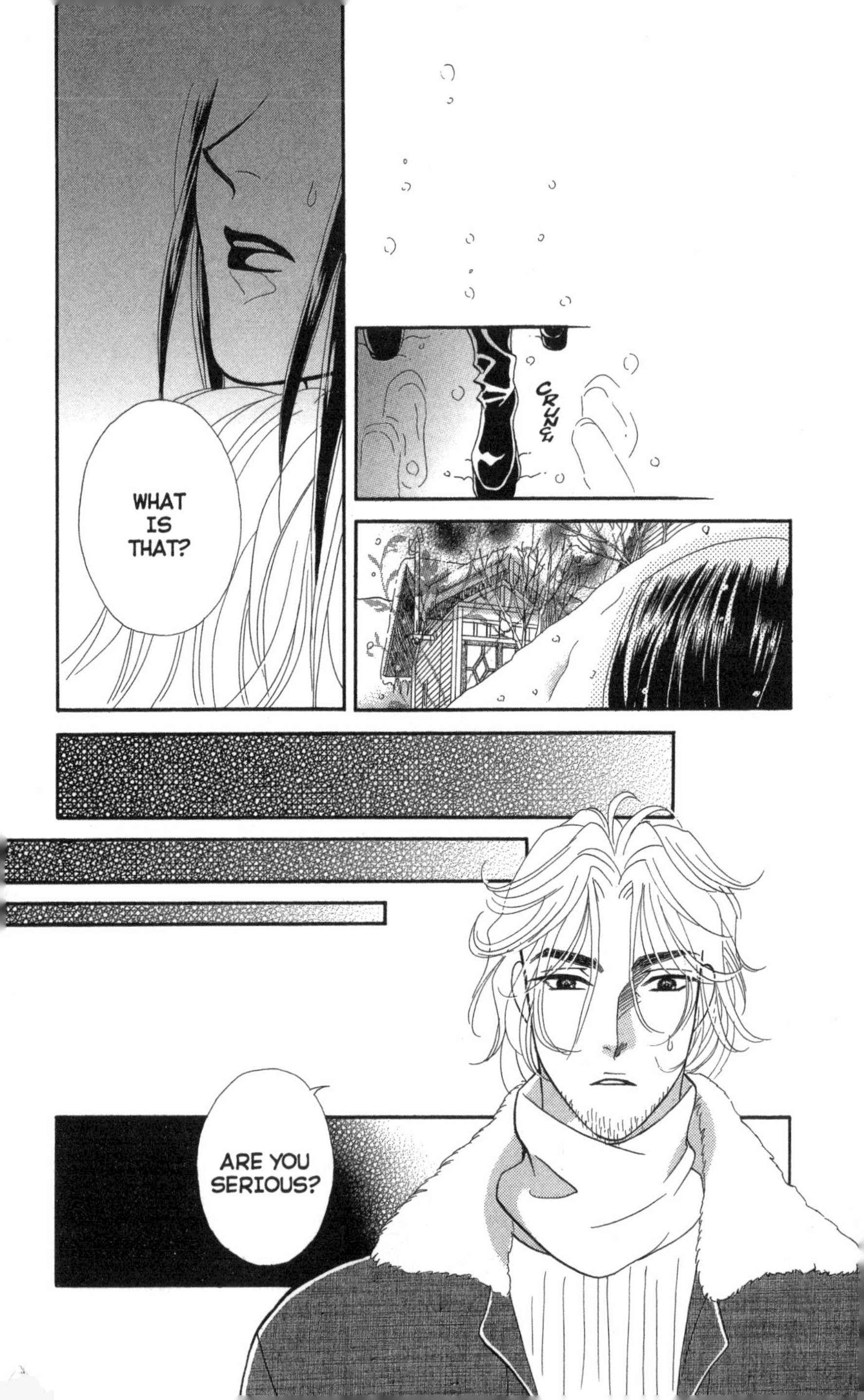
CRUNCH
WHAT IS THAT?
ARE YOU SERIOUS?

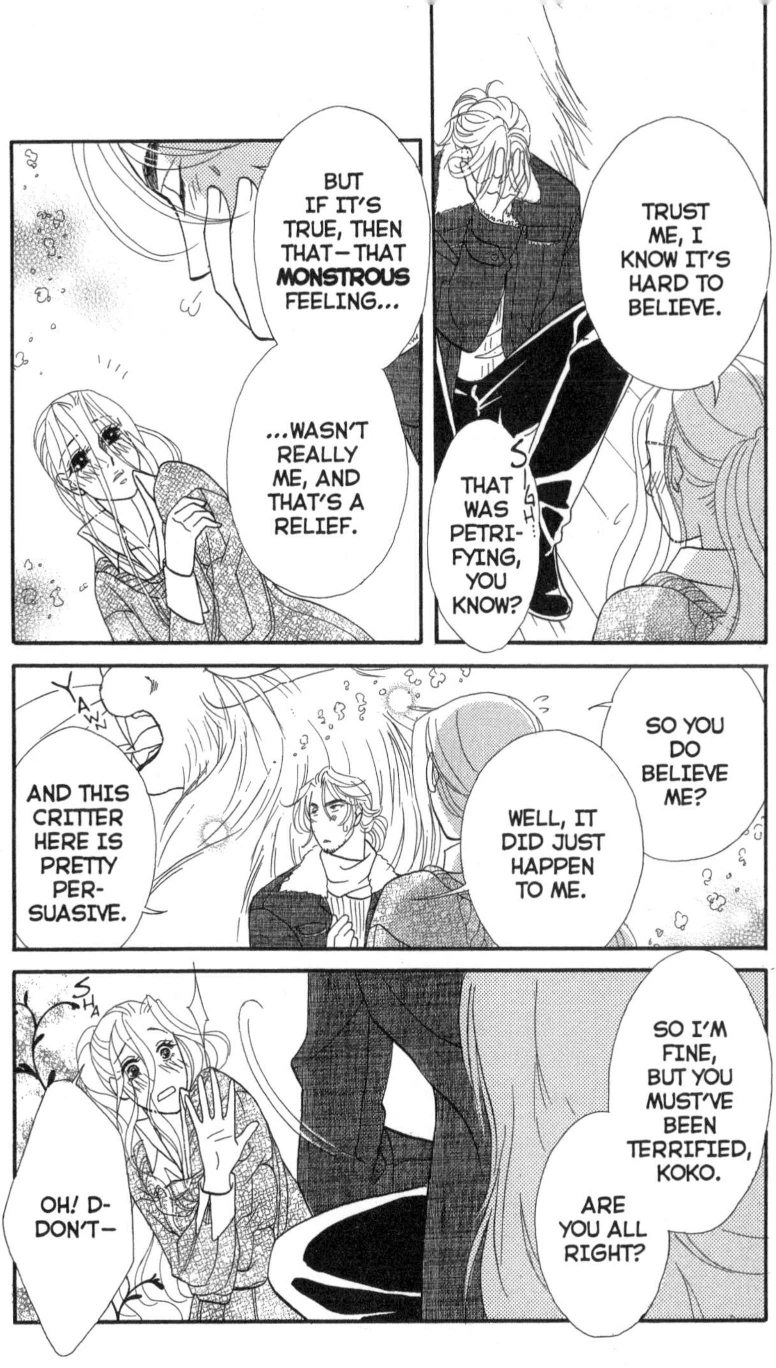
TRUST ME, I KNOW IT'S HARD TO BELIEVE.
SIGH...
THAT WAS PETRI-FYING, YOU KNOW?
BUT IF IT'S TRUE, THEN THAT—THAT **MONSTROUS** FEELING...
...WASN'T REALLY ME, AND THAT'S A RELIEF.
SO YOU DO BELIEVE ME?
WELL, IT DID JUST HAPPEN TO ME.
YAWN
AND THIS CRITTER HERE IS PRETTY PER-SUASIVE.
SO I'M FINE, BUT YOU MUST'VE BEEN TERRIFIED, KOKO.
ARE YOU ALL RIGHT?
SHA
OH! D-DON'T—

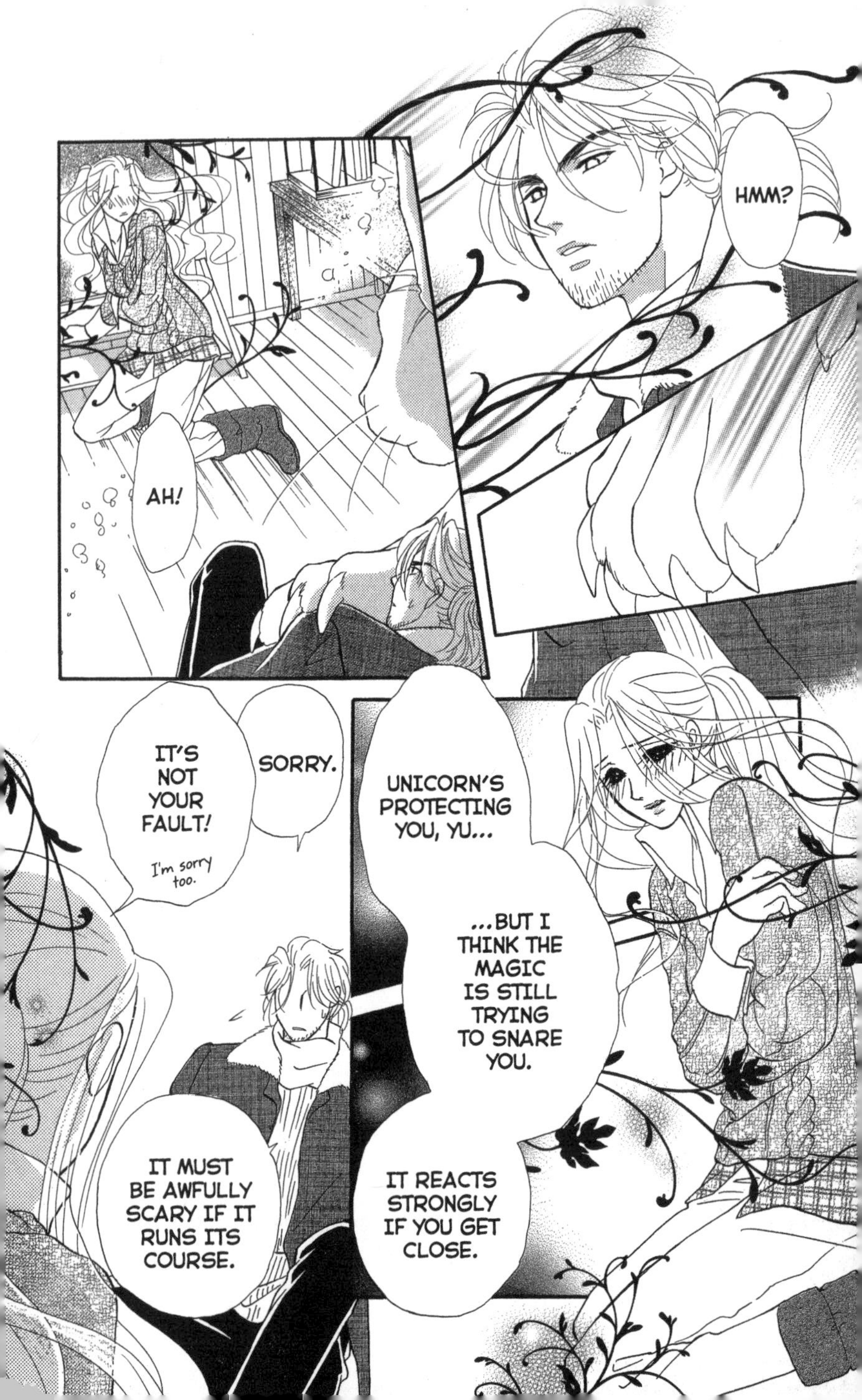
HMM?
AH!
UNICORN'S PROTECTING YOU, YU...
...BUT I THINK THE MAGIC IS STILL TRYING TO SNARE YOU.
IT REACTS STRONGLY IF YOU GET CLOSE.
SORRY.
IT'S NOT YOUR FAULT!
I'm sorry too.
IT MUST BE AWFULLY SCARY IF IT RUNS ITS COURSE.

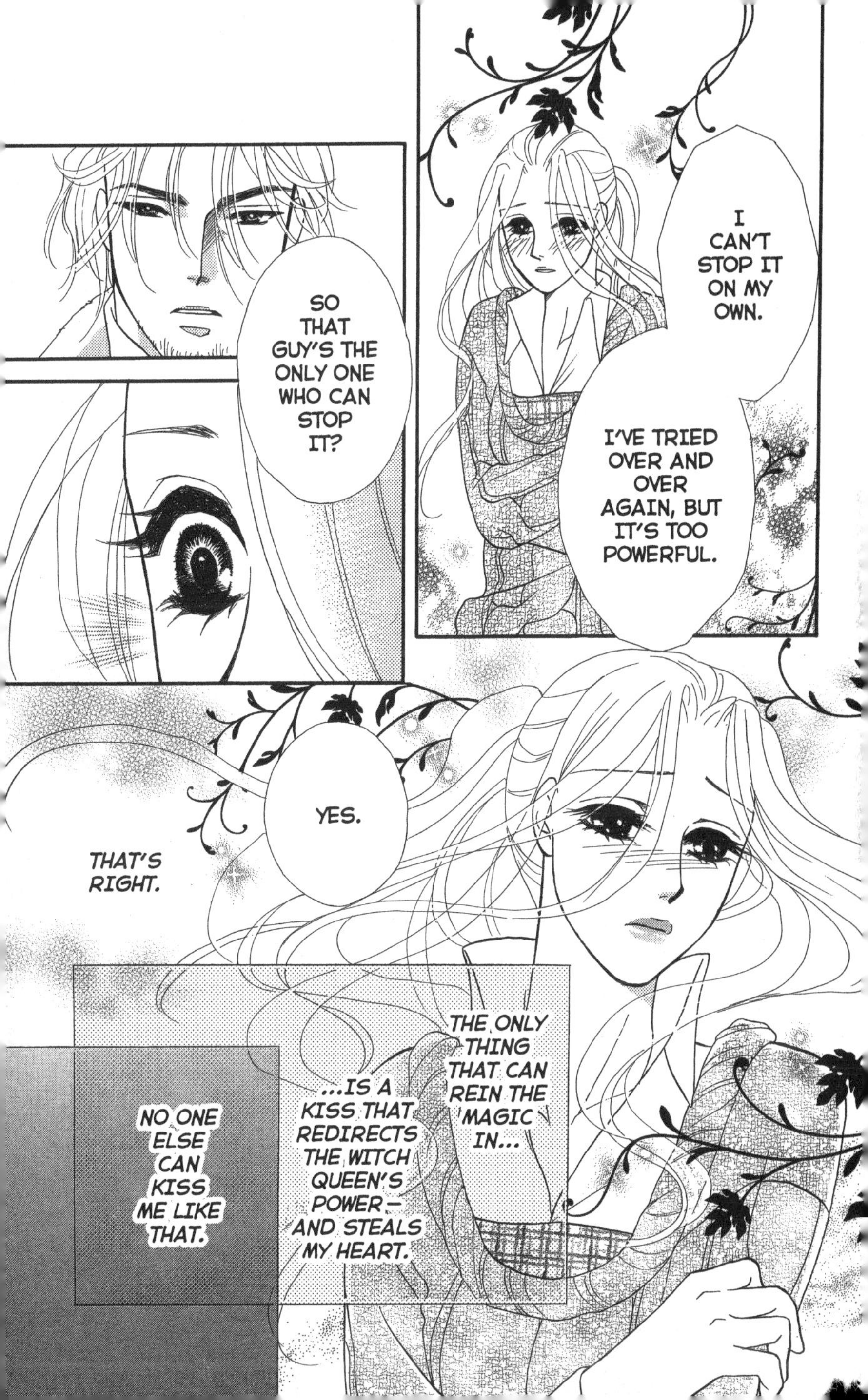
I CAN'T STOP IT ON MY OWN.
I'VE TRIED OVER AND OVER AGAIN, BUT IT'S TOO POWERFUL.
SO THAT GUY'S THE ONLY ONE WHO CAN STOP IT?
YES.
THAT'S RIGHT.
THE ONLY THING THAT CAN REIN THE MAGIC IN...
...IS A KISS THAT REDIRECTS THE WITCH QUEEN'S POWER—AND STEALS MY HEART.
NO ONE ELSE CAN KISS ME LIKE THAT.

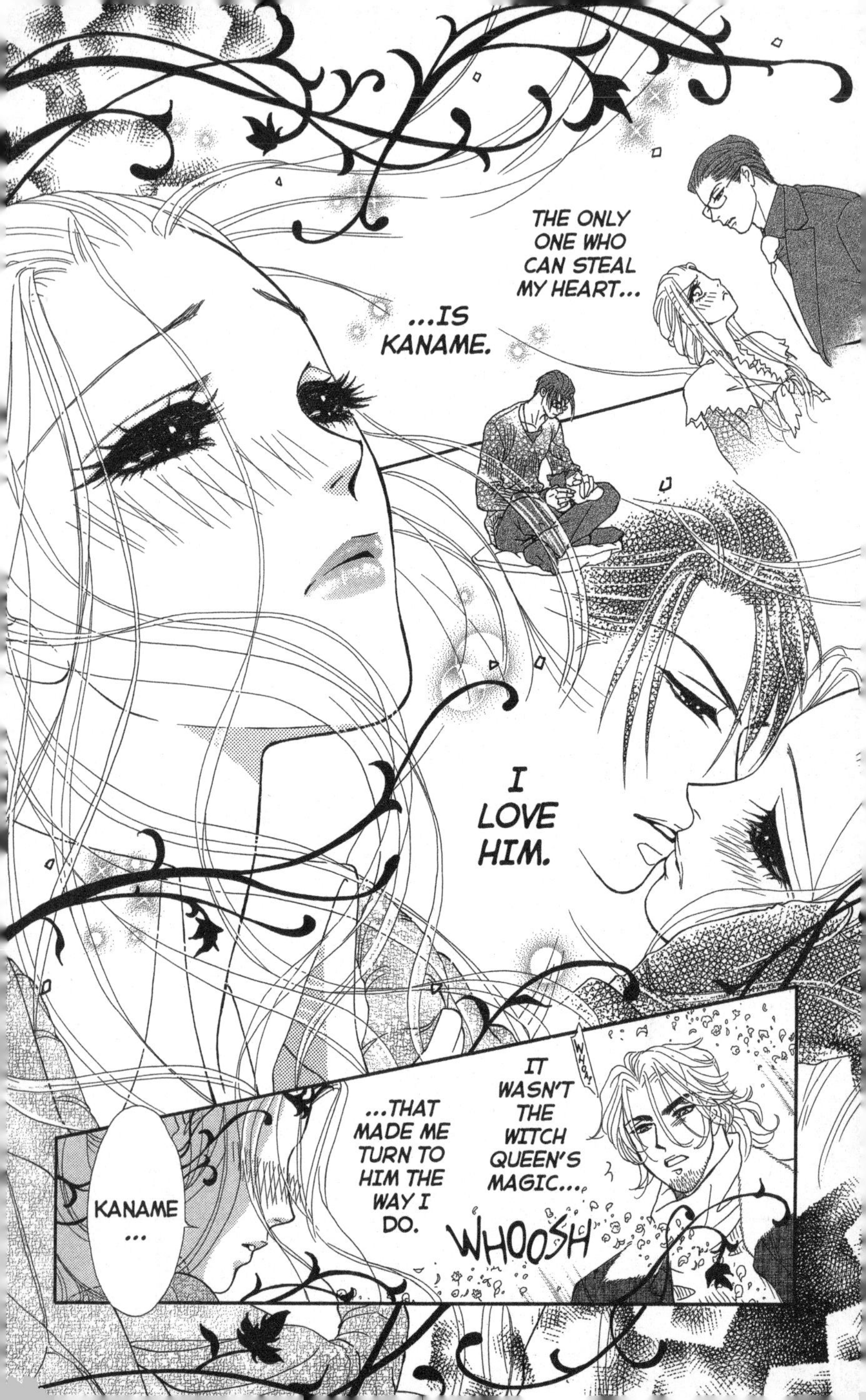
THE ONLY ONE WHO CAN STEAL MY HEART...
...IS KANAME.
I LOVE HIM.
WHOA!
IT WASN'T THE WITCH QUEEN'S MAGIC...
...THAT MADE ME TURN TO HIM THE WAY I DO.
WHOOSH
KANAME ...

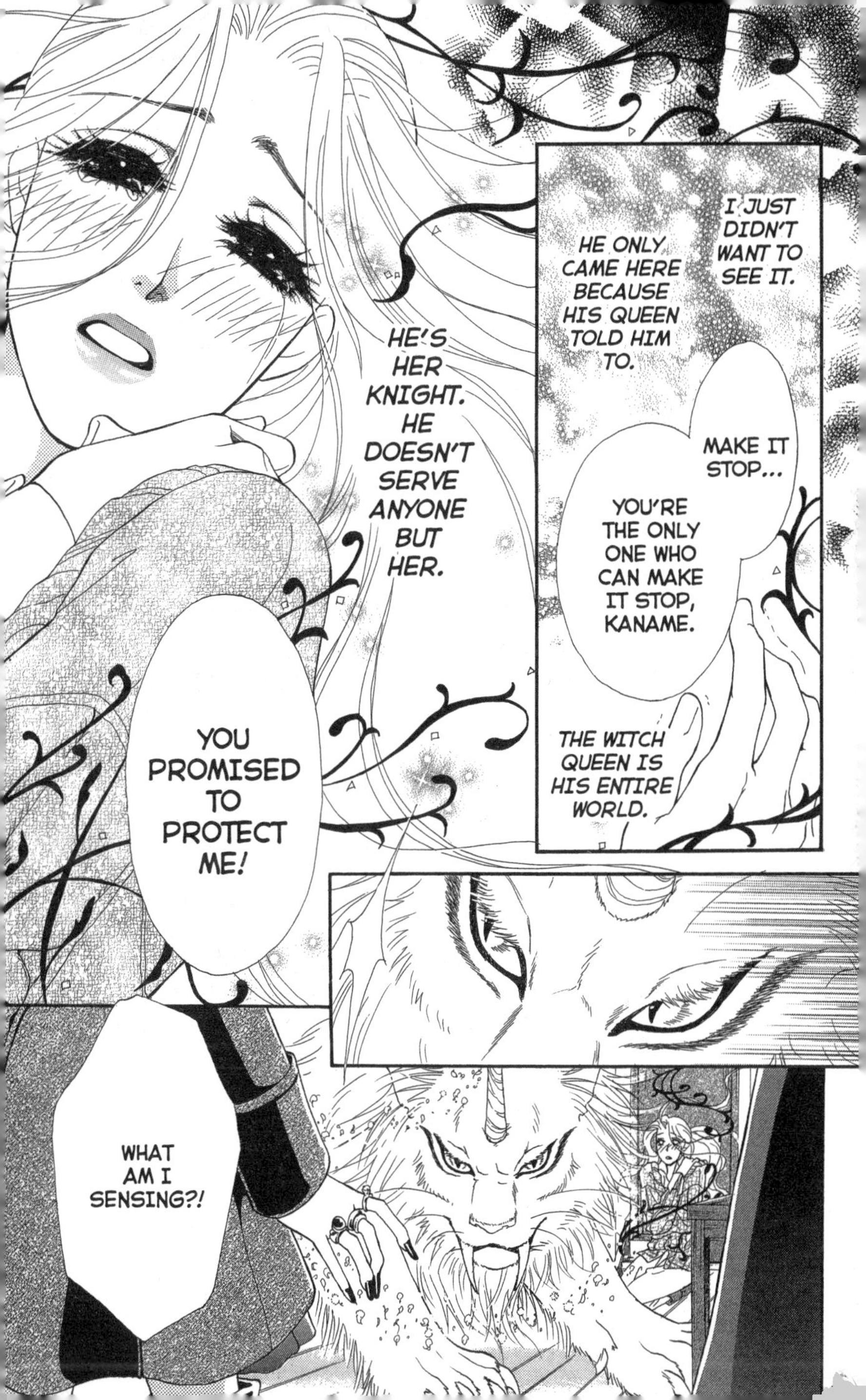
I JUST DIDN'T WANT TO SEE IT.
HE ONLY CAME HERE BECAUSE HIS QUEEN TOLD HIM TO.
MAKE IT STOP...
YOU'RE THE ONLY ONE WHO CAN MAKE IT STOP, KANAME.
THE WITCH QUEEN IS HIS ENTIRE WORLD.
HE'S HER KNIGHT. HE DOESN'T SERVE ANYONE BUT HER.
YOU PROMISED TO PROTECT ME!
WHAT AM I SENSING?!

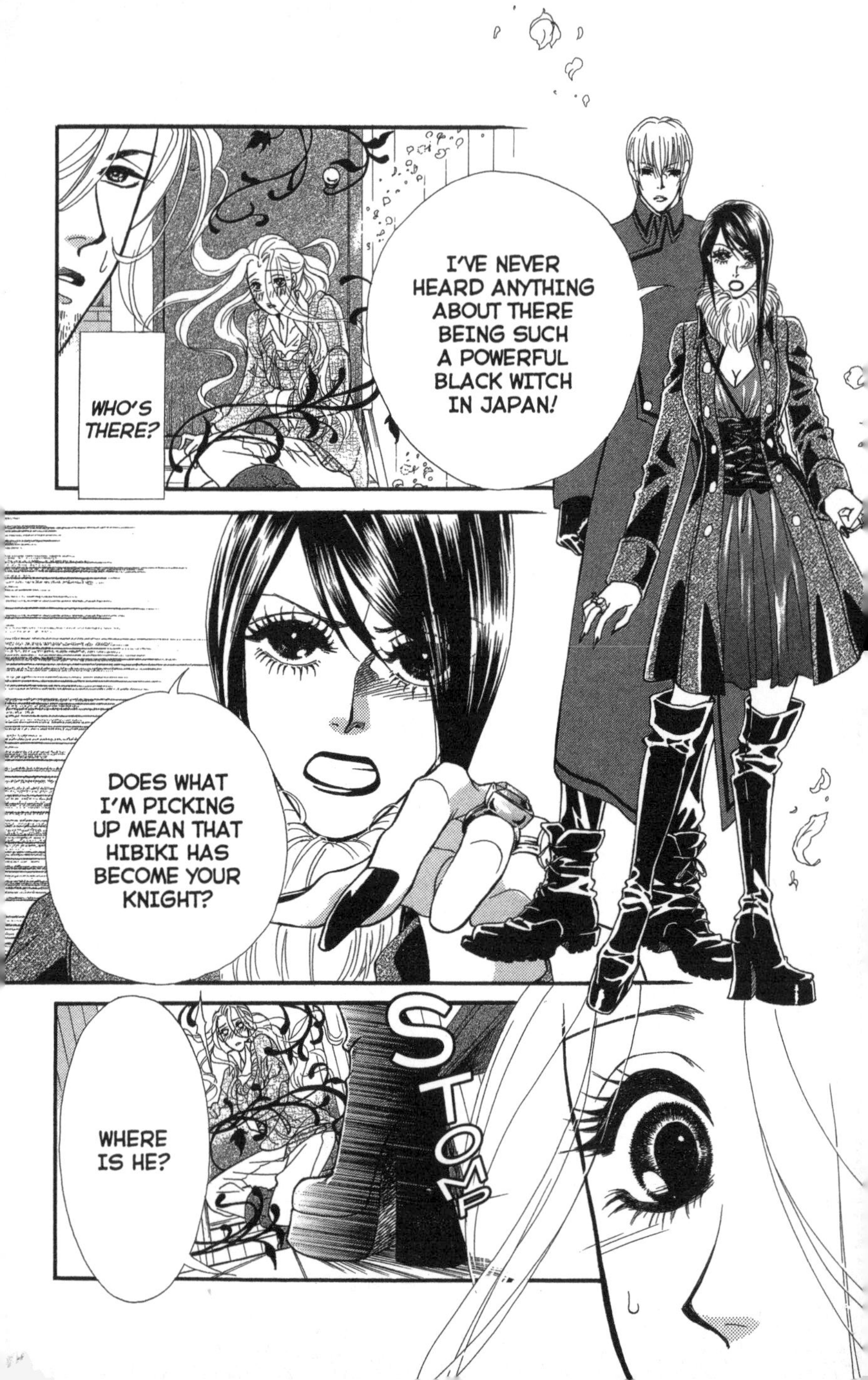
I'VE NEVER HEARD ANYTHING ABOUT THERE BEING SUCH A POWERFUL BLACK WITCH IN JAPAN!
WHO'S THERE?
DOES WHAT I'M PICKING UP MEAN THAT HIBIKI HAS BECOME YOUR KNIGHT?
STOMP
WHERE IS HE?

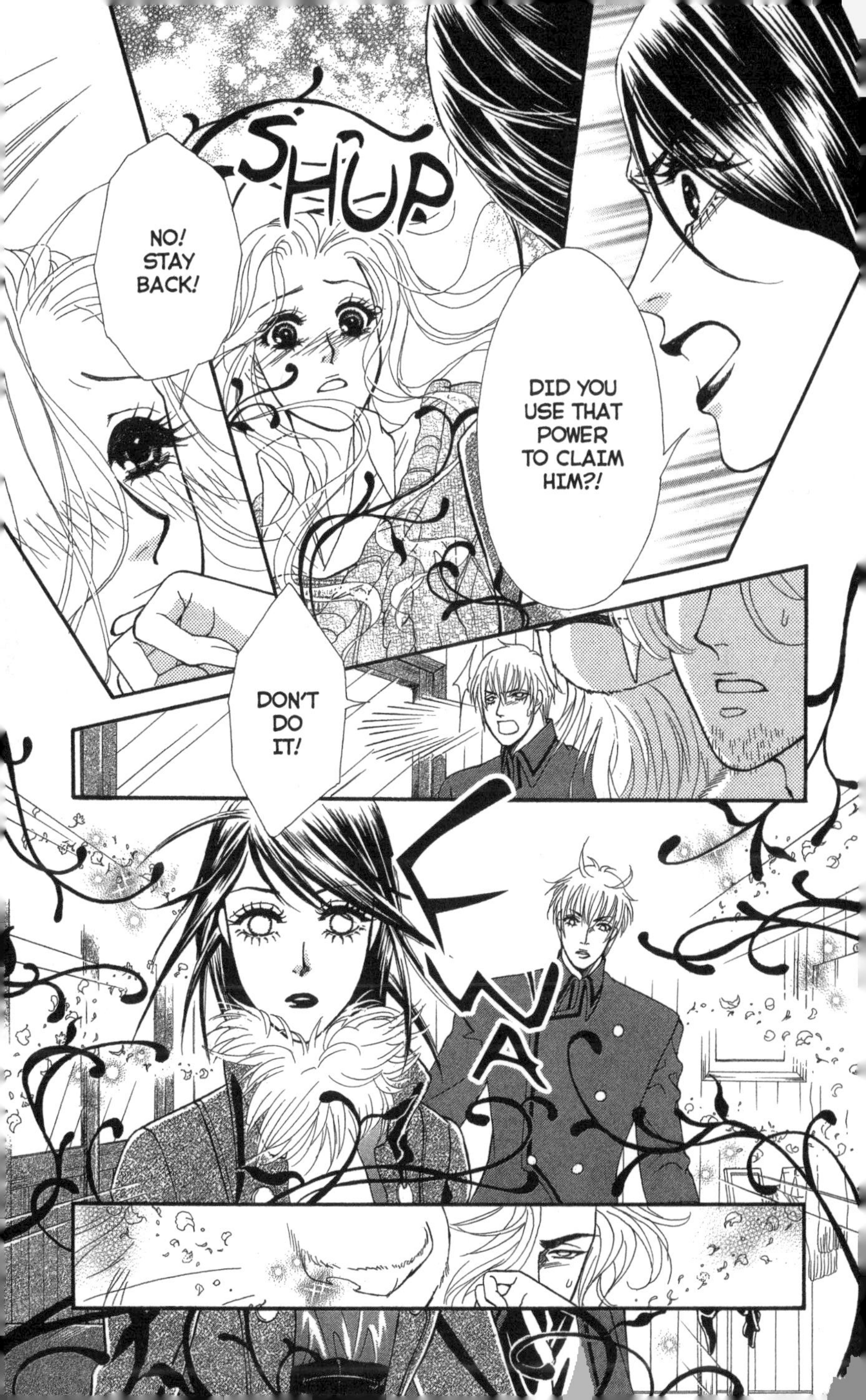
DID YOU USE THAT POWER TO CLAIM HIM?!
SHUP
NO! STAY BACK!
DON'T DO IT!
WA

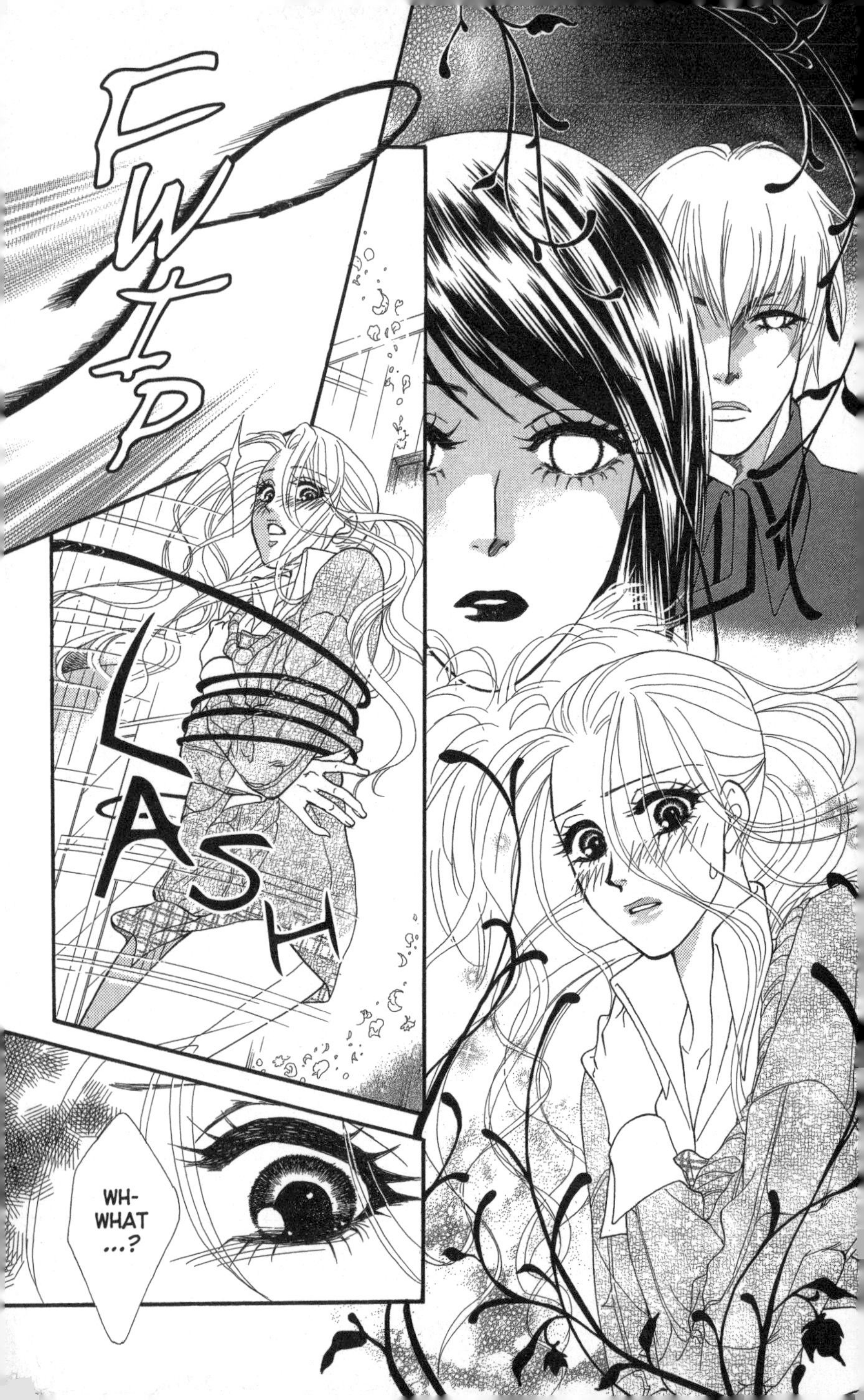
FWIP
LASH
WH-WHAT ...?

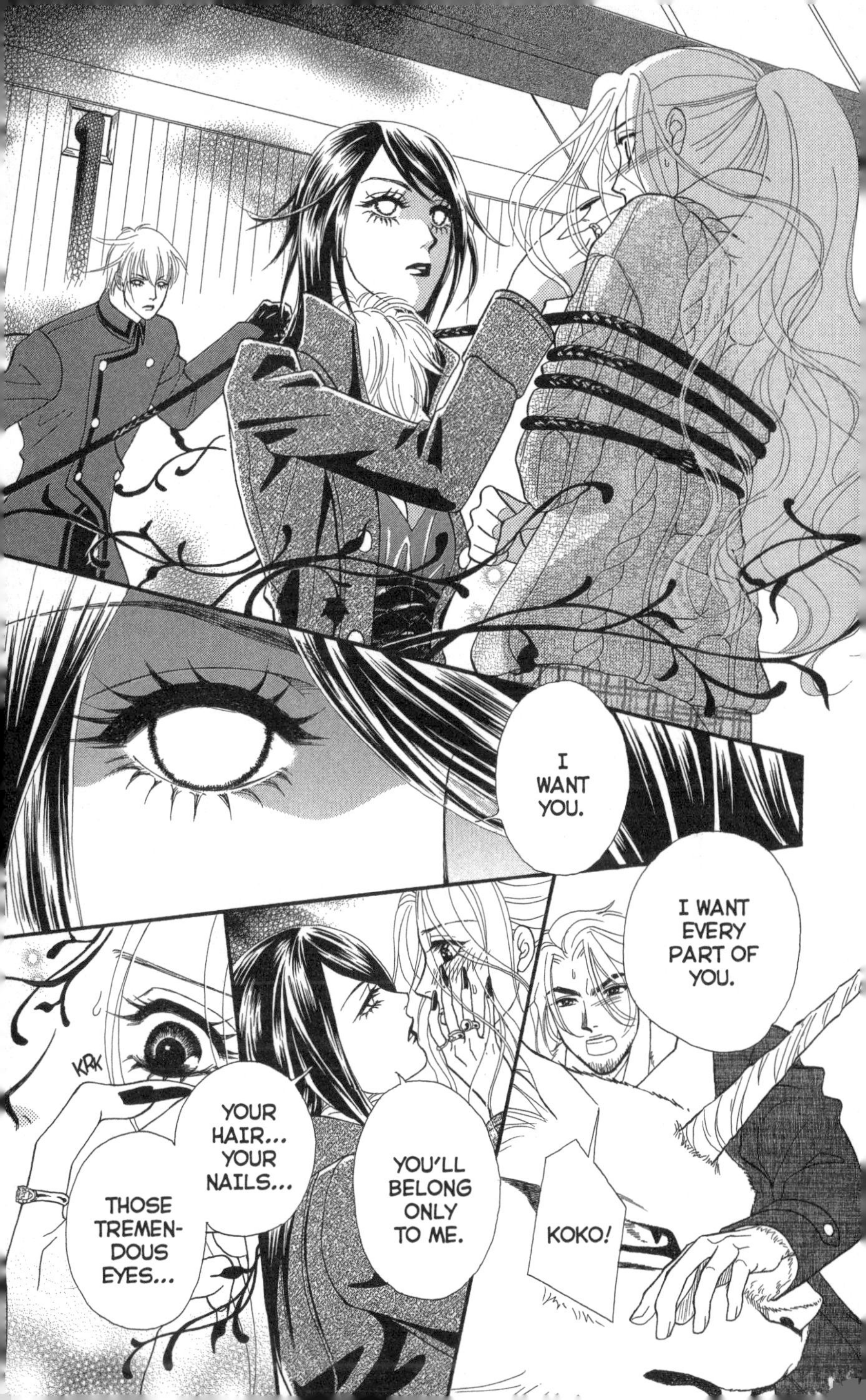
I WANT YOU.
I WANT EVERY PART OF YOU.
KOKO!
YOU'LL BELONG ONLY TO ME.
YOUR HAIR... YOUR NAILS...
THOSE TREMEN-DOUS EYES...
KRK

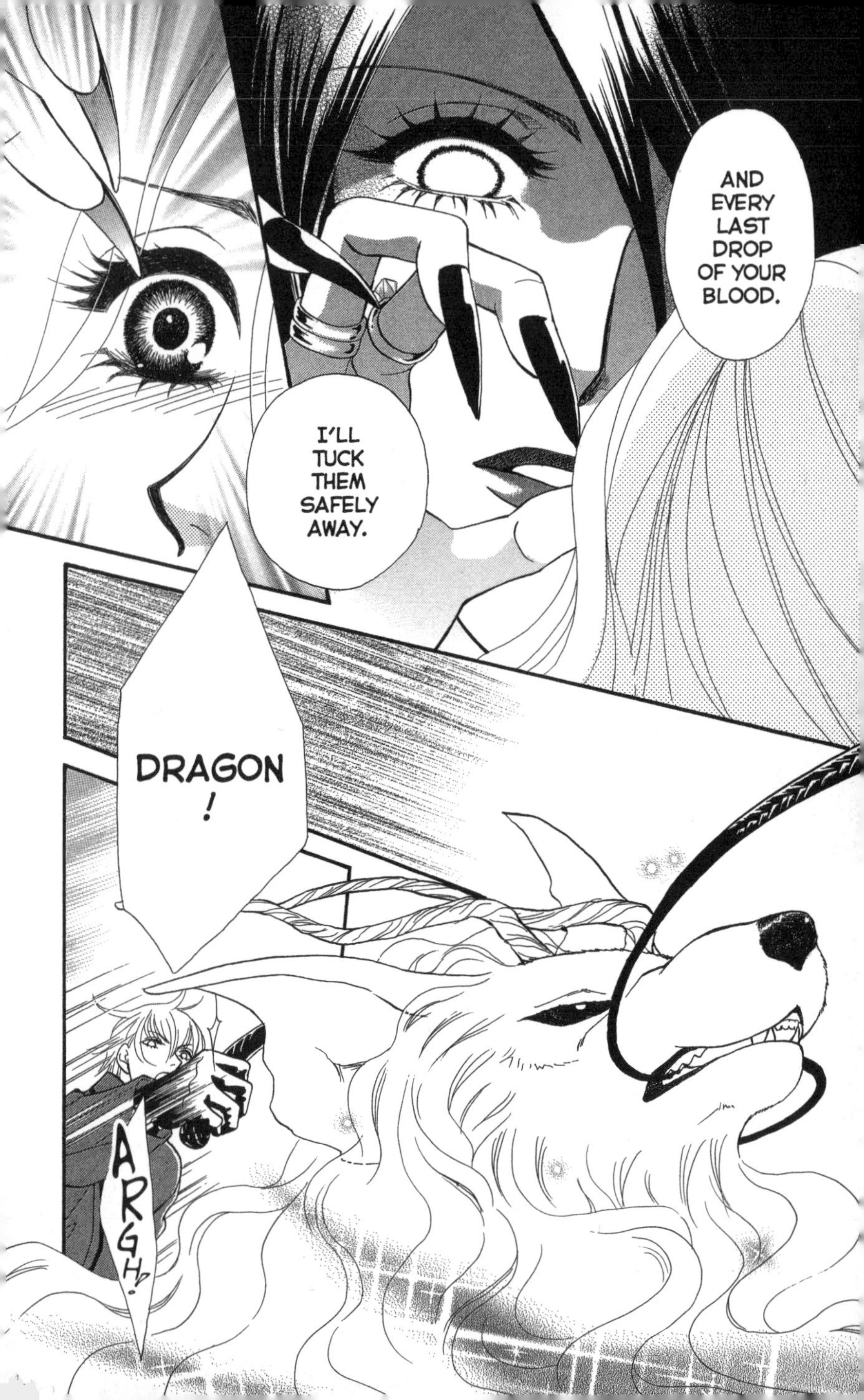
AND EVERY LAST DROP OF YOUR BLOOD.
I'LL TUCK THEM SAFELY AWAY.
DRAGON!
ARGH!

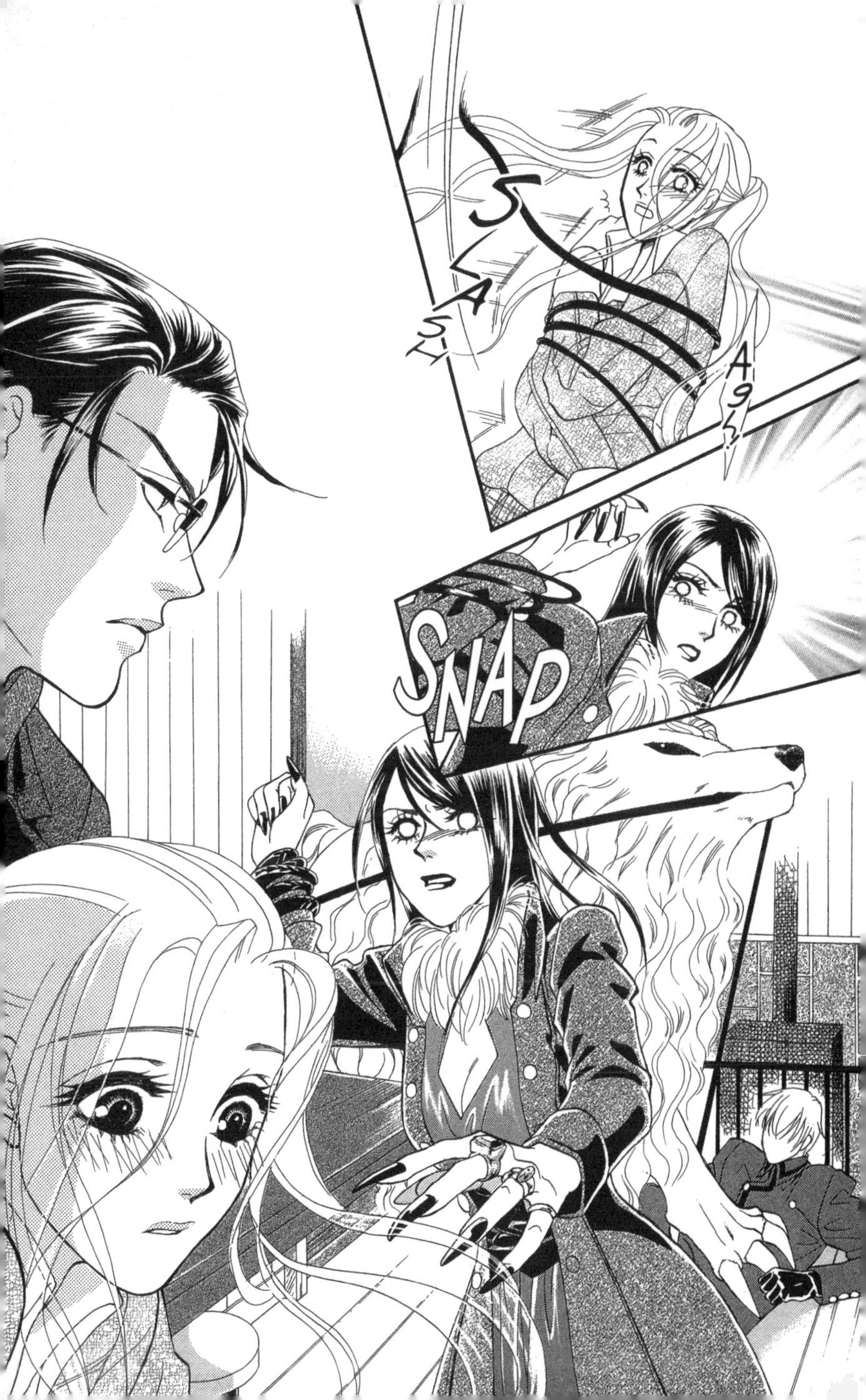
AGH!
SLASH
SNAP

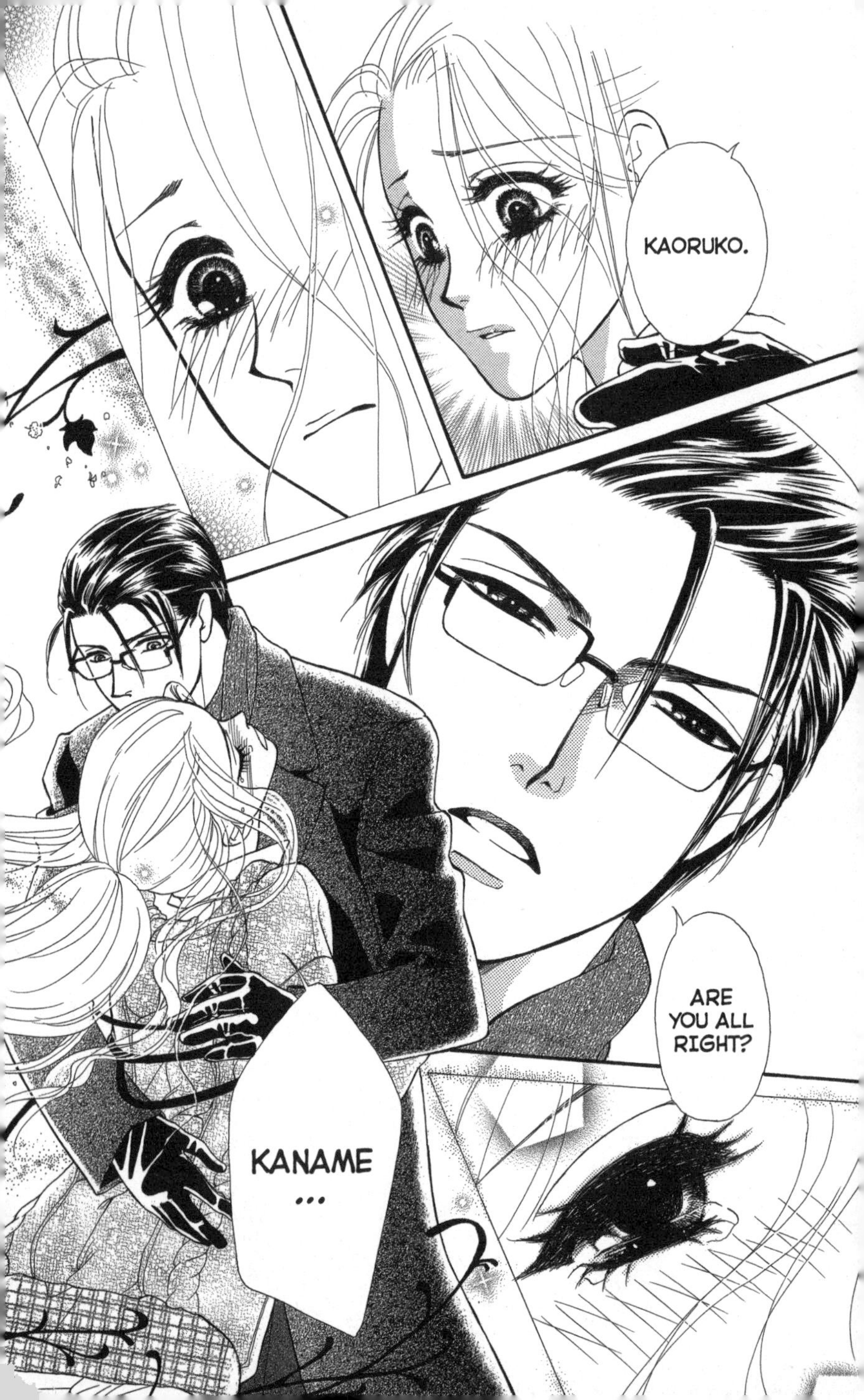
KAORUKO.
ARE YOU ALL RIGHT?
KANAME ...

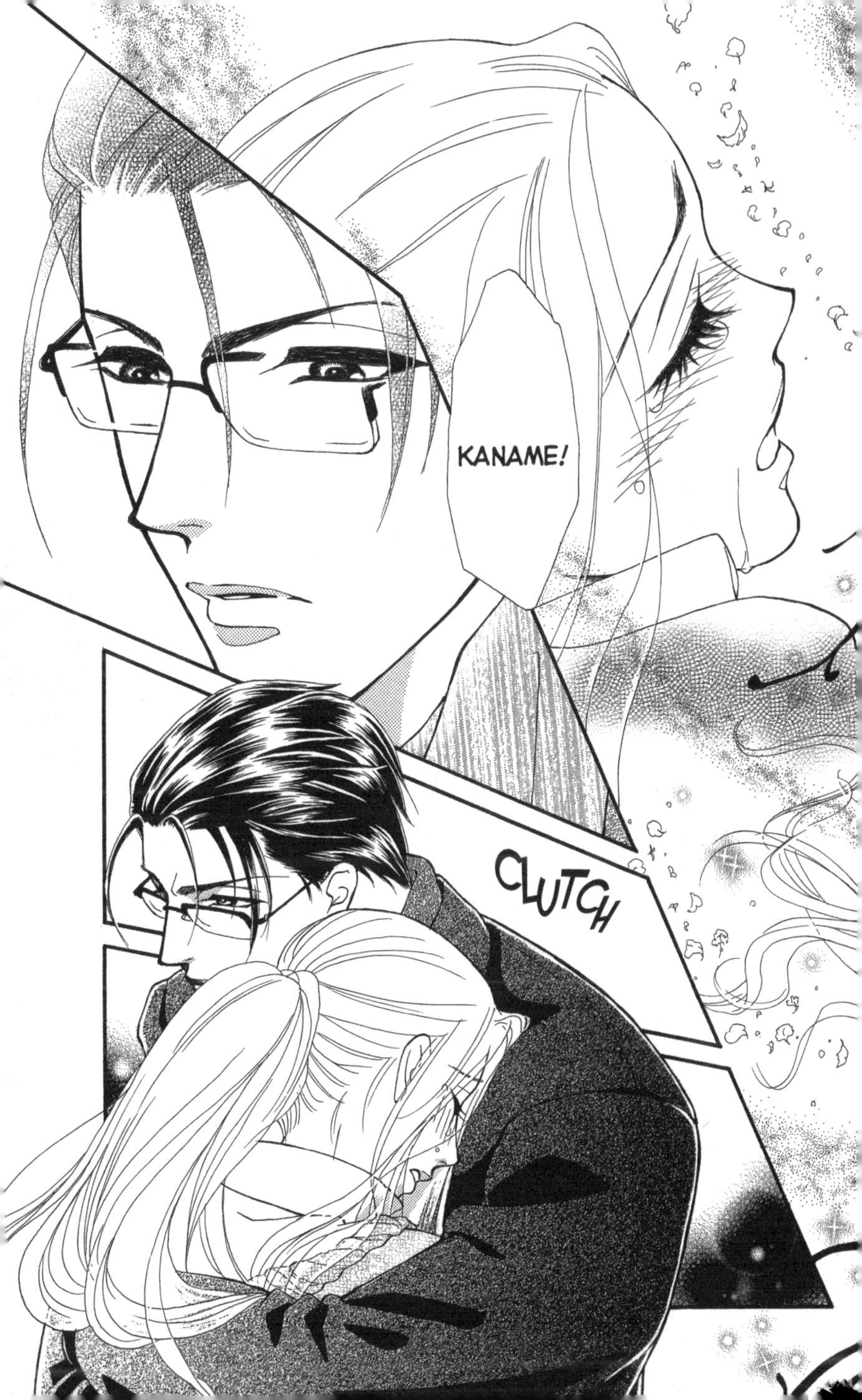
KANAME!
CLUTCH

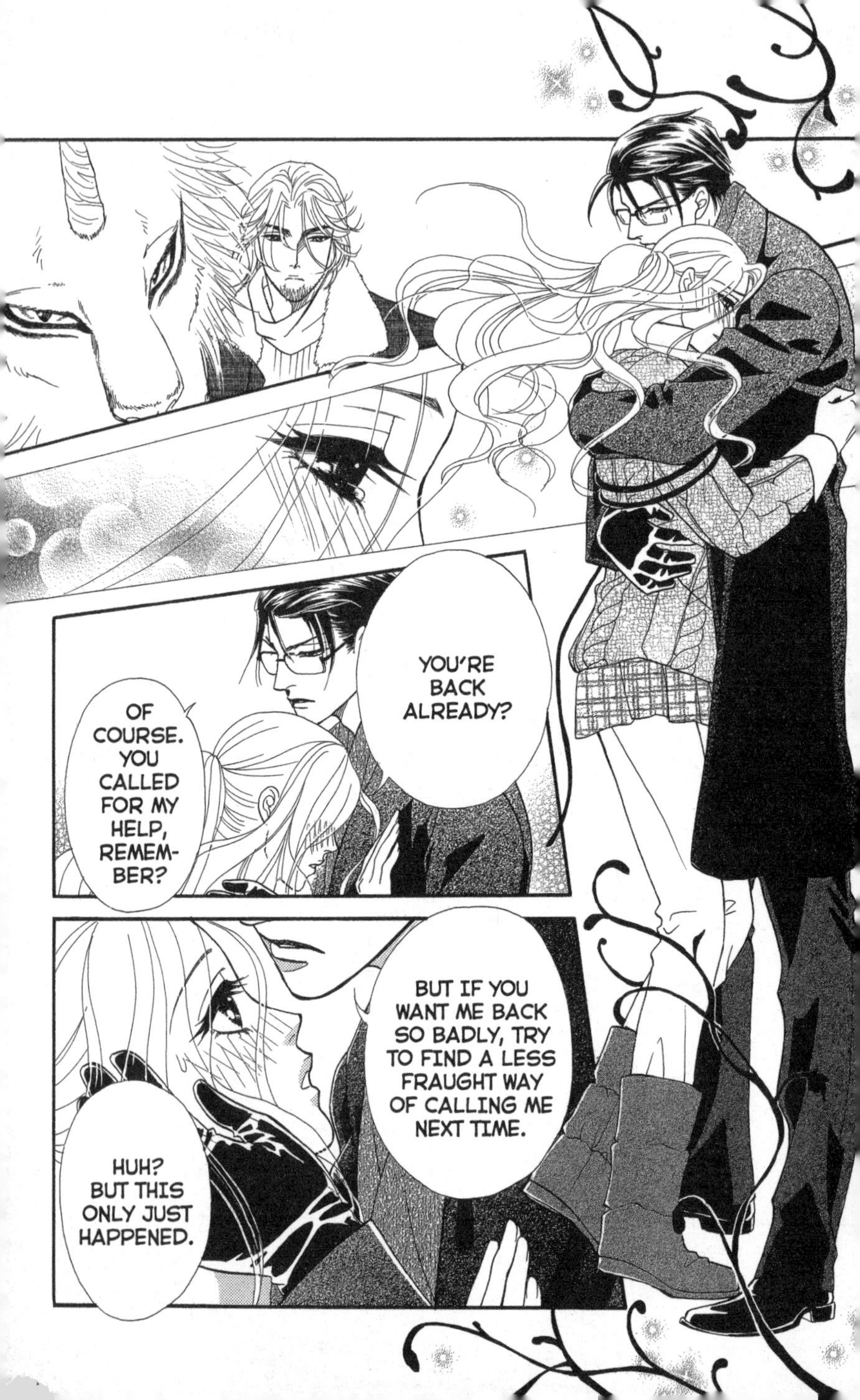
YOU'RE BACK ALREADY?
OF COURSE. YOU CALLED FOR MY HELP, REMEMBER?
BUT IF YOU WANT ME BACK SO BADLY, TRY TO FIND A LESS FRAUGHT WAY OF CALLING ME NEXT TIME.
HUH? BUT THIS ONLY JUST HAPPENED.

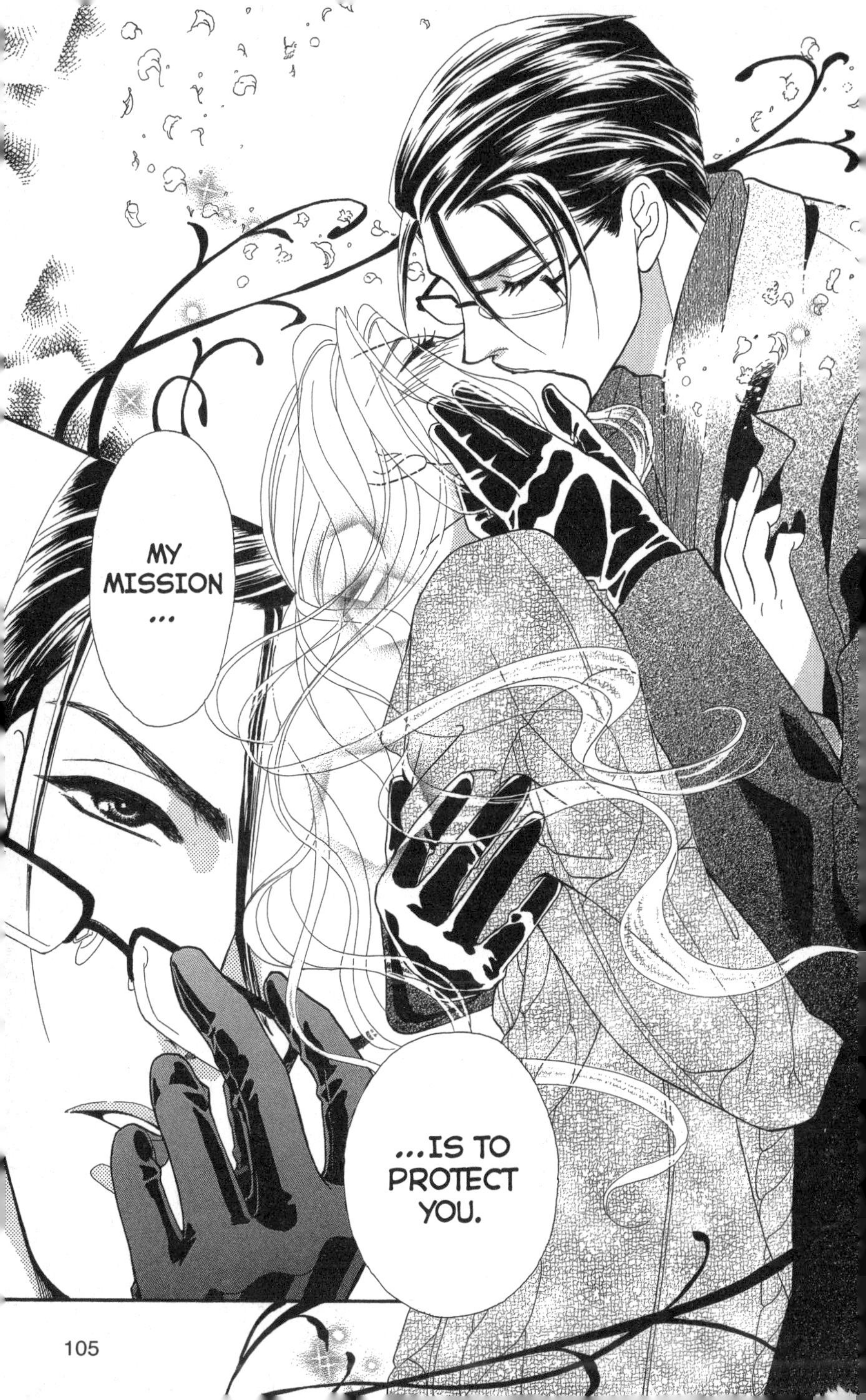
MY MISSION ...
...IS TO PROTECT YOU.

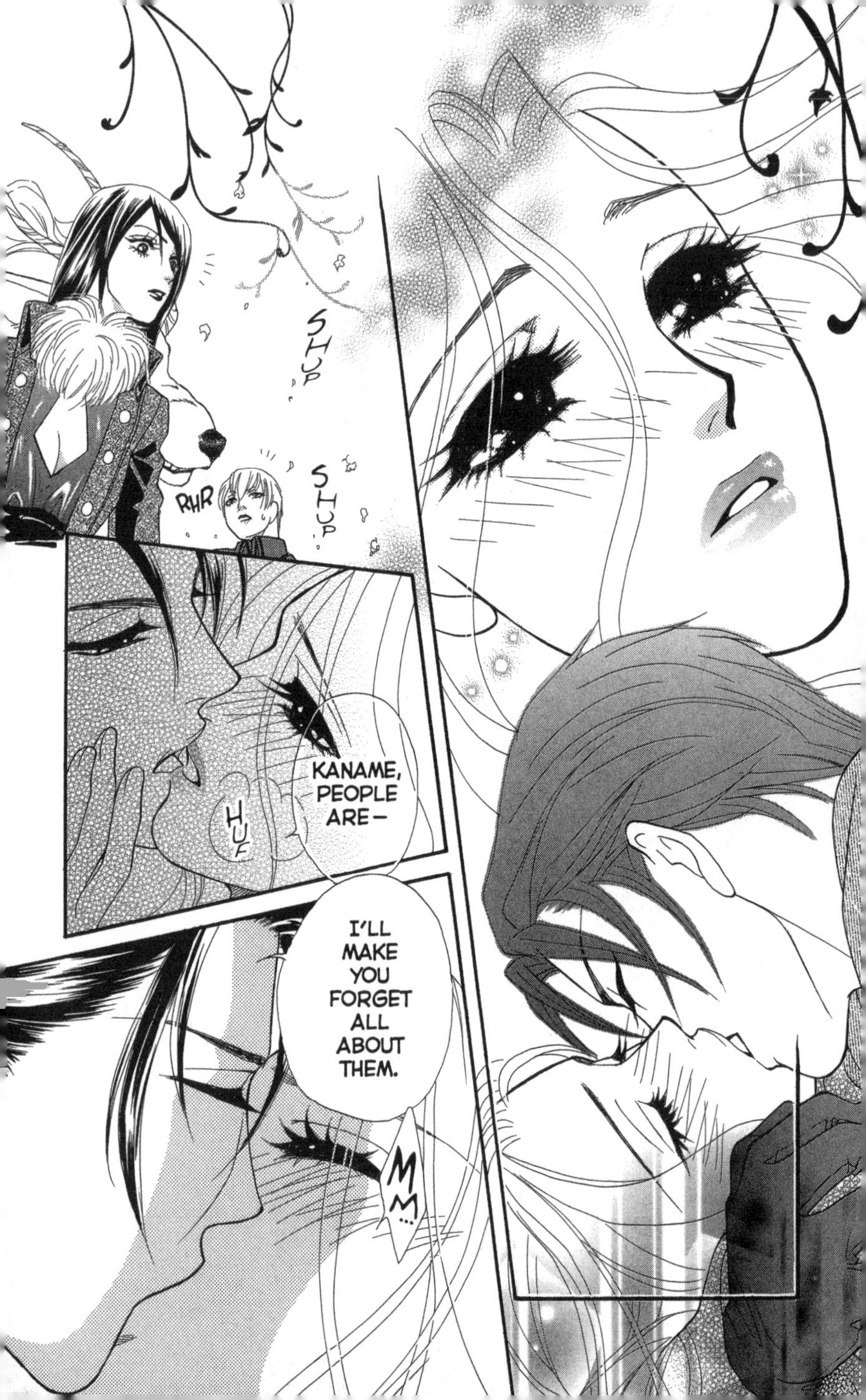
SHUP
SHUP
RHR
KANAME, PEOPLE ARE—
HUF
I'LL MAKE YOU FORGET ALL ABOUT THEM.
MM...

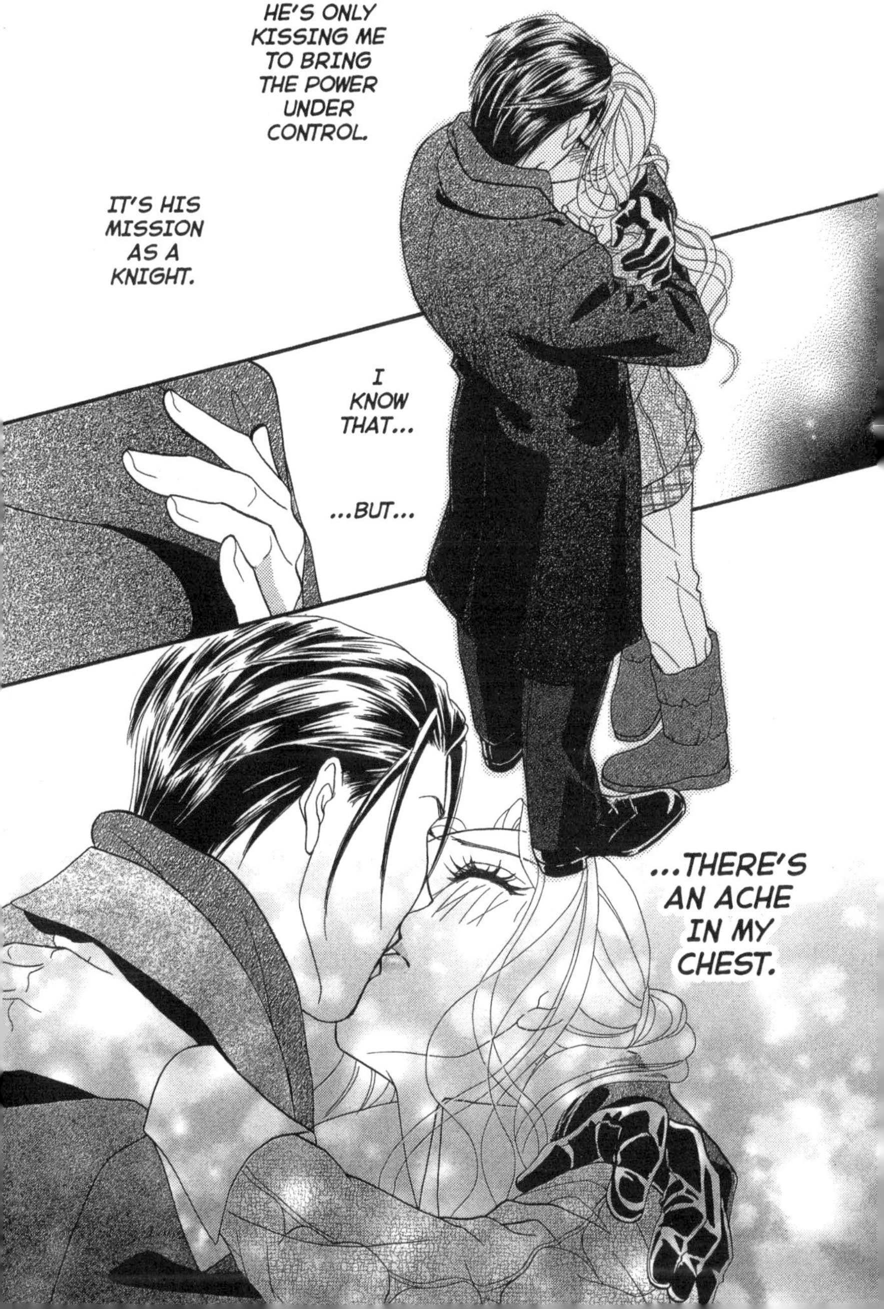
HE'S ONLY KISSING ME TO BRING THE POWER UNDER CONTROL.
IT'S HIS MISSION AS A KNIGHT.
I KNOW THAT...
...BUT...
...THERE'S AN ACHE IN MY CHEST.

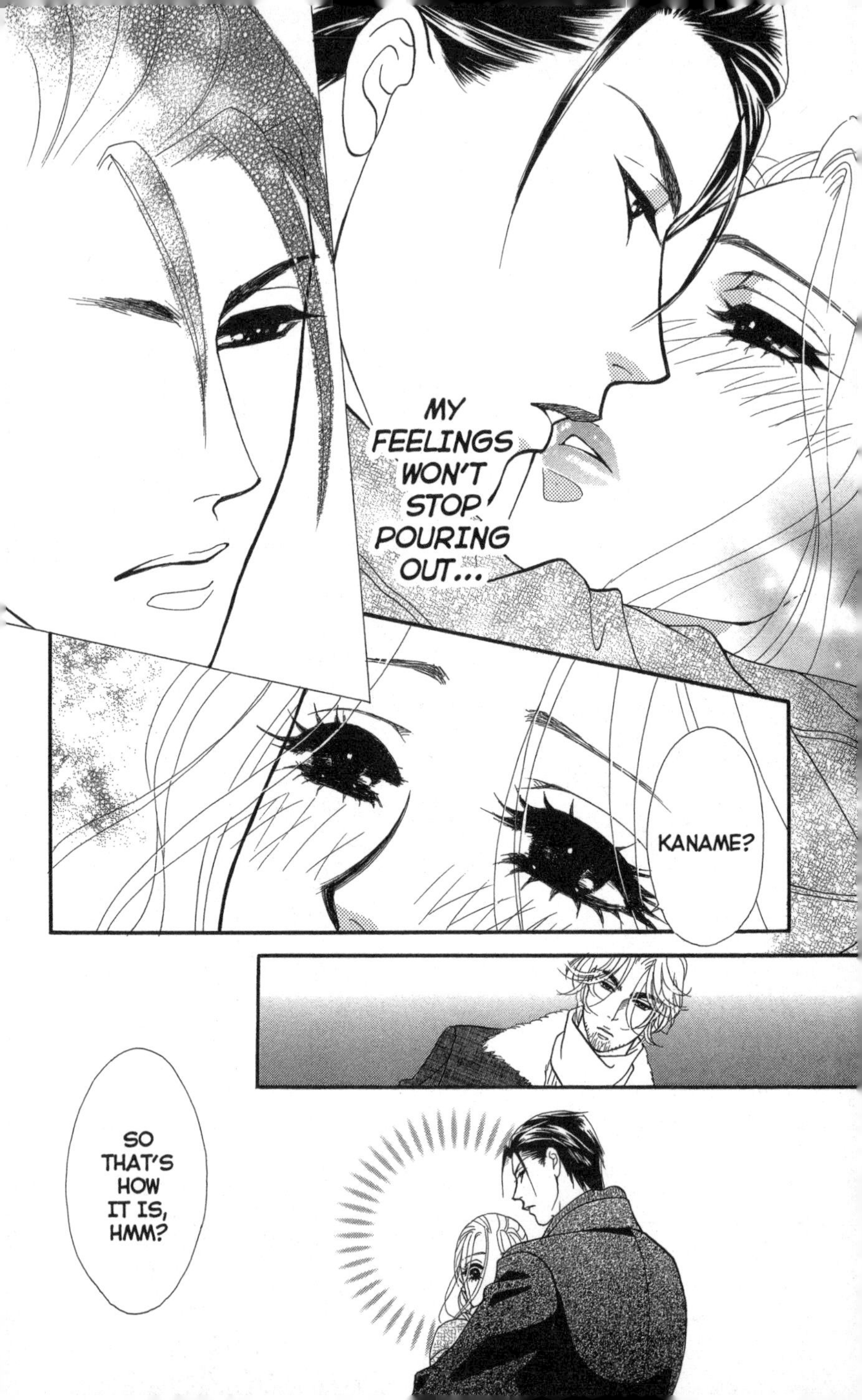
MY FEELINGS WON'T STOP POURING OUT...
KANAME?
SO THAT'S HOW IT IS, HMM?

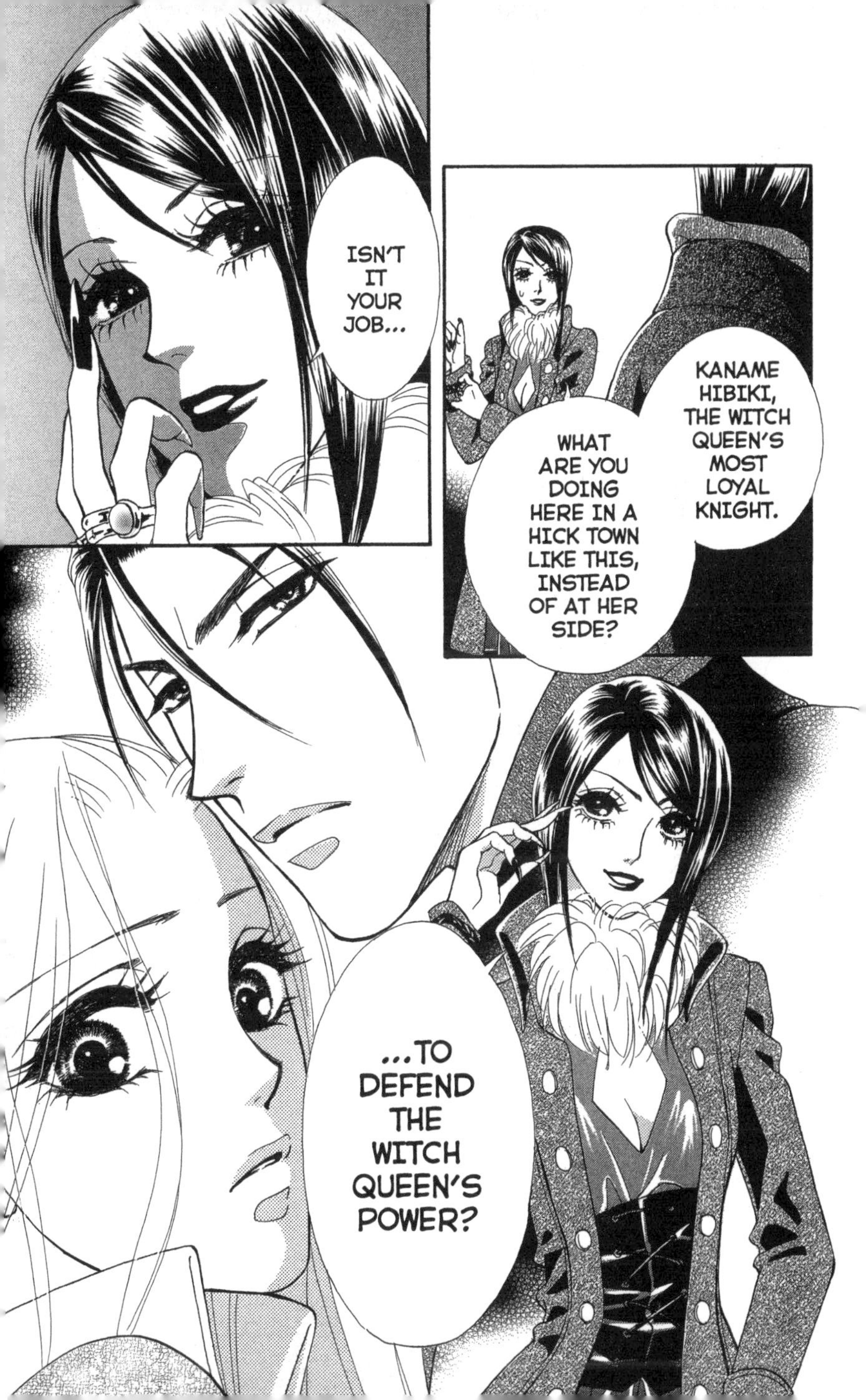
KANAME HIBIKI, THE WITCH QUEEN'S MOST LOYAL KNIGHT.
WHAT ARE YOU DOING HERE IN A HICK TOWN LIKE THIS, INSTEAD OF AT HER SIDE?
ISN'T IT YOUR JOB...
...TO DEFEND THE WITCH QUEEN'S POWER?

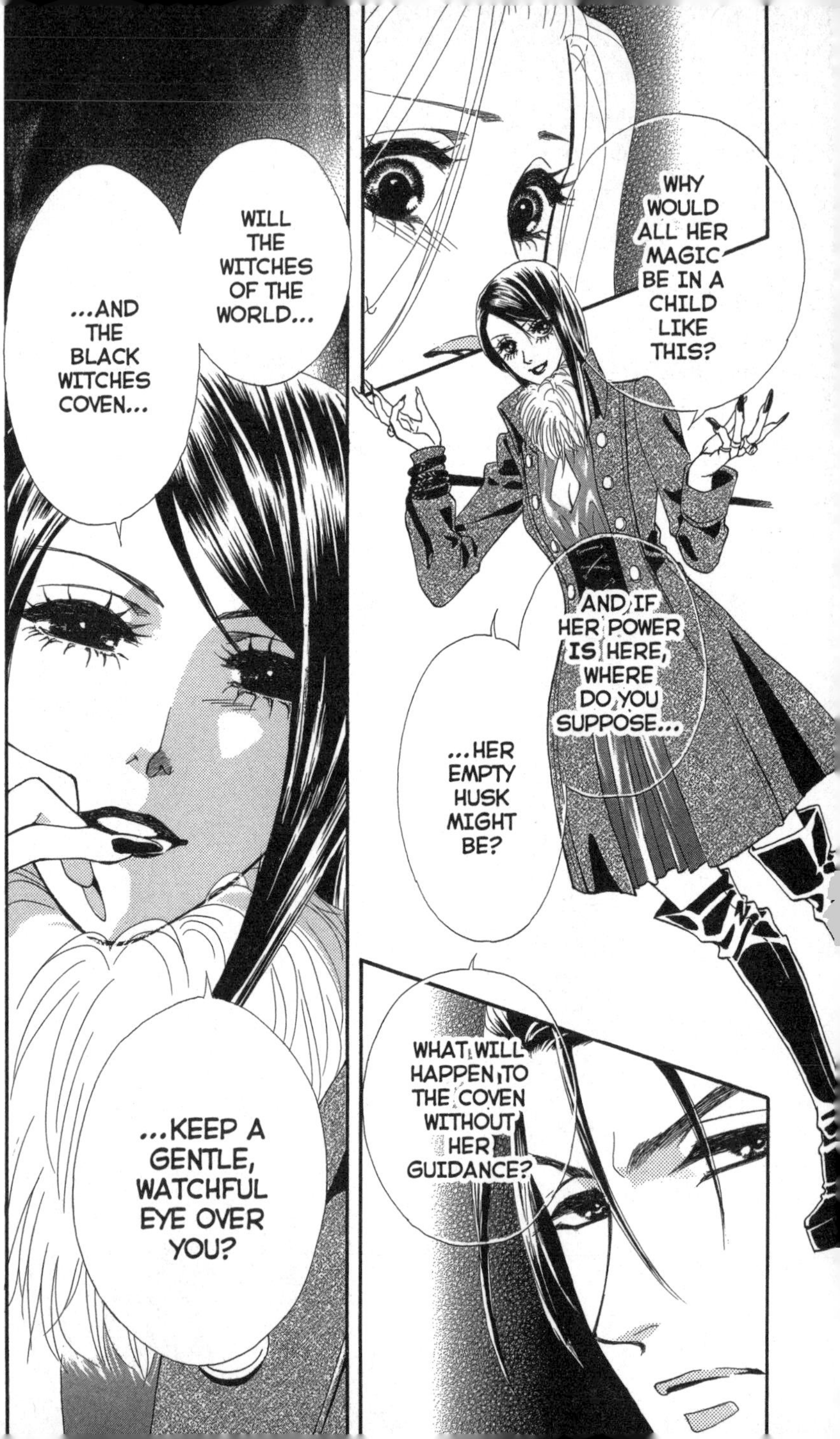
WHY WOULD ALL HER MAGIC BE IN A CHILD LIKE THIS?
AND IF HER POWER **IS** HERE, WHERE DO YOU SUPPOSE...
...HER EMPTY HUSK MIGHT BE?
WHAT WILL HAPPEN TO THE COVEN WITHOUT HER GUIDANCE?
WILL THE WITCHES OF THE WORLD...
...AND THE BLACK WITCHES COVEN...
...KEEP A GENTLE, WATCHFUL EYE OVER YOU?

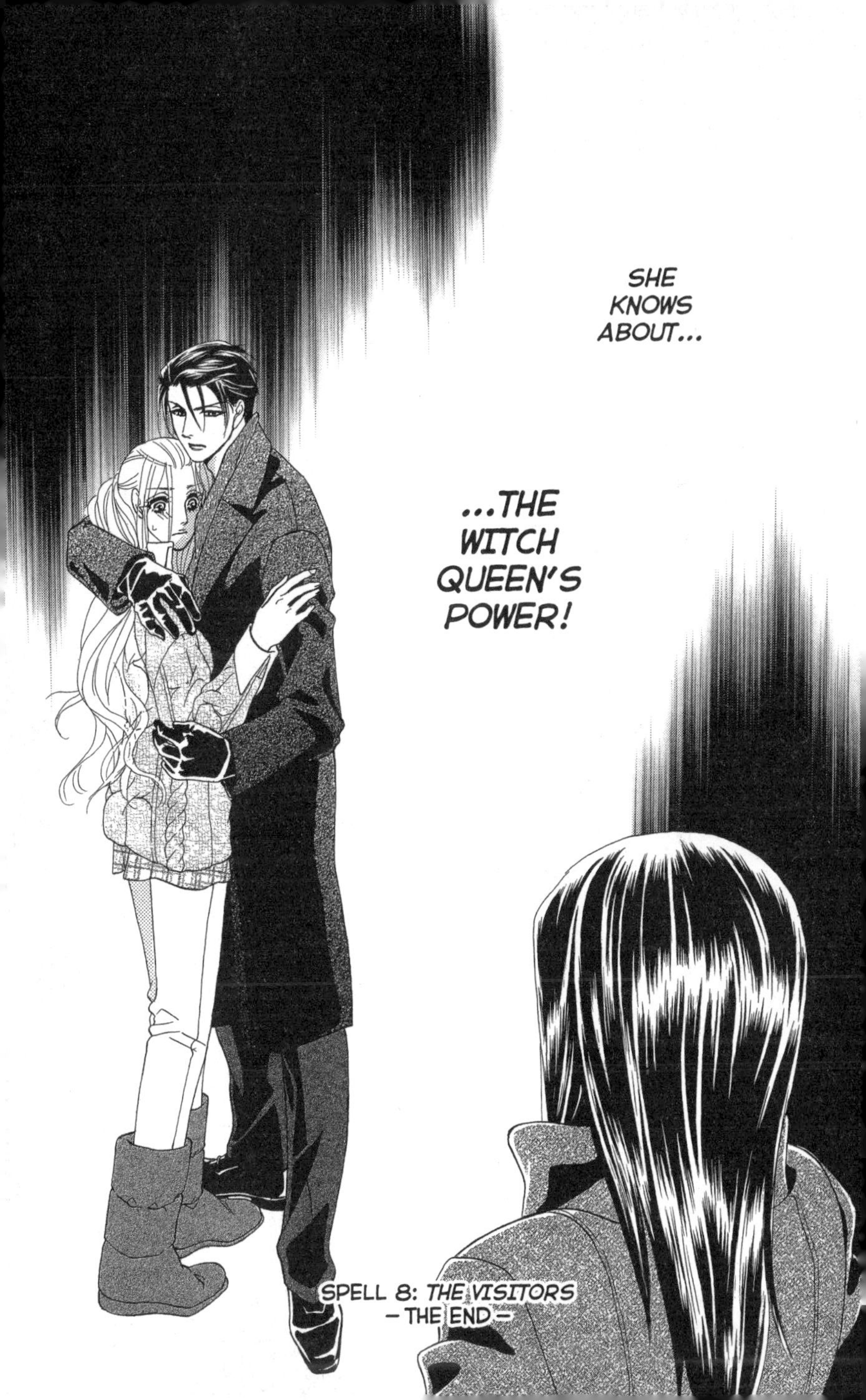
SHE KNOWS ABOUT...
...THE WITCH QUEEN'S POWER!
SPELL 8: THE VISITORS
—THE END—

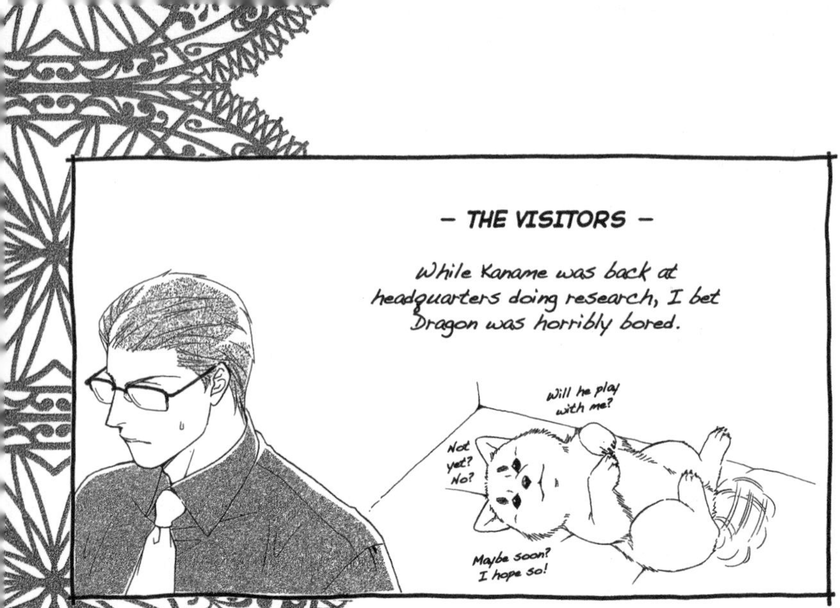
– THE VISITORS –
While Kaname was back at headquarters doing research, I bet Dragon was horribly bored.
Will he play with me?
Not yet? No?
Maybe soon? I hope so!

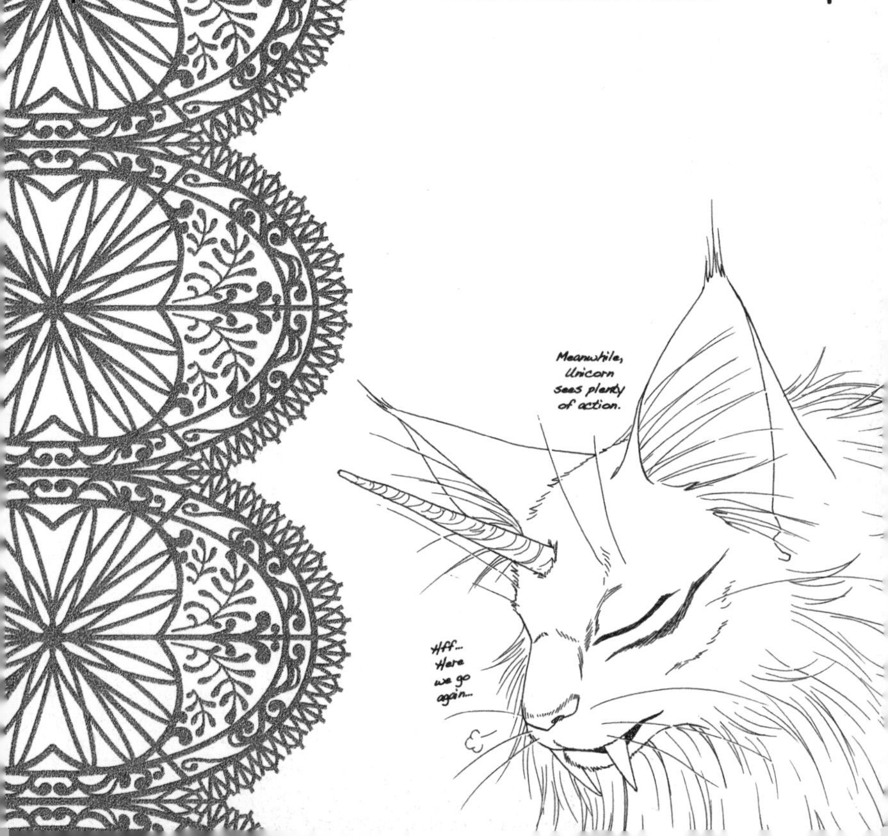
Meanwhile, Unicorn sees plenty of action.
Hff... Here we go again...

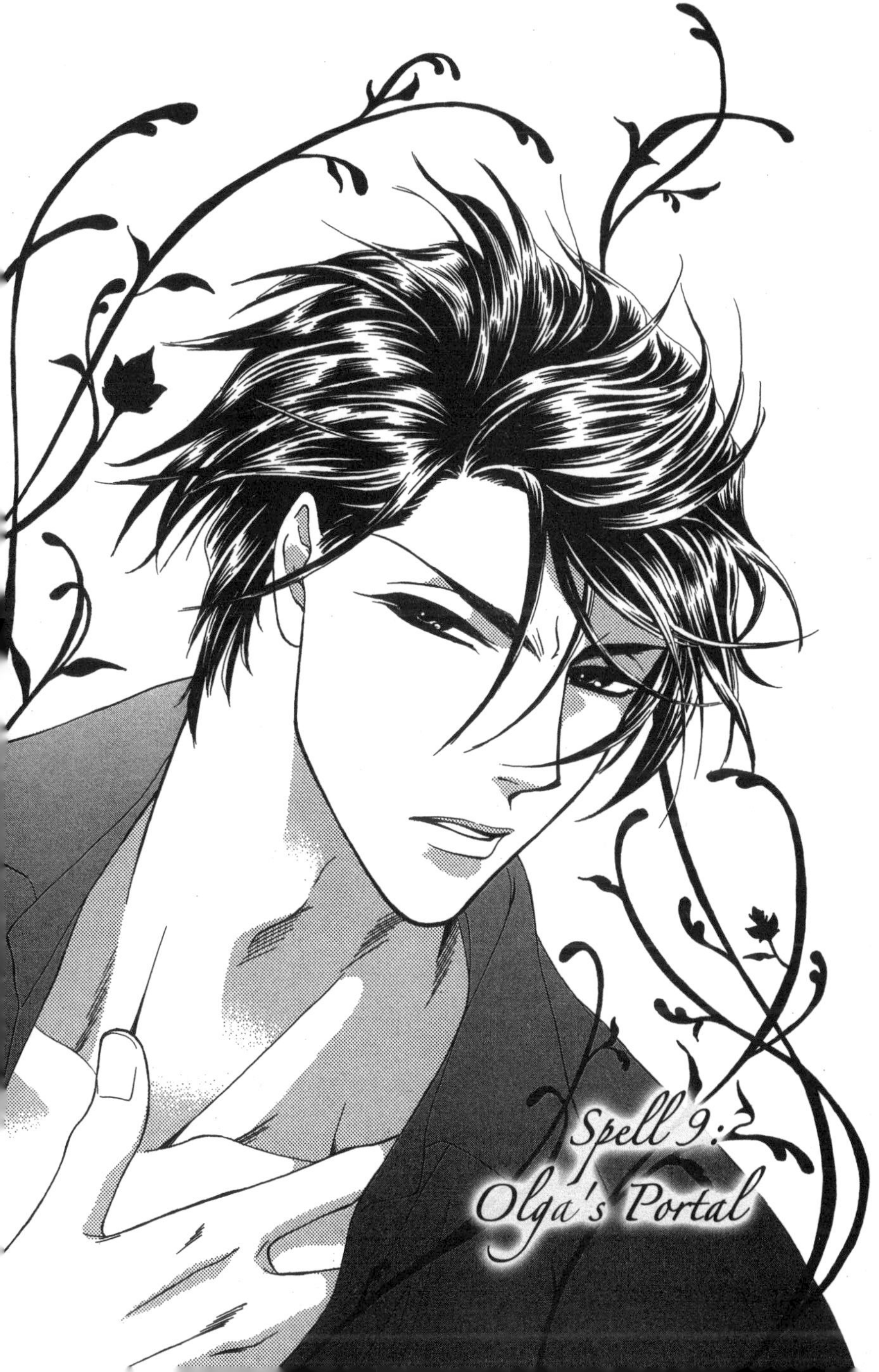
Spell 9:
Olga's Portal

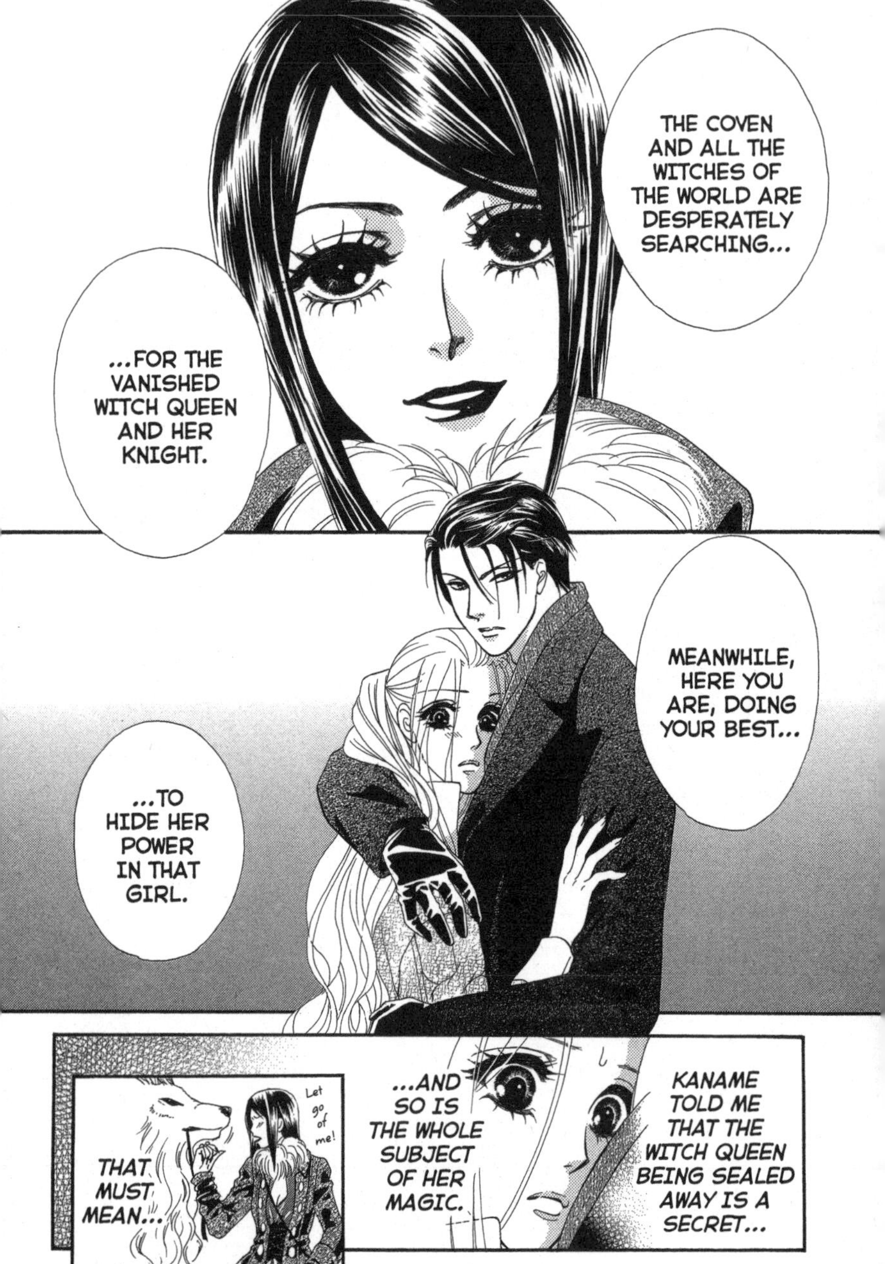
THE COVEN AND ALL THE WITCHES OF THE WORLD ARE DESPERATELY SEARCHING...
...FOR THE VANISHED WITCH QUEEN AND HER KNIGHT.
MEANWHILE, HERE YOU ARE, DOING YOUR BEST...
...TO HIDE HER POWER IN THAT GIRL.
KANAME TOLD ME THAT THE WITCH QUEEN BEING SEALED AWAY IS A SECRET...
...AND SO IS THE WHOLE SUBJECT OF HER MAGIC.
Let go of me!
THAT MUST MEAN...

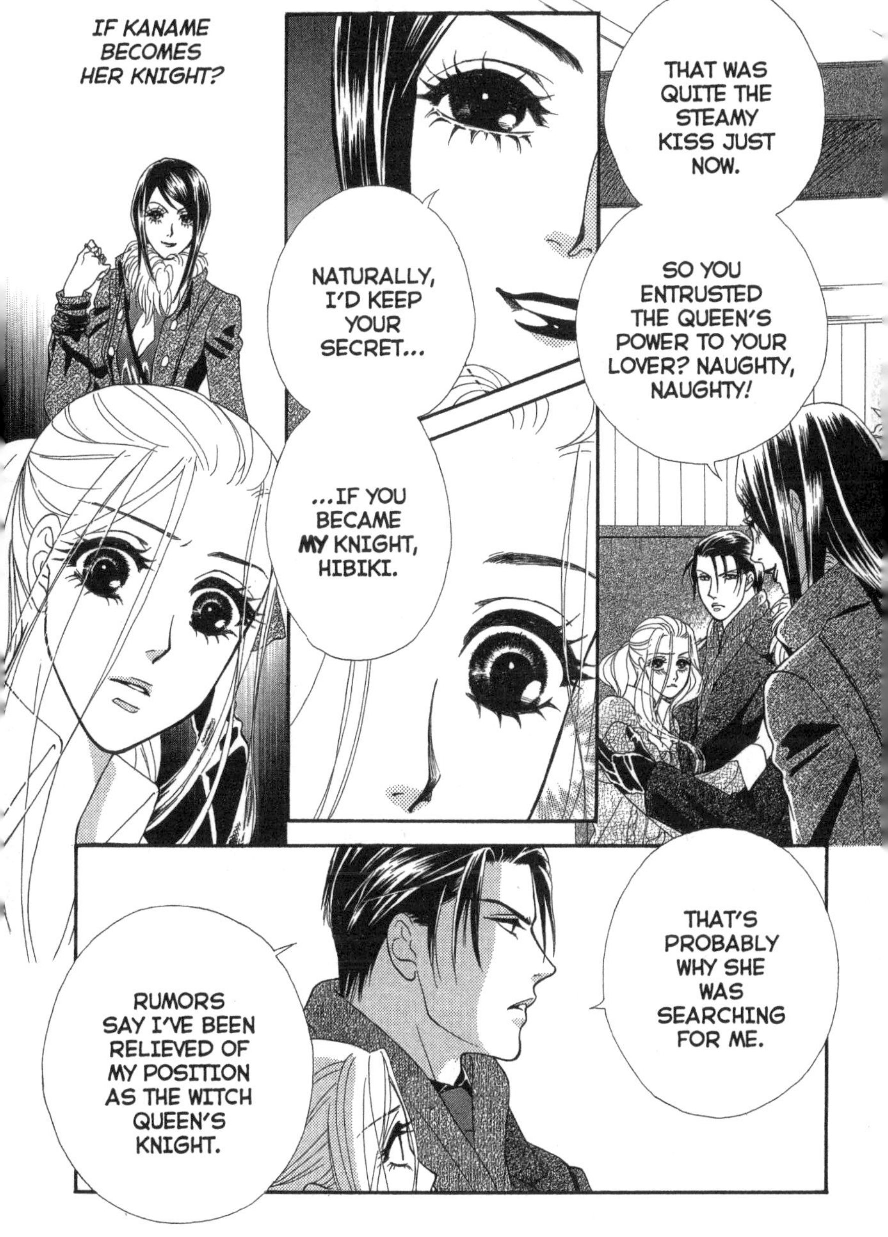

THAT WAS QUITE THE STEAMY KISS JUST NOW.
SO YOU ENTRUSTED THE QUEEN'S POWER TO YOUR LOVER? NAUGHTY, NAUGHTY!
NATURALLY, I'D KEEP YOUR SECRET...
...IF YOU BECAME MY KNIGHT, HIBIKI.
IF KANAME BECOMES HER KNIGHT?
THAT'S PROBABLY WHY SHE WAS SEARCHING FOR ME.
RUMORS SAY I'VE BEEN RELIEVED OF MY POSITION AS THE WITCH QUEEN'S KNIGHT.

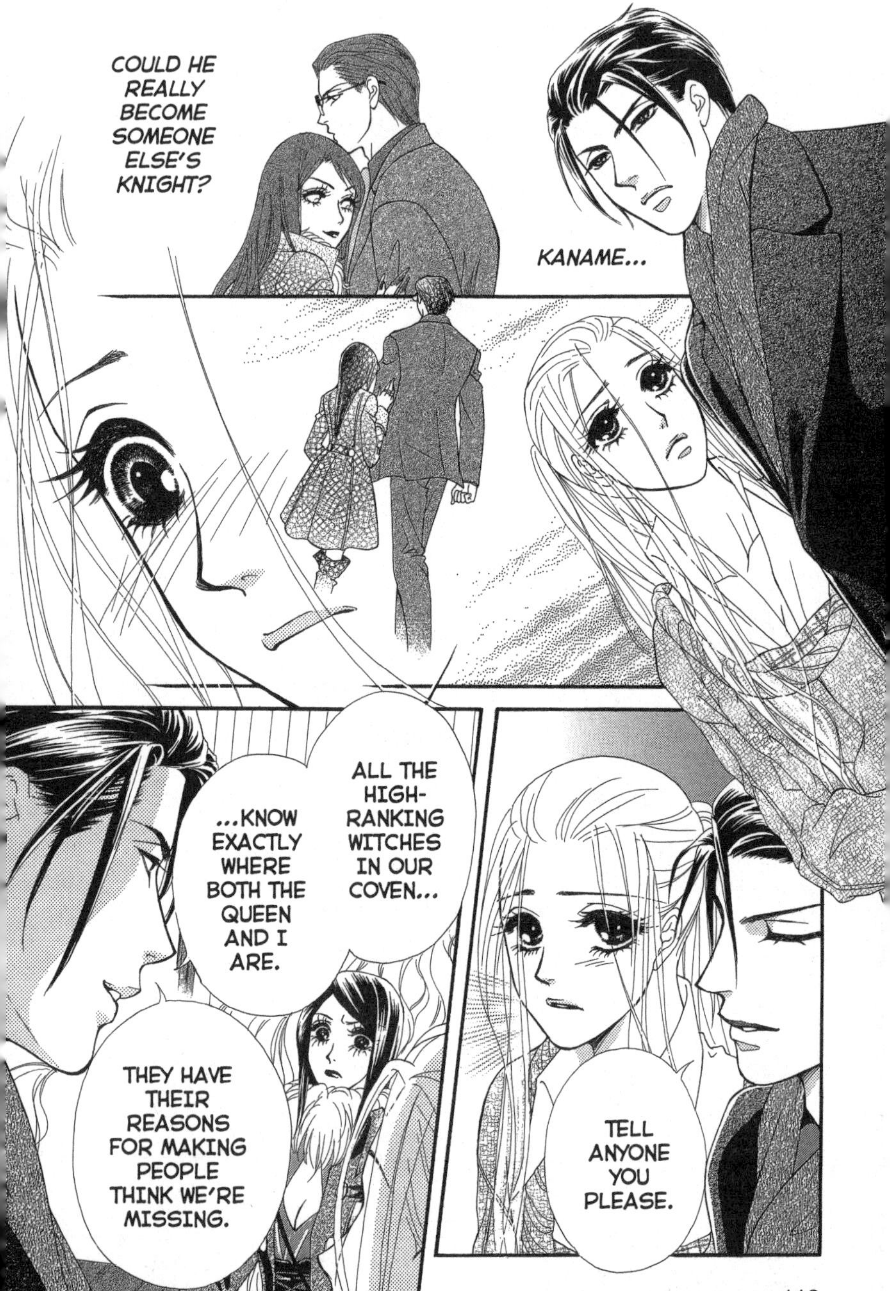

KANAME...
COULD HE REALLY BECOME SOMEONE ELSE'S KNIGHT?
TELL ANYONE YOU PLEASE.
ALL THE HIGH-RANKING WITCHES IN OUR COVEN...
...KNOW EXACTLY WHERE BOTH THE QUEEN AND I ARE.
THEY HAVE THEIR REASONS FOR MAKING PEOPLE THINK WE'RE MISSING.

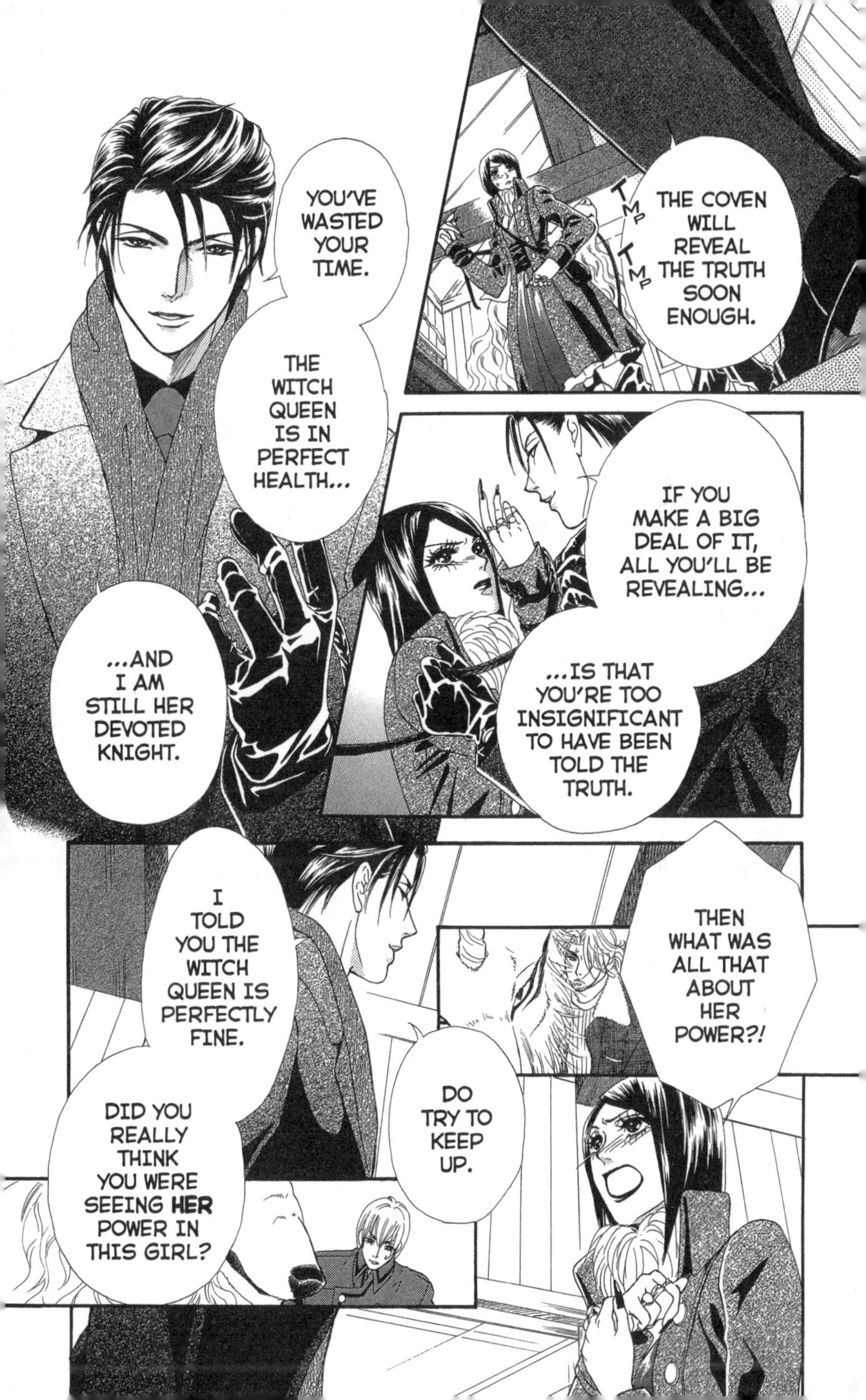
YOU'VE WASTED YOUR TIME.
THE WITCH QUEEN IS IN PERFECT HEALTH...
...AND I AM STILL HER DEVOTED KNIGHT.
TMP TMP TMP
THE COVEN WILL REVEAL THE TRUTH SOON ENOUGH.
IF YOU MAKE A BIG DEAL OF IT, ALL YOU'LL BE REVEALING...
...IS THAT YOU'RE TOO INSIGNIFICANT TO HAVE BEEN TOLD THE TRUTH.
THEN WHAT WAS ALL THAT ABOUT HER POWER?!
I TOLD YOU THE WITCH QUEEN IS PERFECTLY FINE.
DO TRY TO KEEP UP.
DID YOU REALLY THINK YOU WERE SEEING **HER** POWER IN THIS GIRL?

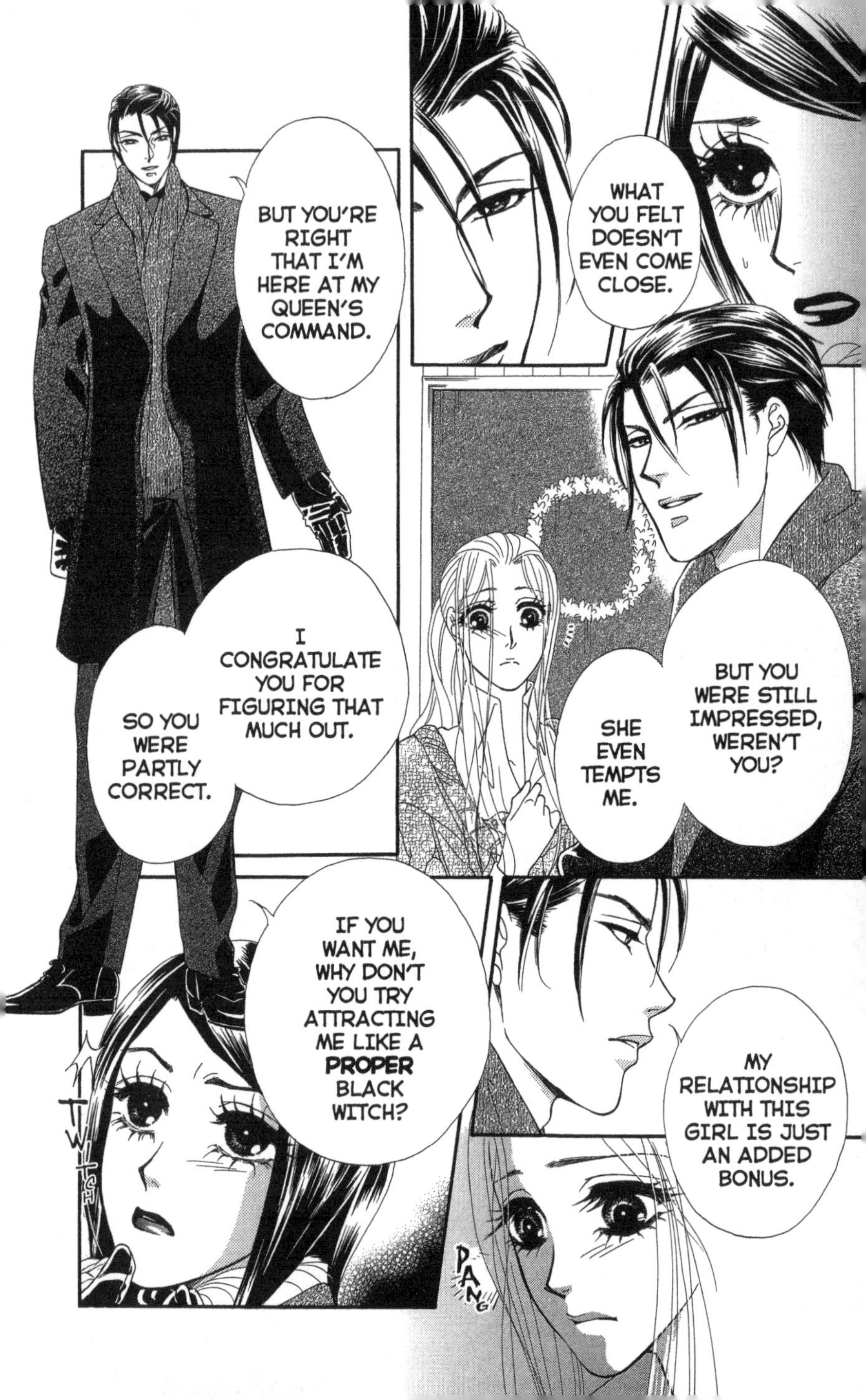
WHAT YOU FELT DOESN'T EVEN COME CLOSE.
BUT YOU WERE STILL IMPRESSED, WEREN'T YOU?
SHE EVEN TEMPTS ME.
BUT YOU'RE RIGHT THAT I'M HERE AT MY QUEEN'S COMMAND.
I CONGRATULATE YOU FOR FIGURING THAT MUCH OUT.
SO YOU WERE PARTLY CORRECT.
MY RELATIONSHIP WITH THIS GIRL IS JUST AN ADDED BONUS.
PANG
IF YOU WANT ME, WHY DON'T YOU TRY ATTRACTING ME LIKE A **PROPER** BLACK WITCH?
TWITCH

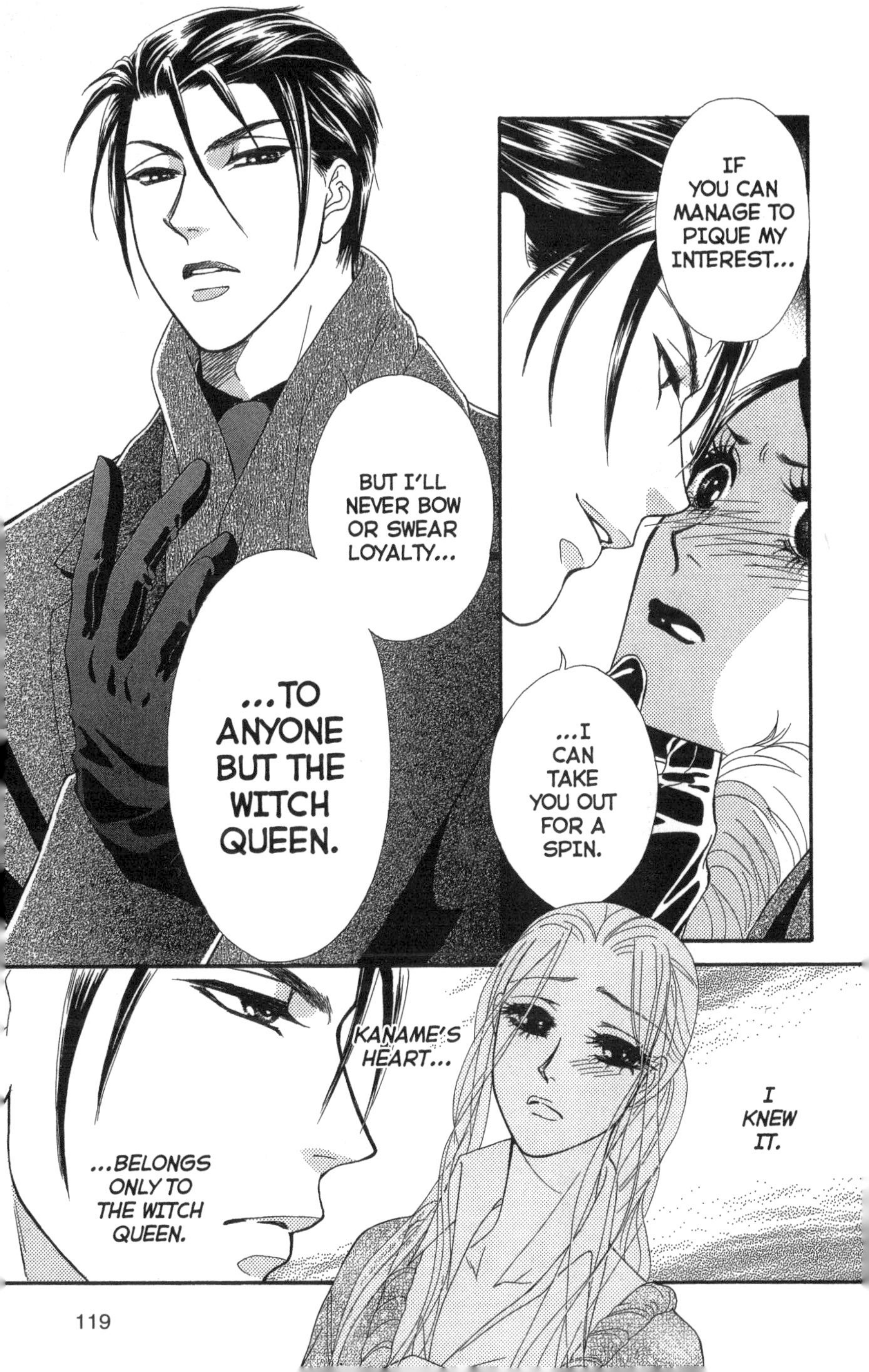
IF YOU CAN MANAGE TO PIQUE MY INTEREST...
...I CAN TAKE YOU OUT FOR A SPIN.
BUT I'LL NEVER BOW OR SWEAR LOYALTY...
...TO ANYONE BUT THE WITCH QUEEN.
I KNEW IT.
KANAME'S HEART...
...BELONGS ONLY TO THE WITCH QUEEN.

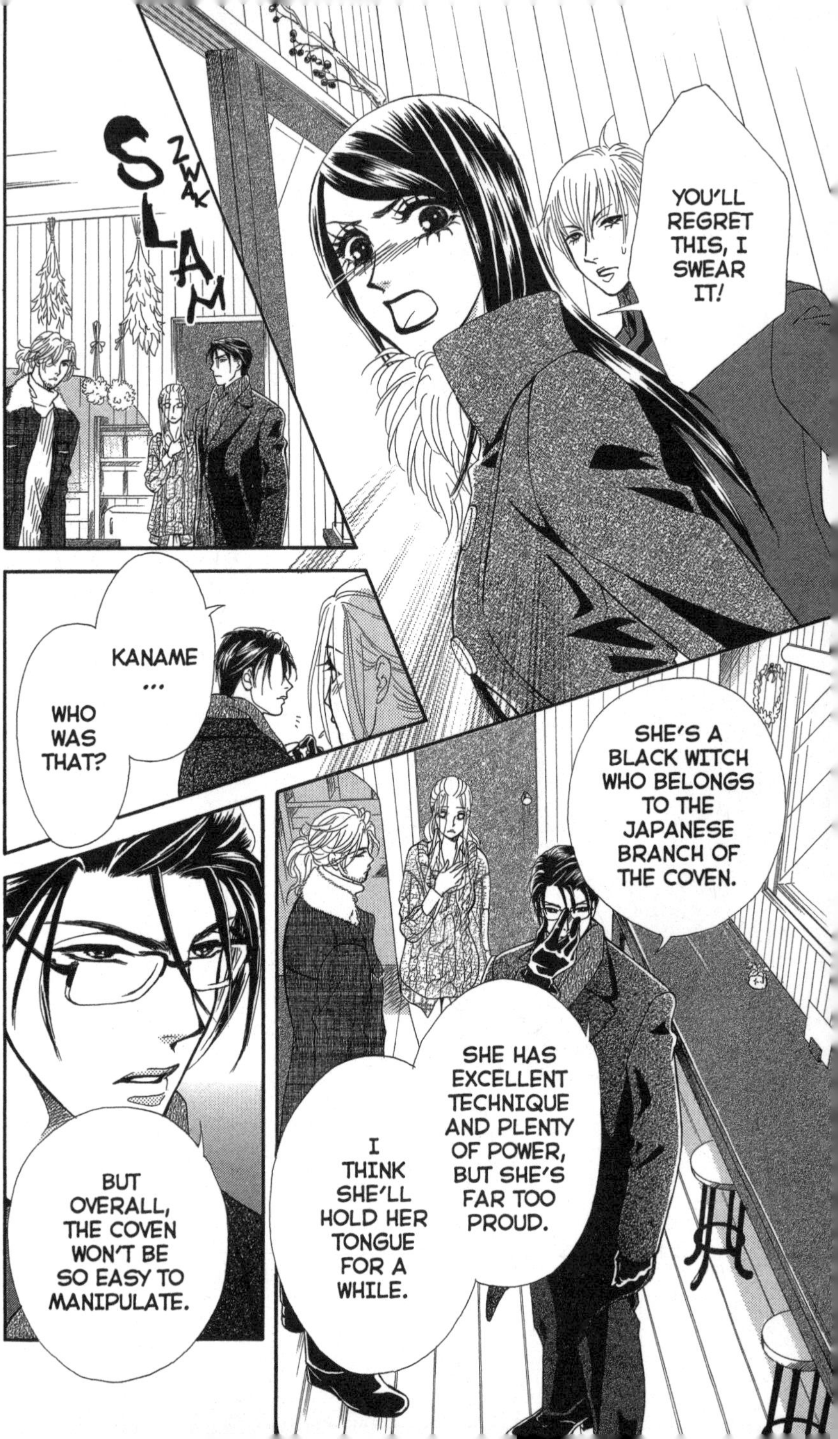

YOU'LL REGRET THIS, I SWEAR IT!
SLAM
ZWAK
KANAME...
WHO WAS THAT?
SHE'S A BLACK WITCH WHO BELONGS TO THE JAPANESE BRANCH OF THE COVEN.
SHE HAS EXCELLENT TECHNIQUE AND PLENTY OF POWER, BUT SHE'S FAR TOO PROUD.
I THINK SHE'LL HOLD HER TONGUE FOR A WHILE.
BUT OVERALL, THE COVEN WON'T BE SO EASY TO MANIPULATE.

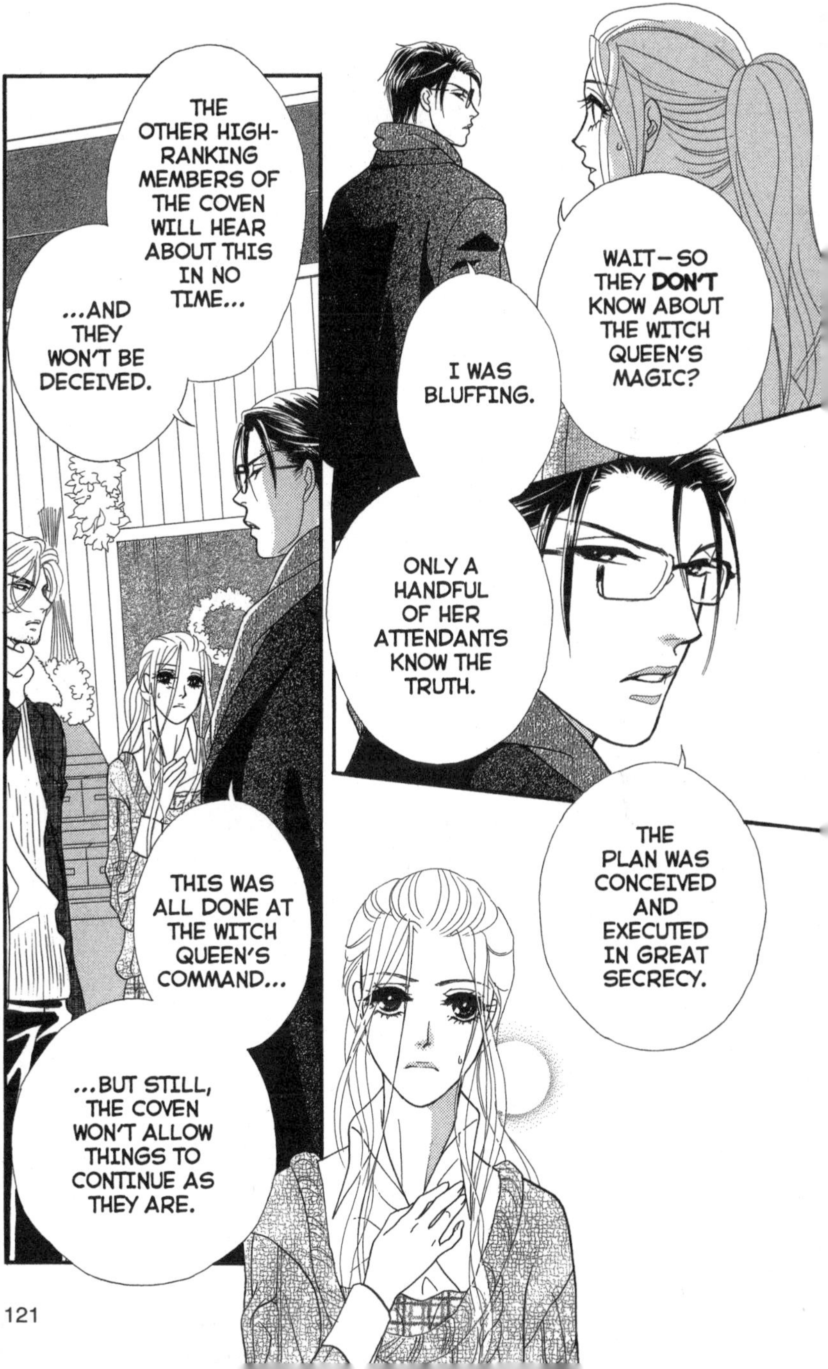
WAIT—SO THEY DON'T KNOW ABOUT THE WITCH QUEEN'S MAGIC?
I WAS BLUFFING.
ONLY A HANDFUL OF HER ATTENDANTS KNOW THE TRUTH.
THE PLAN WAS CONCEIVED AND EXECUTED IN GREAT SECRECY.
THE OTHER HIGH-RANKING MEMBERS OF THE COVEN WILL HEAR ABOUT THIS IN NO TIME...
...AND THEY WON'T BE DECEIVED.
THIS WAS ALL DONE AT THE WITCH QUEEN'S COMMAND...
...BUT STILL, THE COVEN WON'T ALLOW THINGS TO CONTINUE AS THEY ARE.

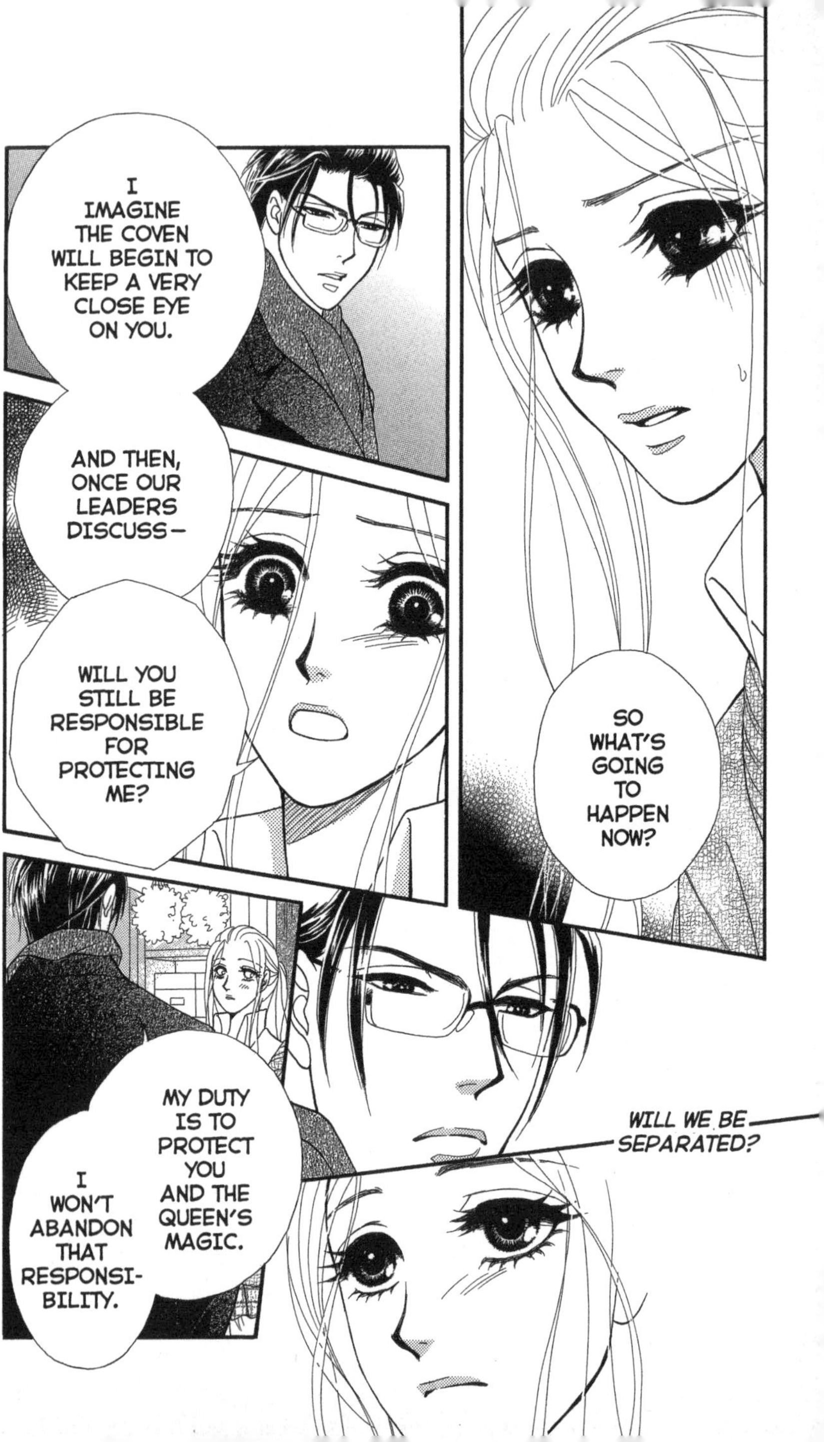
SO WHAT'S GOING TO HAPPEN NOW?
I IMAGINE THE COVEN WILL BEGIN TO KEEP A VERY CLOSE EYE ON YOU.
AND THEN, ONCE OUR LEADERS DISCUSS—
WILL YOU STILL BE RESPONSIBLE FOR PROTECTING ME?
MY DUTY IS TO PROTECT YOU AND THE QUEEN'S MAGIC.
I WON'T ABANDON THAT RESPONSIBILITY.
WILL WE BE SEPARATED?

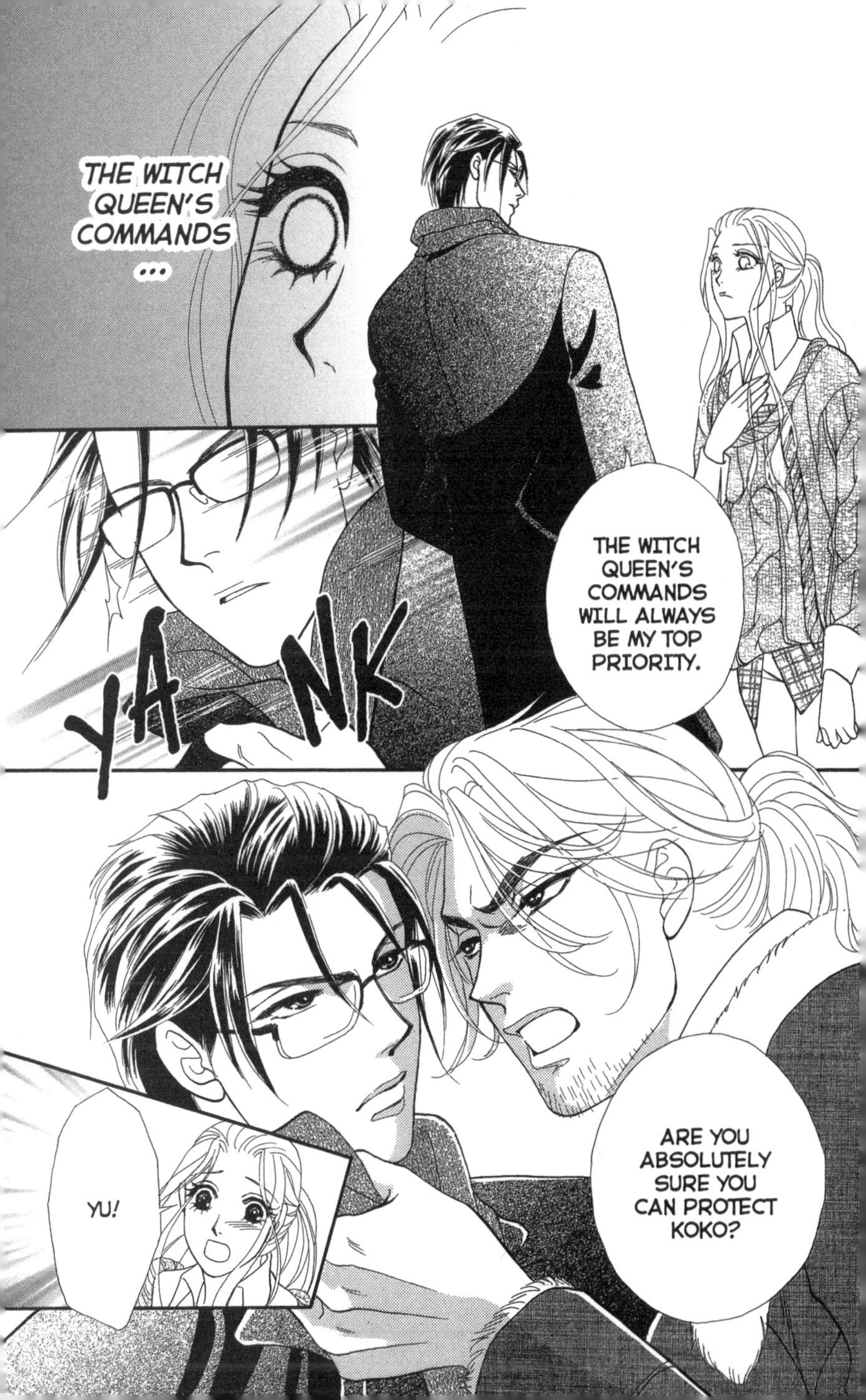
THE WITCH QUEEN'S COMMANDS WILL ALWAYS BE MY TOP PRIORITY.
THE WITCH QUEEN'S COMMANDS ...
YANK
ARE YOU ABSOLUTELY SURE YOU CAN PROTECT KOKO?
YU!

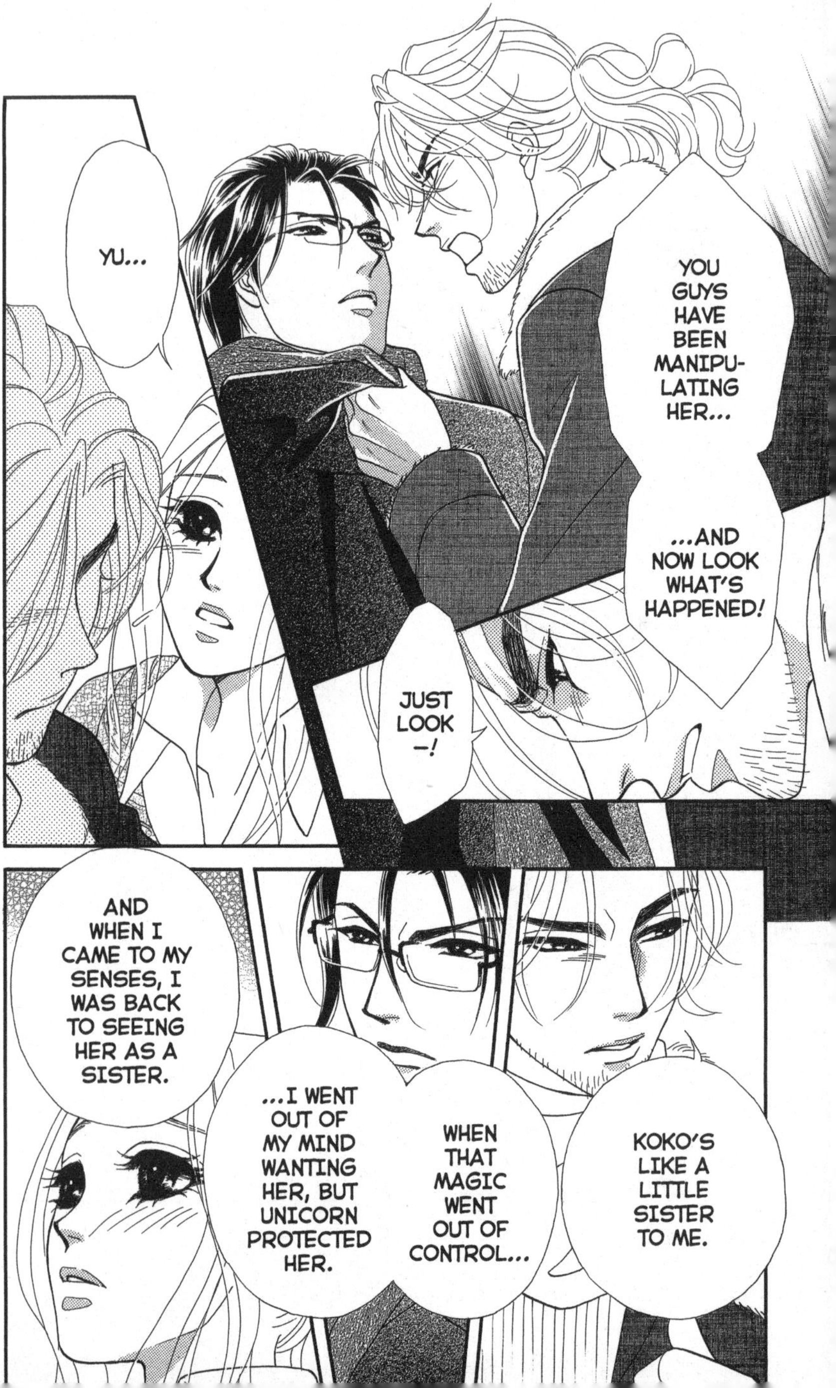
YOU GUYS HAVE BEEN MANIPU-LATING HER...
...AND NOW LOOK WHAT'S HAPPENED!
JUST LOOK—!
YU...
KOKO'S LIKE A LITTLE SISTER TO ME.
WHEN THAT MAGIC WENT OUT OF CONTROL...
...I WENT OUT OF MY MIND WANTING HER, BUT UNICORN PROTECTED HER.
AND WHEN I CAME TO MY SENSES, I WAS BACK TO SEEING HER AS A SISTER.

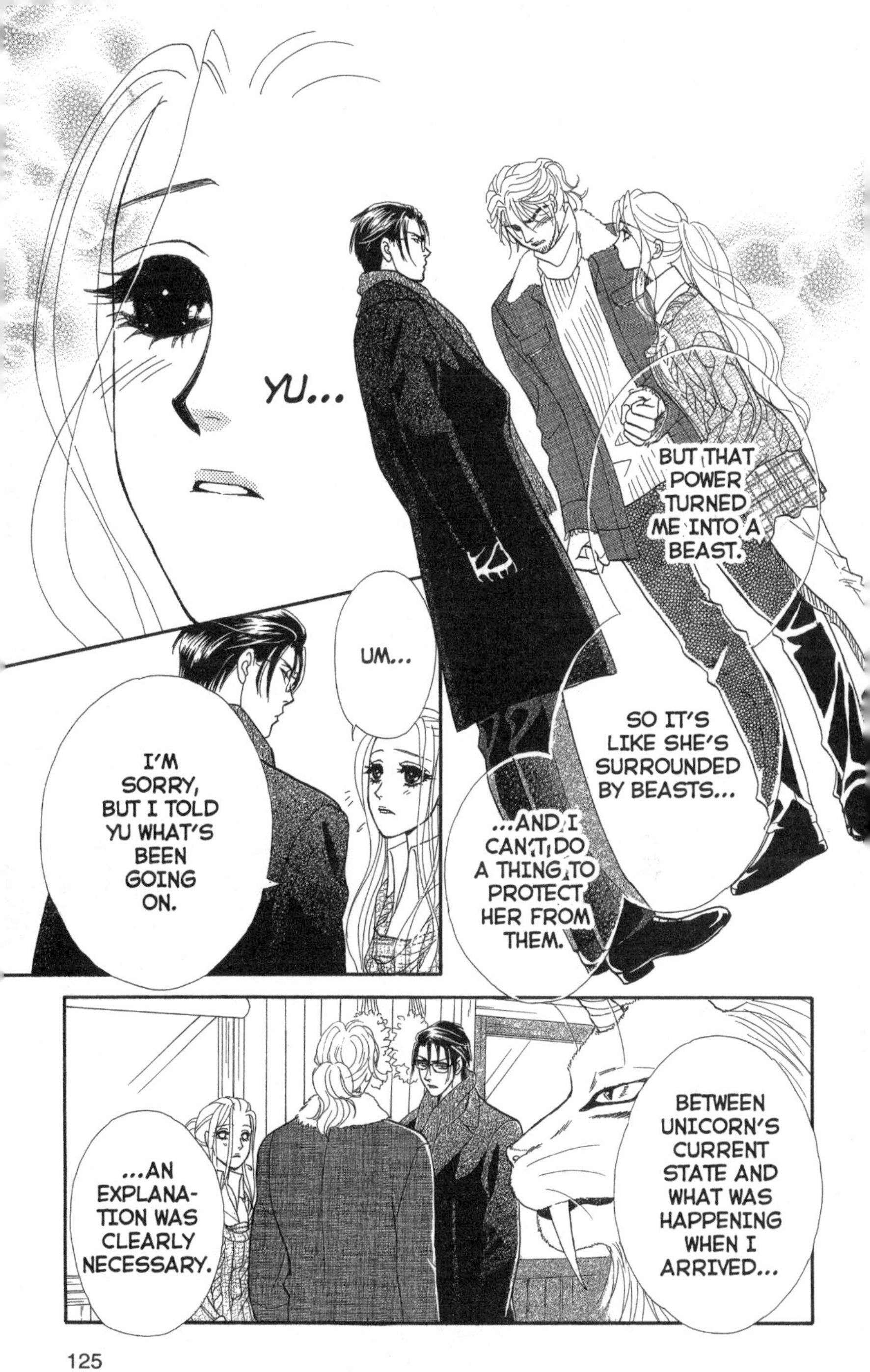
BUT THAT POWER TURNED ME INTO A BEAST.
SO IT'S LIKE SHE'S SURROUNDED BY BEASTS...
...AND I CAN'T DO A THING TO PROTECT HER FROM THEM.
YU...
UM...
I'M SORRY, BUT I TOLD YU WHAT'S BEEN GOING ON.
BETWEEN UNICORN'S CURRENT STATE AND WHAT WAS HAPPENING WHEN I ARRIVED...
...AN EXPLANATION WAS CLEARLY NECESSARY.

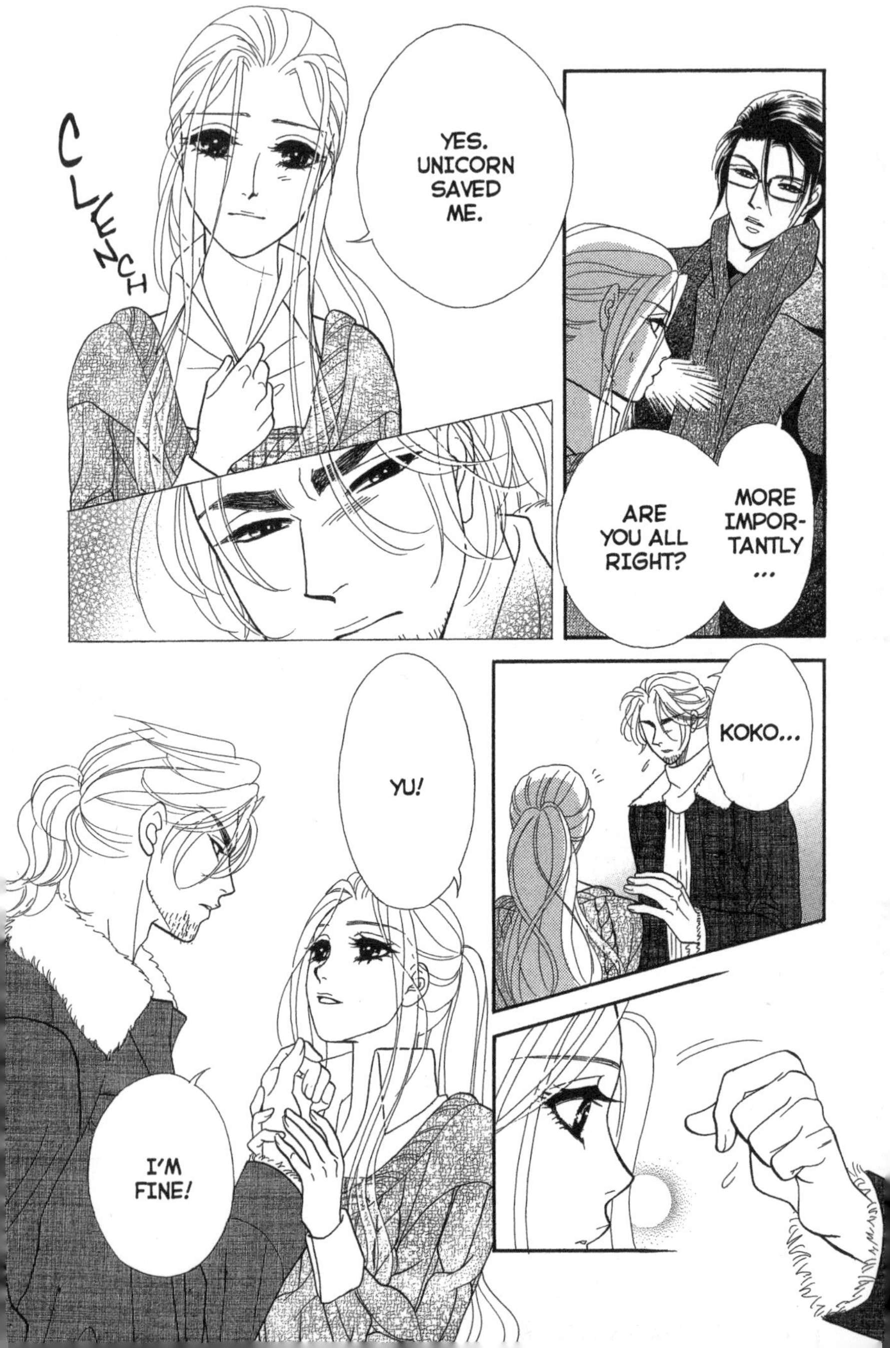
MORE IMPORTANTLY...
ARE YOU ALL RIGHT?
YES. UNICORN SAVED ME.
CLENCH
KOKO...
YU!
I'M FINE!

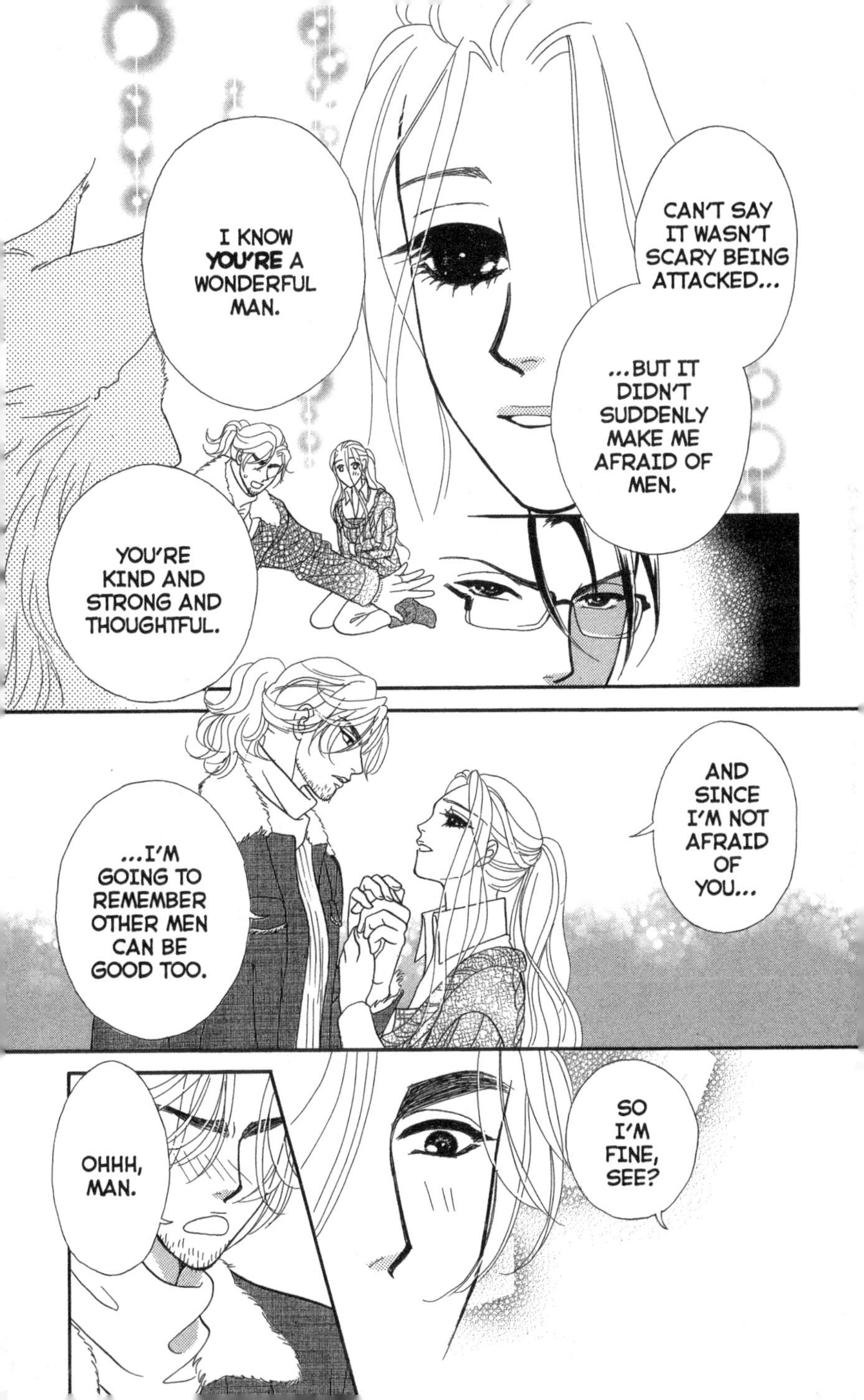
CAN'T SAY IT WASN'T SCARY BEING ATTACKED...
...BUT IT DIDN'T SUDDENLY MAKE ME AFRAID OF MEN.
I KNOW **YOU'RE** A WONDERFUL MAN.
YOU'RE KIND AND STRONG AND THOUGHTFUL.
AND SINCE I'M NOT AFRAID OF YOU...
...I'M GOING TO REMEMBER OTHER MEN CAN BE GOOD TOO.
SO I'M FINE, SEE?
OHHH, MAN.

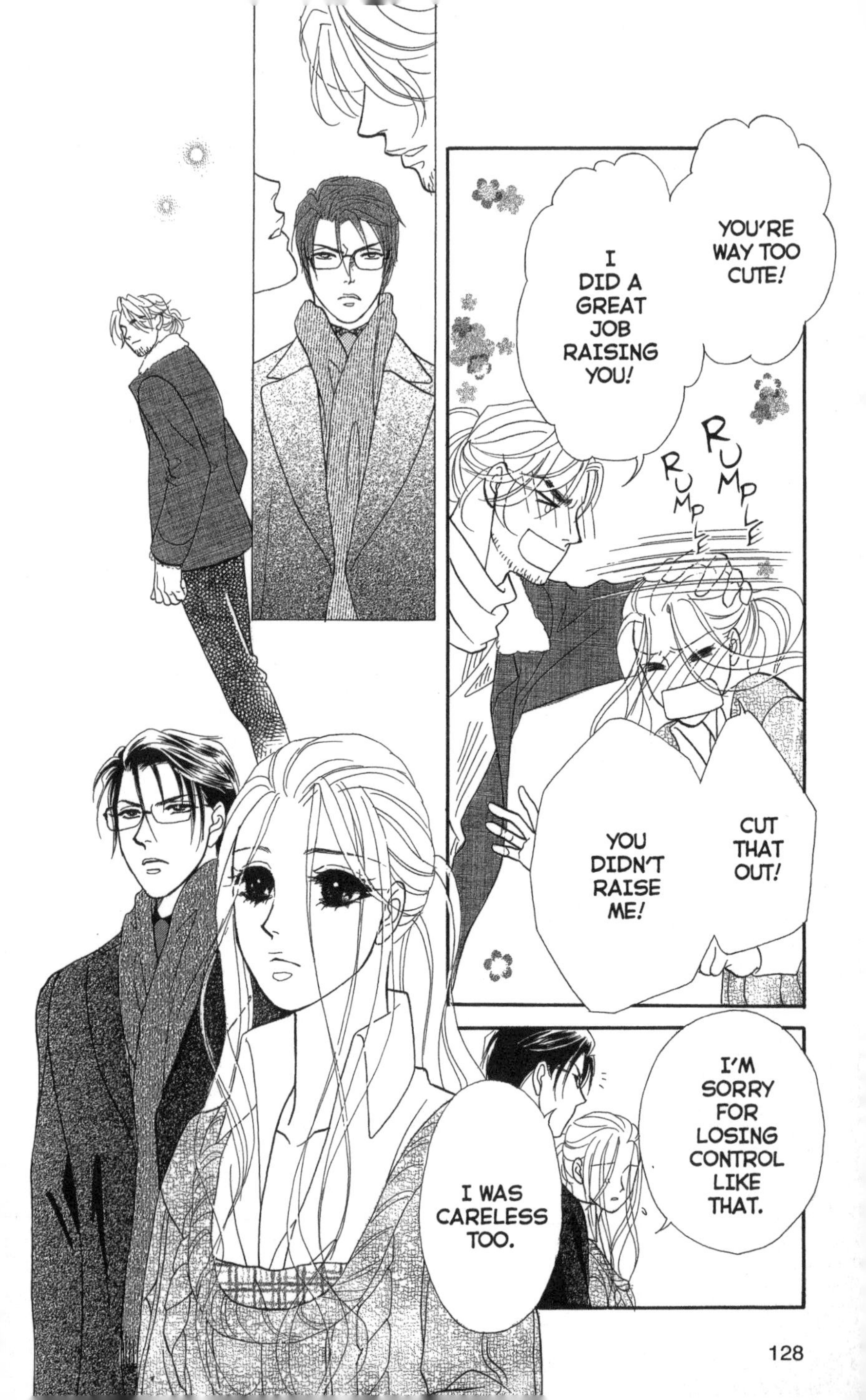
YOU'RE WAY TOO CUTE!
I DID A GREAT JOB RAISING YOU!
RUMPLE
RUMPLE
CUT THAT OUT!
YOU DIDN'T RAISE ME!
I'M SORRY FOR LOSING CONTROL LIKE THAT.
I WAS CARELESS TOO.

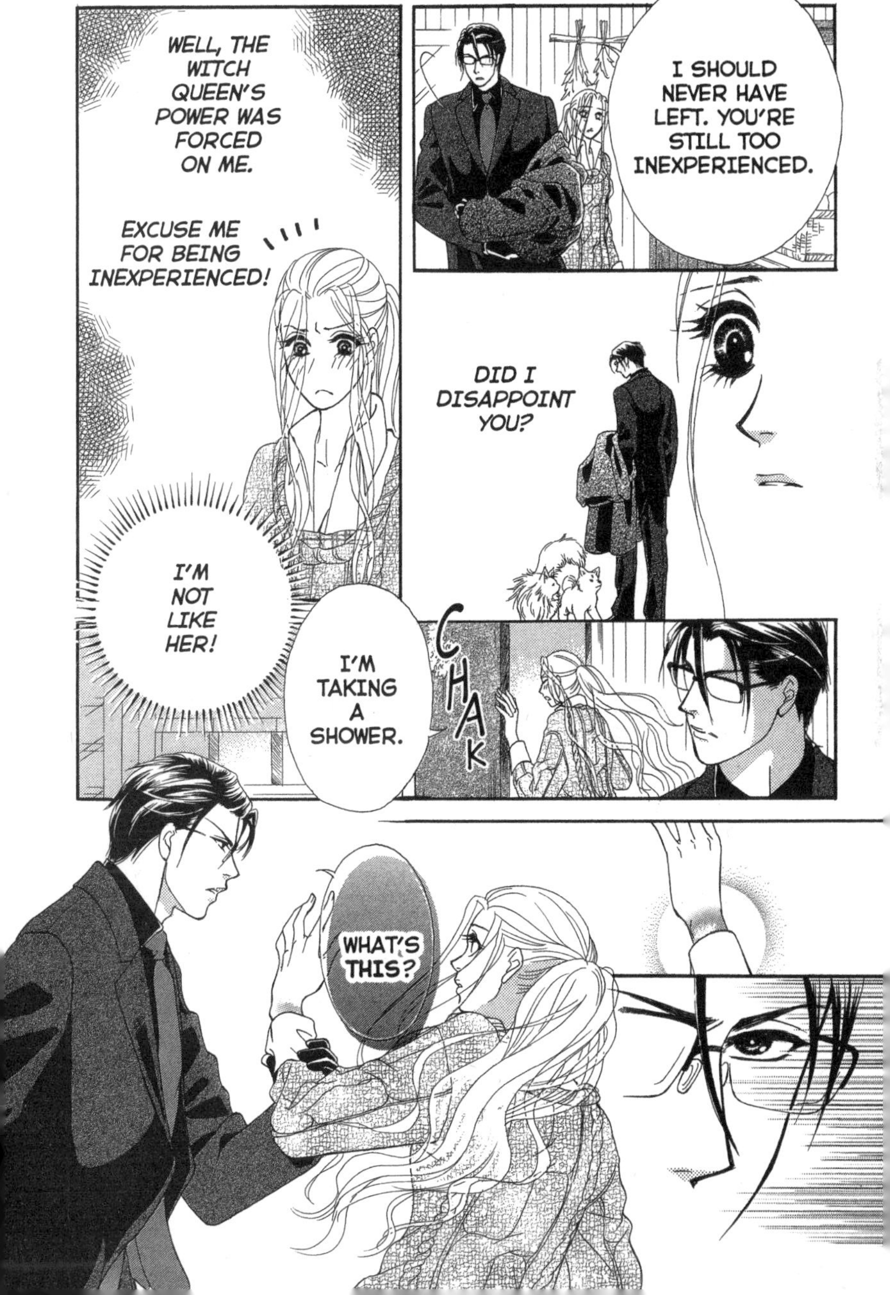

I SHOULD NEVER HAVE LEFT. YOU'RE STILL TOO INEXPERIENCED.
DID I DISAPPOINT YOU?
I'M TAKING A SHOWER.
CHAK
WELL, THE WITCH QUEEN'S POWER WAS FORCED ON ME.
EXCUSE ME FOR BEING INEXPERIENCED!
I'M NOT LIKE HER!
WHAT'S THIS?

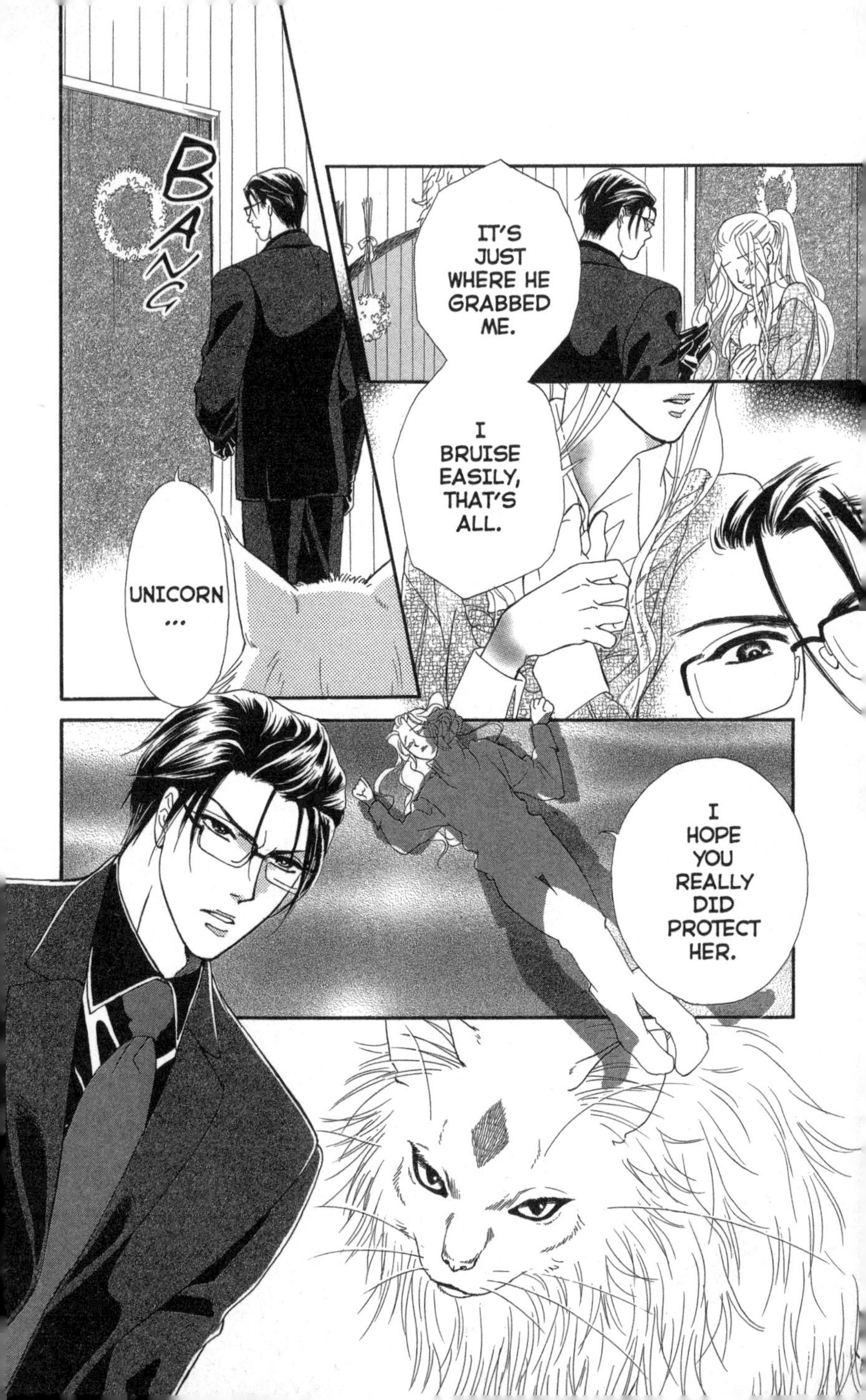
IT'S JUST WHERE HE GRABBED ME.
I BRUISE EASILY, THAT'S ALL.
BANG
UNICORN ...
I HOPE YOU REALLY DID PROTECT HER.

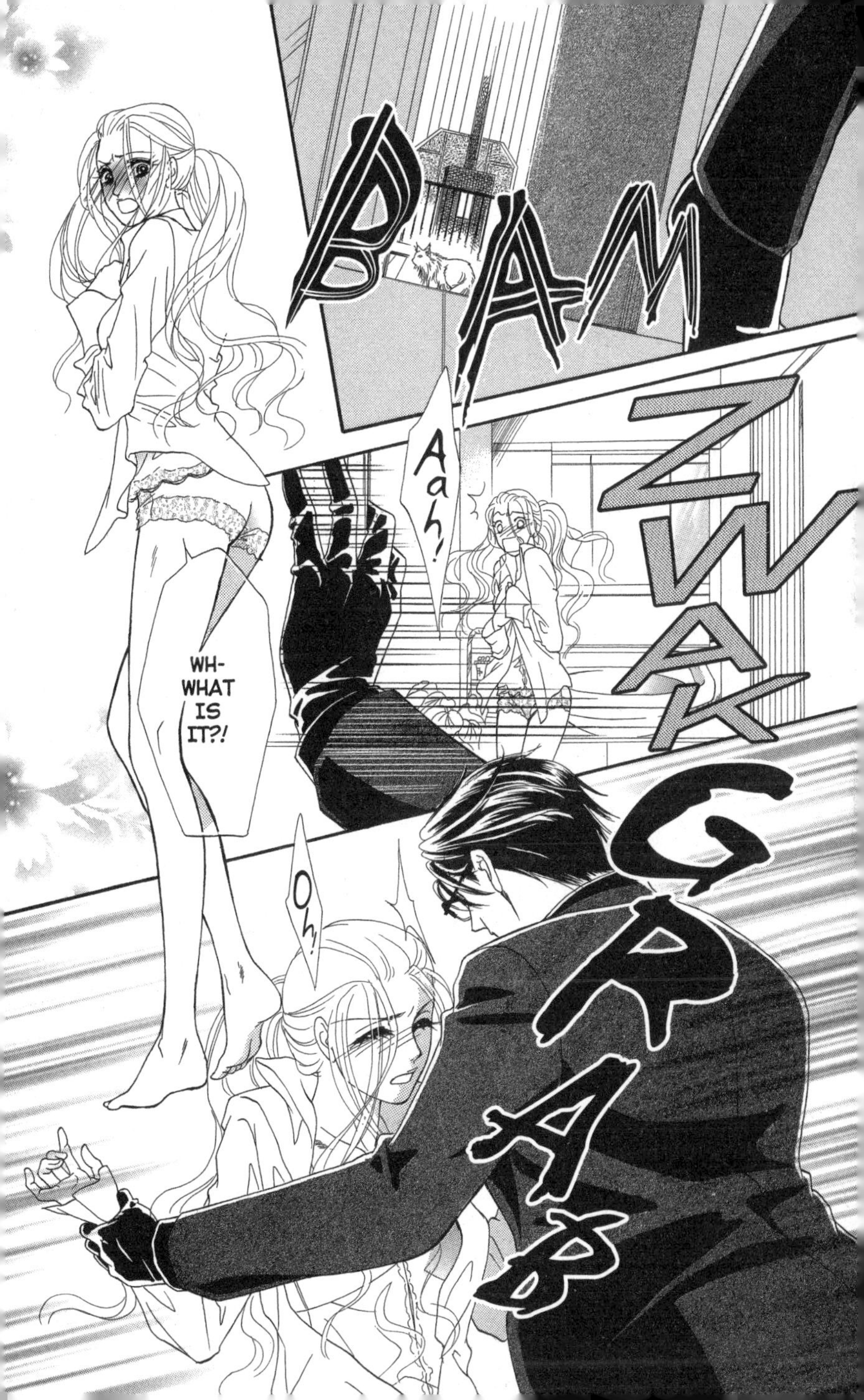
BAM
ZWAK
Aah!
GRAB
Oh!
WH-WHAT IS IT?!

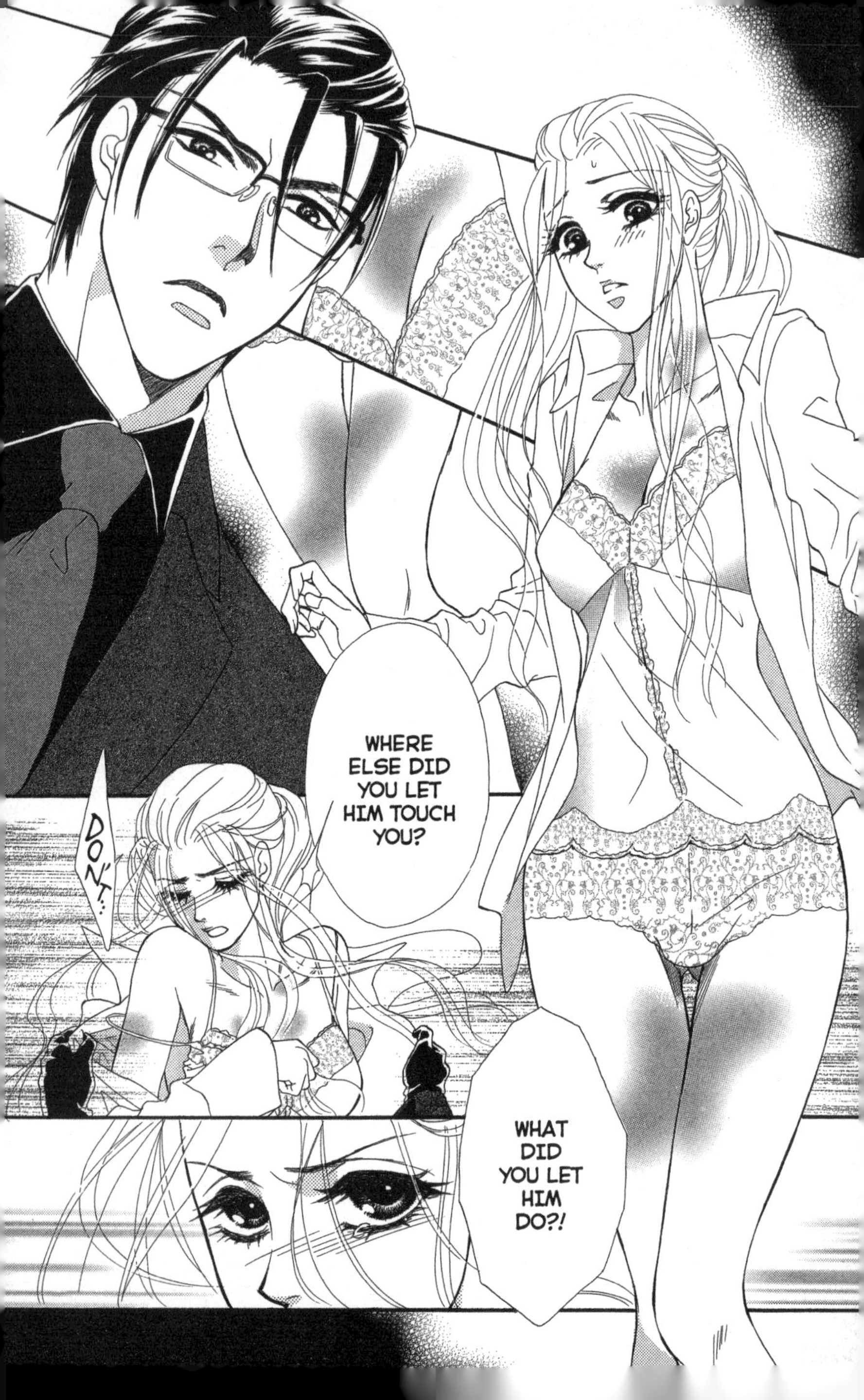
WHERE ELSE DID YOU LET HIM TOUCH YOU?
DON'T...
WHAT DID YOU LET HIM DO?!

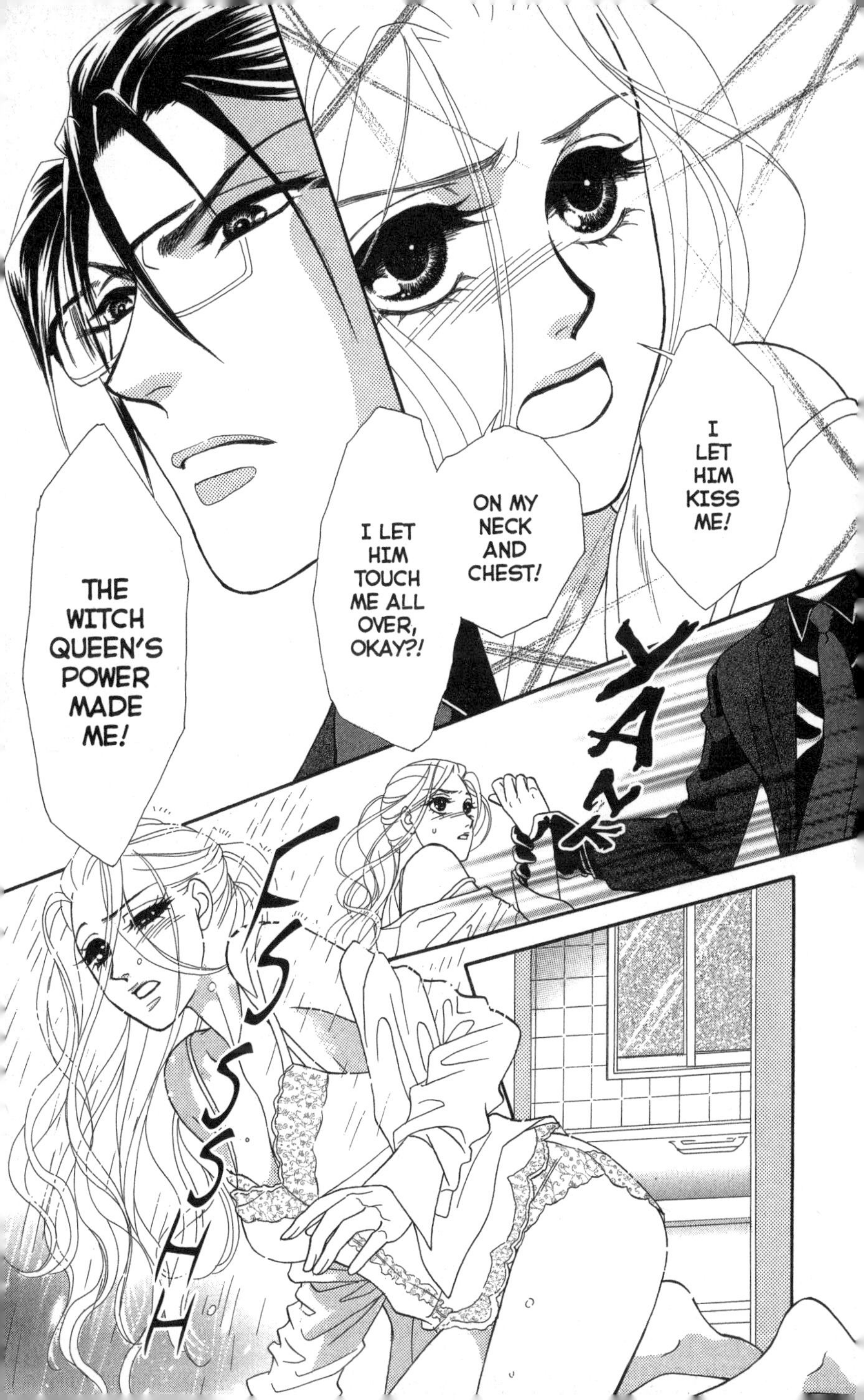
I LET HIM KISS ME!
ON MY NECK AND CHEST!
I LET HIM TOUCH ME ALL OVER, OKAY?!
THE WITCH QUEEN'S POWER MADE ME!
YANK
FSSSHH

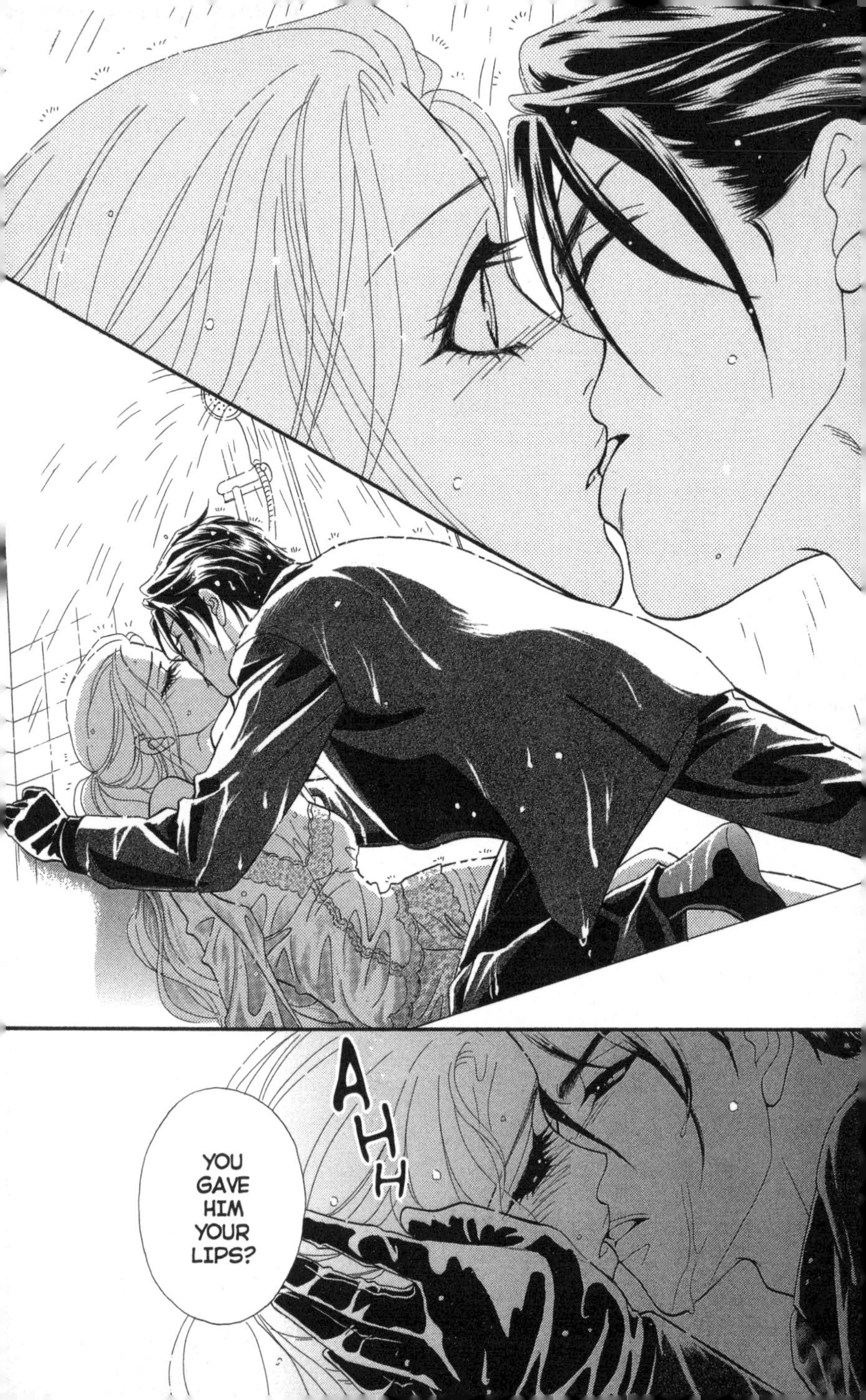
AHH
YOU GAVE HIM YOUR LIPS?

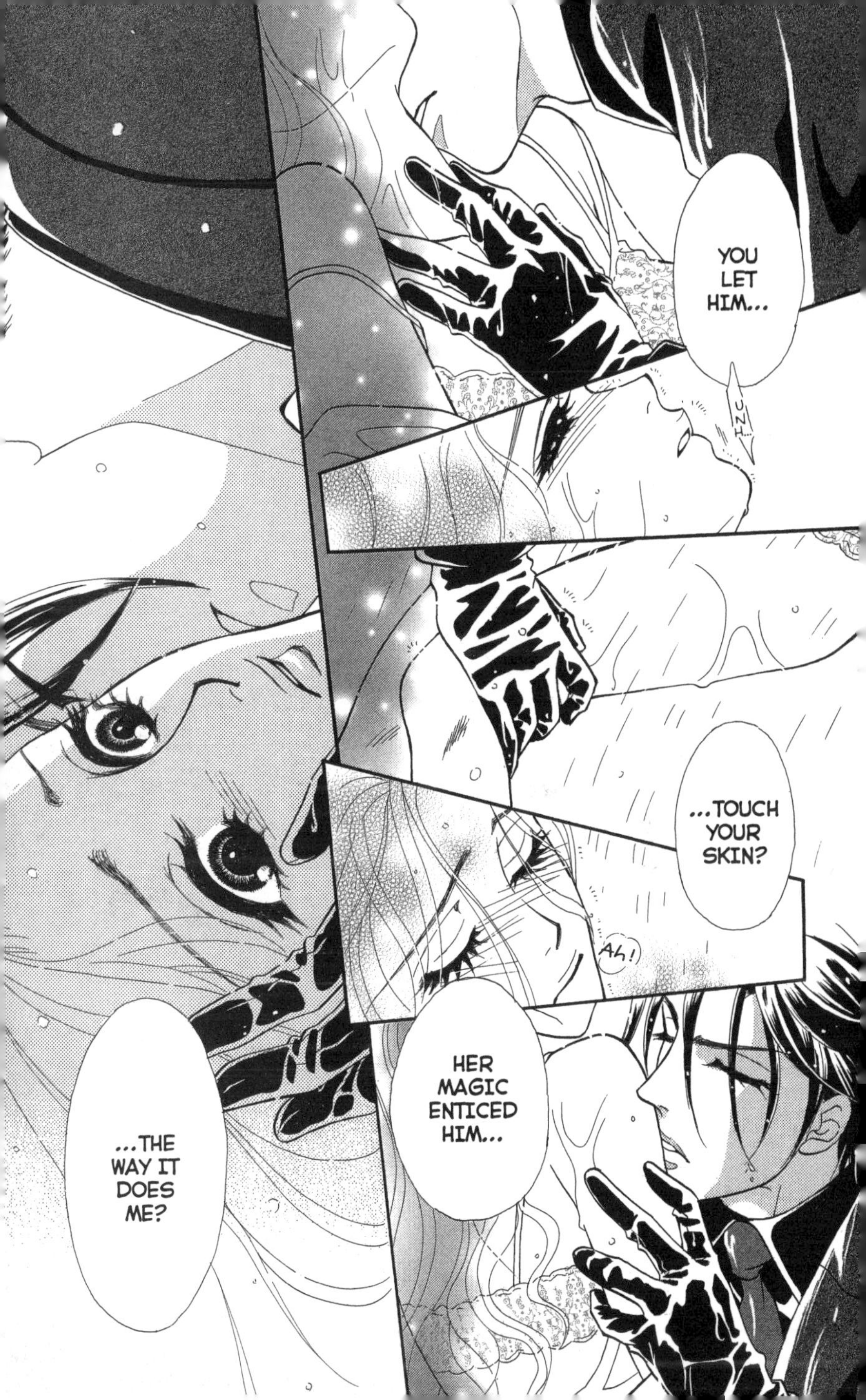
YOU LET HIM...
UNH...
...TOUCH YOUR SKIN?
AH!
HER MAGIC ENTICED HIM...
...THE WAY IT DOES ME?

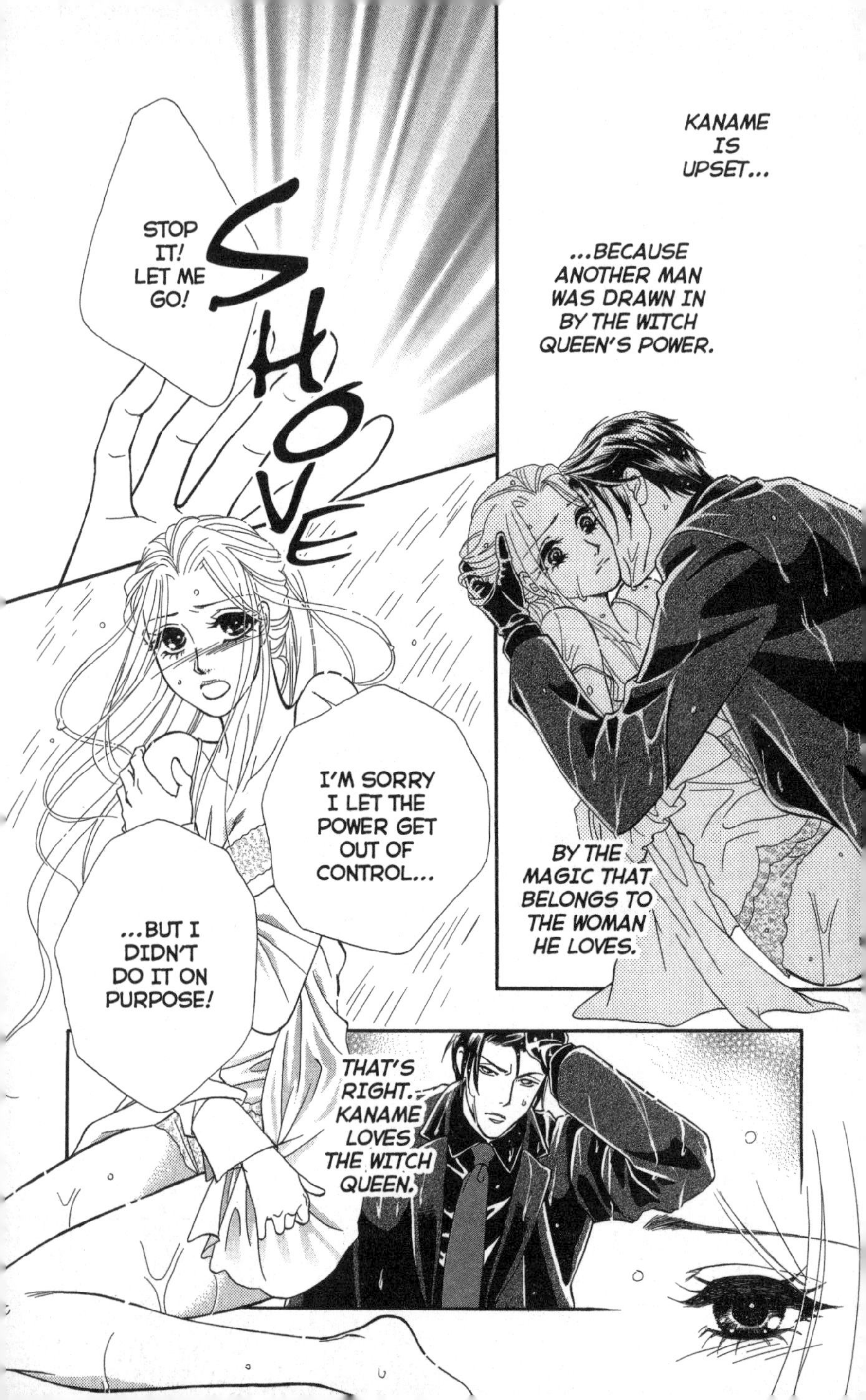
KANAME IS UPSET...
...BECAUSE ANOTHER MAN WAS DRAWN IN BY THE WITCH QUEEN'S POWER.
BY THE MAGIC THAT BELONGS TO THE WOMAN HE LOVES.
STOP IT! LET ME GO!
SHOVE
I'M SORRY I LET THE POWER GET OUT OF CONTROL...
...BUT I DIDN'T DO IT ON PURPOSE!
THAT'S RIGHT. KANAME LOVES THE WITCH QUEEN.

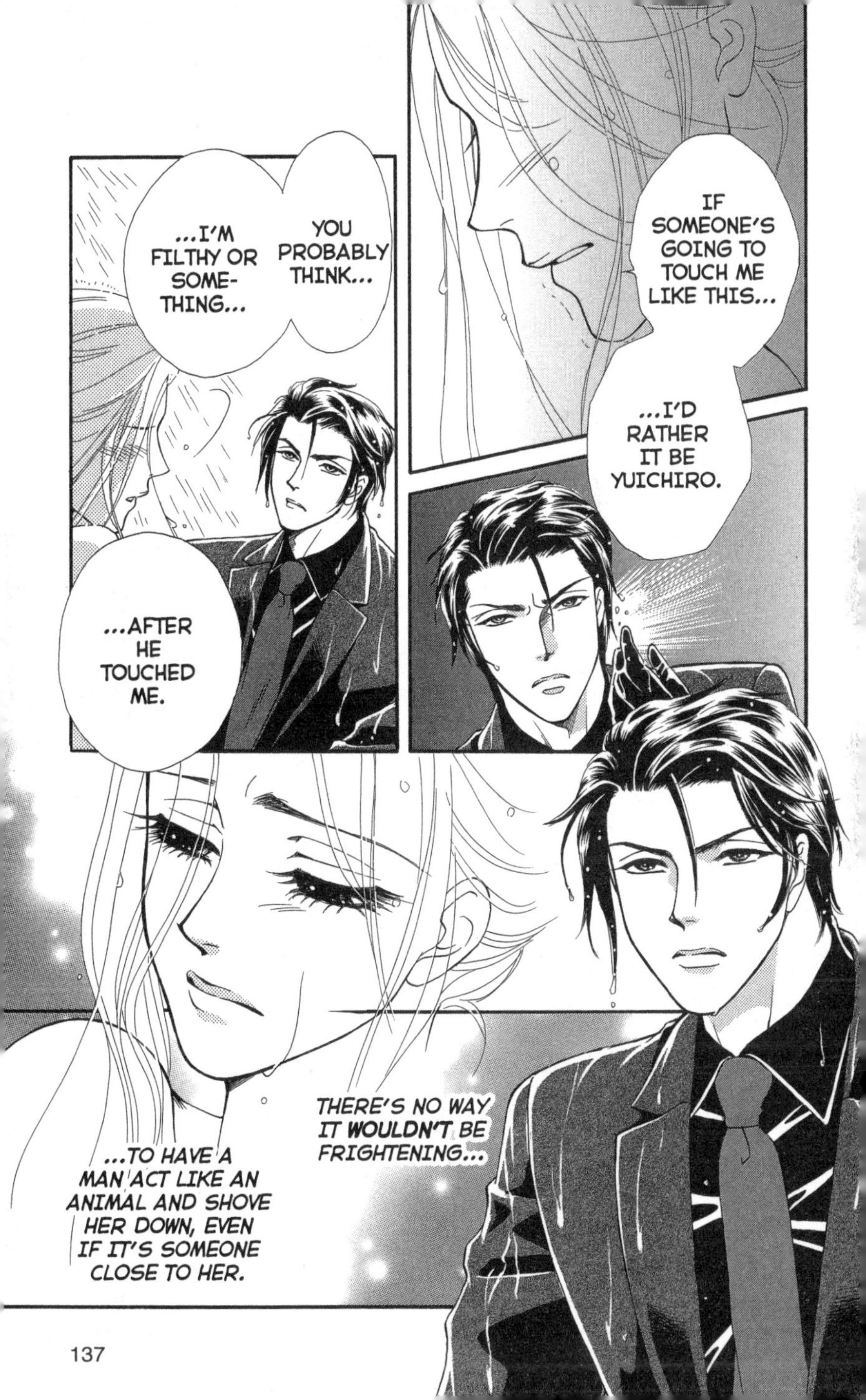
IF SOMEONE'S GOING TO TOUCH ME LIKE THIS...
...I'D RATHER IT BE YUICHIRO.
YOU PROBABLY THINK...
...I'M FILTHY OR SOME-THING...
...AFTER HE TOUCHED ME.
THERE'S NO WAY IT **WOULDN'T** BE FRIGHTENING...
...TO HAVE A MAN ACT LIKE AN ANIMAL AND SHOVE HER DOWN, EVEN IF IT'S SOMEONE CLOSE TO HER.

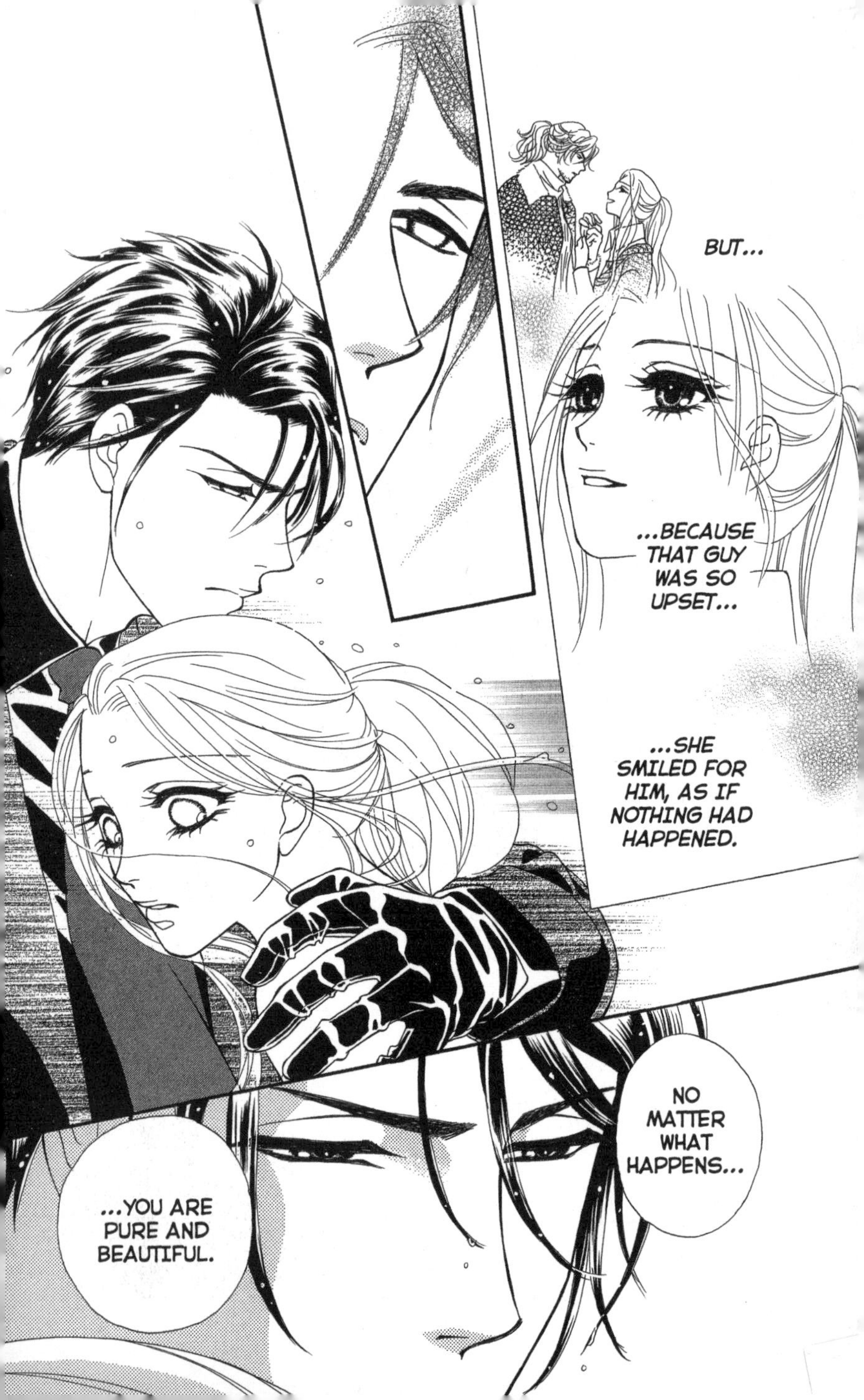
BUT...
...BECAUSE THAT GUY WAS SO UPSET...
...SHE SMILED FOR HIM, AS IF NOTHING HAD HAPPENED.
NO MATTER WHAT HAPPENS...
...YOU ARE PURE AND BEAUTIFUL.

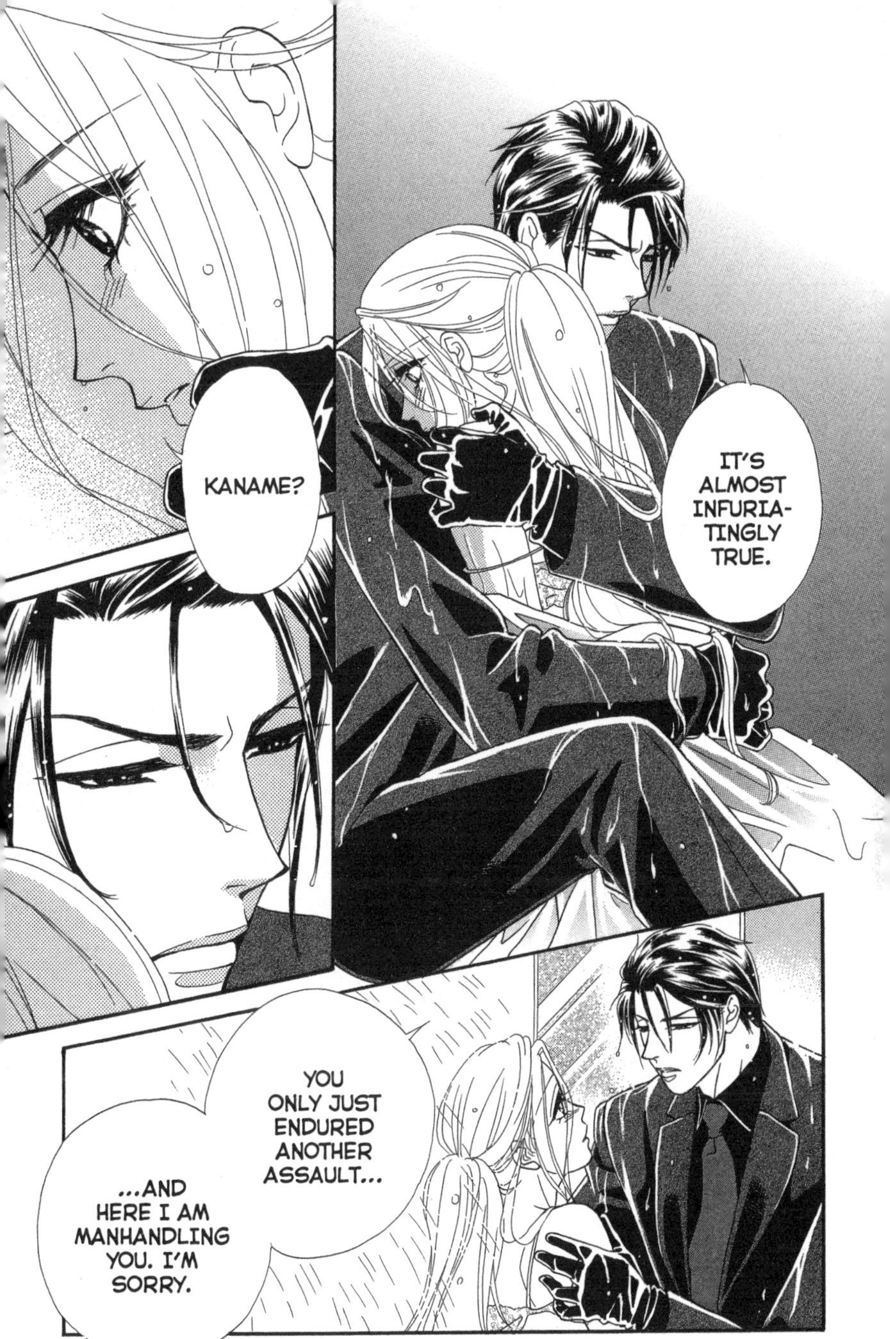
IT'S ALMOST INFURIA-TINGLY TRUE.
KANAME?
YOU ONLY JUST ENDURED ANOTHER ASSAULT...
...AND HERE I AM MANHANDLING YOU. I'M SORRY.

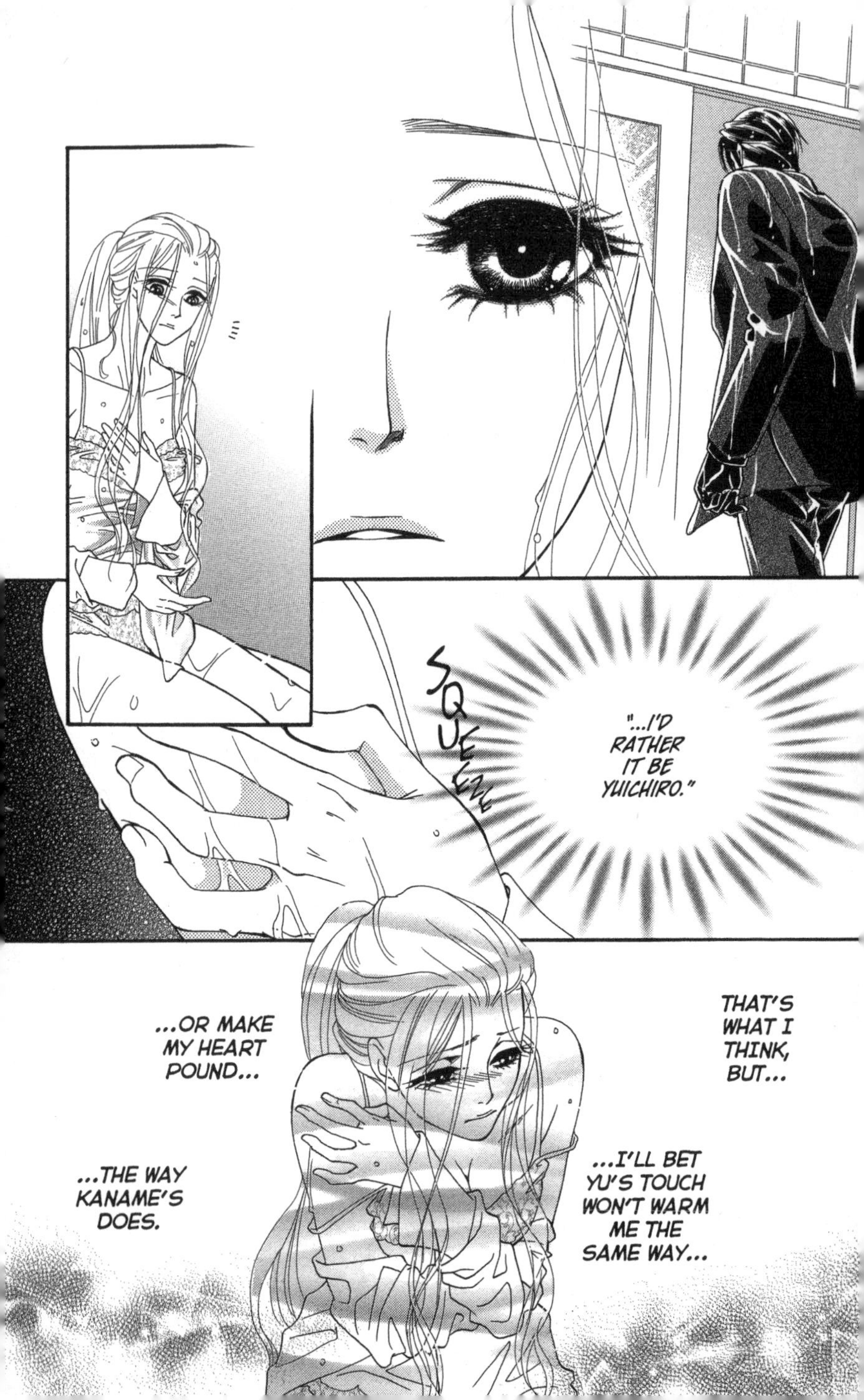
"...I'D RATHER IT BE YUICHIRO."
SQUEEZE
THAT'S WHAT I THINK, BUT...
...I'LL BET YU'S TOUCH WON'T WARM ME THE SAME WAY...
...OR MAKE MY HEART POUND...
...THE WAY KANAME'S DOES.

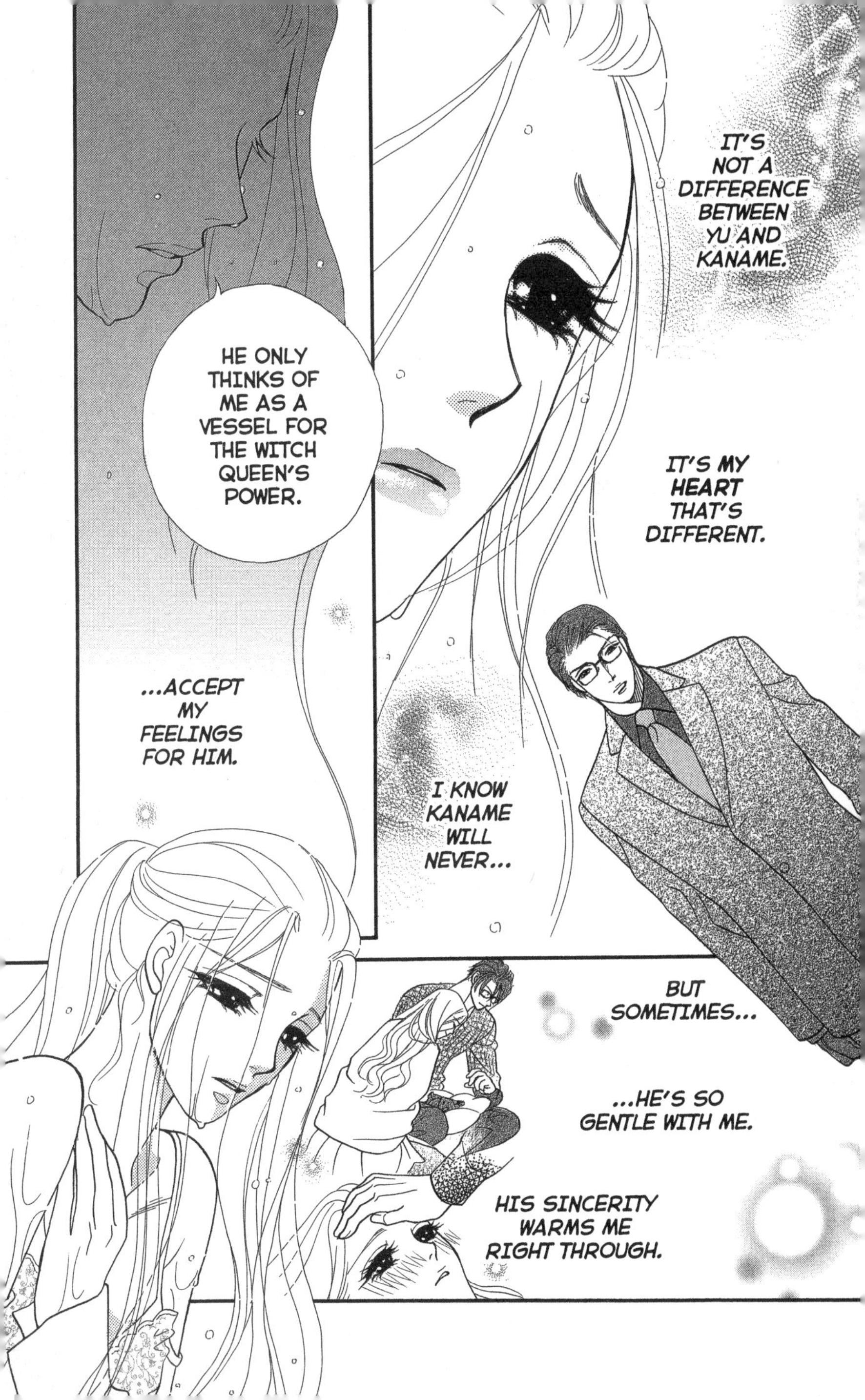
IT'S NOT A DIFFERENCE BETWEEN YU AND KANAME.
IT'S MY HEART THAT'S DIFFERENT.
I KNOW KANAME WILL NEVER...
HE ONLY THINKS OF ME AS A VESSEL FOR THE WITCH QUEEN'S POWER.
...ACCEPT MY FEELINGS FOR HIM.
BUT SOMETIMES...
...HE'S SO GENTLE WITH ME.
HIS SINCERITY WARMS ME RIGHT THROUGH.

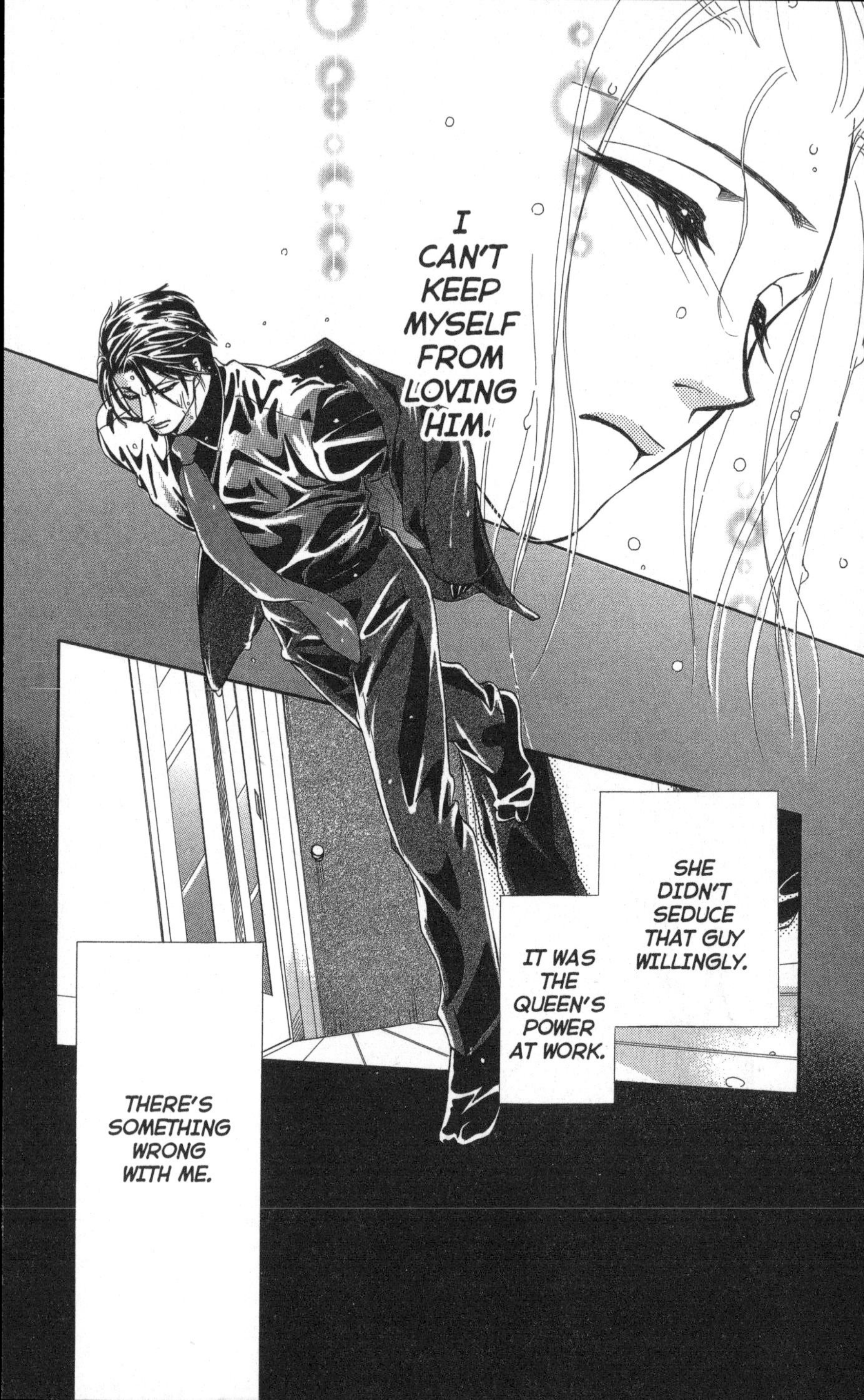
I CAN'T KEEP MYSELF FROM LOVING HIM.
SHE DIDN'T SEDUCE THAT GUY WILLINGLY.
IT WAS THE QUEEN'S POWER AT WORK.
THERE'S SOMETHING WRONG WITH ME.

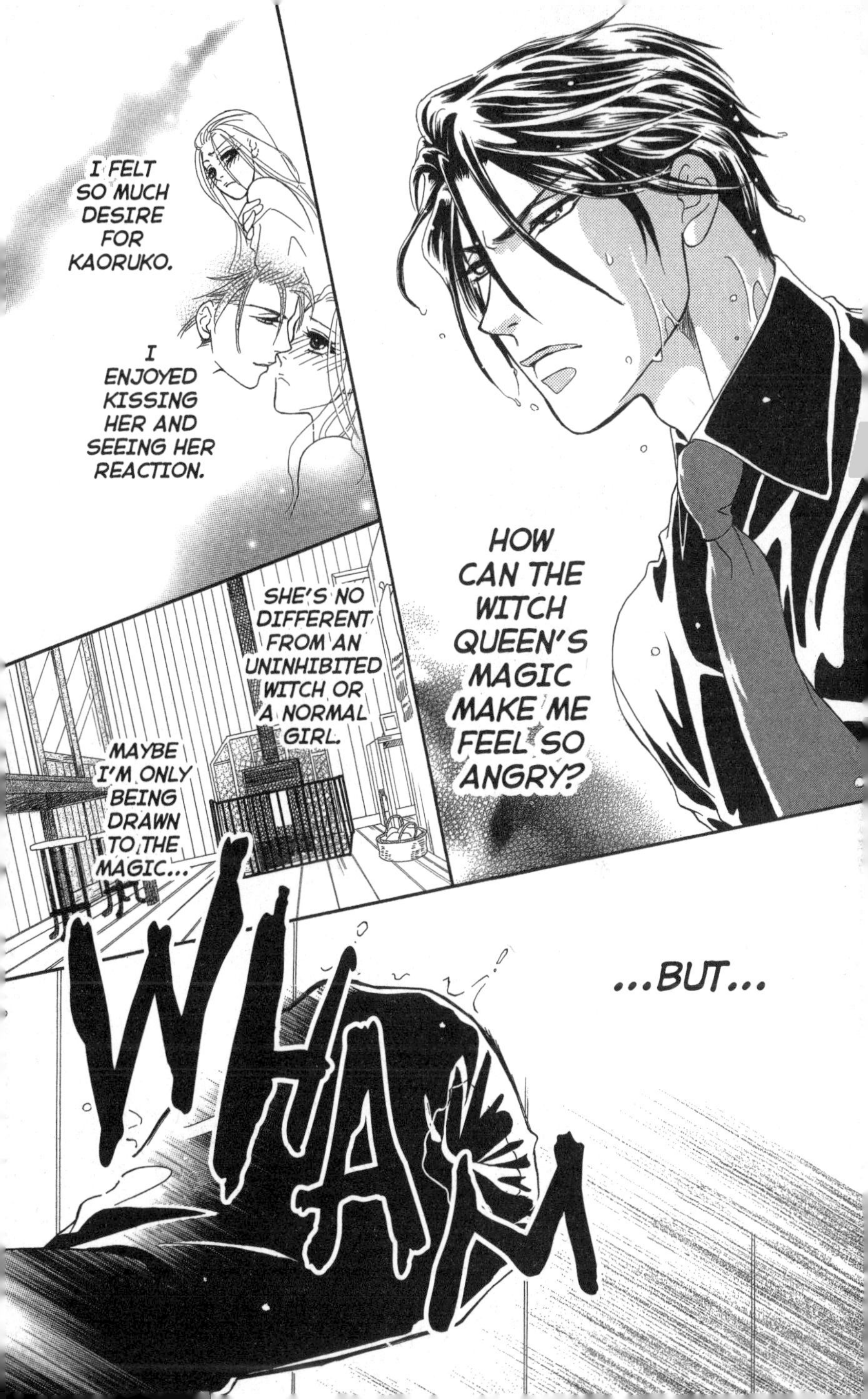
HOW CAN THE WITCH QUEEN'S MAGIC MAKE ME FEEL SO ANGRY?
I FELT SO MUCH DESIRE FOR KAORUKO.
I ENJOYED KISSING HER AND SEEING HER REACTION.
SHE'S NO DIFFERENT FROM AN UNINHIBITED WITCH OR A NORMAL GIRL.
MAYBE I'M ONLY BEING DRAWN TO THE MAGIC...
...BUT...
WHAM

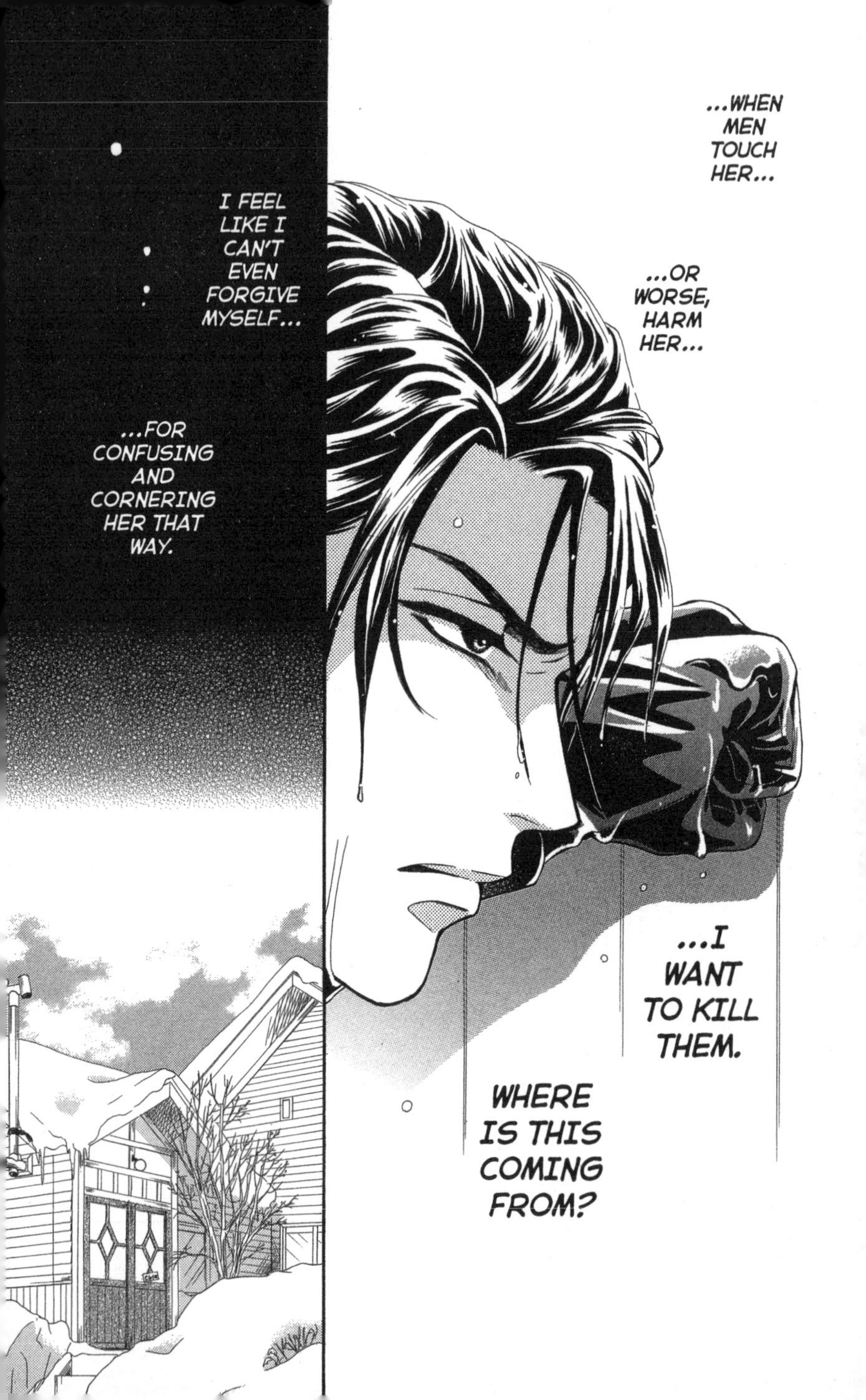
...WHEN MEN TOUCH HER...
...OR WORSE, HARM HER...
...I WANT TO KILL THEM.
WHERE IS THIS COMING FROM?
I FEEL LIKE I CAN'T EVEN FORGIVE MYSELF...
...FOR CONFUSING AND CORNERING HER THAT WAY.

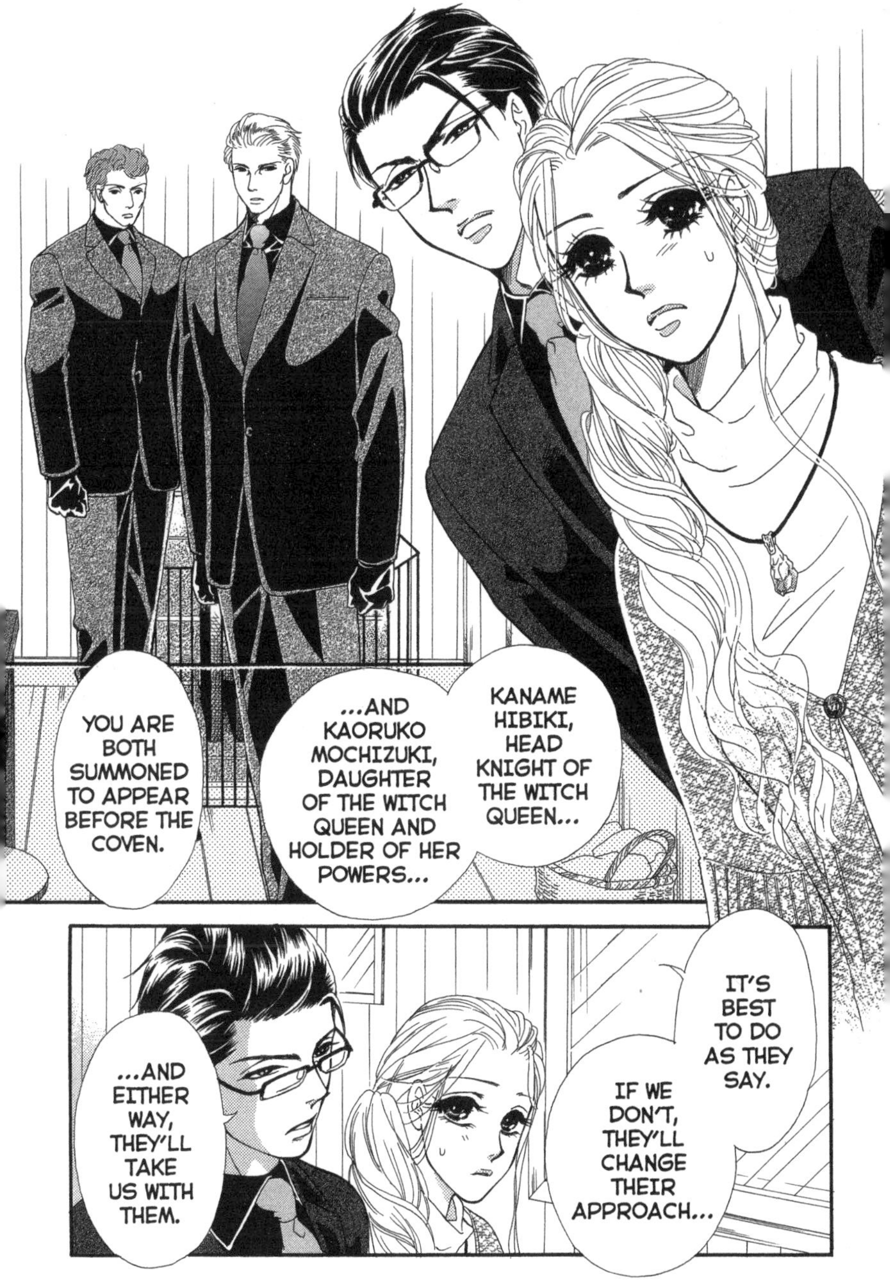
KANAME HIBIKI, HEAD KNIGHT OF THE WITCH QUEEN...
...AND KAORUKO MOCHIZUKI, DAUGHTER OF THE WITCH QUEEN AND HOLDER OF HER POWERS...
YOU ARE BOTH SUMMONED TO APPEAR BEFORE THE COVEN.
IT'S BEST TO DO AS THEY SAY.
IF WE DON'T, THEY'LL CHANGE THEIR APPROACH...
...AND EITHER WAY, THEY'LL TAKE US WITH THEM.

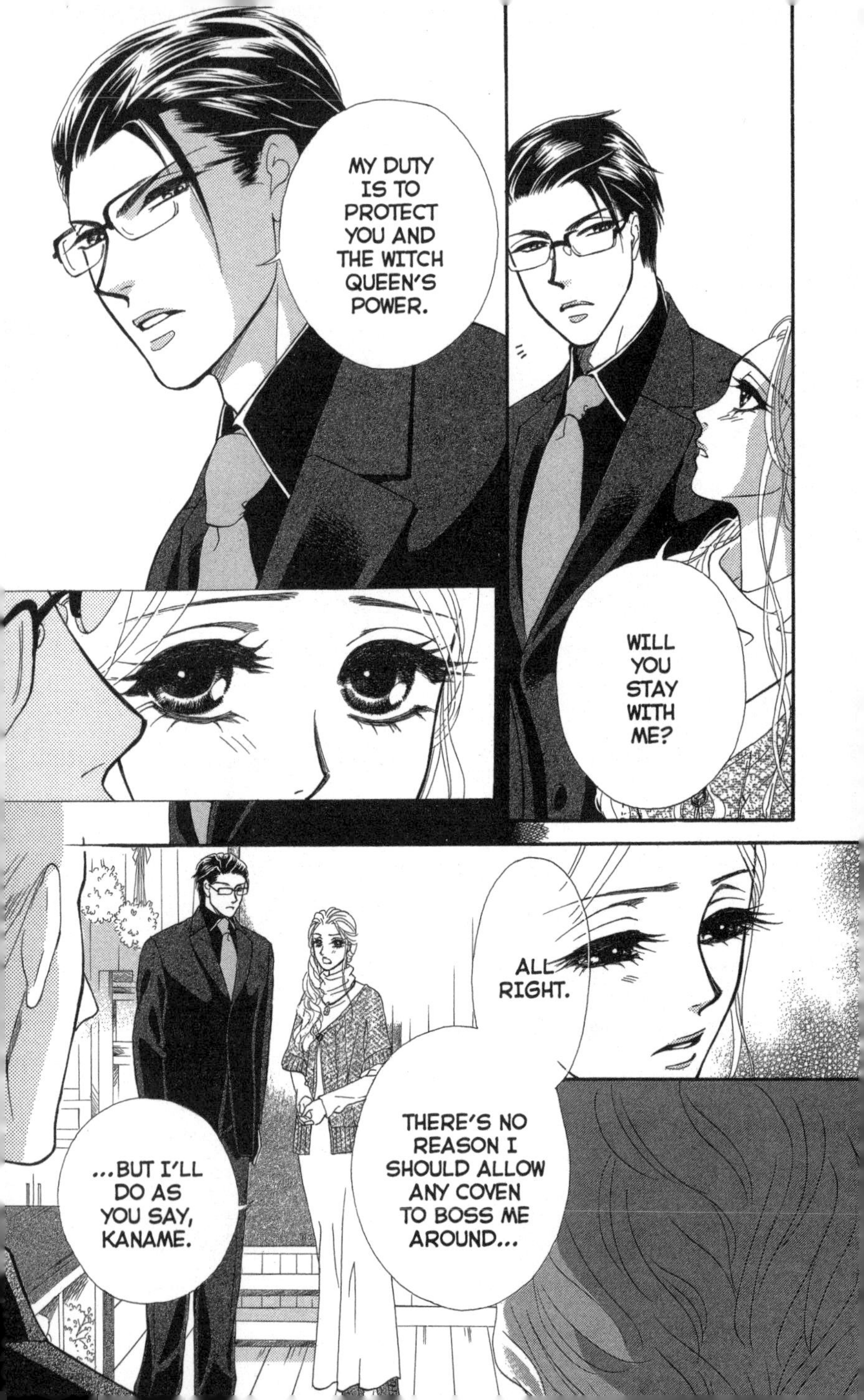
WILL YOU STAY WITH ME?
MY DUTY IS TO PROTECT YOU AND THE WITCH QUEEN'S POWER.
ALL RIGHT.
THERE'S NO REASON I SHOULD ALLOW ANY COVEN TO BOSS ME AROUND...
...BUT I'LL DO AS YOU SAY, KANAME.

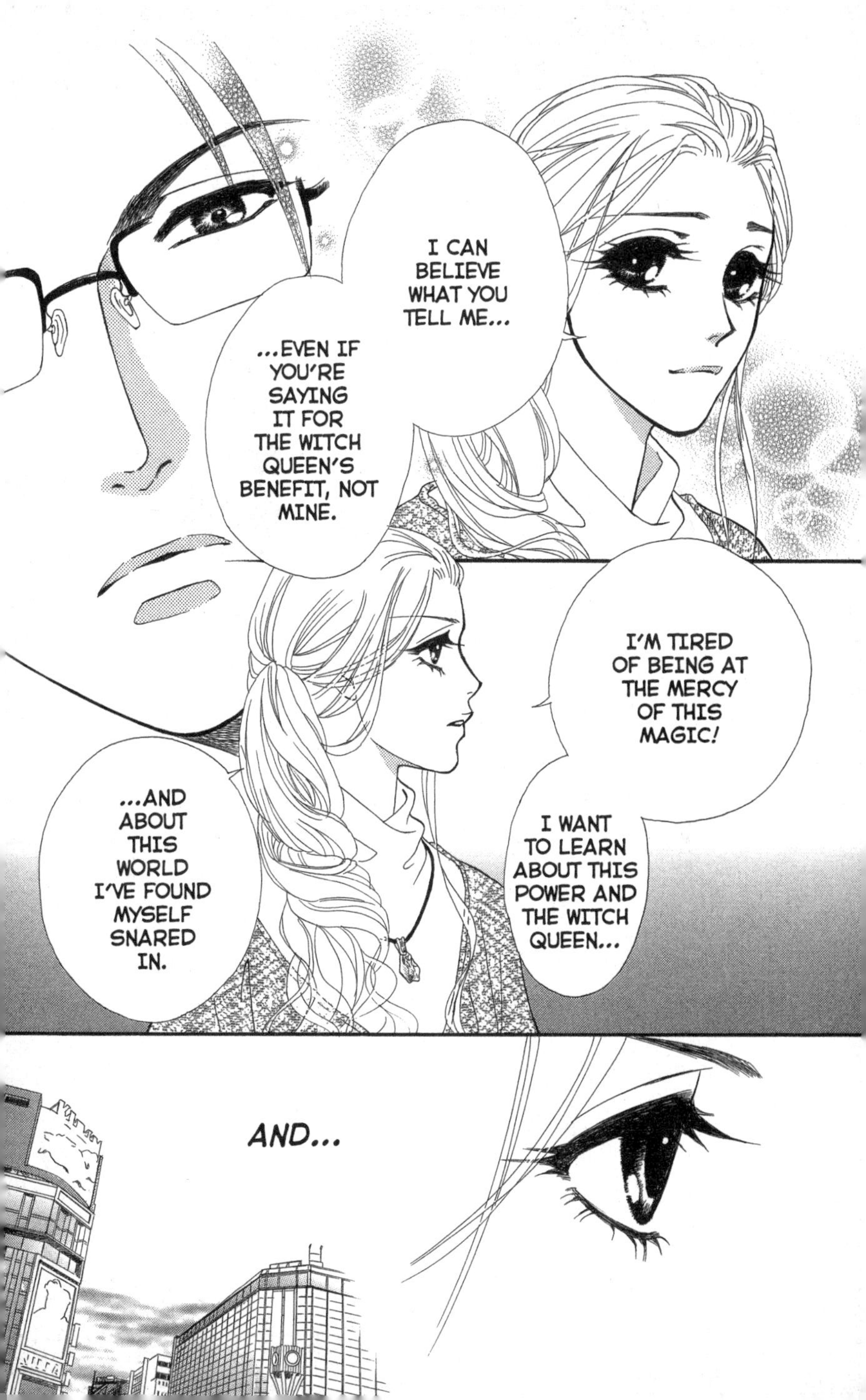
I CAN BELIEVE WHAT YOU TELL ME...
...EVEN IF YOU'RE SAYING IT FOR THE WITCH QUEEN'S BENEFIT, NOT MINE.
I'M TIRED OF BEING AT THE MERCY OF THIS MAGIC!
I WANT TO LEARN ABOUT THIS POWER AND THE WITCH QUEEN...
...AND ABOUT THIS WORLD I'VE FOUND MYSELF SNARED IN.
AND...

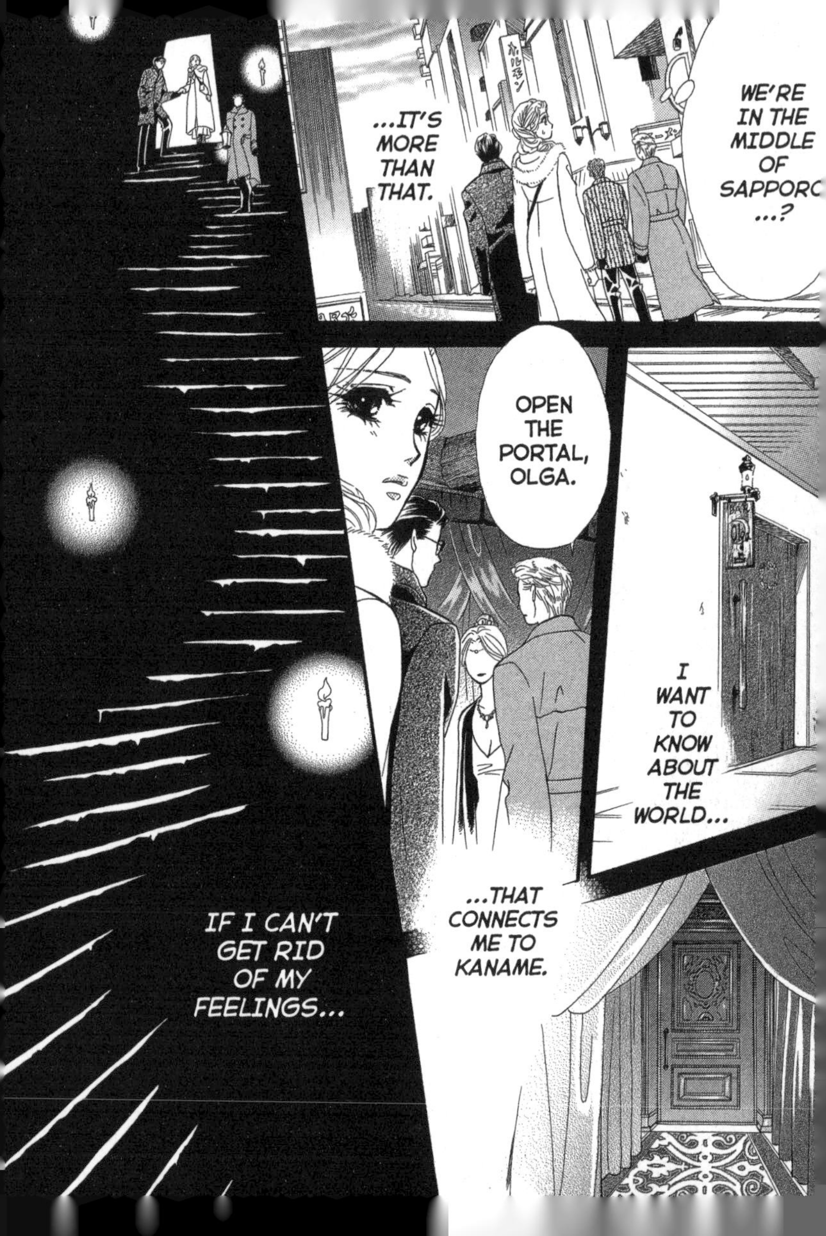
WE'RE IN THE MIDDLE OF SAPPORO ...?
...IT'S MORE THAN THAT.
I WANT TO KNOW ABOUT THE WORLD...
OPEN THE PORTAL, OLGA.
...THAT CONNECTS ME TO KANAME.
IF I CAN'T GET RID OF MY FEELINGS...

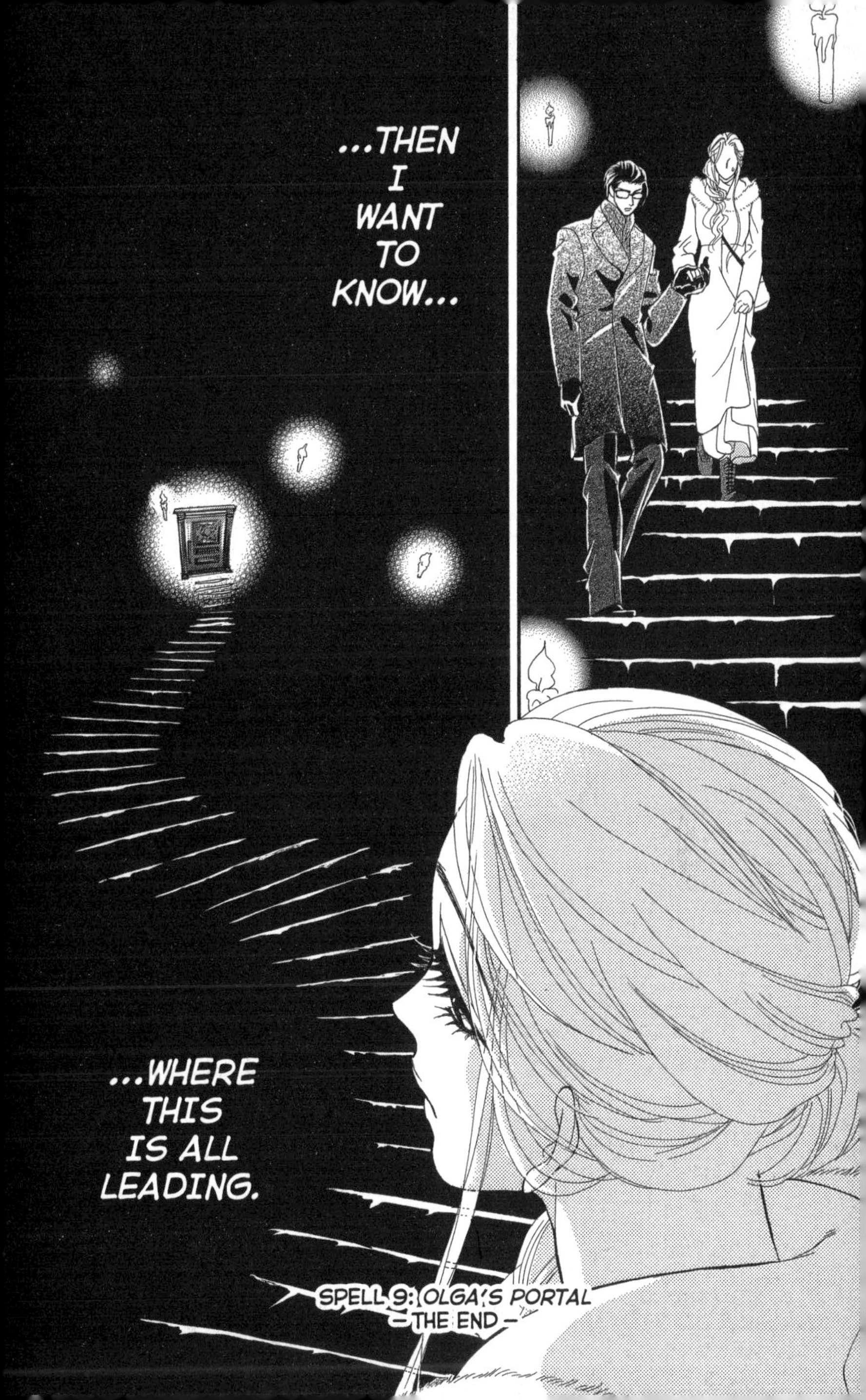
...THEN I WANT TO KNOW...
...WHERE THIS IS ALL LEADING.
SPELL 9: OLGA'S PORTAL
—THE END—

– OLGA'S PORTAL –

The whip the other knight was holding
was based on a bullwhip.

From my research, I know that it's a
beautiful work of art made of braided
leather. I feel like I wouldn't mind
owning one, even if I'd never use it.
(I don't think I would! Ha ha)

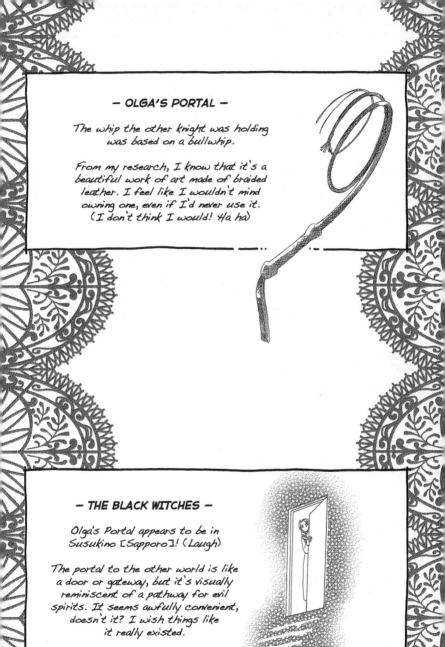

– THE BLACK WITCHES –

Olga's Portal appears to be in
Susukino [Sapporo]! (Laugh)

The portal to the other world is like
a door or gateway, but it's visually
reminiscent of a pathway for evil
spirits. It seems awfully convenient,
doesn't it? I wish things like
it really existed.

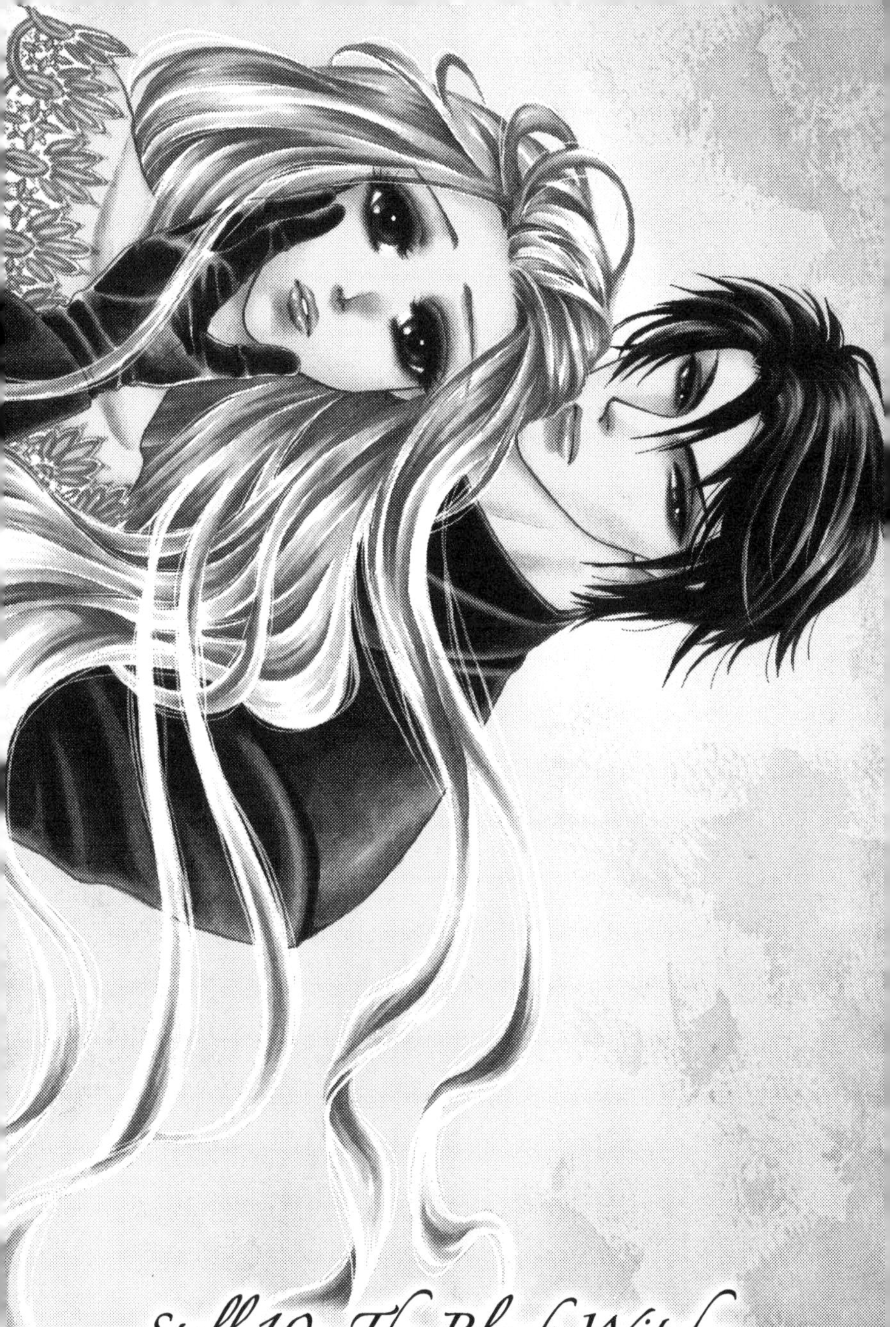

Spell 10: The Black Witches

This is the first chapter in the entire series where not a single beast makes an appearance, so I drew them here!

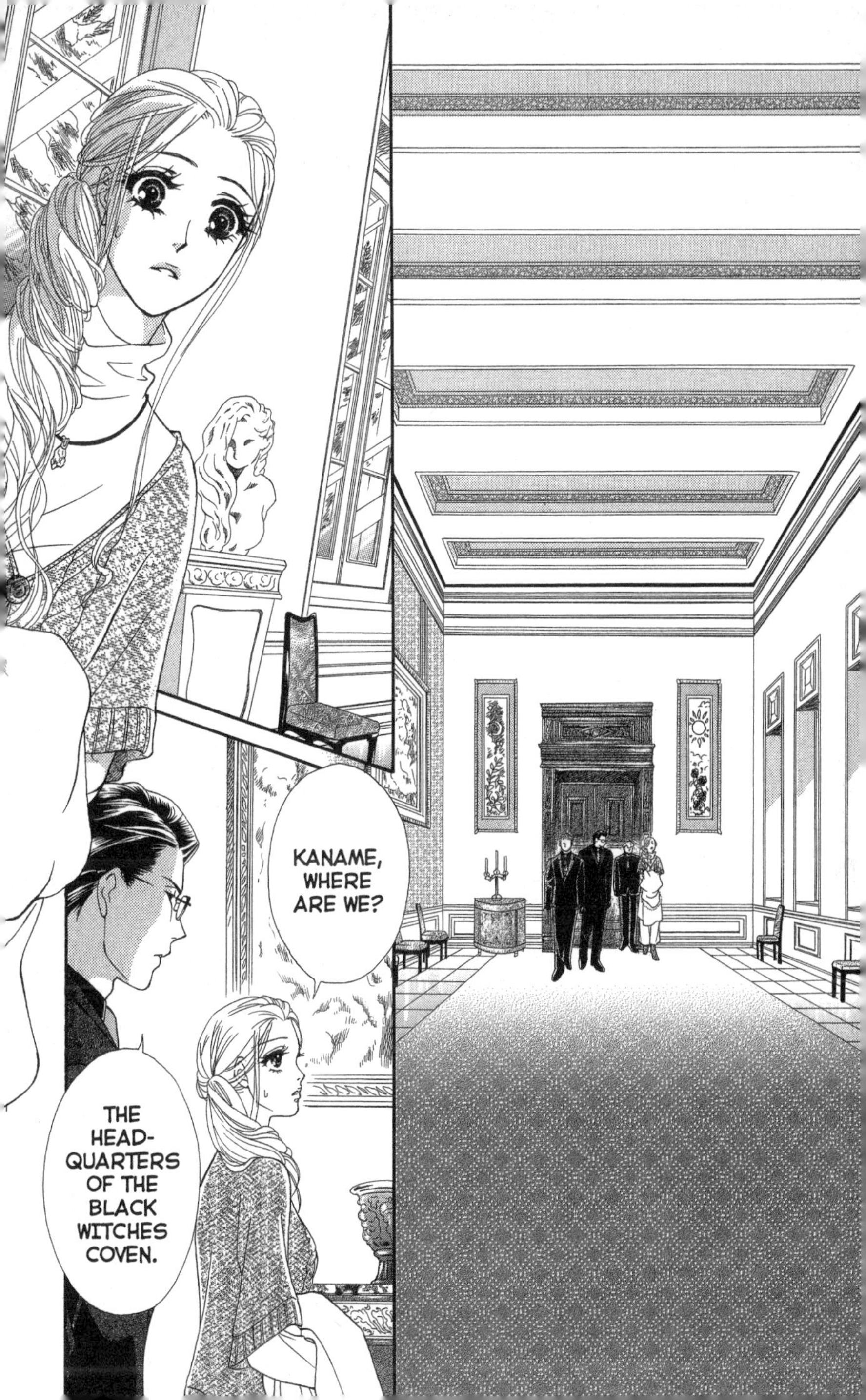
KANAME, WHERE ARE WE?
THE HEAD-QUARTERS OF THE BLACK WITCHES COVEN.

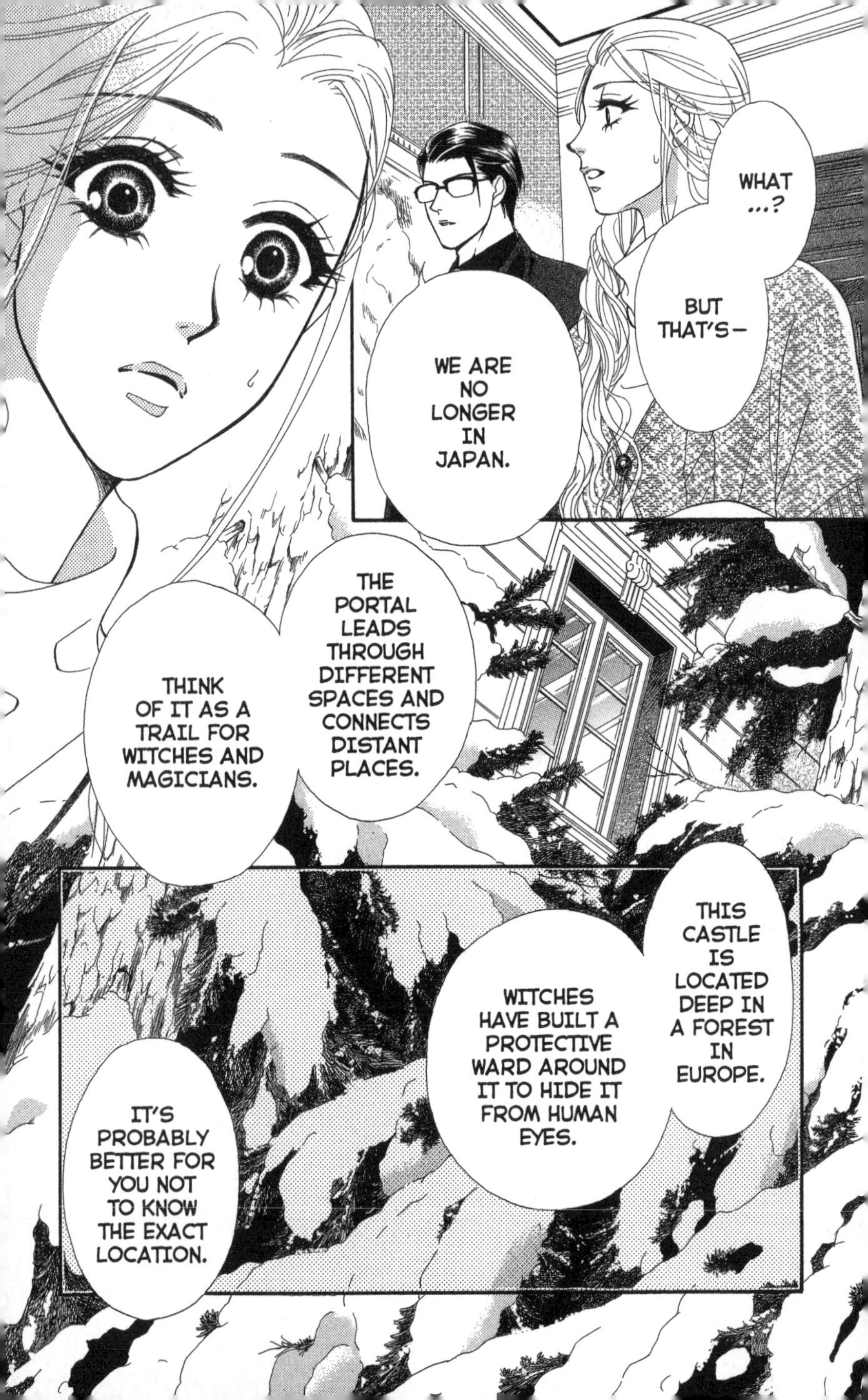
WHAT ...?
BUT THAT'S—
WE ARE NO LONGER IN JAPAN.
THE PORTAL LEADS THROUGH DIFFERENT SPACES AND CONNECTS DISTANT PLACES.
THINK OF IT AS A TRAIL FOR WITCHES AND MAGICIANS.
THIS CASTLE IS LOCATED DEEP IN A FOREST IN EUROPE.
WITCHES HAVE BUILT A PROTECTIVE WARD AROUND IT TO HIDE IT FROM HUMAN EYES.
IT'S PROBABLY BETTER FOR YOU NOT TO KNOW THE EXACT LOCATION.

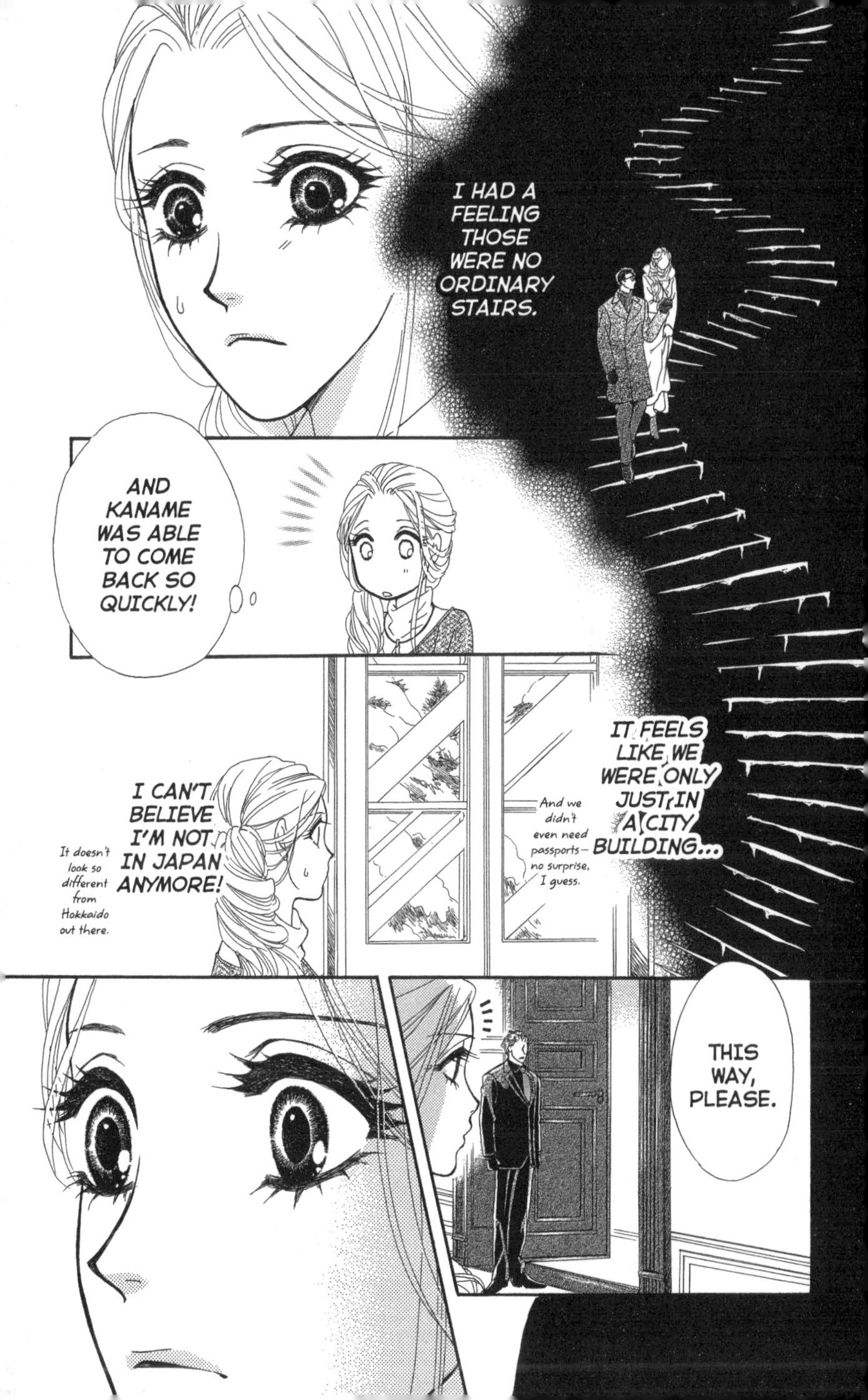
I HAD A FEELING THOSE WERE NO ORDINARY STAIRS.
IT FEELS LIKE WE WERE ONLY JUST IN A CITY BUILDING...
AND KANAME WAS ABLE TO COME BACK SO QUICKLY!
And we didn't even need passports—no surprise, I guess.
I CAN'T BELIEVE I'M NOT IN JAPAN ANYMORE!
It doesn't look so different from Hokkaido out there.
THIS WAY, PLEASE.

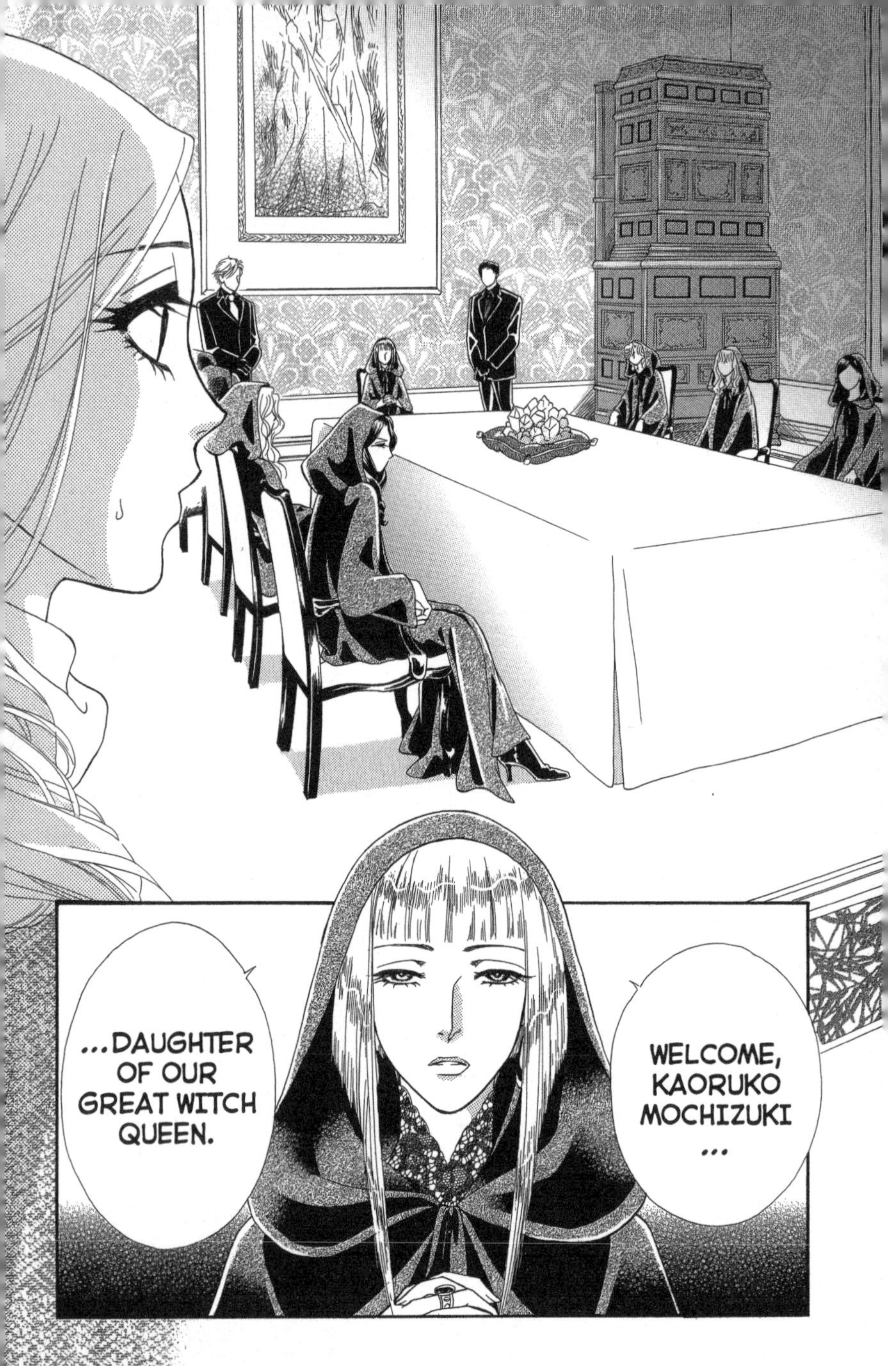
WELCOME, KAORUKO MOCHIZUKI ...
...DAUGHTER OF OUR GREAT WITCH QUEEN.

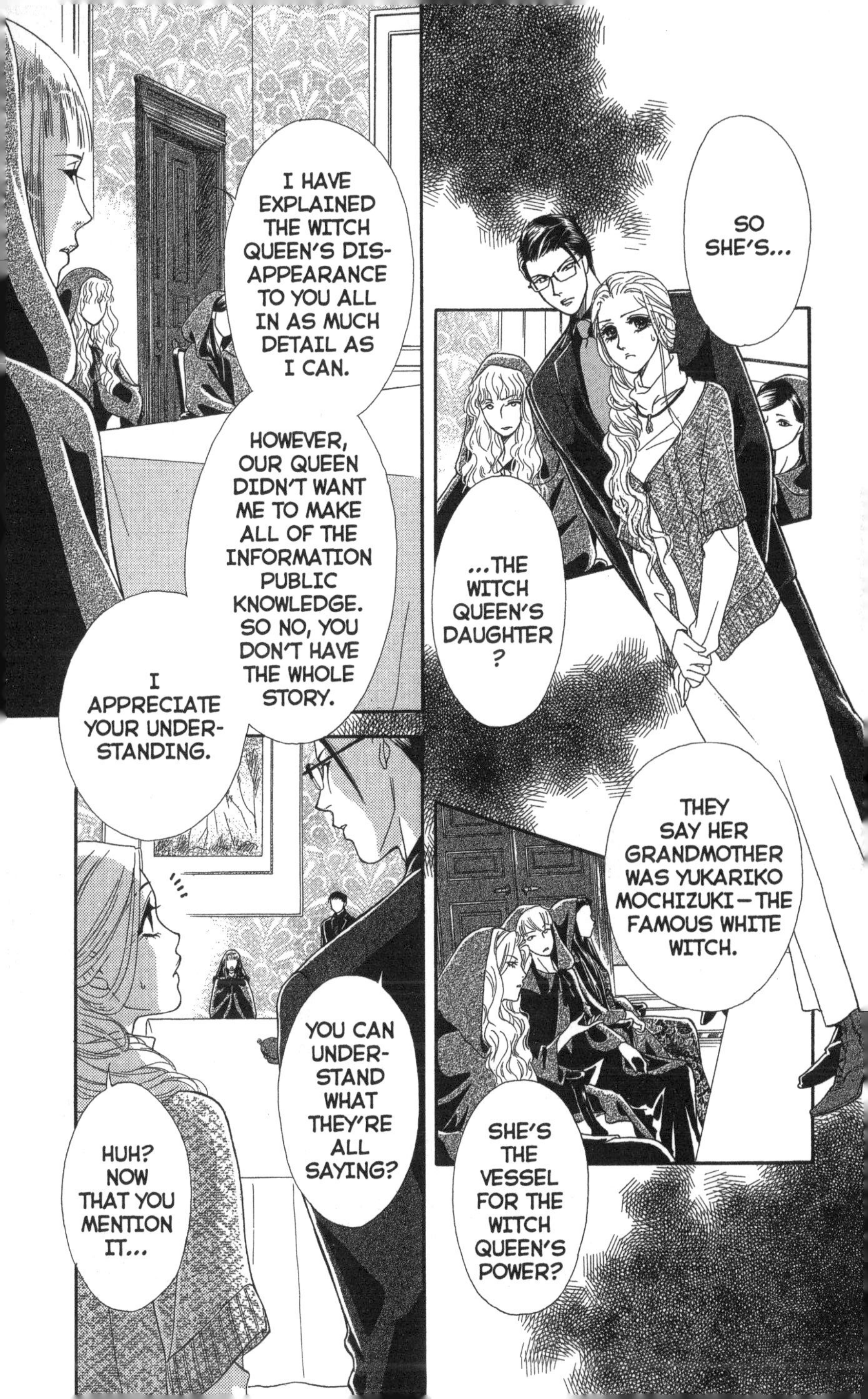
SO SHE'S...
...THE WITCH QUEEN'S DAUGHTER?
THEY SAY HER GRANDMOTHER WAS YUKARIKO MOCHIZUKI—THE FAMOUS WHITE WITCH.
SHE'S THE VESSEL FOR THE WITCH QUEEN'S POWER?
I HAVE EXPLAINED THE WITCH QUEEN'S DISAPPEARANCE TO YOU ALL IN AS MUCH DETAIL AS I CAN.
HOWEVER, OUR QUEEN DIDN'T WANT ME TO MAKE ALL OF THE INFORMATION PUBLIC KNOWLEDGE. SO NO, YOU DON'T HAVE THE WHOLE STORY.
I APPRECIATE YOUR UNDERSTANDING.
YOU CAN UNDERSTAND WHAT THEY'RE ALL SAYING?
HUH? NOW THAT YOU MENTION IT...

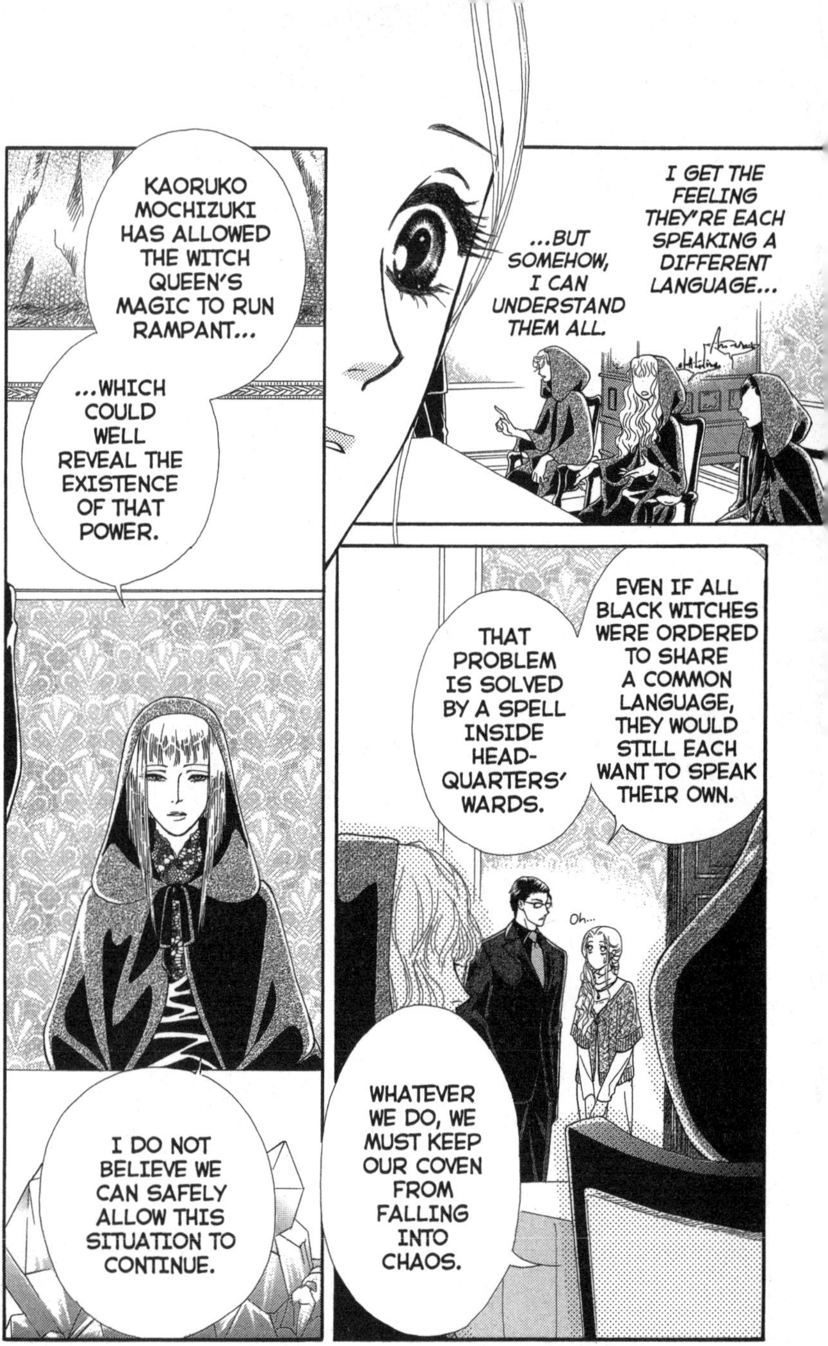
I GET THE FEELING THEY'RE EACH SPEAKING A DIFFERENT LANGUAGE...
...BUT SOMEHOW, I CAN UNDERSTAND THEM ALL.
KAORUKO MOCHIZUKI HAS ALLOWED THE WITCH QUEEN'S MAGIC TO RUN RAMPANT...
...WHICH COULD WELL REVEAL THE EXISTENCE OF THAT POWER.
EVEN IF ALL BLACK WITCHES WERE ORDERED TO SHARE A COMMON LANGUAGE, THEY WOULD STILL EACH WANT TO SPEAK THEIR OWN.
THAT PROBLEM IS SOLVED BY A SPELL INSIDE HEAD-QUARTERS' WARDS.
Oh...
WHATEVER WE DO, WE MUST KEEP OUR COVEN FROM FALLING INTO CHAOS.
I DO NOT BELIEVE WE CAN SAFELY ALLOW THIS SITUATION TO CONTINUE.

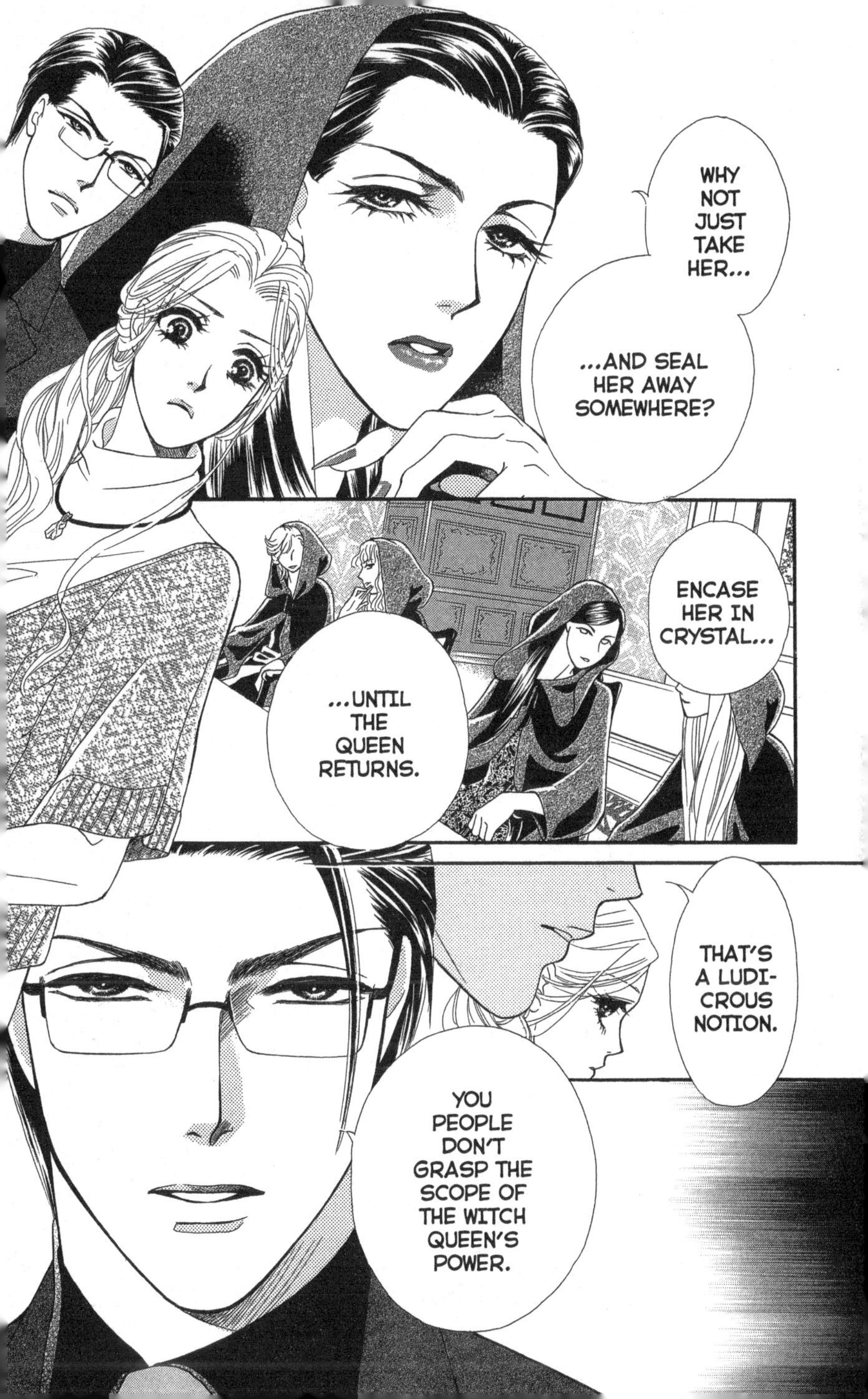
WHY NOT JUST TAKE HER...
...AND SEAL HER AWAY SOMEWHERE?
ENCASE HER IN CRYSTAL...
...UNTIL THE QUEEN RETURNS.
THAT'S A LUDI-CROUS NOTION.
YOU PEOPLE DON'T GRASP THE SCOPE OF THE WITCH QUEEN'S POWER.

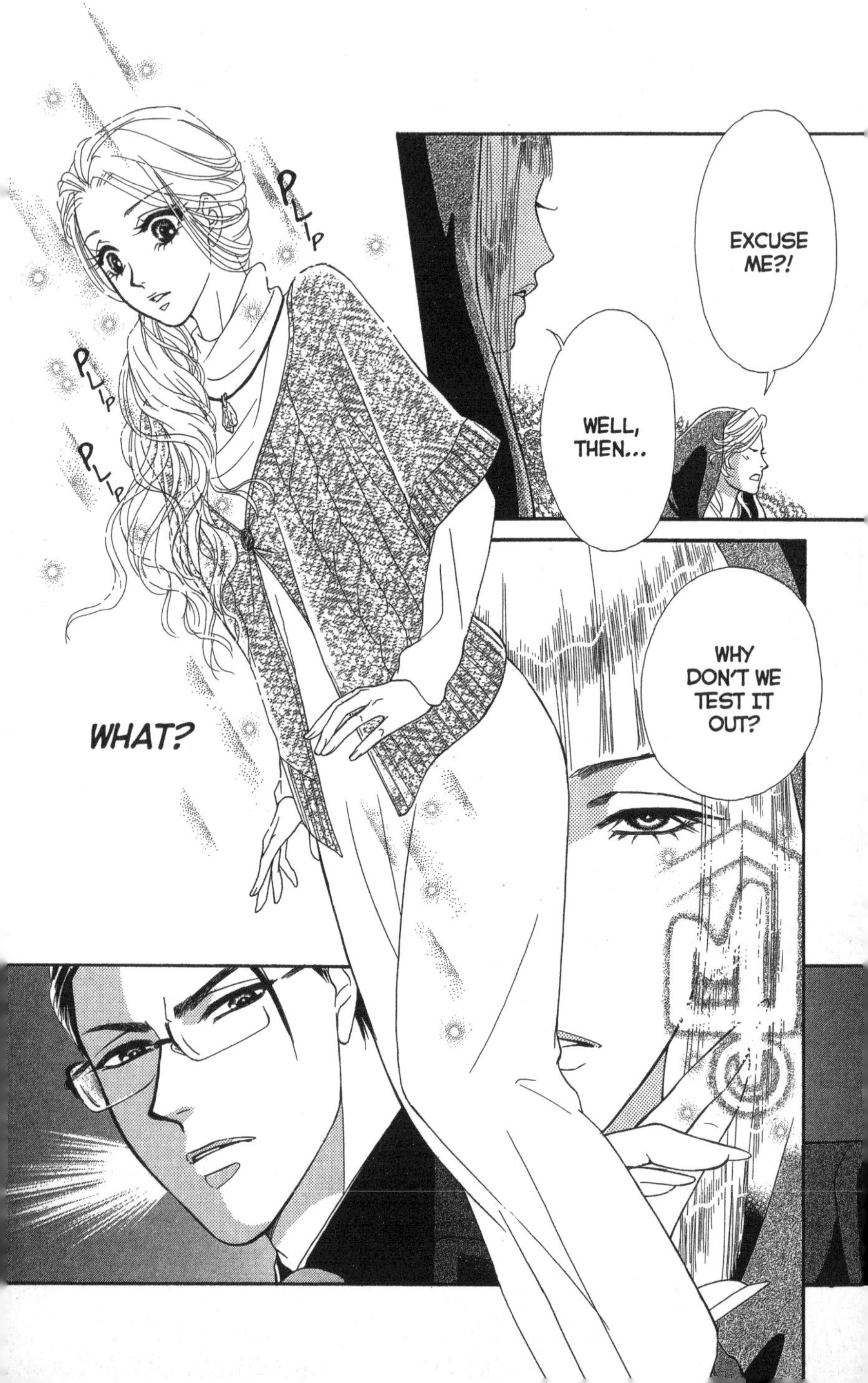
EXCUSE ME?!
WELL, THEN...
WHY DON'T WE TEST IT OUT?
PLIP
PLIP
PLIP
WHAT?

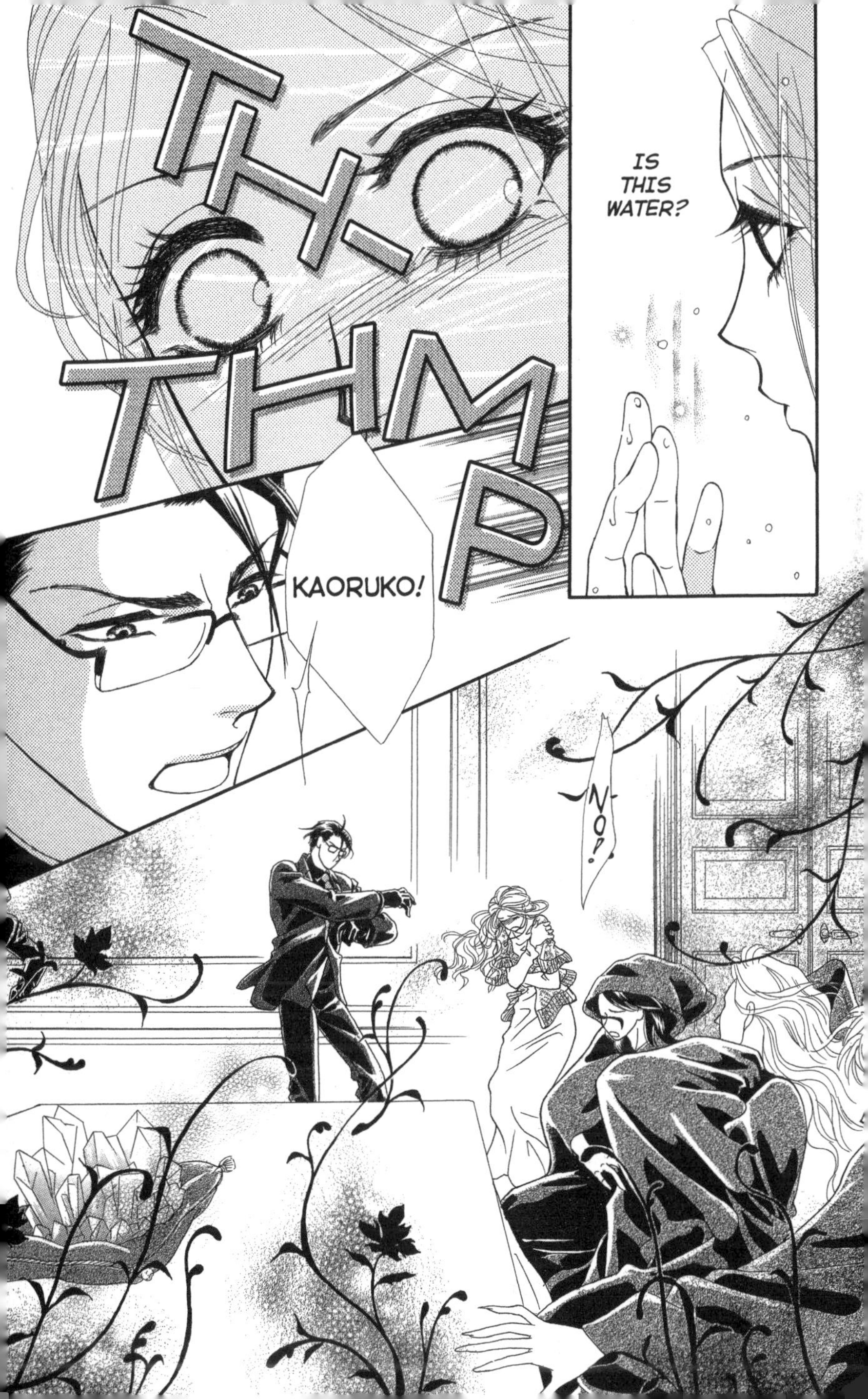
IS THIS WATER?
TH-THMP
KAORUKO!
NO!

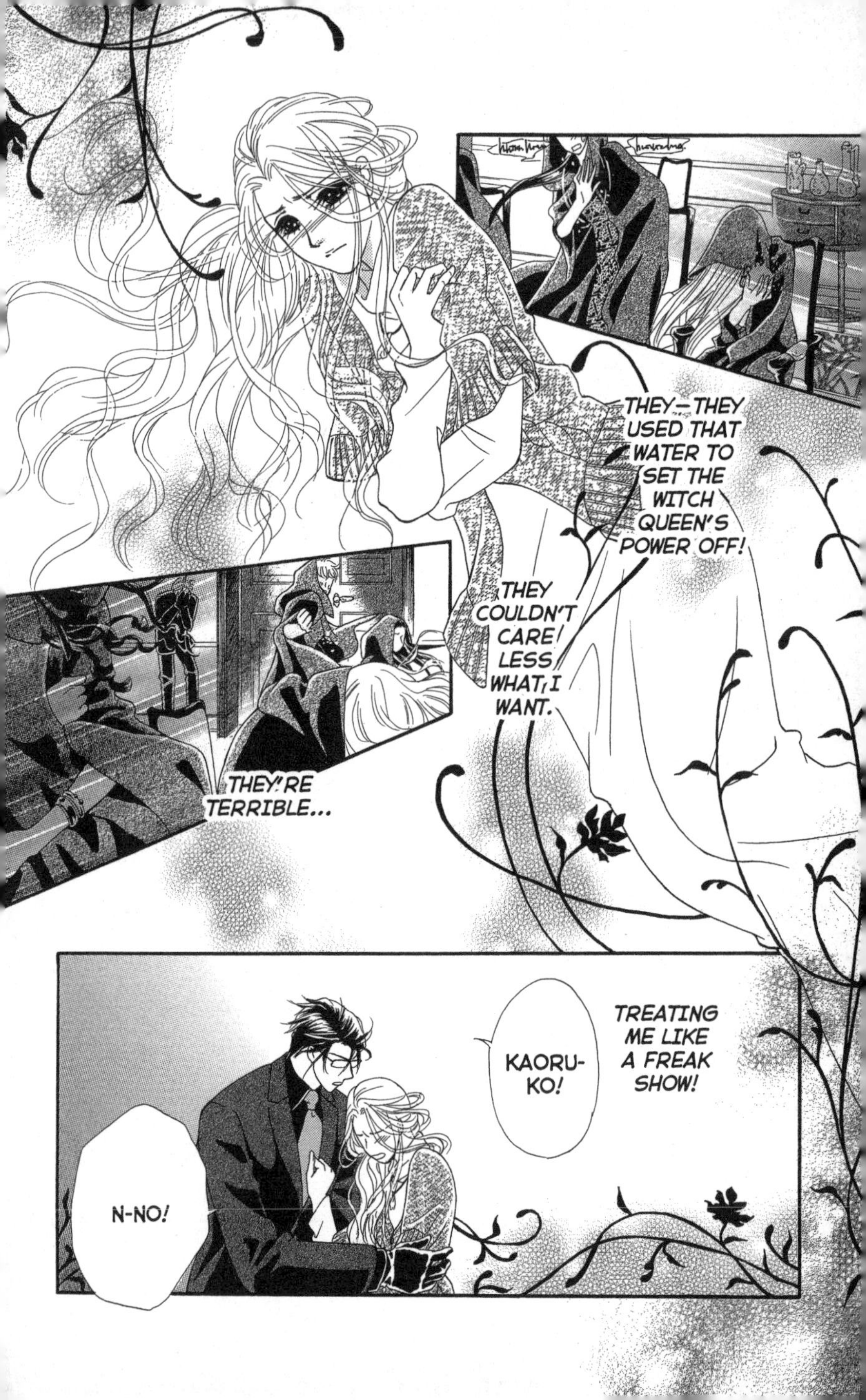
THEY—THEY USED THAT WATER TO SET THE WITCH QUEEN'S POWER OFF!
THEY COULDN'T CARE LESS WHAT I WANT.
THEY'RE TERRIBLE...
TREATING ME LIKE A FREAK SHOW!
KAORU-KO!
N-NO!

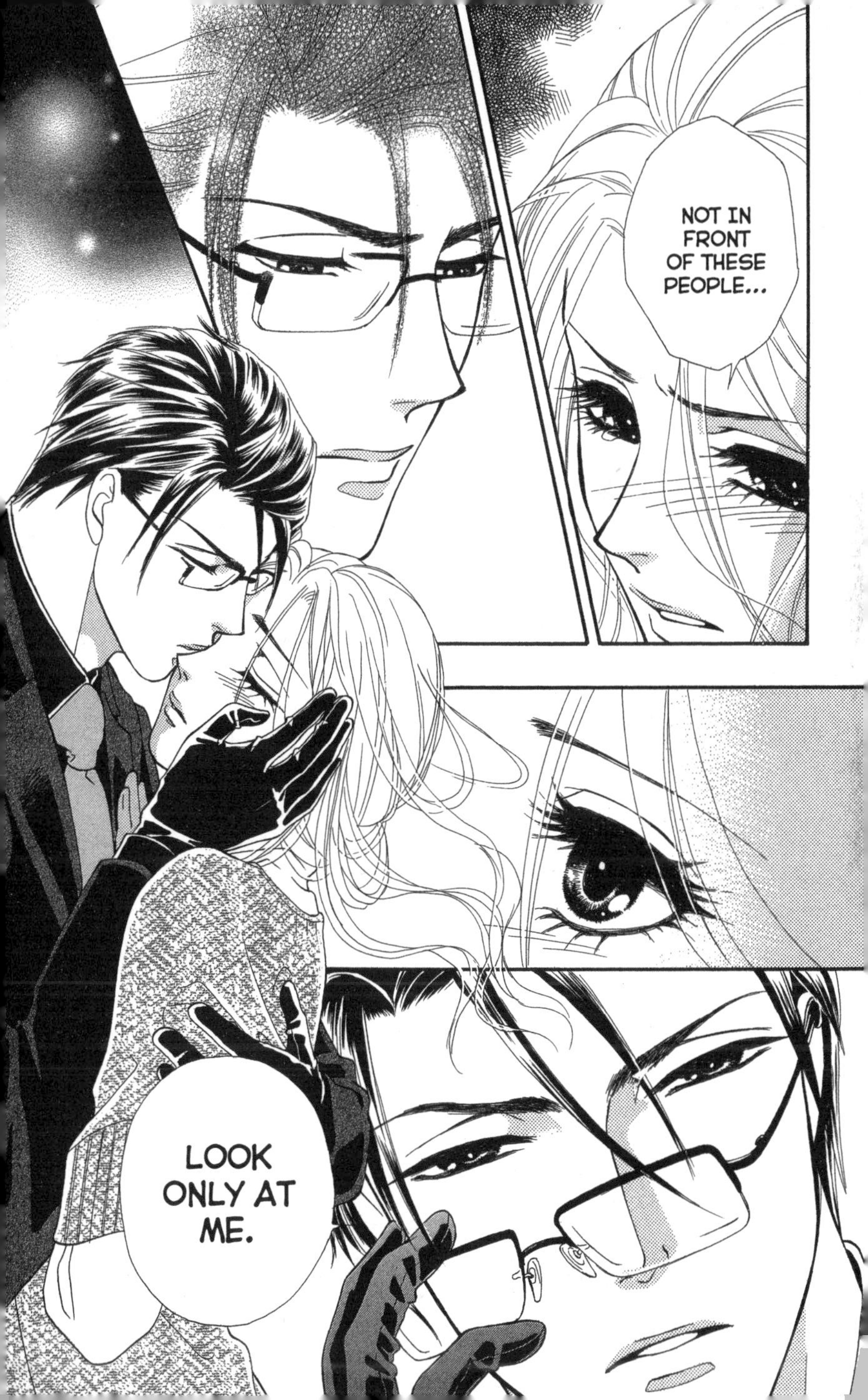
NOT IN FRONT OF THESE PEOPLE...
LOOK ONLY AT ME.

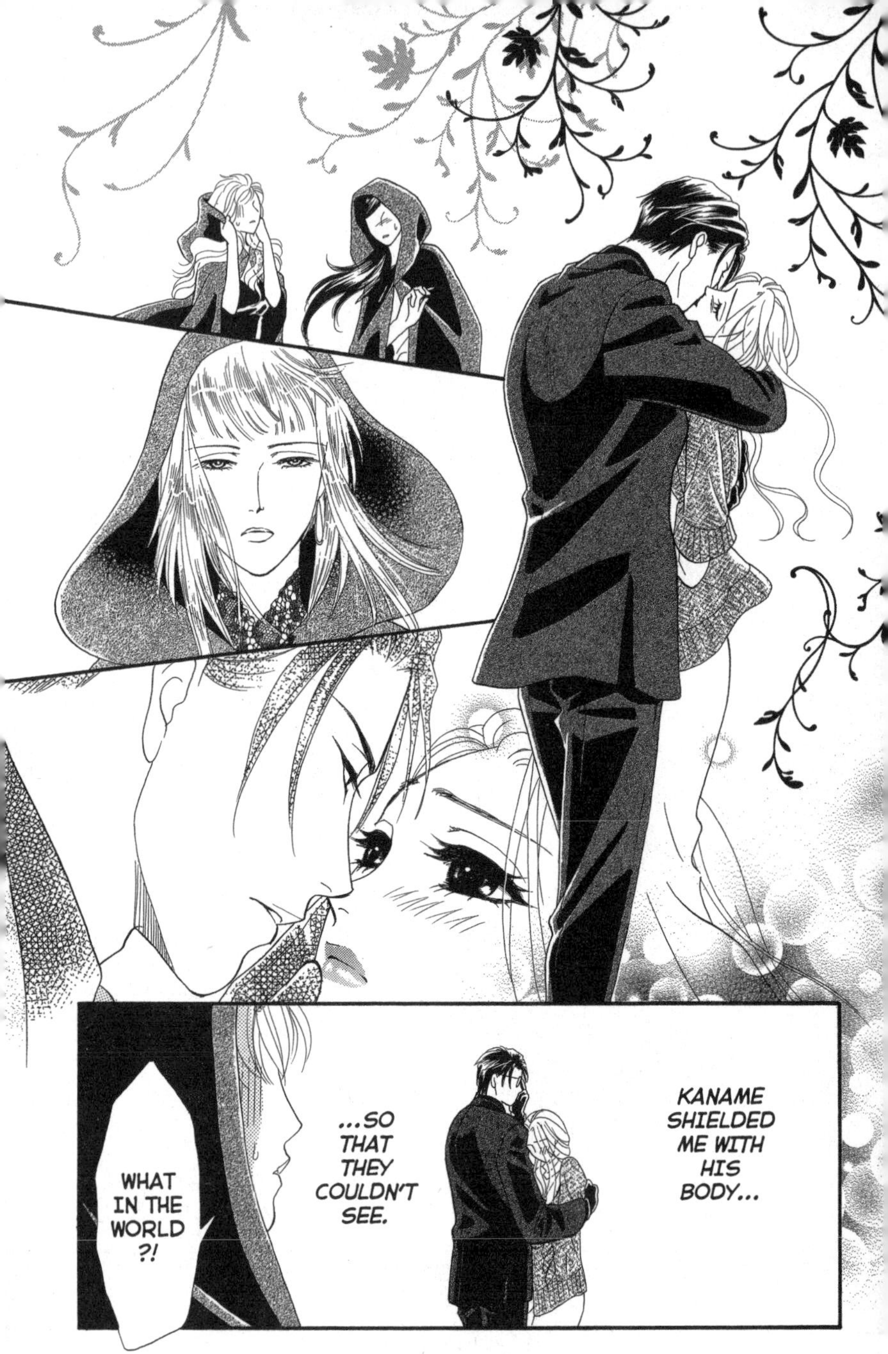
KANAME SHIELDED ME WITH HIS BODY...
...SO THAT THEY COULDN'T SEE.
WHAT IN THE WORLD?!

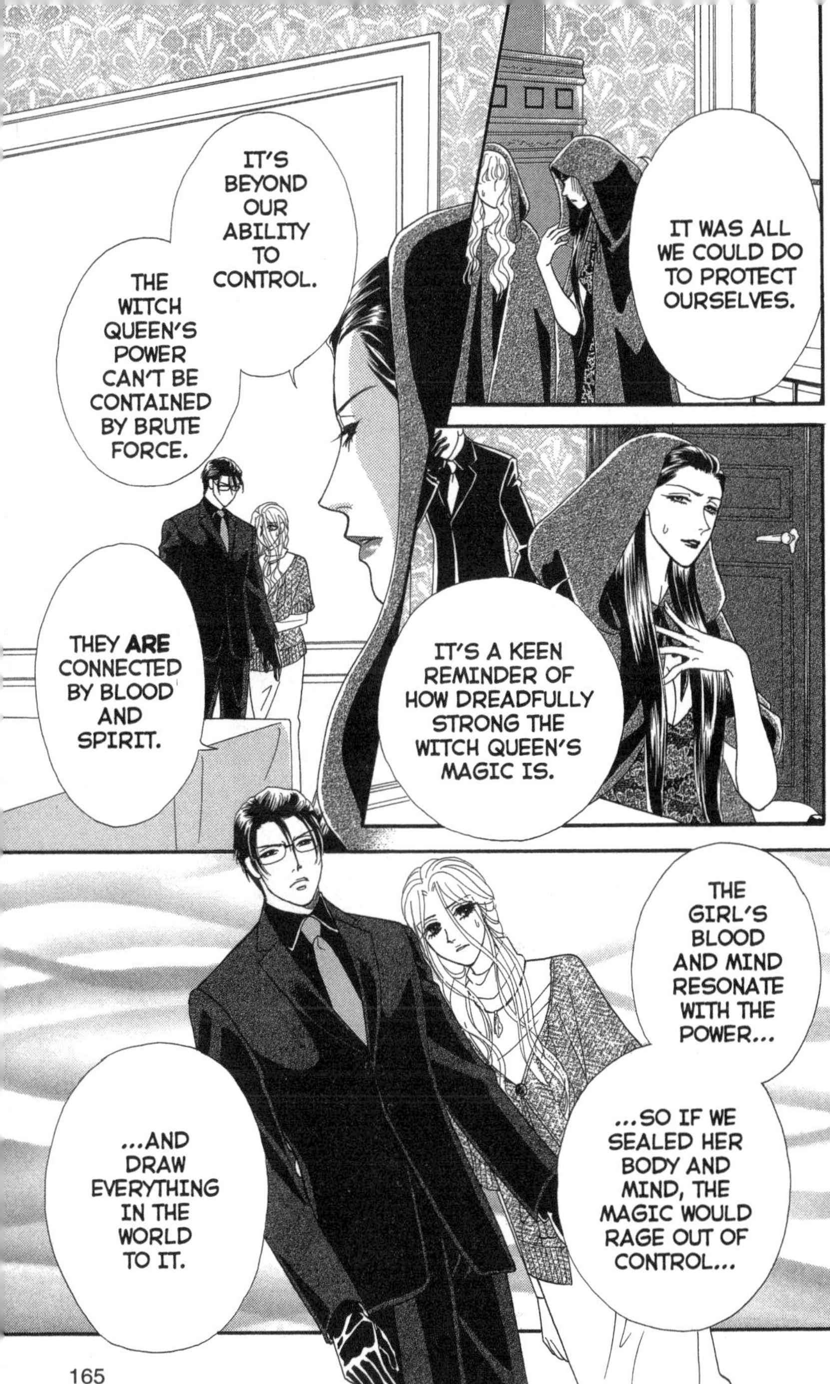
IT WAS ALL WE COULD DO TO PROTECT OURSELVES.
IT'S A KEEN REMINDER OF HOW DREADFULLY STRONG THE WITCH QUEEN'S MAGIC IS.
IT'S BEYOND OUR ABILITY TO CONTROL.
THE WITCH QUEEN'S POWER CAN'T BE CONTAINED BY BRUTE FORCE.
THEY **ARE** CONNECTED BY BLOOD AND SPIRIT.
THE GIRL'S BLOOD AND MIND RESONATE WITH THE POWER...
...SO IF WE SEALED HER BODY AND MIND, THE MAGIC WOULD RAGE OUT OF CONTROL...
...AND DRAW EVERYTHING IN THE WORLD TO IT.

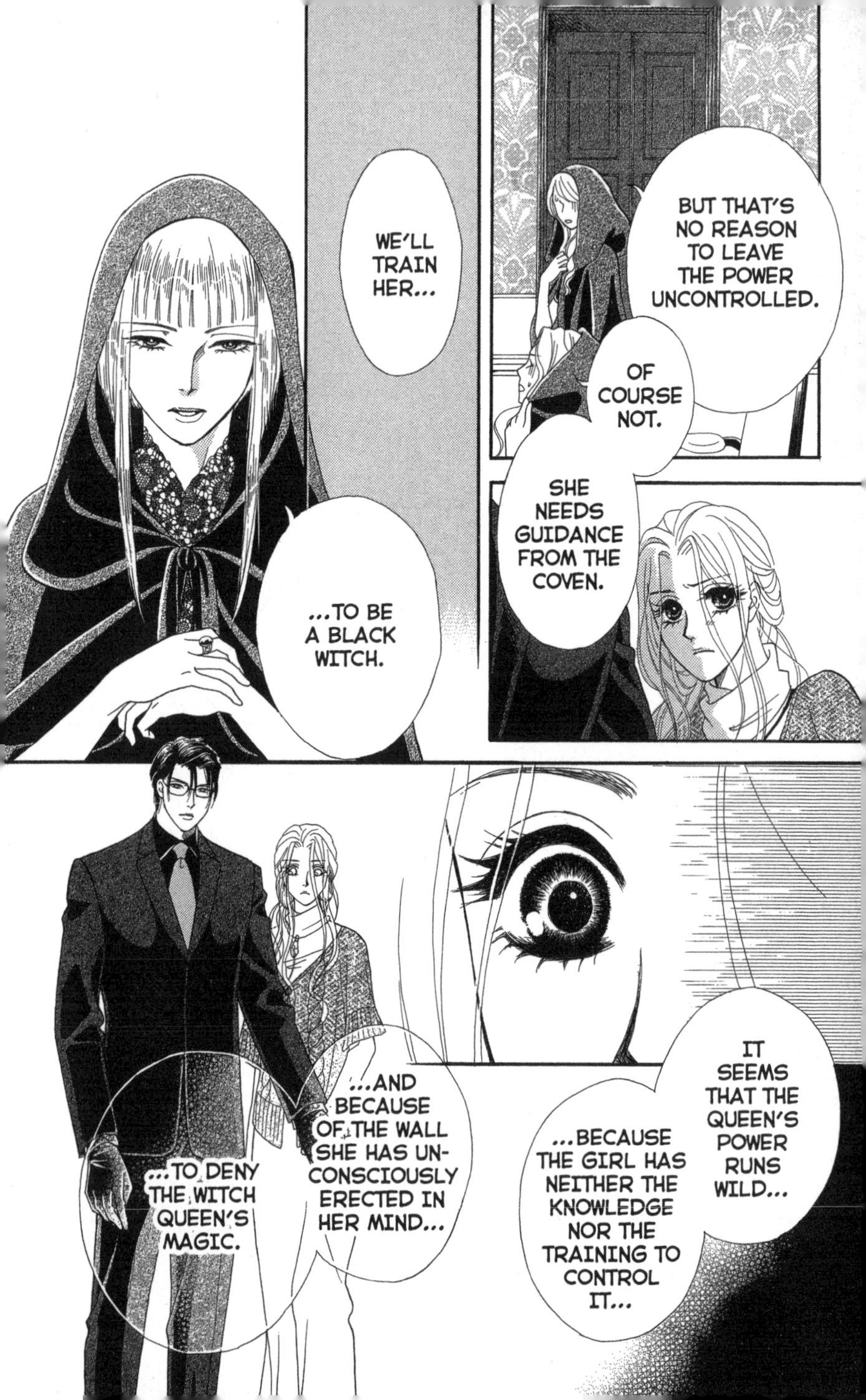
BUT THAT'S NO REASON TO LEAVE THE POWER UNCONTROLLED.
OF COURSE NOT.
SHE NEEDS GUIDANCE FROM THE COVEN.
WE'LL TRAIN HER...
...TO BE A BLACK WITCH.
IT SEEMS THAT THE QUEEN'S POWER RUNS WILD...
...BECAUSE THE GIRL HAS NEITHER THE KNOWLEDGE NOR THE TRAINING TO CONTROL IT...
...AND BECAUSE OF THE WALL SHE HAS UN-CONSCIOUSLY ERECTED IN HER MIND...
...TO DENY THE WITCH QUEEN'S MAGIC.

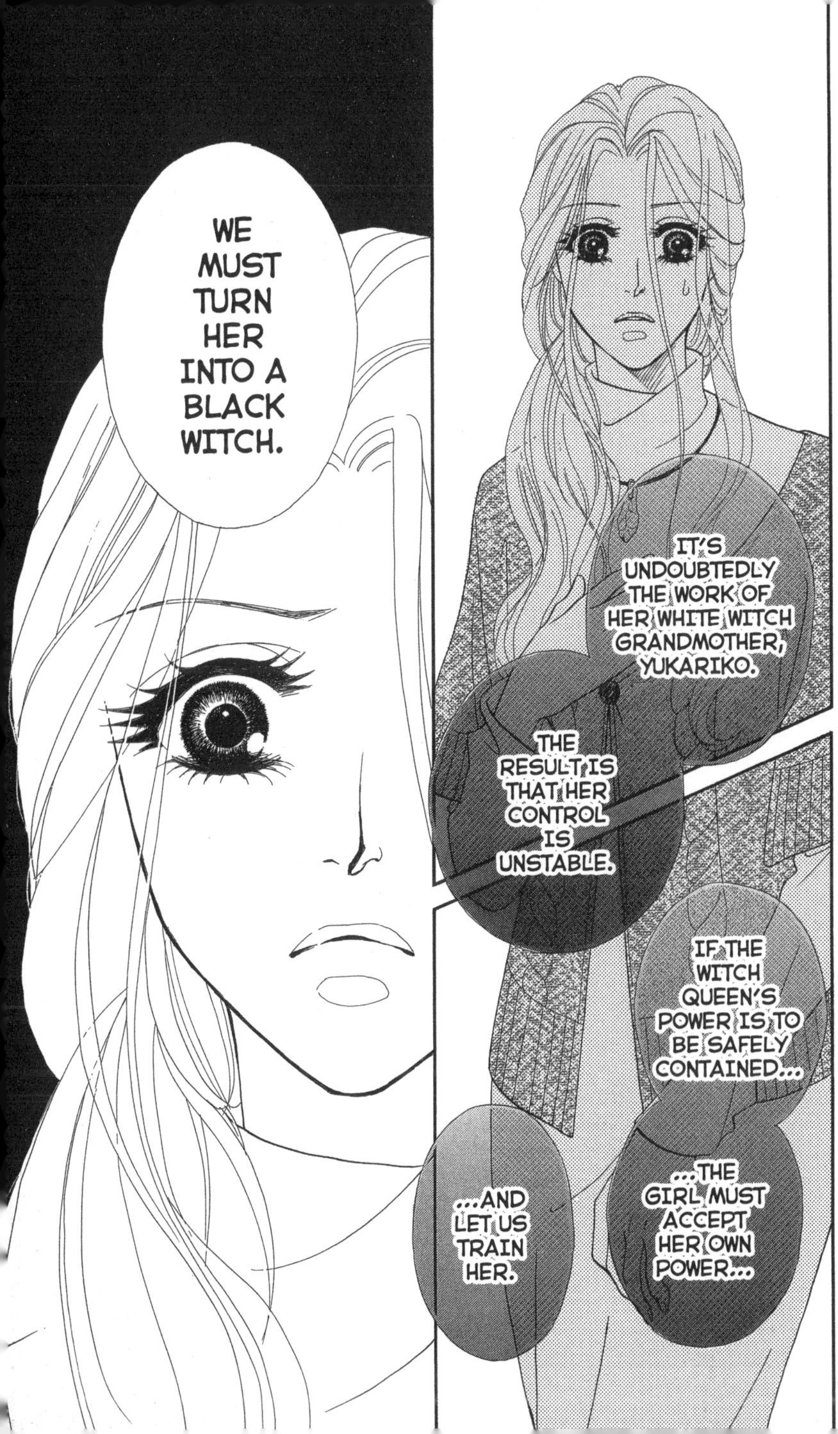

IT'S UNDOUBTEDLY THE WORK OF HER WHITE WITCH GRANDMOTHER, YUKARIKO.
THE RESULT IS THAT HER CONTROL IS UNSTABLE.
IF THE WITCH QUEEN'S POWER IS TO BE SAFELY CONTAINED...
...THE GIRL MUST ACCEPT HER OWN POWER...
...AND LET US TRAIN HER.
WE MUST TURN HER INTO A BLACK WITCH.

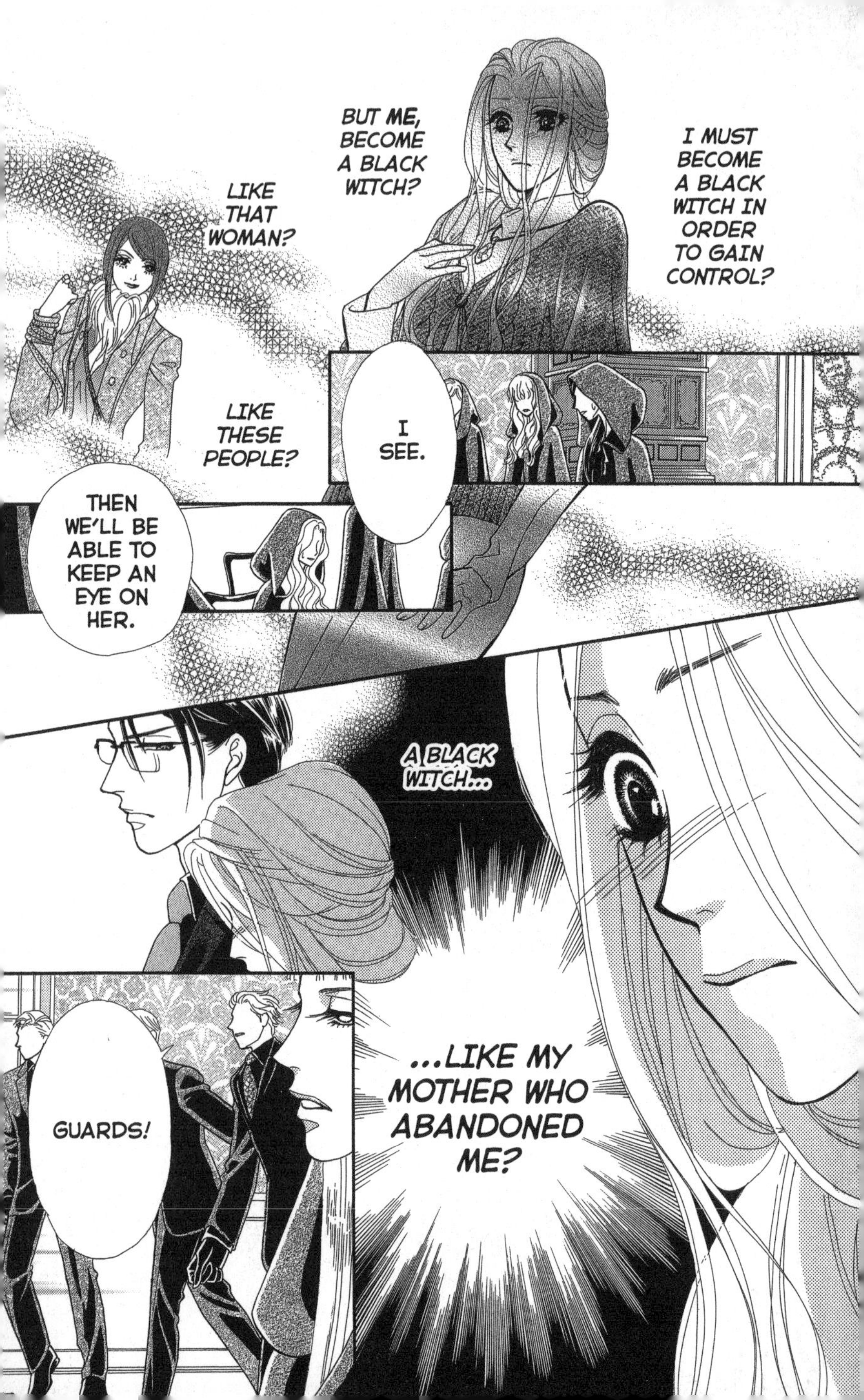
I MUST BECOME A BLACK WITCH IN ORDER TO GAIN CONTROL?
BUT ME, BECOME A BLACK WITCH?
LIKE THAT WOMAN?
I SEE.
LIKE THESE PEOPLE?
THEN WE'LL BE ABLE TO KEEP AN EYE ON HER.
A BLACK WITCH...
...LIKE MY MOTHER WHO ABANDONED ME?
GUARDS!

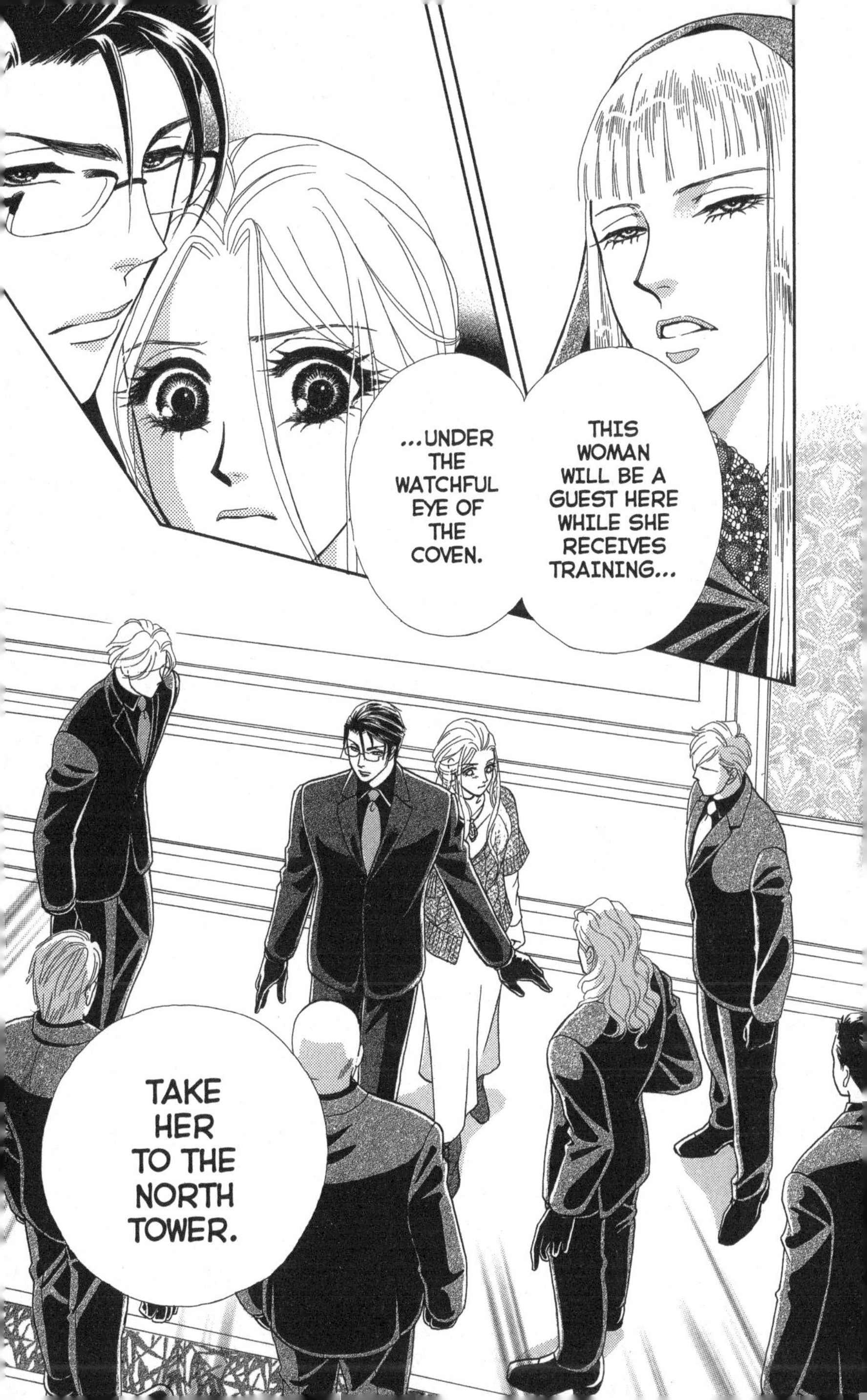
THIS WOMAN WILL BE A GUEST HERE WHILE SHE RECEIVES TRAINING...
...UNDER THE WATCHFUL EYE OF THE COVEN.
TAKE HER TO THE NORTH TOWER.

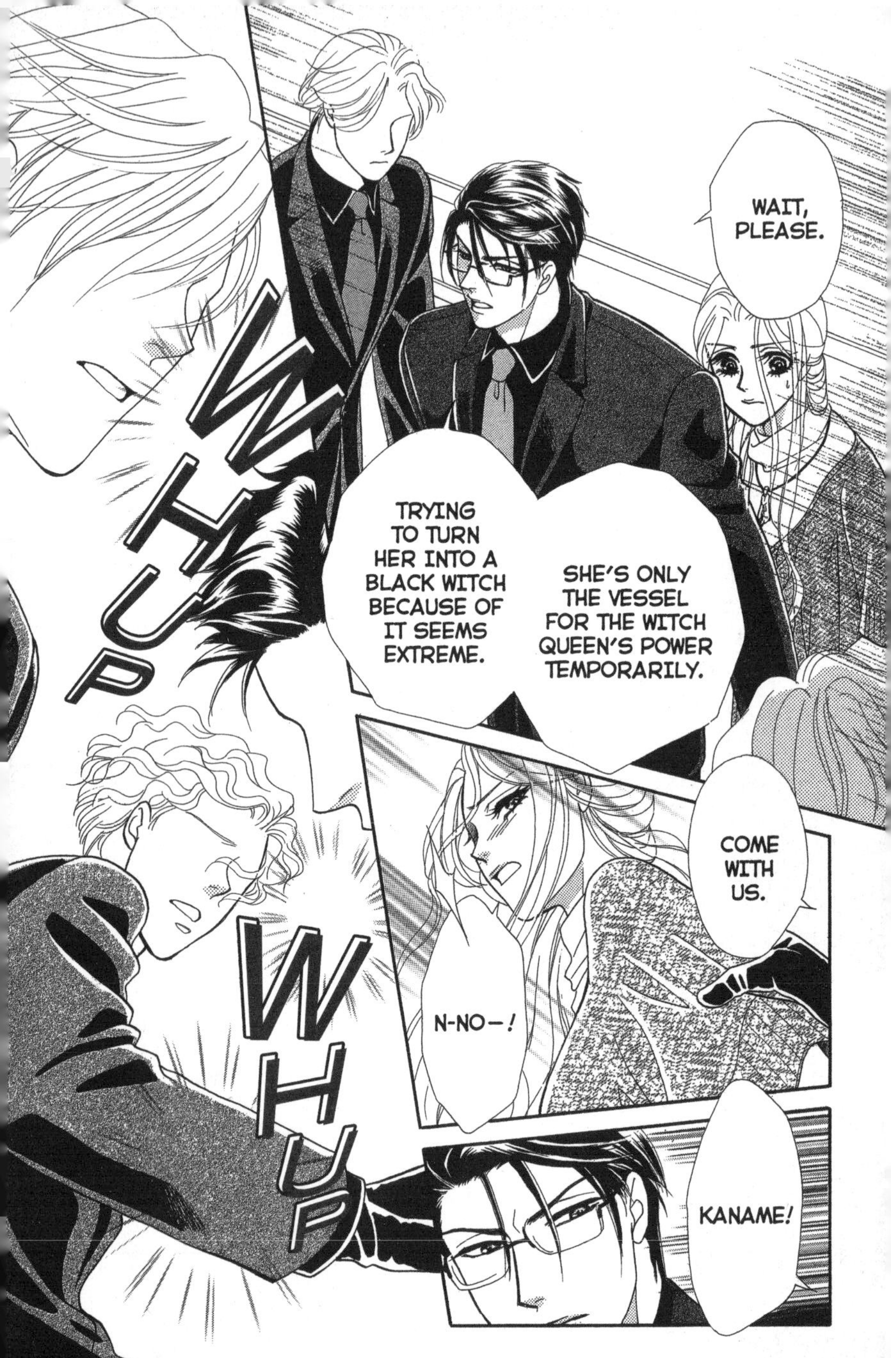
WAIT, PLEASE.
SHE'S ONLY THE VESSEL FOR THE WITCH QUEEN'S POWER TEMPORARILY.
TRYING TO TURN HER INTO A BLACK WITCH BECAUSE OF IT SEEMS EXTREME.
COME WITH US.
N-NO—!
KANAME!
WHUP
WHUP

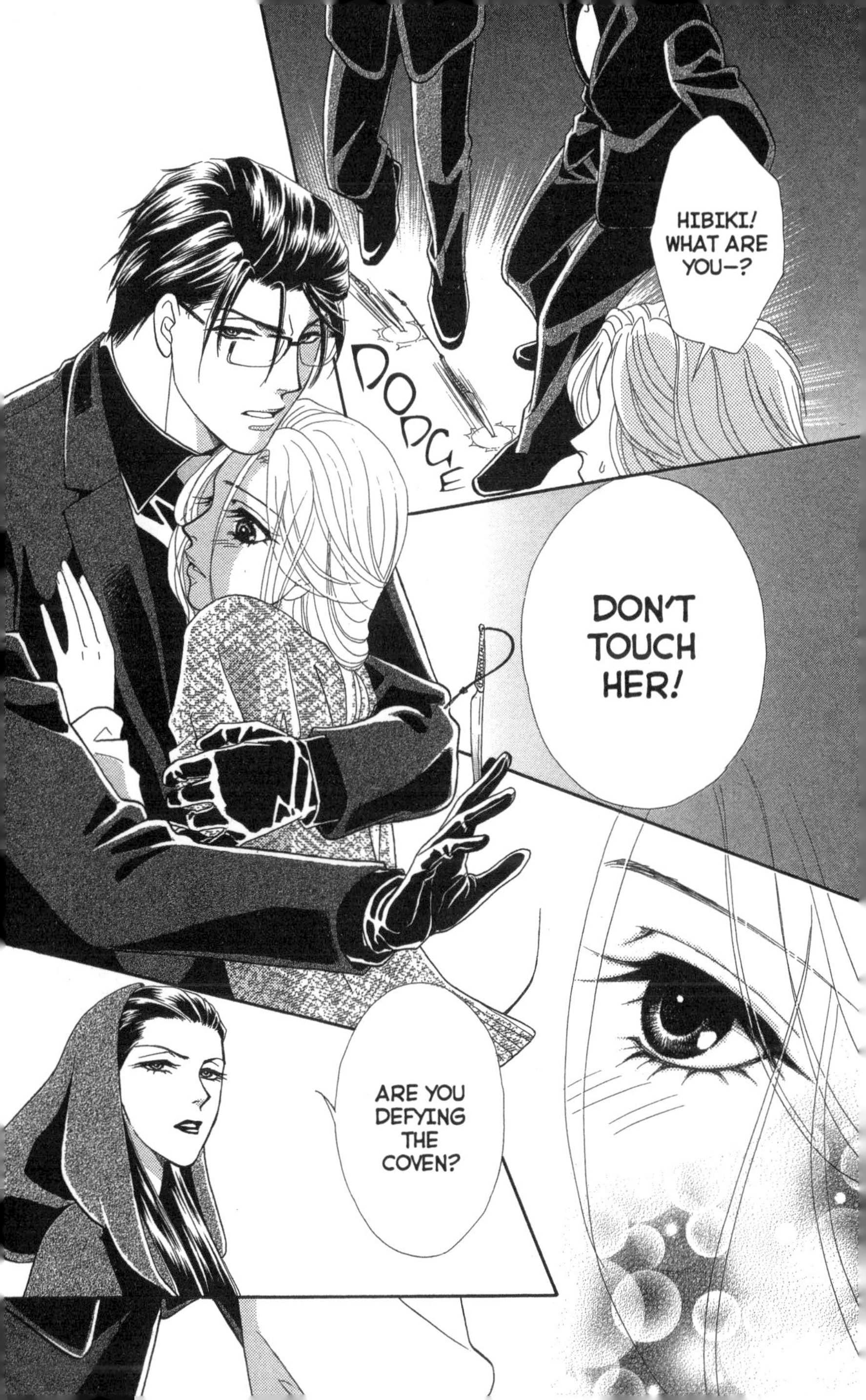
HIBIKI! WHAT ARE YOU—?
DODGE
DON'T TOUCH HER!
ARE YOU DEFYING THE COVEN?

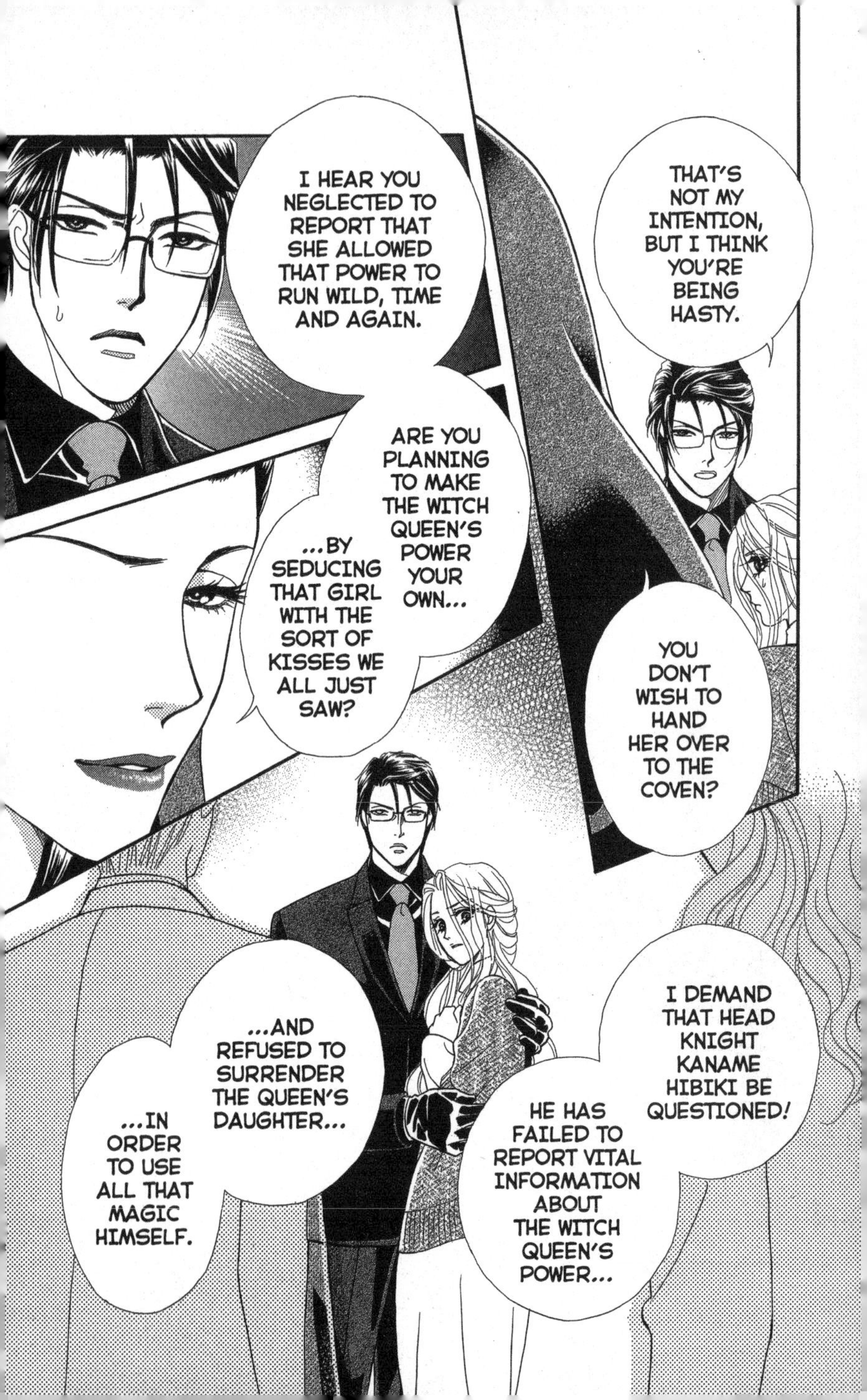
THAT'S NOT MY INTENTION, BUT I THINK YOU'RE BEING HASTY.
YOU DON'T WISH TO HAND HER OVER TO THE COVEN?
I HEAR YOU NEGLECTED TO REPORT THAT SHE ALLOWED THAT POWER TO RUN WILD, TIME AND AGAIN.
ARE YOU PLANNING TO MAKE THE WITCH QUEEN'S POWER YOUR OWN...
...BY SEDUCING THAT GIRL WITH THE SORT OF KISSES WE ALL JUST SAW?
I DEMAND THAT HEAD KNIGHT KANAME HIBIKI BE QUESTIONED!
HE HAS FAILED TO REPORT VITAL INFORMATION ABOUT THE WITCH QUEEN'S POWER...
...AND REFUSED TO SURRENDER THE QUEEN'S DAUGHTER...
...IN ORDER TO USE ALL THAT MAGIC HIMSELF.

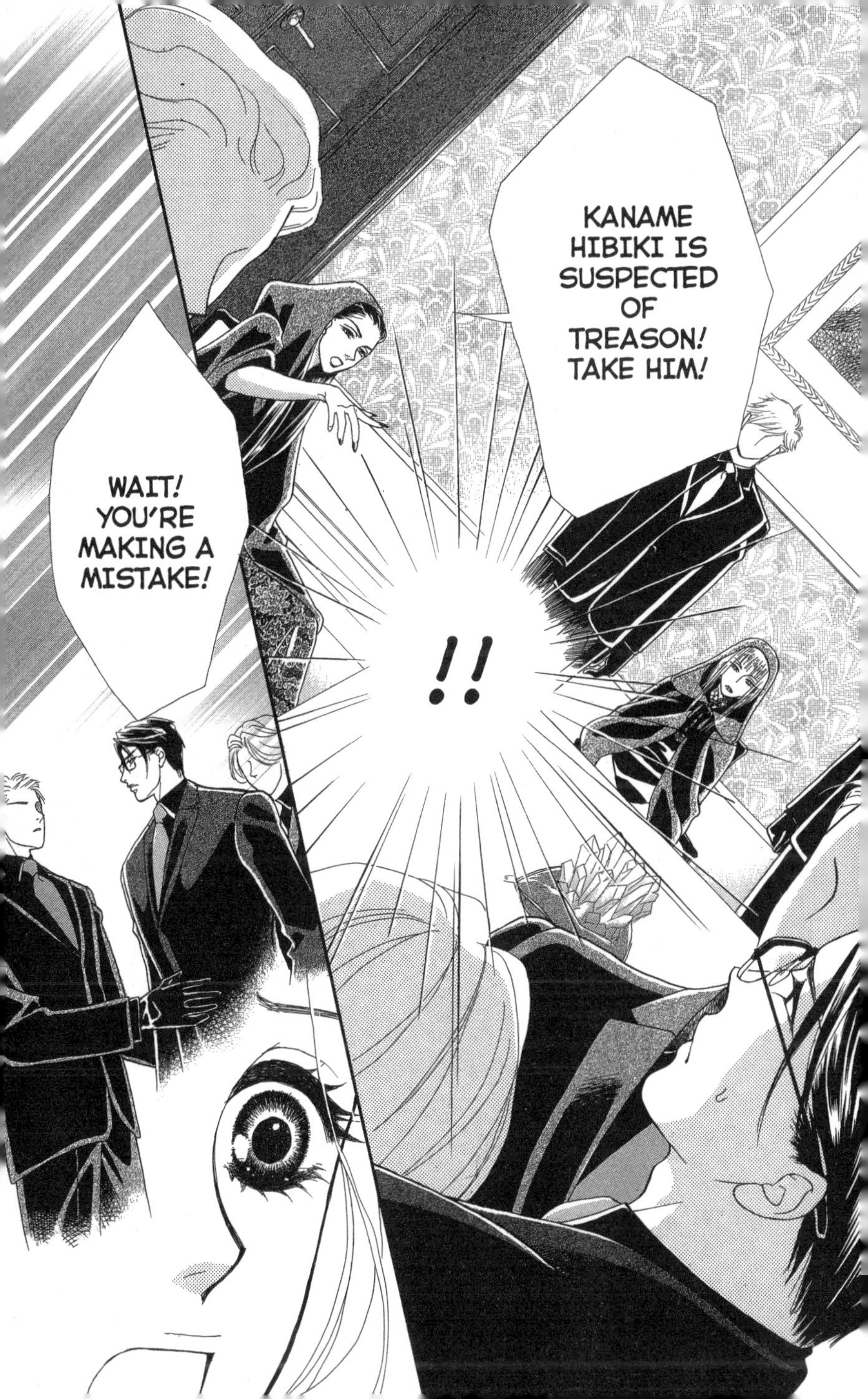
KANAME HIBIKI IS SUSPECTED OF TREASON! TAKE HIM!
WAIT! YOU'RE MAKING A MISTAKE!
!!

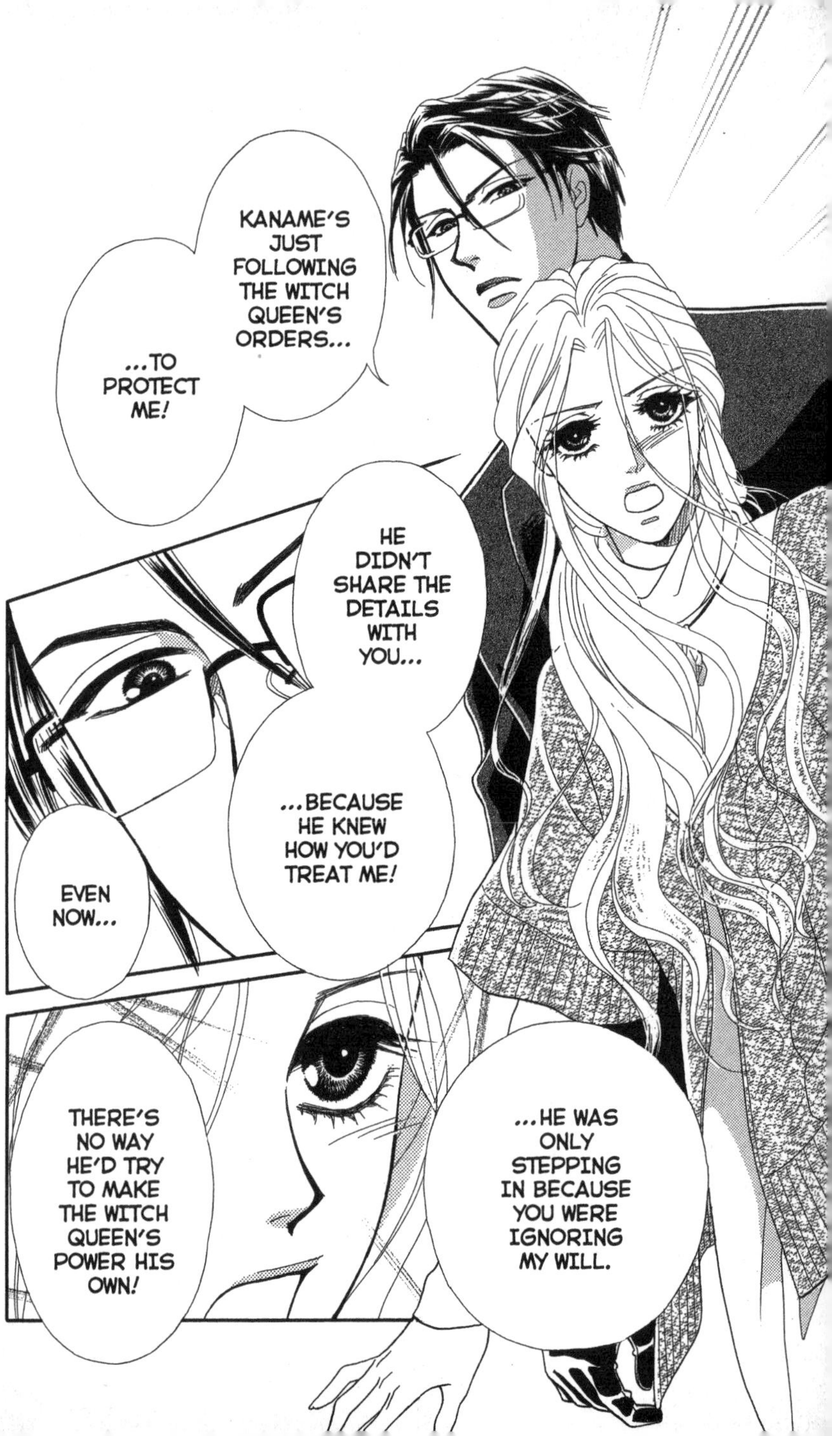
KANAME'S JUST FOLLOWING THE WITCH QUEEN'S ORDERS...
...TO PROTECT ME!
HE DIDN'T SHARE THE DETAILS WITH YOU...
...BECAUSE HE KNEW HOW YOU'D TREAT ME!
EVEN NOW...
...HE WAS ONLY STEPPING IN BECAUSE YOU WERE IGNORING MY WILL.
THERE'S NO WAY HE'D TRY TO MAKE THE WITCH QUEEN'S POWER HIS OWN!

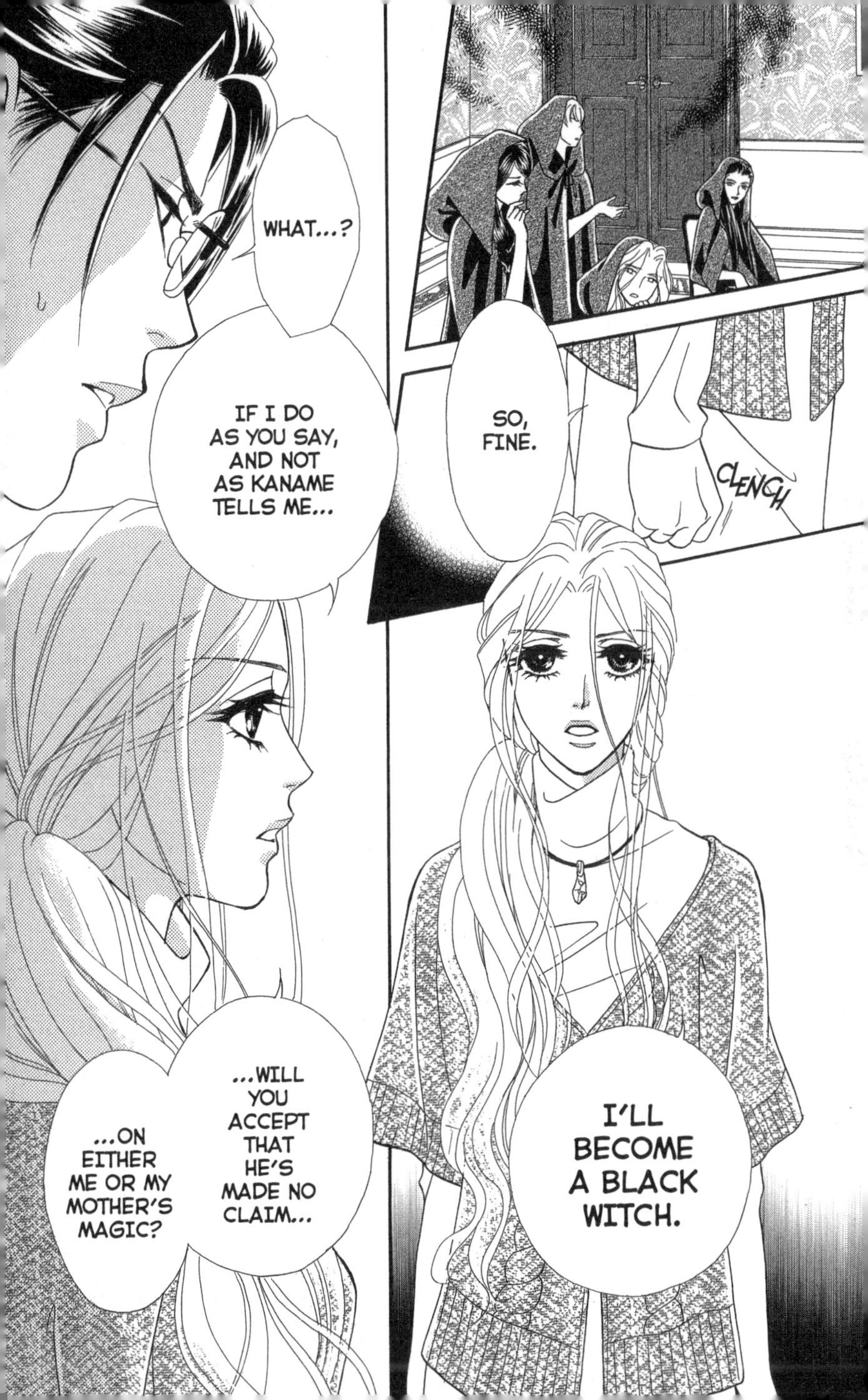
SO, FINE.
CLENCH
I'LL BECOME A BLACK WITCH.
WHAT...?
IF I DO AS YOU SAY, AND NOT AS KANAME TELLS ME...
...WILL YOU ACCEPT THAT HE'S MADE NO CLAIM...
...ON EITHER ME OR MY MOTHER'S MAGIC?

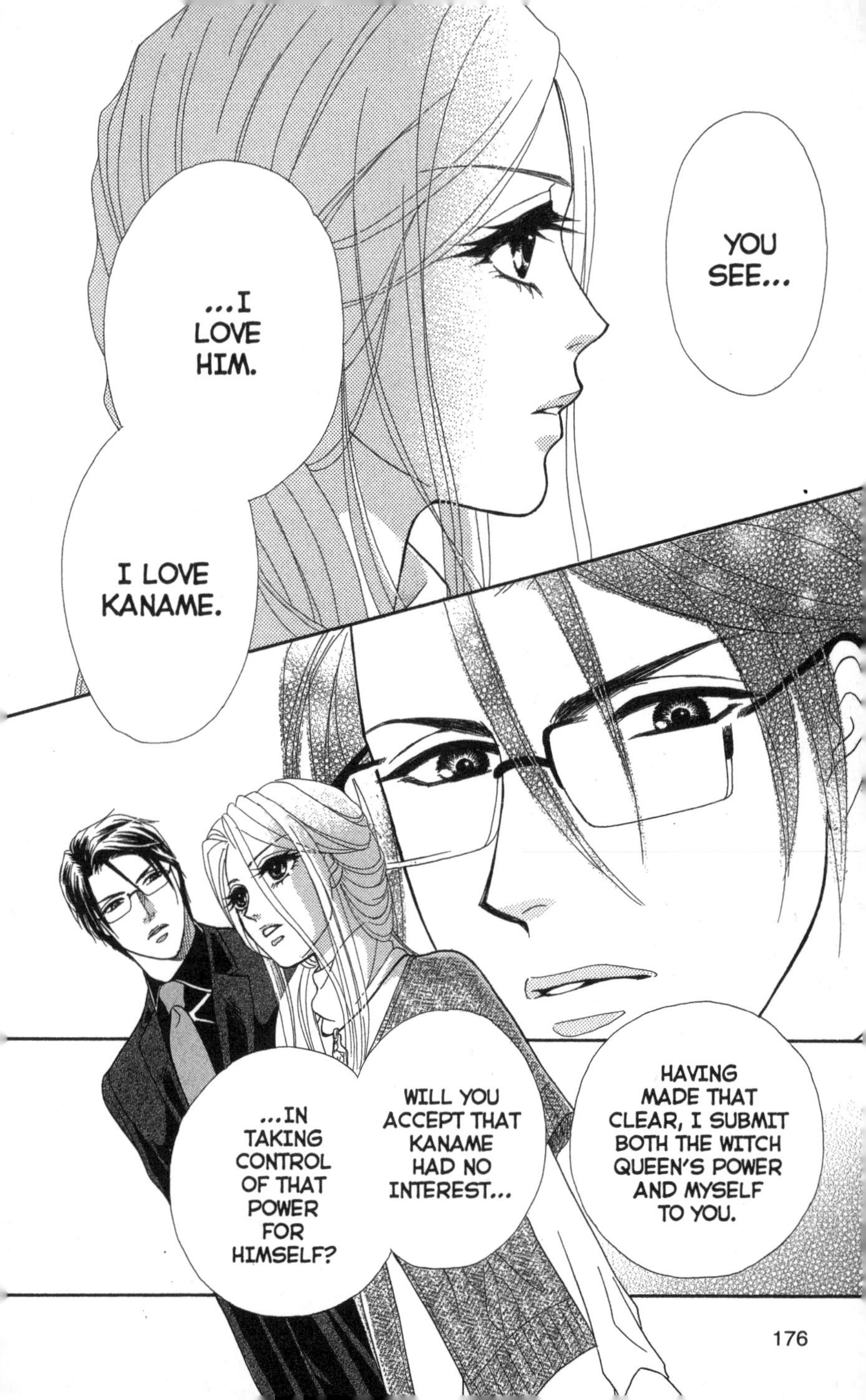
YOU SEE...
...I LOVE HIM.
I LOVE KANAME.
HAVING MADE THAT CLEAR, I SUBMIT BOTH THE WITCH QUEEN'S POWER AND MYSELF TO YOU.
WILL YOU ACCEPT THAT KANAME HAD NO INTEREST...
...IN TAKING CONTROL OF THAT POWER FOR HIMSELF?

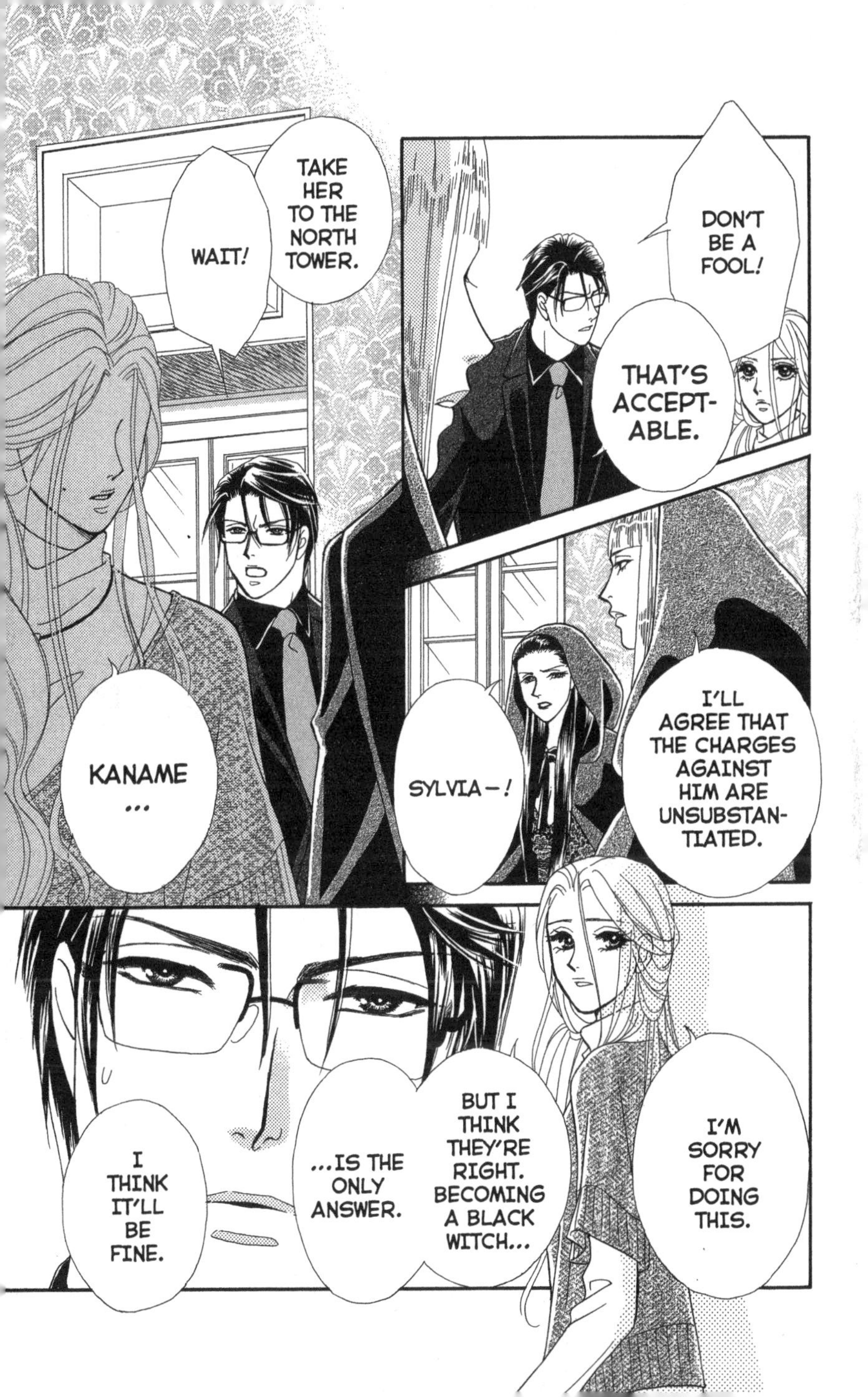
DON'T BE A FOOL!
THAT'S ACCEPTABLE.
I'LL AGREE THAT THE CHARGES AGAINST HIM ARE UNSUBSTANTIATED.
SYLVIA—!
TAKE HER TO THE NORTH TOWER.
WAIT!
KANAME...
I'M SORRY FOR DOING THIS.
BUT I THINK THEY'RE RIGHT. BECOMING A BLACK WITCH...
...IS THE ONLY ANSWER.
I THINK IT'LL BE FINE.

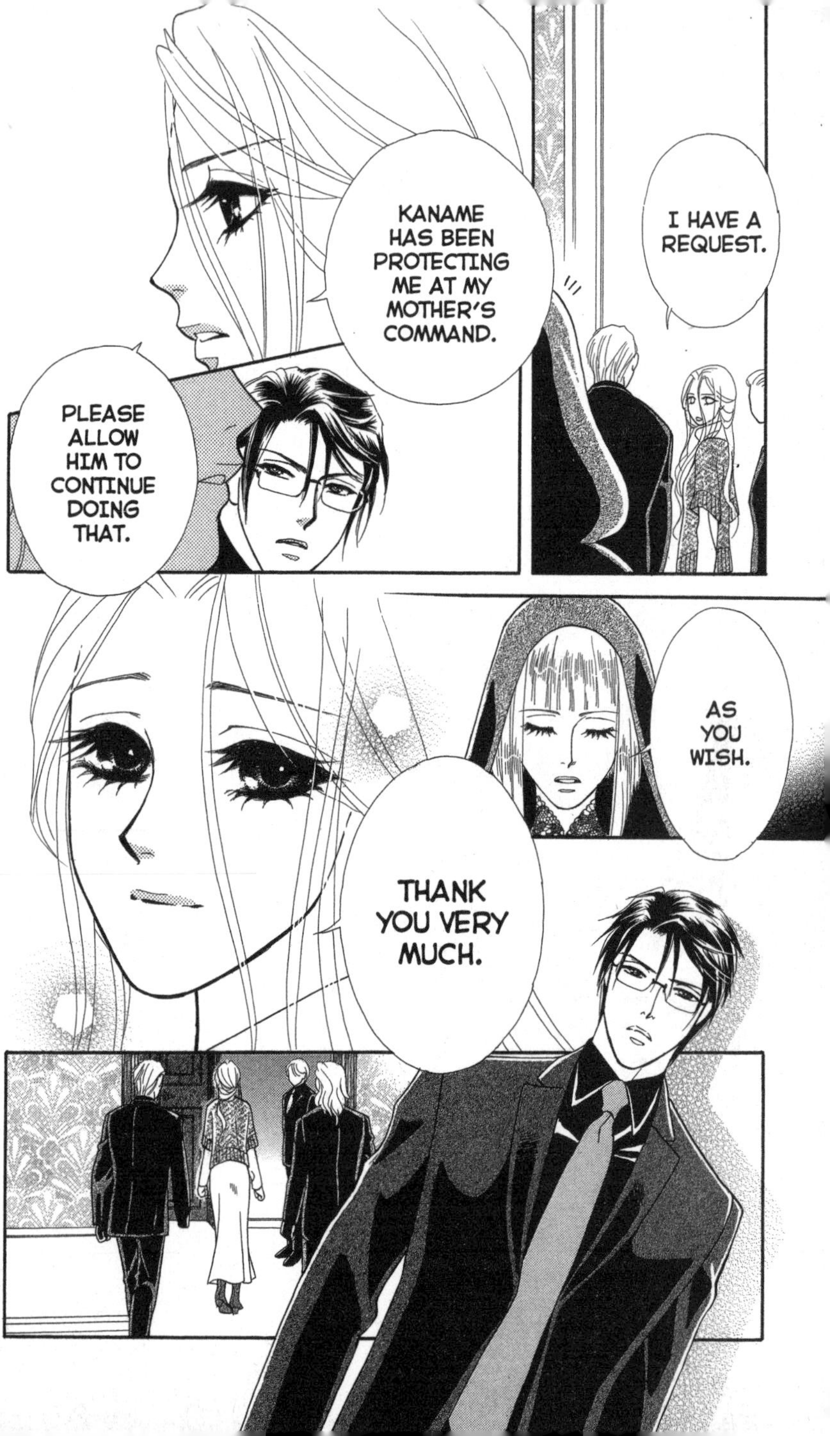
I HAVE A REQUEST.
KANAME HAS BEEN PROTECTING ME AT MY MOTHER'S COMMAND.
PLEASE ALLOW HIM TO CONTINUE DOING THAT.
AS YOU WISH.
THANK YOU VERY MUCH.

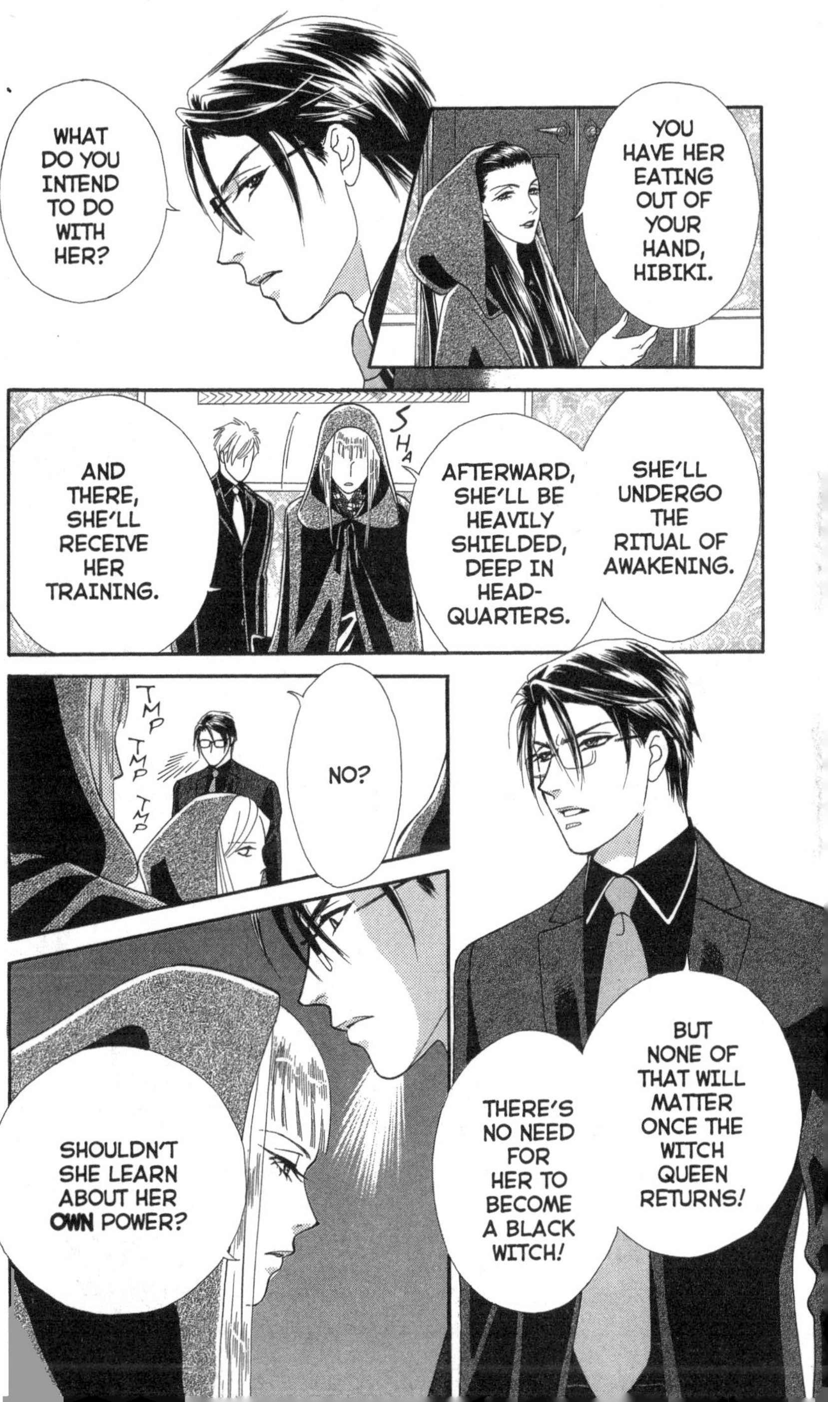
YOU HAVE HER EATING OUT OF YOUR HAND, HIBIKI.
WHAT DO YOU INTEND TO DO WITH HER?
SHE'LL UNDERGO THE RITUAL OF AWAKENING.
AFTERWARD, SHE'LL BE HEAVILY SHIELDED, DEEP IN HEAD-QUARTERS.
SHA
AND THERE, SHE'LL RECEIVE HER TRAINING.
NO?
TMP TMP TMP
SHOULDN'T SHE LEARN ABOUT HER **OWN** POWER?
THERE'S NO NEED FOR HER TO BECOME A BLACK WITCH!
BUT NONE OF THAT WILL MATTER ONCE THE WITCH QUEEN RETURNS!

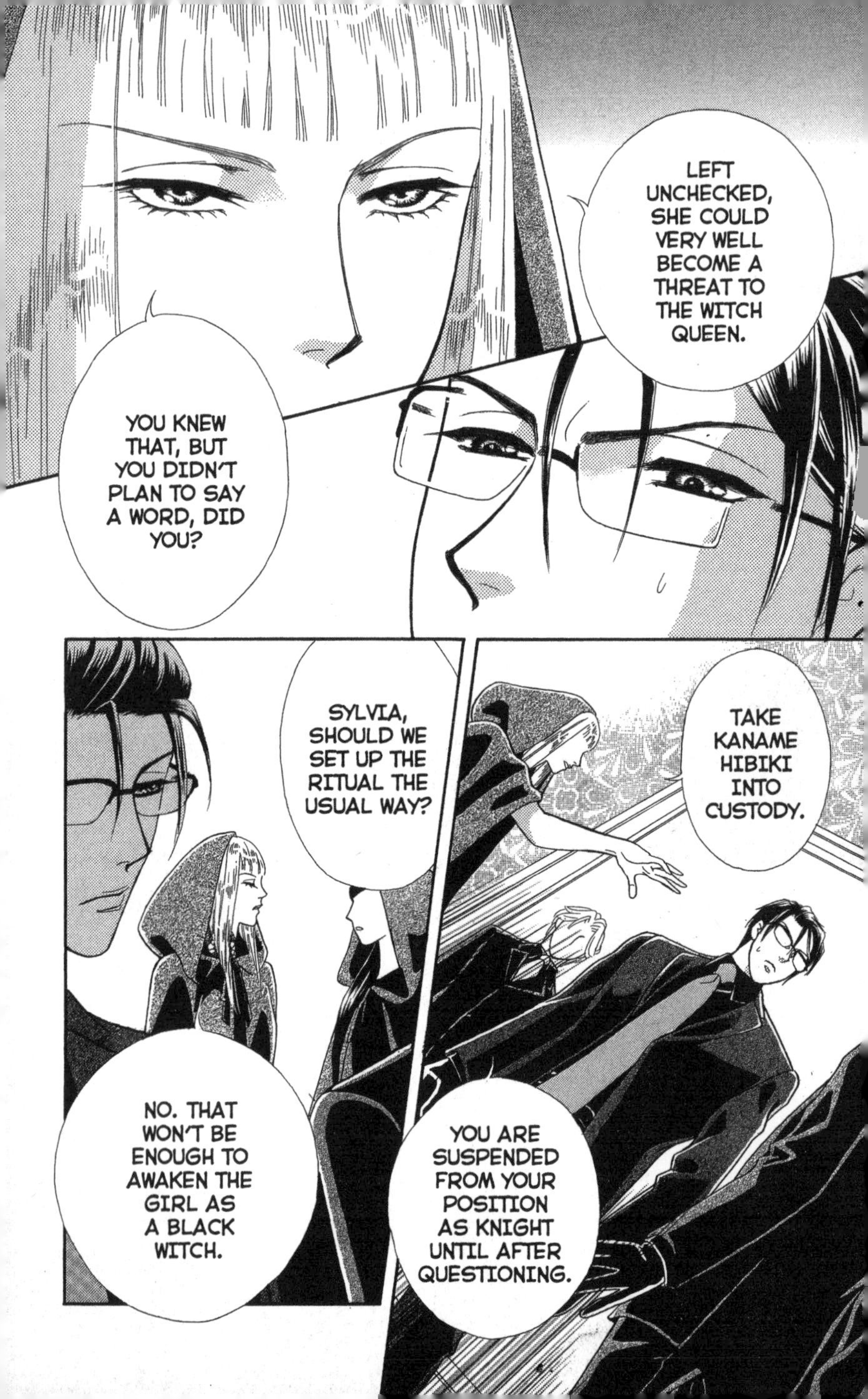
LEFT UNCHECKED, SHE COULD VERY WELL BECOME A THREAT TO THE WITCH QUEEN.
YOU KNEW THAT, BUT YOU DIDN'T PLAN TO SAY A WORD, DID YOU?
TAKE KANAME HIBIKI INTO CUSTODY.
YOU ARE SUSPENDED FROM YOUR POSITION AS KNIGHT UNTIL AFTER QUESTIONING.
SYLVIA, SHOULD WE SET UP THE RITUAL THE USUAL WAY?
NO. THAT WON'T BE ENOUGH TO AWAKEN THE GIRL AS A BLACK WITCH.

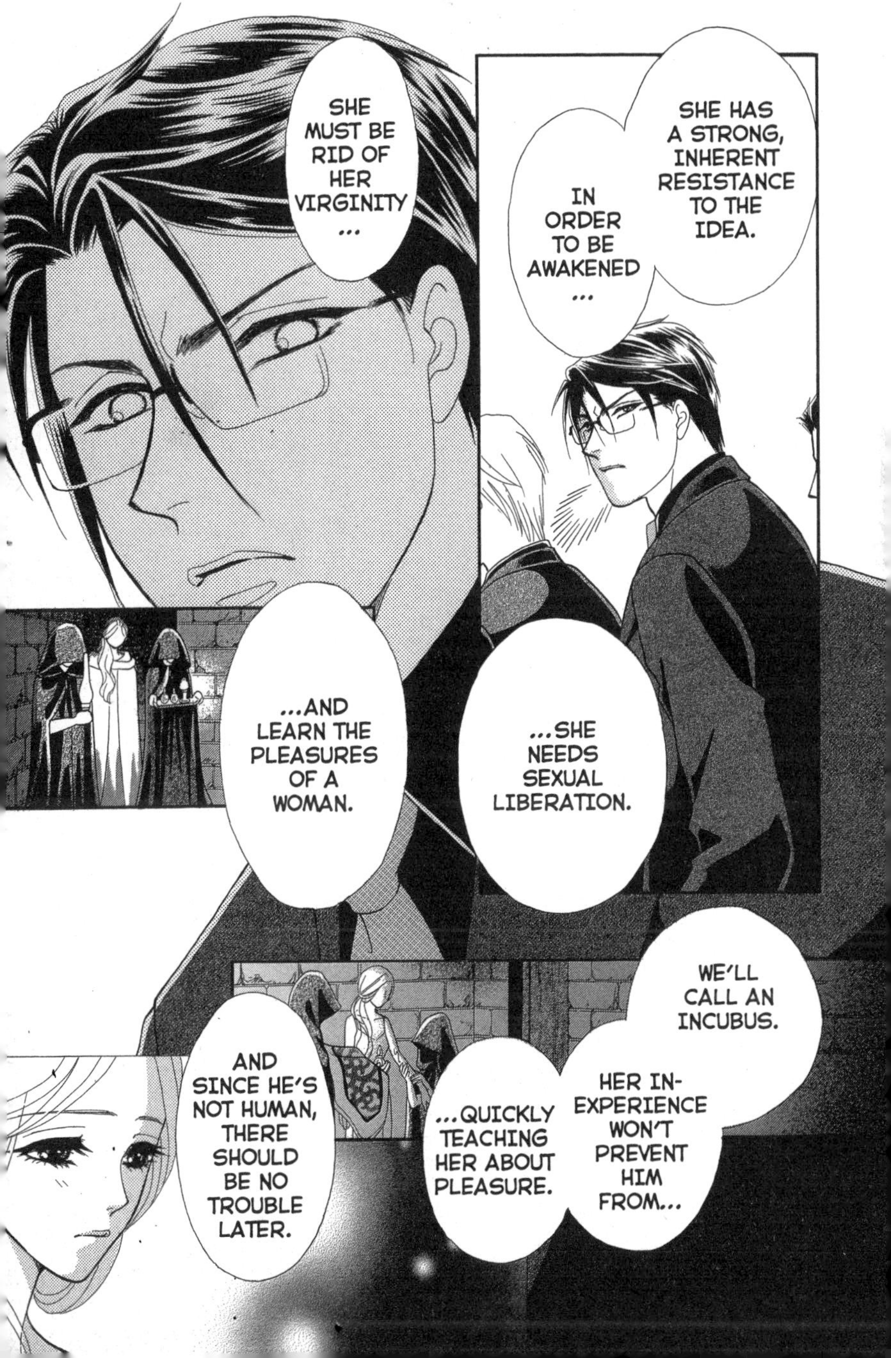
SHE HAS A STRONG, INHERENT RESISTANCE TO THE IDEA.
IN ORDER TO BE AWAKENED...
SHE MUST BE RID OF HER VIRGINITY...
...SHE NEEDS SEXUAL LIBERATION.
...AND LEARN THE PLEASURES OF A WOMAN.
WE'LL CALL AN INCUBUS.
HER IN-EXPERIENCE WON'T PREVENT HIM FROM...
...QUICKLY TEACHING HER ABOUT PLEASURE.
AND SINCE HE'S NOT HUMAN, THERE SHOULD BE NO TROUBLE LATER.

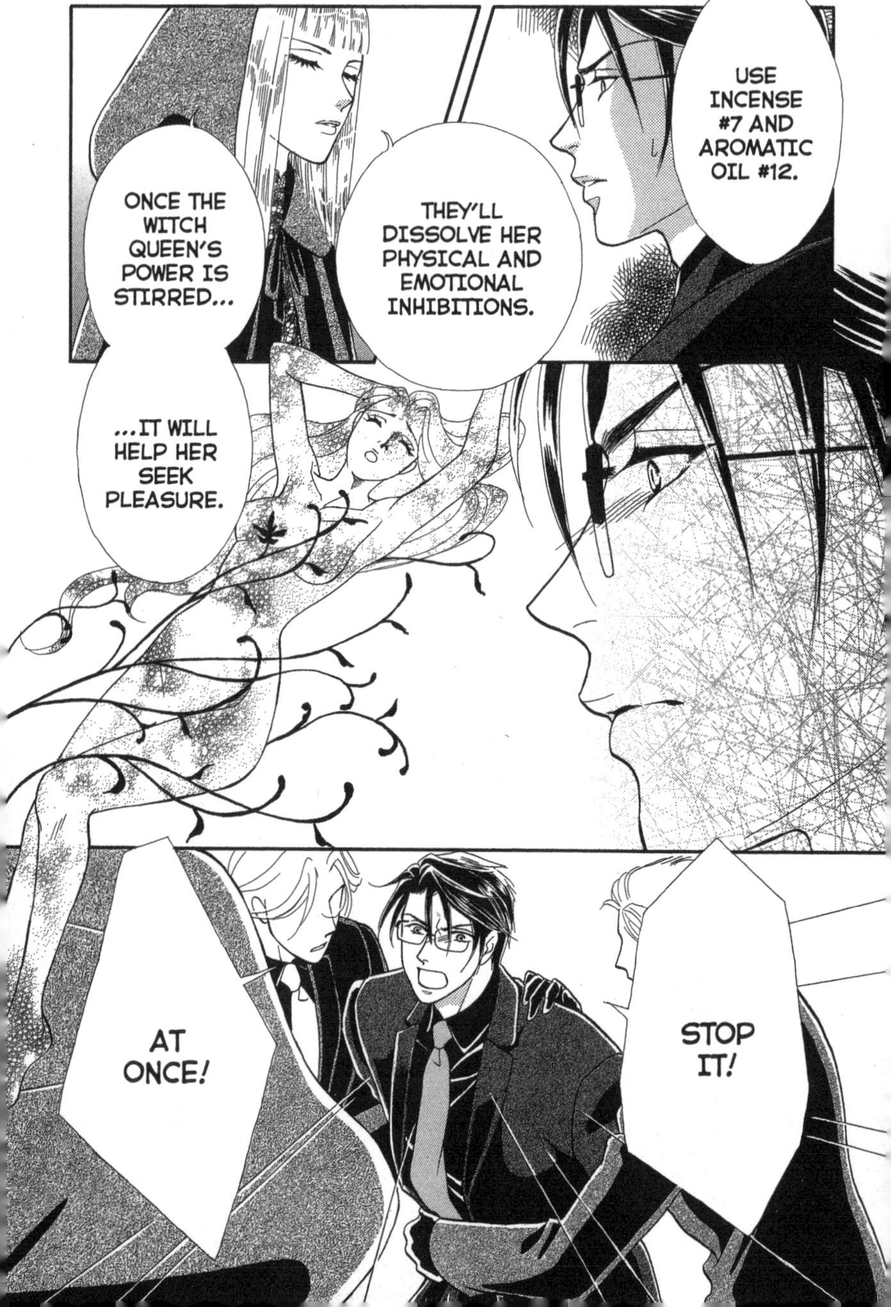
USE INCENSE #7 AND AROMATIC OIL #12.
THEY'LL DISSOLVE HER PHYSICAL AND EMOTIONAL INHIBITIONS.
ONCE THE WITCH QUEEN'S POWER IS STIRRED...
...IT WILL HELP HER SEEK PLEASURE.
STOP IT!
AT ONCE!

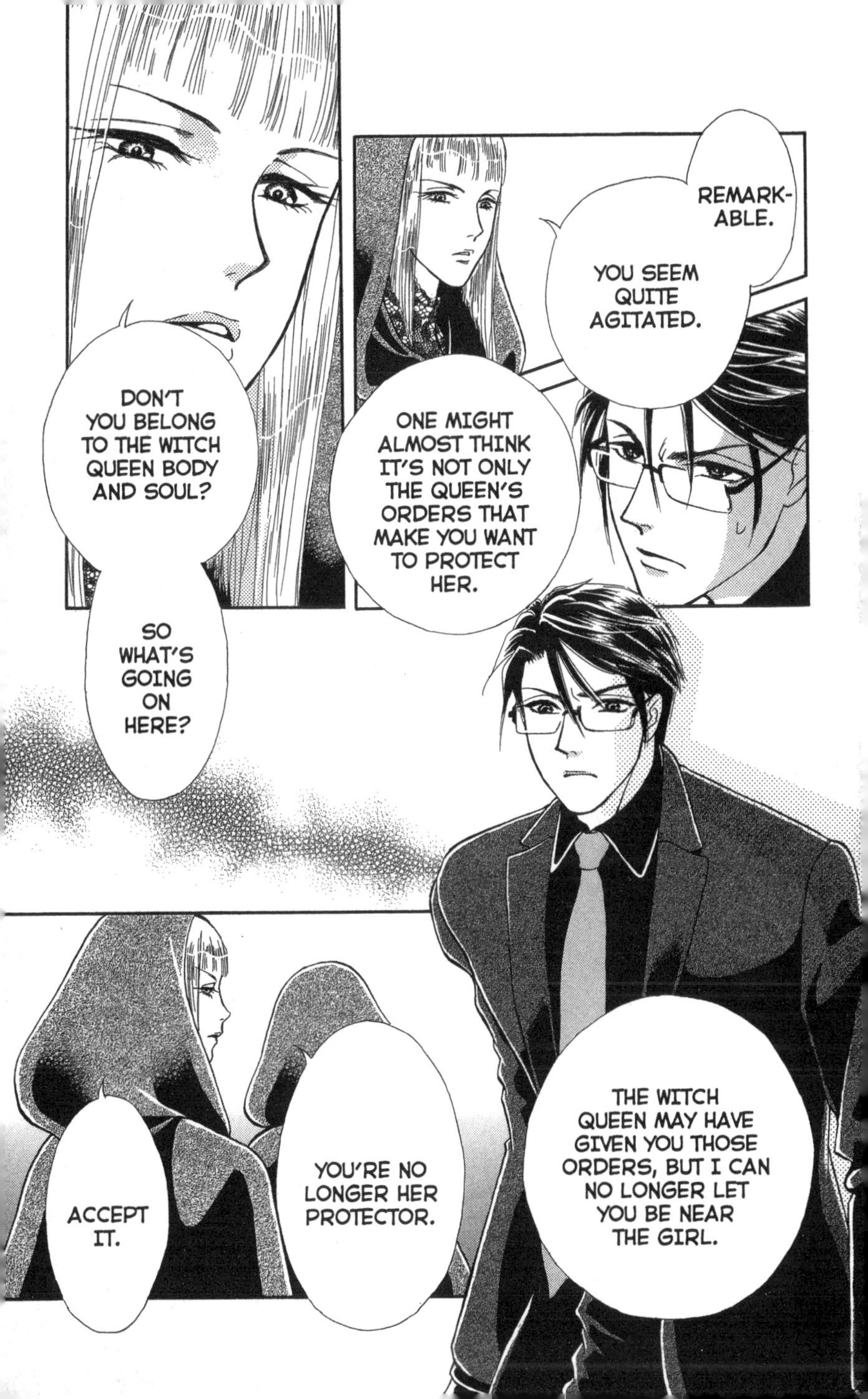
REMARK-ABLE.
YOU SEEM QUITE AGITATED.
ONE MIGHT ALMOST THINK IT'S NOT ONLY THE QUEEN'S ORDERS THAT MAKE YOU WANT TO PROTECT HER.
DON'T YOU BELONG TO THE WITCH QUEEN BODY AND SOUL?
SO WHAT'S GOING ON HERE?
THE WITCH QUEEN MAY HAVE GIVEN YOU THOSE ORDERS, BUT I CAN NO LONGER LET YOU BE NEAR THE GIRL.
YOU'RE NO LONGER HER PROTECTOR.
ACCEPT IT.

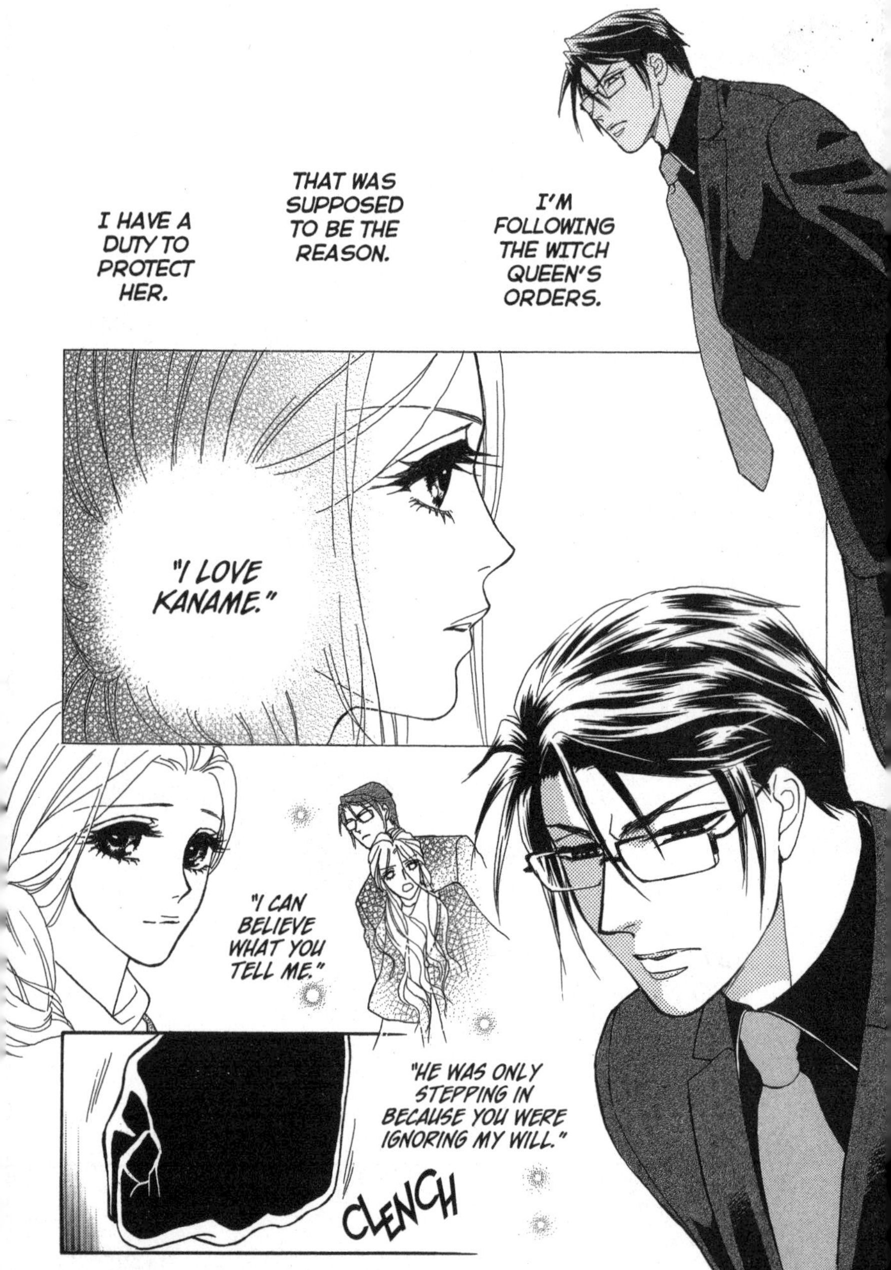
I'M FOLLOWING THE WITCH QUEEN'S ORDERS.
THAT WAS SUPPOSED TO BE THE REASON.
I HAVE A DUTY TO PROTECT HER.
"I LOVE KANAME."
"I CAN BELIEVE WHAT YOU TELL ME."
"HE WAS ONLY STEPPING IN BECAUSE YOU WERE IGNORING MY WILL."
CLENCH

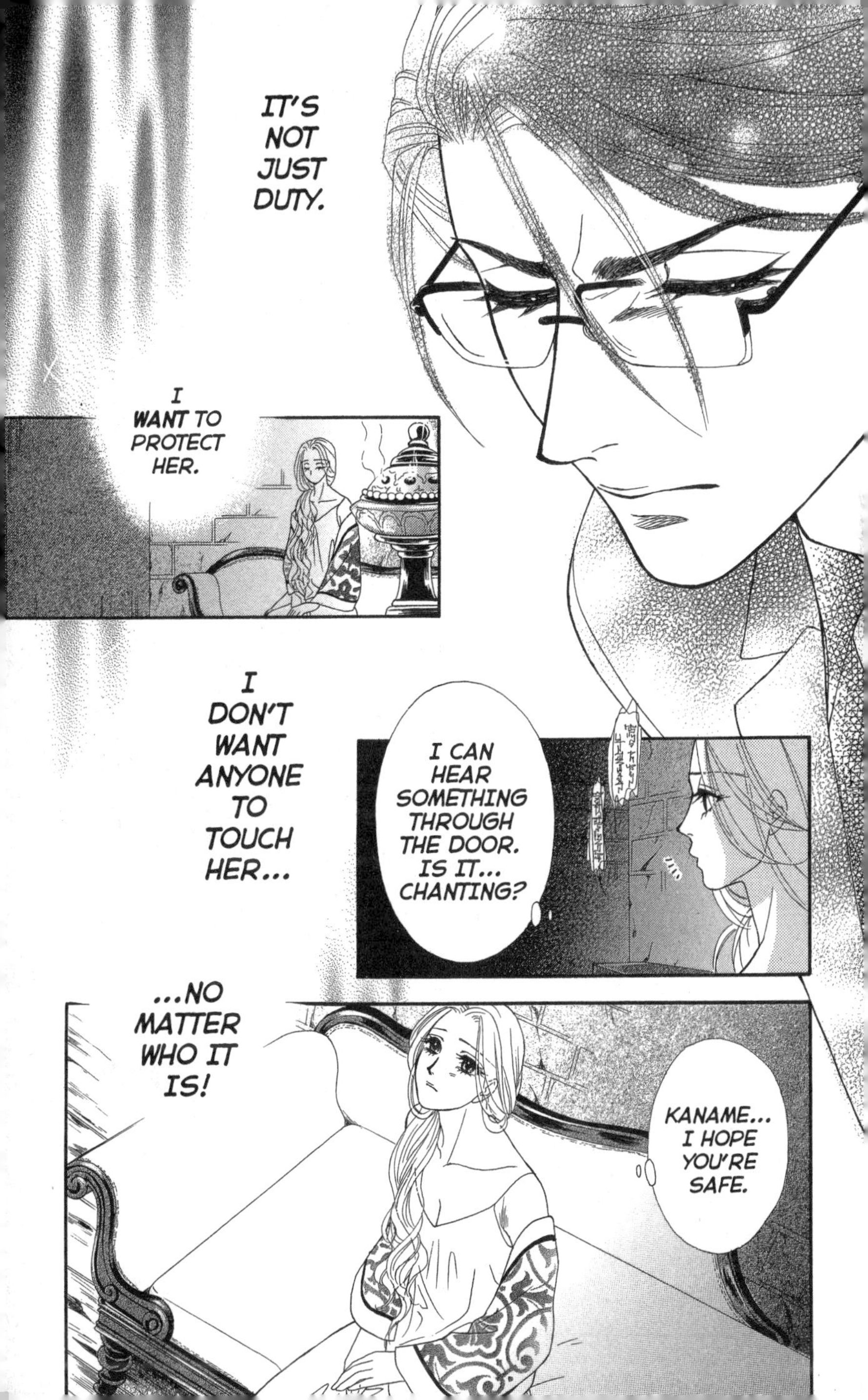
IT'S NOT JUST DUTY.
I WANT TO PROTECT HER.
I CAN HEAR SOMETHING THROUGH THE DOOR. IS IT... CHANTING?
I DON'T WANT ANYONE TO TOUCH HER...
...NO MATTER WHO IT IS!
KANAME... I HOPE YOU'RE SAFE.

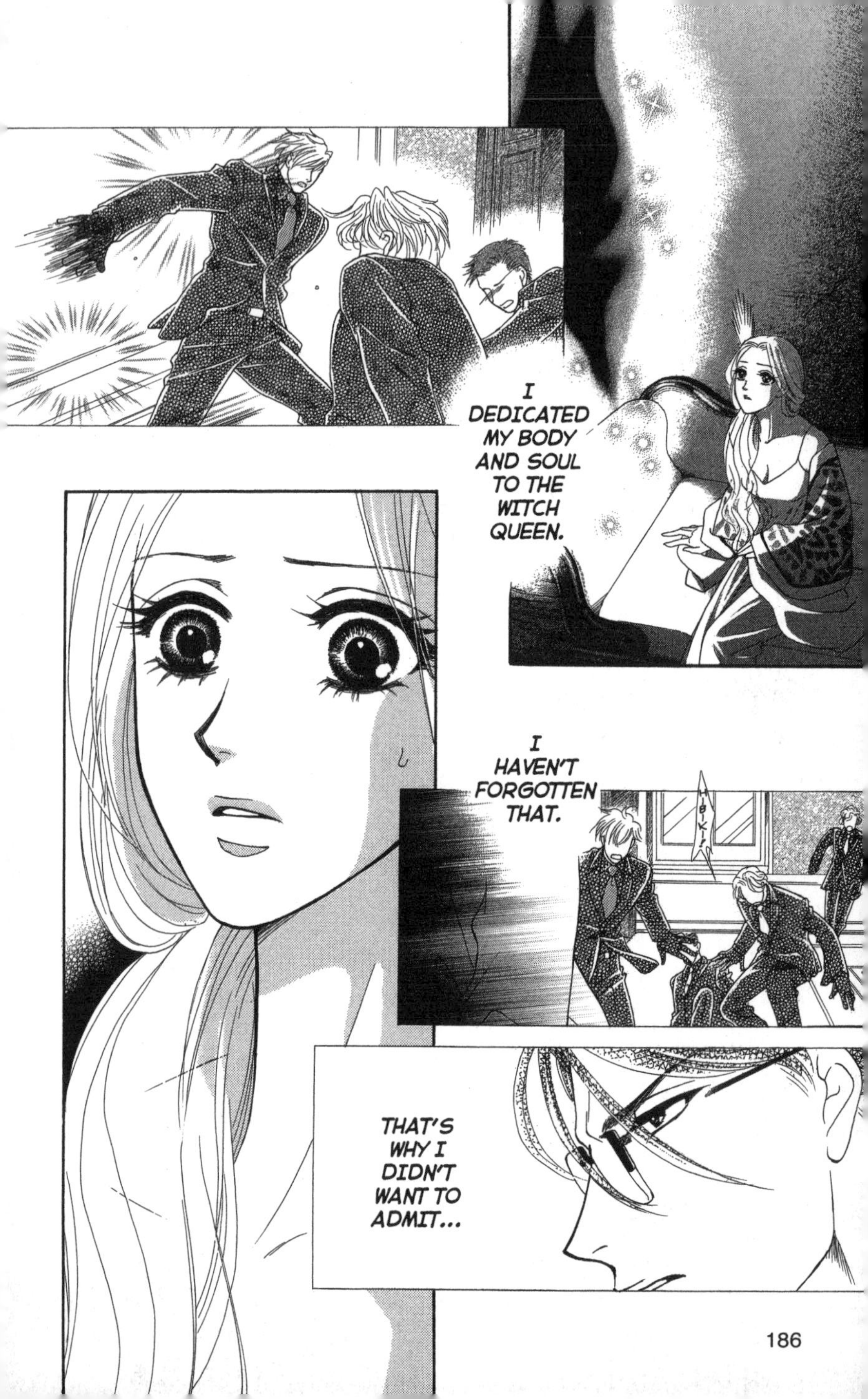
I DEDICATED MY BODY AND SOUL TO THE WITCH QUEEN.
I HAVEN'T FORGOTTEN THAT.
HIBIKI!?
THAT'S WHY I DIDN'T WANT TO ADMIT...

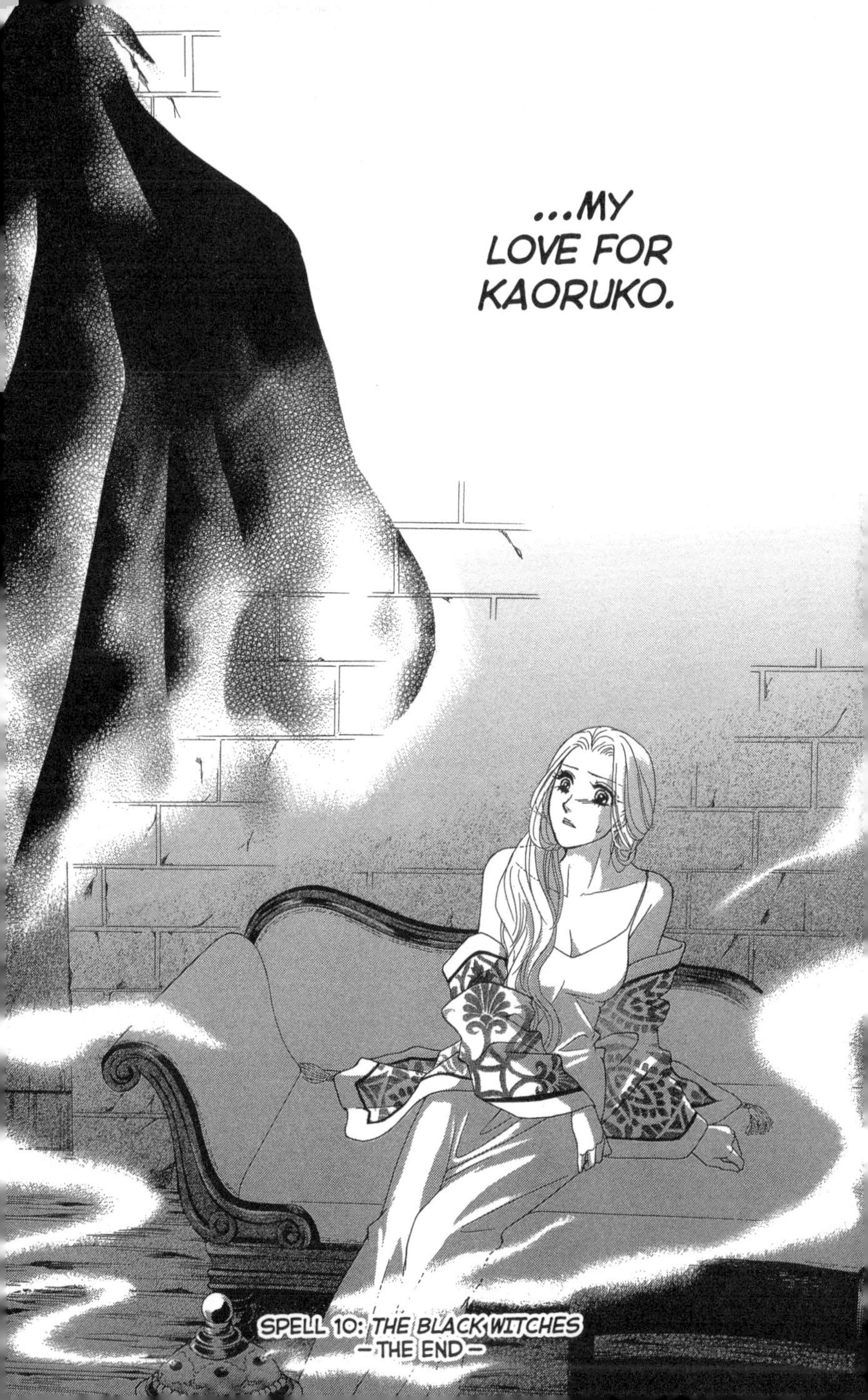
...MY LOVE FOR KAORUKO.
SPELL 10: THE BLACK WITCHES
–THE END–

AFTERWORD

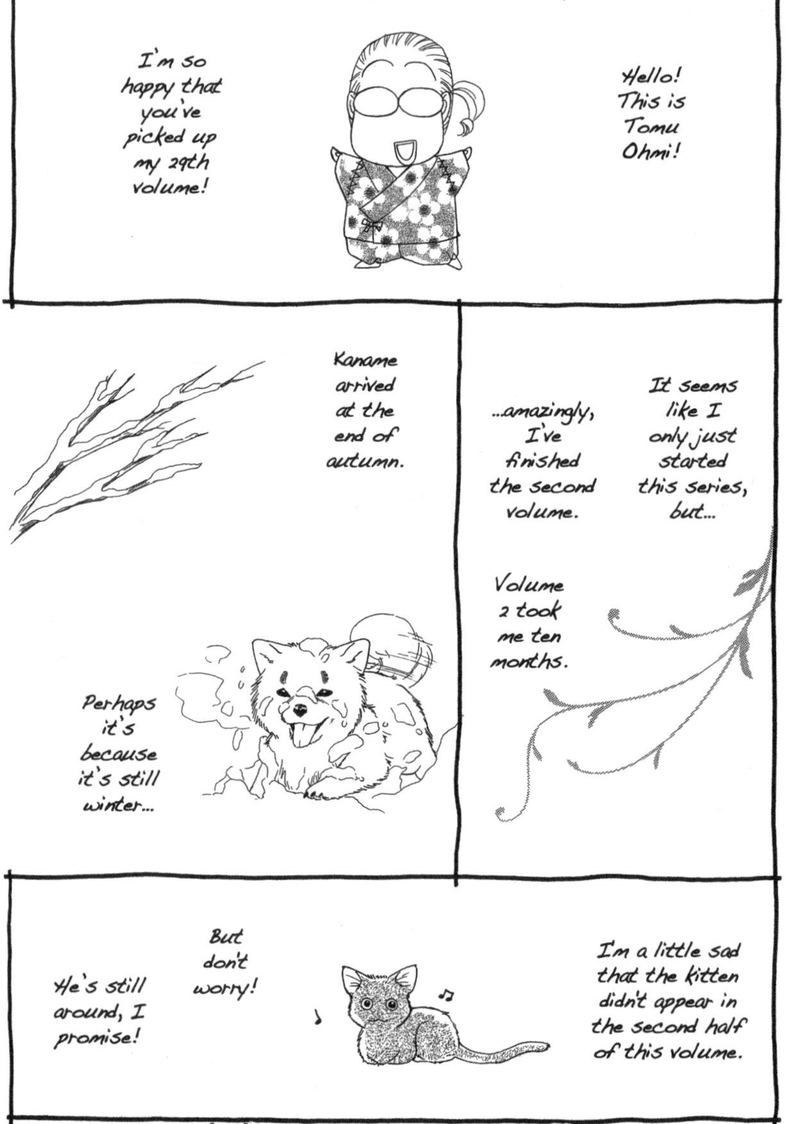
Hello! This is Tomu Ohmi!
I'm so happy that you've picked up my 29th volume!
It seems like I only just started this series, but...
...amazingly, I've finished the second volume.
Volume 2 took me ten months.
Kaname arrived at the end of autumn.
Perhaps it's because it's still winter...
I'm a little sad that the kitten didn't appear in the second half of this volume.
But don't worry!
He's still around, I promise!

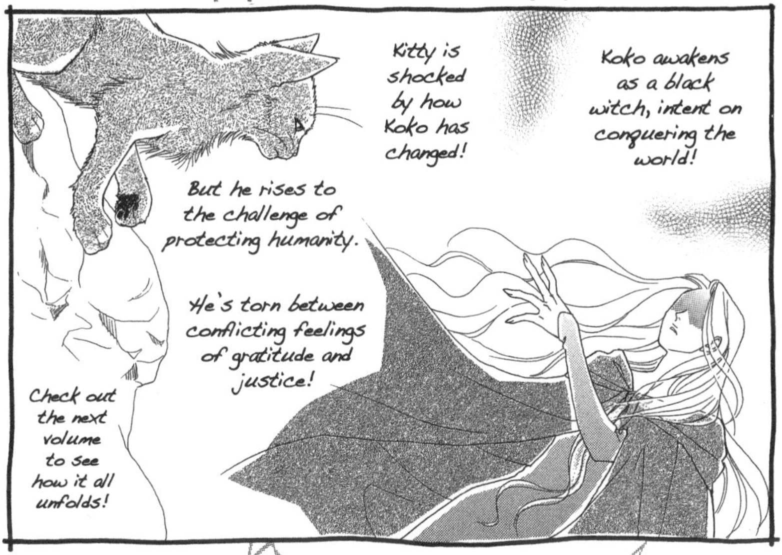
Koko awakens as a black witch, intent on conquering the world!
Kitty is shocked by how Koko has changed!
But he rises to the challenge of protecting humanity.
He's torn between conflicting feelings of gratitude and justice!
Check out the next volume to see how it all unfolds!

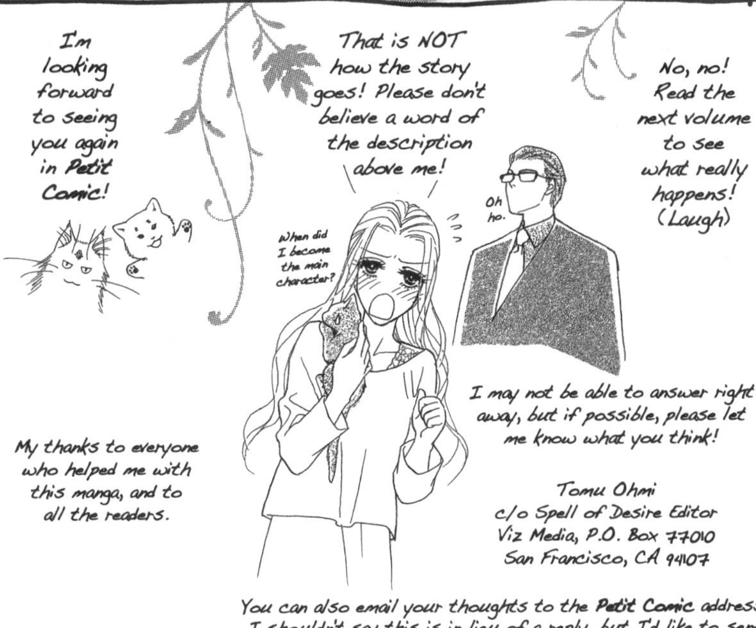
No, no! Read the next volume to see what really happens! (Laugh)
That is NOT how the story goes! Please don't believe a word of the description above me!
Oh ho.
When did I become the main character?
I'm looking forward to seeing you again in **Petit Comic**!
I may not be able to answer right away, but if possible, please let me know what you think!
Tomu Ohmi
c/o Spell of Desire Editor
Viz Media, P.O. Box 77010
San Francisco, CA 94107
My thanks to everyone who helped me with this manga, and to all the readers.

You can also email your thoughts to the **Petit Comic** address. I shouldn't say this is in lieu of a reply, but I'd like to send you a New Year's greeting card, so please include your address.

A WITCH'S FAMILIAR...

...IS A BLACK CAT, OF COURSE!

Yay! ♥ This is my 29th book!! Thank you very much for picking this up! For this volume, I added a lot of extra material to the chapters that ran in the magazine. I hope you'll be happy with the extra pages!

               –Tomu Ohmi

Author Bio

Born on May 25, Tomu Ohmi debuted with *Kindan no Koi wo Shiyoh* in 2000. She is presently working on *Petit Comic* projects like *Spell of Desire*. Her previous series, *Midnight Secretary*, is available from VIZ Media. Ohmi lives in Hokkaido, and she likes beasts, black tea and pretty women.

Spell of Desire

VOLUME 2
Shojo Beat Edition

STORY AND ART BY
TOMU OHMI

MAJO NO BIYAKU Vol. 2
by Tomu OHMI
© 2012 Tomu OHMI
All rights reserved.
Original Japanese edition published by SHOGAKUKAN.
English translation rights in the United States of America, Canada, the
United Kingdom, and Ireland arranged with SHOGAKUKAN.

English Adaptation/Ysabet Reinhardt MacFarlane
Translation/JN Productions
Touch-up Art & Lettering/Monalisa de Asis
Design/Izumi Evers
Editor/Amy Yu

Printed in the U.S.A.

Published by VIZ Media, LLC
P.O. Box 77010
San Francisco, CA 94107

10 9 8 7 6 5 4 3 2 1
First printing, November 2014

www.viz.com

This is the last page.

In keeping with the original Japanese comic format, this book reads from right to left—so action, sound effects, and word balloons are completely reversed. This preserves the orientation of the original artwork—plus, it's fun! Check out the diagram shown here to get the hang of things, and then turn to the other side of the book to get started!